History of Christian Education

History of Christian Education

by
C. B. Eavey

MOODY PRESS
CHICAGO

Second Printing, 1965

Printed in the United States of America

Contents

Foreword

To understand Christian education, one must first gain a clear idea of the nature of education in general. Meanings given the word "education" vary greatly. To some persons it includes all the forces that influence human development. Others so limit the meaning as to make education equivalent to nothing more than teaching. In its widest meaning education includes both individual and social development.

Basically, education is a process of change undergone by human beings as they interact with their environment. In each and every situation he meets from the beginning of life, the individual interacts with what makes up his environment at the moment. This interaction is experience. Every experience changes the individual. In other words, he learns. Learning, then, is an activity of a learner responding to his environment. The learner is no blank tablet on which the environment writes impressions. As he actively appropriates impressions, the learner develops and thus becomes capable not only of responding in a different manner to his environment but also of reacting to new phases of it.

Along with ability to learn and develop, human beings have the power of language and the skill to record it. Thus they preserve records of the results of experience and transmit these results to others. Animals have innate ability to respond instinctively to an environment they are able to change but little. With a fixed inherited mental equipment, animals do not have insight in the measure possessed by man. Neither do animals have the higher mental processes characteristic of man. Moreover, animals are without the power of language. Consequently, animals of any generation start just where those of every previous generation began. Only man can benefit from the outcomes of the experience of those who preceded. The child, unlike the young of animals, learns largely from the results of experience transmitted from generation to generation.

From the moment of birth, the normal child meets situations, has experiences, undergoes changes, continually learns, and develops. Learning is, of course, dependent upon conditions and experiences; what the individual does determines what and how much he learns. However, it is safe to say that a human being learns more during the first five years of life than during any other five-year period. Three different ways in which he undergoes change and learns give rise to three corresponding types of education.

The first kind of change takes place apart from guidance. Because there is no arranging of conditions, no planning at all, this type of education may be called *natural education*. The individual learns from anything that happens to provide him with content for experience. If he is hungry, he acts to satisfy his felt need for food, and he learns from the experience thus induced. If he loses something, he hunts for it, and he learns from the experiences he has while seeking it. If he feels insecure, he tries to satisfy the need for safety, and he learns from the resulting effort and activity.

Natural education is unorganized; it has no planned end or purpose. At one moment the individual learns this lesson and at the next moment some other lesson entirely unrelated to the first. About the only unity among the many lessons learned is that it is the same person who is learning them. Obviously, there is also some unity among learning experiences of any given kind. On the whole, however, natural education moves toward no goal. Nevertheless, this type of education is the source of a large part of what both the individual and the race learns.

A second type of change in human beings is the change resulting from informal teaching. Guiding the child in dressing, telling him in everyday contacts how he should or should not behave, or showing him how to perform a task in the home, are examples of *informal education*. This has more purpose and makes for more definite results in learning than natural education does. However, the purpose is that of the person who guides the learning rather than the purpose of the learner. And the outcomes are, typically, those sought by the guide.

Informal education is relatively unorganized; in general, the situations met by the learner arise out of conditions as they come along instead of being planned. Like natural learning, informal learning moves from one condition to another without overall design or intent on the part of those who guide. The purpose the learning serves is essentially an immediate purpose related to the outcome of a certain kind of activity rather than a long-range central one. Because the general purpose of those who guide informally is to train the learner right, this type of education has somewhat more unity than natural education has. But, since this purpose is general and usually involves many persons who guide in varied ways, it does not give informal education any great amount of unity.

A third type of education is *formal education,* the kind most people have in mind when they use the word "education." Formal education is intentional; it means the introduction of control into experience for the purpose of changing pupils in specific ways. Where the school, the church, or other organized agency directs the experience of the learner toward the realization of certain desired ends, there formal education is being carried on.

Whether such education is good or bad depends upon three things: the ends sought, the content taught, and the quality of teaching. The best content will not make for good education if the purpose is vague or wrong. The highest end and the noblest goals will never be reached if teaching is ineffectively done. Learning under formal teaching may be no better organized than natural and informal learning are. If the control introduced into experience is without plan or system, learning will be haphazard or unsystematized. The sad fact is that formal education can be a hindrance instead of a help to good learning.

When one thinks clearly about the nature of education, he sees that education is inevitable. Man, an active being, lives in an environment to which he begins to react as soon as he is born. Reacting, he learns; learning, he becomes able to respond more and more to his environment. An individual becomes educated by the process of living even when there is no purpose of educating him and no planning in the process.

It is a misconception of education to think of it as being done only in a school. Education is an ongoing process as broad as experience itself. An individual is educated by everything he experiences from the cradle to the grave. Every event of his life is a factor in his education. Every person with whom he has contact shares unconsciously or consciously in his education. His most effective teachers are his father and mother, his brothers and sisters, his grandparents and uncles and aunts and cousins, his playmates and friends and associates, his own children—every person with whom he has relations. Education of some kind is always being carried on and is utterly inescapable. To be alive is to become educated.

For right understanding of Christian education one must have a clear idea not only of the nature of general education but of the nature of religious education also. General education, as noted above, is concerned with changes in human beings resulting from reaction to the environment and with the outcomes of these changes. Religious education recognizes the existence of the divine in the environment of men; it is education founded upon and inspired by faith in a divine being. It is education which has for its purpose, first, the gaining of personal religious faith through the individual's interacting with his environment and, second, development in that faith.

Religious education involves changes in human beings making for right relationship with God—right thinking about Him, right attitudes toward Him, and right conduct before Him. General education involves whatever is necessary to "the perfection of our nature"—changes making for health and growth for the body, knowledge for the mind, beauty for the feelings, moral goodness for the will, and efficiency for living. General education can be carried on without regard to religious education, but it will be incomplete. Religious education may go on with little heed to general education, but it will be unreal and inadequate. Education apart from religion is defective, falling short of its goal of making perfect an imperfect being—one who can find completion only in right relationship with the Author of his being.

Religion is part of the nature of a human being, so much a part that he cannot escape it. It holds him even against his will. It pervades his whole being and controls both his personal and his social development. From first to last, his interaction with his environment is controlled by religious attitudes and religious ideas. Being endowed with reason, man must think. The thought of a reasoning being is but a factor that relates him to his infinite, eternal Creator.

Religion is so built into man as to be at the very heart of his nature.

Religious education is as much a part of the life of man as religion itself, for, wherever religion is, there religious education is going on. Religious education is as inevitable as general education is; a human being can escape the one no more than he can the other. General education includes religious education, and religious education is general education conscious of its true goal. To be alive is to become not only educated but to become religiously educated, though the forms religious education takes are as varied as the forms assumed by religion itself. No student of history can doubt the existence of religion, and Daniel Webster rightly said that nowhere and never "has religious education been excluded from the education of youth."

To gain true understanding of Christian education, either in history or in the present, one must also have a correct conception of the nature of Christianity. Christian education has no existence in its own right; it is wholly dependent on Christianity and exists solely for the sake of Christianity. Without education, Christianity would not continue to exist, yet there is no Christian education where there is no Christianity.

Just what is Christianity? Is it merely one among a number of religions? From the standpoint of its being an organized system of religious truth, Christianity can properly be called a "religion." As such, it would be all right to classify it among Mohammedanism, Buddhism, Shintoism, Confucianism, and other great religions. But Christianity is more than a mere religion. In its origin, the word "religion" means respect for what is sacred. Religion is man's sense of need to be rightly related to the ultimate powers of the universe, and the impulse which leads him to seek to fulfill this need. Therefore, a religion is any system of faith in and worship of a supreme Being, or a god or gods.

In reality, Christianity is something quite different from this. When its Founder is set alongside the founder of other religions, He is seen to be more than human. Jesus is God. And God is not just "a supreme Being, or a god" among gods. He is the ultimate reality, an absolute, personal Spirit, dependent upon Himself alone, and the source of all being.

By an act of His omnipotent and sovereign will, God, for His own glory, created a universe out of nothing. After creating the universe and everything else therein, God brought into being man, the highest form of His creative activity. "And the LORD God formed man of the dust of the ground, and breathed into his nostrils the breath of life; and man became a living soul" (Gen. 2:7).

On his physical side, therefore, man "is of the earth, earthy" but in his real or spiritual essence he is of God—the breath of God is the life of his soul, his actual being. On his earthy side, man has a physical body similar to that of animals, but he is far superior to the animals because he alone of all creatures bears the image of God. When created man resembled God in being, in righteousness, and in holiness. As a rational creature he was able to think and, within the limits of his finite nature, to apprehend truth. As the offspring of God, he is the object of God's most tender care.

In loving-kindness, God instructed man in regard to His plans and His wishes for him. Subject to God, man was to rule over everything in the world and to bring it under his dominion for his use and God's glory. But he was not to partake of the nature of the world. Instead, he was to be content with life in the spirit—with living out the life God had breathed into him. This, in spite of God's loving instruction, man chose not to do. He chose instead to yield to the appeal, "Ye shall be as gods, knowing good and evil." Deceived by Satan, he deliberately chose to try to obtain knowledge he would have been much better off not to have acquired. In self-assertion he set himself against his Creator.

"In the day that thou eatest thereof thou shalt surely die" (Gen. 2:17). The threatened penalty of death was immediately executed. The heavenly in man's spirit and body was extinguished, the divine which set him above the world departed from him, and he became a being subject to the evil and sin, the bondage and corruption, the blindness and self-deception of a purely earthly existence. Knowledge of good and evil did become his though in distorted form. Man knows only too well what evil is, but the little knowledge he has of good is of a good only as it would have been had he chosen to obey God. Not only was man's nature marred but he totally lost all spiritual life; he became dead in trespasses and sins, and subject in his entire being to the power of the Devil.

Every person born into the world inherits this corrupted fallen nature, for none other can be transmitted to offspring. Hence every child of Adam is born with a nature that has in it no spark of divine life. There is in man no power of deliverance from his universal depravity and death in sin. No amount of improvement, no attainment in morality, no culture, no education—Christian or other—can make man a son of God and a renewed bearer of His image. By nature man is dead and he remains dead, in spite of everything he does and everything done to him, until through grace God imparts a new life.

In love, God sent His Son as a man to make it possible for man to have a new life. By His obedience to God, Jesus Christ regained for man what Adam lost by his disobedience. In Christ is restored the life that was lost in Adam. The concern of Christian education, its purpose, and all its activities have to do with the process of restoration. As is true of education in general, Christian education is interaction with the environment—interaction resulting in changes in the individual. In its actual and fundamental essence, Christian education is the interaction of the soul with its environment—God.

Two kinds of change occur when Christian education is effective. First, the soul is made alive. A person who hears the Gospel of the grace of God and yields to the drawing of the Holy Spirit undergoes the greatest change possible to a human being, the change from death in sin to life in Christ. No human effort can effect this change; it is a miracle wrought by God. It may take place as the person meets God in some natural way, or through informal teaching, or as an outcome of formal teaching. But always it is God who works the change as the soul responds to Him.

The soul being made alive, the task of Christian education is to build Christian personality—to bring to perfection in Christ Jesus the soul that He made alive. The ideal of perfection applies only to Christians as perfect in the substitutionary perfection of Christ. In the after-work as in the original work of making alive, it is God's power that operates. The life of any Christian is a series of miraculous changes wrought by God. As the soul alive in Christ responds to God, the new man is liberated from the shackles that keep him bound in personality, and the barriers that prevent the mind of Christ in him from expressing itself are removed. The channels of his life are cleared of obstructions so that he becomes mature as a son of God. Thus is accomplished the restoration of the image-bearer of God. As one generation seeks to make it possible in the next, there will come a time when all God's children shall stand side by side complete in Christ.

There is a vast difference between Christianity as it is and Christianity as it is practiced even in so-called Christian circles. Actually, Christianity is the life of God being lived in the soul; Christianity as it is practiced is often an imitation of the genuine—a product of corrupted paganized views of men tinged with some of the symbols of Christianity. There are those interested in education who take this faulty Christian practice and further dilute it to suit their human thinking. Consequently, much of what passes for Christian education is not at all a fruit of genuine Christianity.

Eve was but the first of a long line of human beings who, setting their own thinking over against the revealed will of God, became enamored with the deceitful beauty of knowledge originating in the human capacity for reason and insight. Through the centuries the principle of the creativity of human thought has held sway in the thinking of mankind, being present often in their thinking on the subject of education. The philosophy founded upon this thinking assumes many forms, but all agree in their emphasis upon the sufficiency of man to cope with his own problems and to live his own life. Always, as in the beginning, there is conflict between two kinds of philosophy, the man-centered and the God-centered. Every philosophy of education, whether it be labeled Christian or not, has for its center either man's ideas or God's revealed truth.

The way of man is not in himself; the finite does not have sufficiency in itself. Without God man's life and experience are meaningless. Men with all their ability to think and reason do not perceive and know Him through earthly wisdom. The meaning of life is rooted in revelation—in God's having made Himself and His will known to man. True Christian education is education in truth as revealed by God. True Christian education is education that centers in God, not in man. A history of education that is truly Christian traces through time the development of that education which began with God, continued to center in God, and is now being carried on under the direction of God. He who created man and who loves man has never ceased to work in and for and through man, education-wise as well as otherwise.

True Christian education is not a concern of narrow interest to some particular movement or organization. No one group of people has a monopoly upon Christian truth. The word "Christian" rightfully belongs to any and every person, church, denomination, organization, association, institution, or movement that is true to the plain simple teachings of the Bible.

Education that is truly Christian subscribes to the following doctrines held originally by the majority of Protestants: the Bible as the inspired Word of God is the supreme authority in everything pertaining to faith and conduct; there is one God, Creator of all things, eternally existing in three persons, Father, Son, and Holy Spirit; Jesus Christ as God manifest in the flesh died on the cross making a perfect sacrifice for our sins, arose from the dead, ascended into Heaven, and is now seated on the right hand of God as our High Priest and Advocate; in this age the Holy Spirit convicts men of sin, regenerates those who believe, and indwells the believer to enable him to live a holy life, to witness, and to serve God; man, created in the image of God, fell into sin and is therefore lost, and only through faith in the Lord Jesus Christ and regeneration by the Holy Spirit can he obtain eternal life; the true Church, the Body of Christ, is composed of all who through saving faith in Christ have been made new creatures; there will be a bodily resurrection of all the dead, of believers to eternal life and of unbelievers to everlasting punishment.

A history of Christian education cannot properly concern itself entirely with schools and classroom teaching. Unquestionably the school has played an important part in the historical development of Christian education. But the educative process extends far beyond the confines of the school. Natural education and informal teaching, whatever the values derived from formal teaching in classroom situations, account for an immense amount of learning in the realm of Christian truth. This learning begins in the family with the care of the infant by the mother, the influence of the home environment upon the child, the training given the child, and with family interrelationships, the natural channel for the transmission of beliefs, experiences, and views of life. The process goes on beyond the family circle, gaining in breadth as the environment of the child widens, bringing him into contact with other people and new objects, new forms of teaching and discipline, one of which—not always the most effective—is the school. Formal teaching is but one factor in learning.

This is particularly true of learning in the realm of the spiritual, both in its foundations and in its course of development. The children of Israel had no schools until near the time of Christ. The Church in obeying the commission of the Lord to go "and teach all nations" has never limited its educational work to the school. The Church did not use to any great extent the school as an organized means for inculcating Christian ideals in the converts from the Roman world or, later on, in those from among the northern barbarians. Even after Christian schools had become common in the latter part of the Middle Ages, they were a small part of the prevailing system of education. And, though accessible to all, they actually served the interests only of those preparing for the professions; the people in general received what preparation they got for Christian living through agencies other than the school.

History has been defined as "His story"—the account of the development by God of His plan for the world, insofar as man has come to knowledge of this development. It has also been said that "history, without God, is a chaos without design or end or aim." Certainly, history has a divine side, for God does reveal Himself in time and unfolds His plan for accomplishing His purposes. But history has also a human side, because it is a record not only of God's activities in connection with human beings but also of the achievements of men themselves. Moreover, to be at all complete, the historical record must take note of the activities of a third being, Satan, who ever seeks to defeat the plan of God, working through men whenever and however he can.

Human history deals with what is known concerning the beginnings of man and his development through time. Sacred history is the story of what is known about human development as this is seen to have been affected by God's dealings with man. Church history is that division of sacred history which treats of all that is known relative to the founding and the development of the kingdom of God on earth. This kingdom comprehends far more than the visible church or churches; it is permanent while the churches as founded by men are temporary. Church history, therefore, has various divisions such as the history of missions, the history of theology, the history of persecution, the history of worship, and the history of Christian education.

Christian faith and Christian education are inseparable; where-ever the first exists, the second is found. Among peoples with religions antedating Christianity—the Chinese, the Assyrians, the Babylonians, the Egyptians, the Greeks—there were systems for the religious teaching of youth. Wherever an active faith exists, there is also education in that faith. Such a faith must have a way to teach its truths. The word "education" is not found in the Bible, but from the very beginning of the Bible record there is emphasis upon education. Accordingly, the historical approach in studying Christian education is helpful. Such approach makes evident how essential education is in God's plan for the progressive revelation He is making of Himself to mankind.

Often men have sought to separate Christian faith and Christian education, which God has joined together. Even more often has Satan sought to contaminate with the ideas of men the pure truth of the living God. Always, along with the setting forth of the light and the glory of God, there exists within and without the church much error. So long as time lasts, the Church militant, in the very nature of things, will have against it the world, the flesh, and the Devil. At all times there are those who, while claiming to be the Lord's own, deny Him by lip and by life.

But the Father has given Christ all power on earth as well as in Heaven. In the end He will triumph and rule supreme with His Church on the throne with Him. Despite the odds against it, there is in true Christian education a rich heritage from the past which will be passed on to generation after generation until His day of triumph dawns. Christian education is increasingly assuming the place it should have in the life and work of the Church of the living God. More than in all past time it has undergone in this present century tremendous growth and development.

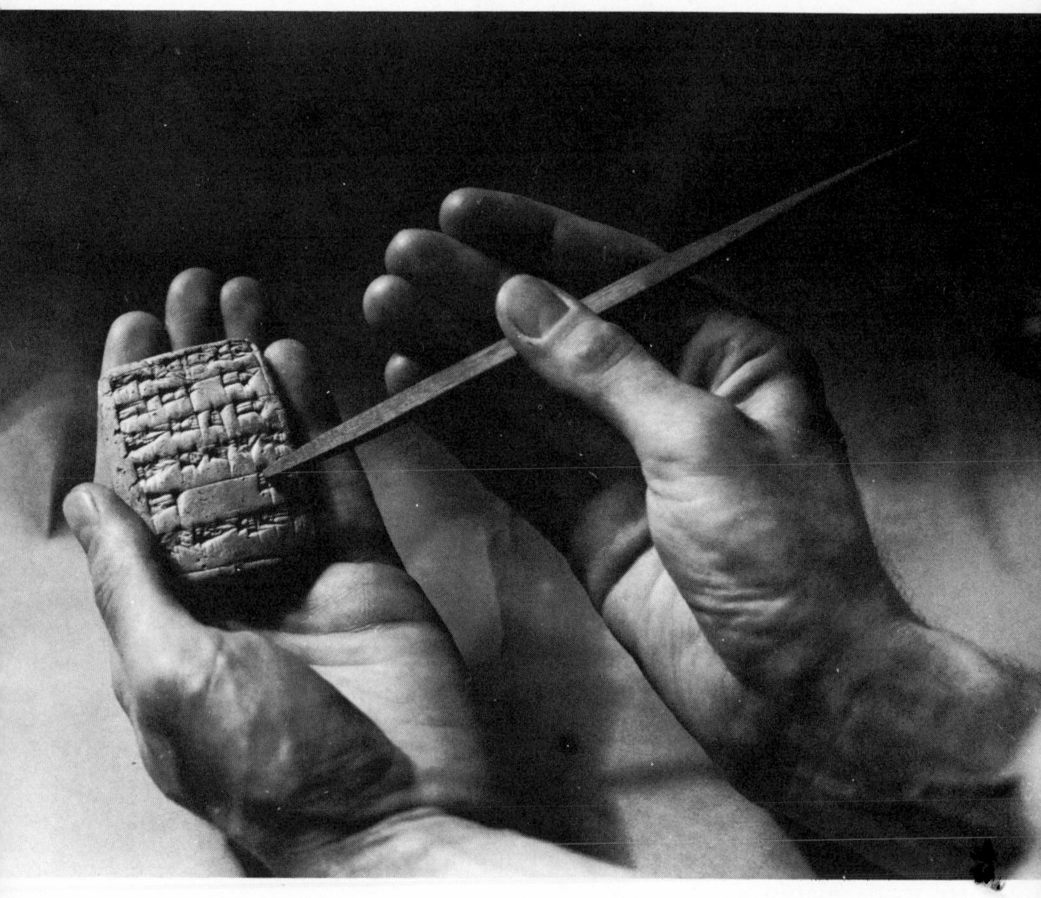

Important to the education of early peoples of Babylonia, Assyria, and Asia Minor was the clay tablet on which were written cuneiform (wedge-shaped) symbols. Hundreds of thousands of these tablets have been found in the Near East with subject matter as widely diverse as hymns and prayers, bills of lading, astronomical observations, and exercises of school boys. Here hands and stylus are shown in correct position for writing on a clay tablet.

(Courtesy of the Oriental Institute, University of Chicago)

1

The Beginnings of Christian Education

THE BIBLE is the record of the history of God's work for and with men. It is the beginning of a special historical revelation within the limits of the general history of mankind—a revelation of the eternal purpose of God for the salvation of men. What God purposed before time began He is carrying out and realizing in time through Christ, man's Redeemer. "The march of the Gospel through the world is the proper theme of world history." One who understands the Bible as the unfolding of God's purpose regards the development of human history from the standpoint of eternity. Such a one sees in history a plan, guided by God, which unfolds in orderly manner as it moves steadily but surely to its goal. History has meaning; it is no unending series of purposeless events accidentally occurring.

The Bible is the history of salvation, not the history of Christian education. God is not dependent upon men, but He does use human agencies in carrying out His purpose. From the day He created him, He made man a worker with Him in the achieving of His plan. It would seem that God might always have been man's direct Teacher if only man had been properly responsive to Him. When man chose not to respond, God used other and more indirect means of instruction. Whatever He would otherwise have done, God has been, and is now, teaching men through human beings. So, while the Bible is not primarily a history of Christian education, it is much concerned with an education which centers in God.

Never does God abandon His plan for His creation, but He does vary His methods, in accordance with man's responses, for carrying out His plan. Accordingly, the story of the education that centers in Him is not the history of a finished product. History shows Christian education as a process in which continuity and change are inseparably united. God, the eternal One who had no beginning, the One who is above the whole course of history, the Source of all that is, originated as Creator the universal plan. All things came into being through His will and are sustained by His creative energies. All things center in Him and will be consummated in Him. Consequently, all things belong to Him. Each creature, including man, is His work and, therefore, His instrument to be used in His own way. So, the education that centers in God, far from being static, must ever be keeping pace with the work God is doing among men. This education must from time to time reformulate its methods in the light of experience to keep them always in harmony with God's manner of working.

God's Plan for Man

"So God created man in his own image, in the image of God created he him; male and female created he them" (Gen. 1:27). The Creator formed the creature; the Creator is infinite, but the creature is finite. Though finite, man was created perfect, for God looked on everything He had made and found it to be "very good."

However, this perfection was not the perfection of maturity. Being immature, man had a divinely ordained need to be educated in a divinely ordained way. To develop man to maturity, God would undoubtedly have maintained between man and Himself the perfect relation that existed in creation. So long as man responded properly to God, this relationship was that of a perfect being to a perfect Creator. But when man presumed to seek knowledge of good and evil for himself, in opposition to God's will and instruction, the perfection of the relationship was terminated.

Upon creating man, God instructed him concerning His will. He was to increase, to people the earth, to subdue the earth, and to rule over everything upon the earth. Also, God instructed man relative to his own means of subsistence as well as that of other living creatures (Gen. 1:28-30). That is, God gave man a work to do and a task to accomplish. Through these he was to bring to full maturity of development the powers and capacities God had placed in him and in the world.

In the instructions God gave, Adam counted not simply as an individual but also as the generic man, the organic representative of the whole human race. So the task assigned him was the start and goal and type of the entire task of man on earth. Two chief facts are to be noted: first, for the effective performance of the task man needs to be educated; second, through performing the task, man individually and collectively is taken further and further along the way in the never-ending process of becoming educated.

Proof of the existence in the earth of conditions not in harmony with the plan of God is found in the instruction given to man to subdue the earth and to rule over it. Bible history indicates that the earth, in spite of the new beginning God was making with the creation of man, was at least partially under the control of a power hostile to God. God placed man in the Garden of Eden "to dress it and to keep it" (Gen. 2:15). Had there been no opposing force, there would have been no need for dressing and keeping. Also, the temptation of man came through a power opposed to God. Furthermore, had all the earth been a place where God had undisputed sway, there would have been no need for a garden. Seemingly, God prepared for man, His highest creation, a special region to give him a place of residence corresponding to his rank and in harmony with the plan God intended him to fulfill.

This plan was that man, under God, should rule the earth, drawing all creation into the purposes of God for redemption from evil and perfection in righteousness. For His own glory, God sought to build the fully perfect man and the fully perfect creation, the fully developed man and the fully developed creation. This had to be done against the opposition of the adversary, the one who, after revolting against God in Heaven, had entered into an eternal mysterious conflict with Him—a conflict of which one phase was now to take place upon the earth.

To take his God-appointed part in this mighty conflict, man had to be prepared—educated, so to speak. Until he was able to rule himself he could not rule the earth for God; unless he first gained mastery over self he could not conquer evil. Only by being placed in a moral conflict, with the possibility of yielding to evil, could man learn how to rule for God. Only through victory over temptation to evil could he attain to freedom of authority necessary to rule the earth and thus bring everything into subjection to God.

The prohibition against eating the fruit of the tree took into consideration the level of understanding of the newly created pair. Along with the prohibition, God gave plain and definite instruction regarding the consequences of disobedience. The conflict into which this brought man was essentially spiritual, for what was involved was the absolute authority of God over man. To Adam and Eve violation was not simply the eating of the fruit but that they chose, by a forbidden way, to become equal with God in respect to the knowledge of good and evil (Gen. 3.5). So the tree was but a sign of the rule of God over man and of the willingness of man to submit his will to God's will. It was a means used by God to educate man and, through educating him, to bring all creation into the glory of complete subjection to God.

Man failed the test. He took his own way—that of indulging in the delights and satisfactions of intellectual exercise, of enjoying the power and pleasure of using his own reasoning, and of seeking to have a greater breadth and depth of intellectual understanding. He forsook God's way—that of unwavering reliance upon what God revealed, of wholehearted acceptance of truth as given by God, and of complete dependence upon God as the only source of the knowledge of good. In short, man chose to put his own puny insufficiency in the place of God's boundless sufficiency. The knowledge of good and evil did become his, but in a form distorted by wrong conceptions of what man can do for himself. The result is a life of unsatisfied longing for the return of a glory that is departed and a perpetual, unavailing attempt to reinstate it.

God's Program of Education

Great was the ruin of man, but great also is the plan of God for him. Even as a sinner man never ceased to be the object of God's love. However, the fall made necessary a change in God's ways of dealing with man. By disobeying, he had asserted himself against God; he had dethroned God and made himself the king on the throne. God's plan had been that He should be the center of man's life, with man dependent upon Him. Instead, man makes self the center of his life; around this self as center he would have the world—and even God—rotate. He looks to self for satisfaction, for redemption, for everything he longs for but cannot find since he banished God from the throne of his heart.

Created in the image of God, the subject of God, assigned the task of ruling the world for God, man should have done the will of God. Had he done so when Satan tempted him, human progress under God's tutelage would have been gradually upward, a continually ascending course of development of man and of creation. With the entrance of sin, all was ruined. Man became subject to death in spirit, soul, and body; the world came under the power of Satan; and the "prince of the power of the air" took up a station "in the heavenly places." In sinning man brought not only himself but also the whole creation into bondage to sin and the author of sin, Satan. Before human development can proceed, redemption from this enslavement must be effected. Consequently a change in God's way of dealing with man became necessary.

In order that His plan for man may be effectively achieved, God must teach man two great lessons—his own insufficiency and God's abundant sufficiency. Man must learn the terrible consequences of having fallen through going contrary to God's command. He must learn his absolute weakness and his utter helplessness. He must be brought to the realization of the impossibility of his accomplishing his own redemption. Sin so blinds man that he cannot see himself as he is. His spiritual understanding is darkened and his reason beclouded. He takes evil for good and good for evil. He glories in the good he mistakenly thinks he has in himself. So long as he believes he is strong and right, he cannot be made to realize that his sufficiency is of God, in whom alone is redemption.

To bring man to this realization, God set up a program of education extending over thousands of years. So much a part of man is his belief in his own sufficiency that he must be taught his utter helplessness in each and every respect. Accordingly, this program made provision for him to test his strength in every direction so that he might finally come to a complete recognition of his powerlessness to do anything at all for himself. Each phase of the program has for its purpose the learning of the lesson of failure in one particular aspect. The overall educative purpose is that man learn from all angles his lost and helpless state. Thus everything human will be finally proved insufficient and man will be shut up to faith in God as the only source of salvation and deliverance.

So God tests man again and again to give him opportunity to become obedient to Him. Each test is in respect to some specific phase of the revelation of His will and plan. But man persists in his rebellion against God; therefore each stage of testing ends with God's judgment upon him for disobedience.

Created in innocence, given a simple test, and instructed about the consequences of disobedience, man chose to disobey. The judgment was death and expulsion from the Garden which meant cessation of intimate relationship with God and being obliged to dwell not in a blessed paradise but in the earth, which was cursed because of his sin. Thereafter, his activities and undertakings while he sojourned here would be in sorrow, pain, and toil. Then his body would return to the ground whence it came.

Since man's conscience had been awakened through the knowledge of good and evil obtained in the fall, God tested him next by giving him freedom to do the good and to abstain from doing the evil. His wicked heart led him only into evil, so God sent upon him the judgment of the flood. Then God put man under the rule of man, making him responsible to govern the world for Him. When he failed in this, God visited upon him the judgment of the confusion of tongues and the setting aside of the nations. Next, God chose a people as His own to whom He tried through centuries of time to give an education in faith. The outcome was unbelief, for which God visited upon them blindness of heart. Then He tested them by law for other centuries, giving them an education in repentance. Once more man failed, for the result was repeated violation of law, unattended by confession of sin. This testing ended in the judgment of the captivities and the dispersion of Israel.

Then God put man under grace, giving him the opportunity to accept Christ as his Redeemer. Man rejects Christ. The tribulation under Antichrist will be the judgment. Finally, there will be the kingdom of glory, a kingdom in which God will appear triumphantly. The judgment upon man for not accepting His rule will be destruction and fiery ruin.

Thus failure is written over the history of man, but the failure is not of God's principles of education but of the human element. Always, His program has been effective with a small number from the whole of mankind. Whenever He was obliged to bring judgment upon men for their sins, there was here and there one who had learned the lesson He taught. Never has the world been without a few godly individuals through whom God carried forward His plan. Men such as Enoch, Noah, Abraham, Joseph, Job, David, Daniel, and the prophets were obedient to Him, even though they did not obey Him perfectly. Unnoticed and even despised by the world, these few kept pure the testimony of God. Through this minority God has advanced His kingdom. In carrying forward His plan, He uses the insignificant and the scorned to the end that men may see the nothingness of the human. He "hath chosen the foolish things of the world to confound the wise" so that man may have nothing to glory in before Him (I Cor. 1:27-29).

Man's Program of Education

God works in the wide scope of the history of the ages to accomplish in and through man the glorious purpose He had for him before He created him. To man God has given free will, which He never violates or takes away. In a sense, then, man is the architect of his own destiny, the maker of his own life, the builder of his own history. Consequently, as he has developed through time, there has come to be a program of education from the human point of view as well as the one carried on by God.

Satan seeks forever and continually to contaminate the pure work of God in and through man, just as he did in the Garden of Eden. The result in education is an admixture composed of elements of the divine, the human, and the demonic. In the beginning, as God sought to teach men directly, the divine was ascendant. When man, instigated by Satan, refused to learn of God, God allowed him freedom to act of and for himself. However, God has never forsaken man; always He stands ready and willing to have him turn from his own poor, weak, inadequate ways and subject himself to God and His perfect way.

In education, as in other aspects of life, there have been during the centuries a few among the many through whom God could work. It is the purpose of this book to trace the education carried on by the few who make God the center of their program. The history of education in general is characterized by less and less of God and more and more of man's thoughts and ideas, influenced at many points by the deceptions of the enemy of God.

The time intervening between the fall of man and the call of Abraham may be called the primitive period of the history of Christian education, or of the education centering in God. Man was created with the power of speech but he developed a language. Preliterate or primitive people have their own peculiar educational practices. Since the Bible is not a book on education, it says nothing directly on the subject. However, valid inferences may properly be drawn.

It is evident from the Biblical record that God dealt directly with the individual prior to the flood. From Noah's time on, the head of the family was the agent through whom God usually conveyed His instructions to the individual. During the primitive period knowledge was imparted by God's authority; therefore it was in itself authoritative. The duty of the individual was to accept it as such and to do as he was taught. The purpose of imparting the knowledge was that man might know and do the will of God.

Knowledge was conveyed even in connection with the placing upon Adam and Eve of the penalty for their sin. The penalty itself was a divine judgment and belongs in the moral realm. Its very pronouncement taught man that sin is violation of the holiness of God and that entrance of sin into his life meant the departure from him of the glory of God. But the words, "it shall bruise thy head, and thou shalt bruise his heel" (Gen. 3:15), state the truth that victory over Satan, the source of sin, shall be with man. As man was defeated, so will it be man who effects the triumph, for in Christ, "the seed of the woman," will the triumph be realized. Thus as God pronounces upon man judgment for sin, He teaches him three basic facts concerning redemption from sin: the incarnation of Christ, the death of Christ, and Christ's victory over sin through death.

In Genesis 3:21 it is said that "the Lord God made coats of skins, and clothed" Adam and Eve. After they had sinned, they used as coverings for their shame aprons of fig leaves, which were much too narrow for them to wrap themselves in. God provided them with coats of skins, adequate in size and well suited to their need. To obtain the skins, lives of animals had to be taken. So, in this matter, two lessons were given man: the inadequacy of his own provision for coping with the outcomes of sin; the perfection of God's provision made through the shedding of blood.

Blood sacrifice was probably basic also in the offerings made by Cain and Abel. It is not certain that Cain's offering was rejected because it was a bloodless one, but it is certain that both Cain and Abel knew God had regarded their offerings as unequal in value. The difference between the two was this: Cain's was a product of his own work and strength; Abel's was an offering of blood, necessitating the death of a guiltless victim. From the statement in Hebrews 11:4 it is manifest that Abel's sacrifice was better than Cain's because it was the acceptable response to truth God had made known to them. Abel was reckoned righteous because of his faith, expressed in his offering. That faith must surely have been in the substitutionary merit of a death not his own.

From this point onward two "ways" run through human history—"the way of Cain" (Jude 11) and the way of Abel. The first is the way of human development apart from God, the way of self-will, of opposition to the truth revealed by God, of a religion of the flesh, of trust in human knowledge and strength, of justification by works, of confidence in the ability of man to achieve for himself, of denial of need for redemption through the means appointed by God. The second is the way of humble dependence on God, of wholehearted submission to His will, of acceptance as truth what He revealed, of the worship of God in sincerity of heart, of complete reliance on Him for everything, of humble acknowledgment that sin deserves death, of the recognition of the total insufficiency of man, of awareness of guilt for which God alone can make atonement, and of expectation that God will bring about the redemption of man through grace. In short, the first is the way of man proud that he knows and can do so much, while the second is the way of man humble in the realization that in God are wisdom and knowledge and redemption.

Those who follow the "way of Cain" accomplish great things, both materially and culturally. The first civilization originated in Cain, and it was a splendid one. It was characterized by a high level of development in the mechanical arts, by many inventions and discoveries, and by much emphasis upon the development of social life. For these to flourish as they did, there must have been an education of no low level. No attainment of civilization is in and of itself contrary to the will of God. He is not opposed to culture as such. He condemns not civilization and culture but the arrogance and pride, the selfishness and hypocrisy, the waywardness and the rebellion of men against Himself so typically present in those who promote culture.

In spite of all the temporal and material splendors of this first civilization, God's judgment was poured out upon it—judgment that was according to the moral state, not the material, the cultural, or anything human. For many centuries God had called upon men to give heed to Him and His ways, but men paid no attention to His call. Gradually even the Sethites, who had originally honored Him, were overcome by the tendencies of the age, with the consequence that the professed people of God lost their identity and everything was given over to wickedness. So great was this wickedness that God sent upon the alienated sinful race destruction by the flood, saving from it Noah, one of the two antediluvians of whom it was said that they "walked with God."

As was noted above, beginning with Noah God conveyed instruction indirectly through an agent rather than directly to the individual. Noah, under God's blessing, is the second head of the human race. There are parallels between what God told him and what He had told Adam. Both were to "be fruitful, and multiply, and replenish the earth." Both were instructed as to food, Adam concerning herbs and Noah concerning the flesh of animals. Both were given divine stipulations: Adam was not to eat of the fruit of the tree of the knowledge of good and evil; Noah was not to eat flesh with the blood in it. In addition, Noah was told that never again would God destroy the earth in a judgment by water. Furthermore, he was instructed concerning the establishment of human government—a necessary barrier against sin's gaining the upper hand if God was not henceforth going to inflict upon mankind an exterminating judgment.

The covenant made by God with Noah gives information about nature and world history. Though Noah's curse and blessing are not directly a part of the covenant, they do constitute its prophetic foundation in that they give the program for the races in the history of the world.

The curse on Canaan, Ham's fourth son, shows that from him will descend an inferior and servile posterity. This prophecy has been verified in history. The Canaanites in Palestine were subjugated by Israel, the Semitic people. In Syria and North Africa, as Phoenicians and Carthaginians, they were conquered by the Persians, Grecians, and Romans, the Japhetic people. Through the centuries other Hamites have been made to feel the heavy hand of the oppressor.

Glorious blessing was to be the portion of Shem. The prophecy has been fulfilled in history through the choosing of the Semitic race as the people of God, the channel of God's redeeming grace to all peoples of the earth. God's revelation has been through Semitic men. Christ, after the flesh, was a descendant of Shem; in Him the blessing of Shem becomes the Gospel for all the world.

The prophetic statement concerning Japheth is that from him would descend the enlarged races. Historically, government, culture, science, and art have been predominantly the marks of peoples descended from Japheth. From his seven sons came the Gentile nations. The ancient Medes were from the line of Madai, and the Greeks were descendants of Japheth through Javan. The Persians were connected with the Medes, and the Romans were related to the Greeks. The people of India and the Germanic nations are genealogically related to the Persians. The origin of the Chinese people is clouded in mystery, but available evidence indicates Japhetic connections. Russia is commonly identified with Magog, Tubal, and Meschech.

Thus the Japhetic race has ruled the earth not only geographically and politically but also intellectually and culturally. The blessing Noah pronounced on Shem emphasized spiritual power, the one on Japheth mentioned a wide extension of cultural and worldly powers. Of Japheth, however, Noah said, "and he shall dwell in the tents of Shem." The channel of revelation was Shem, but the Japhethites, or Gentiles, were to be sharers in his spiritual benefits. This prophecy has been and is being fulfilled in history as Gentiles are made partakers with God's chosen people of the blessing of salvation through Christ.

Confusion of Language and Religion

The civilization that began with Noah had its end, as such, in the confounding of languages and the scattering abroad of men "upon the face of all the earth." Left to their own devices, governed by human beings instead of God, men became lifted up in pride and vainglory. Satisfied with themselves, they developed a plan that they thought might hold them together—the building of a city and a tower "whose top may reach unto heaven." There is nothing in the Biblical record to shed light on the nature of the education that prevailed in the time of this civilization, but it is certain to have been much opposed to God. Since the top of the tower was to reach to Heaven, it must have expressed defiance against Him, or at least an attempt to rival Him. They hoped through its construction to make a name for themselves, not to honor God. And they built it to prevent their dispersion, thus disobeying the command of God to replenish the earth.

Lest they in their strength of human oneness go on to greater lengths in their opposition to Him, God visited upon them the judgment of the confusion of tongues. This is a judgment against which the world has been struggling in vain ever since it was executed. The confounding of language is far more than mere confusing of speech; it involves a confusing also of the thought patterns, a breaking down of the uniformity of mental life. In place of the uniformity that existed with one language and one speech, there came to be wide differences in thought, feeling, and outlook on life. This meant great variations in the conceptions of different peoples in respect to the total content and product of human thinking.

Of far greater significance than the confounding of speech was the spiritual confusion which resulted from the setting aside of the oneness of the race. Never, anywhere in the world, have men been without "a belief in Spiritual Beings." Originally, they believed in one God who reveals Himself in nature, in conscience, and in history. God who "really is not far from any of us" seeks men continually, yearning that they should seek Him "if haply they might feel after him, and find him" (Acts 17:27). Ever since the fall, the life of man has been one of groping, of seeking blindly after God. Satan, forever the arch deceiver, gave mankind's search for God a false direction. Through his working, the conception of God and spirit remaining with man from the original revelation was distorted, the revelation in nature misinterpreted, and the revelation in conscience perverted. Such corrupting of the original revelation characterizes all heathen religion, whatever its present level of development.

All heathen religion begins with animism, or the belief that spirits determine and control the actions of all things in the world—the forces of nature, things animate, and things inanimate. Early man believes that present in everything is a spirit or a "double" of itself which causes its activities, be these the activities of man or those of natural things. Every stone, tree, animal, weapon, utensil, human being—every form of material existence, whether animate or inanimate—possesses a soul, the so-called "double." The number of souls, or spirits, is infinite; a supernatural world exists side by side with the natural world, and the one is just as real as the other.

A spirit is deemed the cause of everything that occurs, be it bad or good. Some spirits, or "doubles," are malevolent and others benevolent, so man must know how to behave in respect to all of them in order to escape the bad and receive the good. As man advances from primitivism, animism continues in various forms, such as the veneration of trees, sacred wells, holy water, and many other objects. Early man believed that "doubles" of the dead returned to the living in their dreams; thus ancestor worship developed. The grave became an altar; many altars and churches have been built over graves or the relics of saints. Egyptian civilization made much of the tomb. Deification of holy men in India and the canonization of holy men in Christendom have been common practice. Thus, the traces of animistic belief which persist to the present are not inconsiderable in number.

Separated from God, the infinite Spirit, man knew no spirit other than his own, hence it was logical for him to attribute to the spirits with which he peopled nature the characteristics of the human spirit. And these nature spirits which he saw were most powerful could be pictured to the imagination only as beings of a higher form of life; hence they must have these human characteristics in higher and stronger measure than the human. Thus developed the superhuman, the essence of the heathen idea of God. And so man in his blindness, deceived by Satan, created his "god" in his own image.

With the confusion of tongues and the resulting confusion in patterns of thinking, there arose varied conceptions of the man-created "god." Each nation, or people, under the influence of Satan, became the creator of its own "god." Even if there were, prior to the Babel judgment, different ideas of nature divinities, there could have been no national types of religion. Such forms of religion could have had their beginning only in the breaking up of the oneness of the human race into separate nations. Since that event there has been variety of national character with a corresponding variety of spiritual and moral ideas and ideals. This last has one common mark: *godlessness.* In creating his own religion, man breaks the first commandment, "Thou shalt have no other gods" and expresses emphatically his opposition against God. But, withal, his conception of the gods he creates for himself has its basis in the idea of God so implanted in his being that it is impossible for him to get away from it.

Summary

At this point it may be well to pause for purposes of orientation. Attempt has been made to show something of the program of education of man that God is carrying out through the ages. Mention was made of the fact that, alongside this program, man, endowed by God with free will, develops his own program. This Satan does his utmost to corrupt and pervert so as to make ineffective the work God would accomplish in and through man. Because of the corrupt nature of mankind, the majority of men respond to Satan instead of God. Therefore, the history of education in general shows that it has come to be characterized by less and less of God and more and more of human thought and activity permeated through and through by Satanic deception.

Attempt was then made to trace the beginnings of man's program of education in the primitive period of human history. Data being scarce, reliance must be placed mostly on inference. During this period knowledge was imparted by God's authority, which men persistently rejected. Just as persistently they sought to follow the "way of Cain," the way of human development apart from God. Humanly speaking, they attain much. But spiritual departure from God and moral wickedness become so great that God destroyed the race by the flood and made a new beginning under Noah and his three sons. Their descendants continued prevailingly in the "way of Cain," exulting in pride and the feeling of human sufficiency. To frustrate their efforts to displace or rival Him, God destroyed the oneness of humanity in speech and in place of habitation. The result was the founding of the nations with their diverse characteristics, their different patterns of thought, and their religions, from which men, influenced by Satan, banished God, in the measure they could, in favor of gods of their own creation.

The call of Abraham and the founding of the nation of Israel marks an important turning point in God's dealing with man. Before the Babel judgment, humanity was one; after this, it existed in many divisions. God had sought unavailingly to get men to turn to Him; instead of so doing they increasingly departed from Him and became worshipers of idols—gods of their own creating. So God called Abraham and made of him a great nation to serve as His witness in the midst of universal godlessness. Through this people chosen for Himself, God would show to all peoples the blessedness of serving the true God, would reveal His plan and purpose for mankind, and would bring forth the Redeemer of all men.

Henceforth, the human race would have two main divisions, Jews and Gentiles. Since the nations had rejected God, there was among them no education centering in Him. Accordingly, it was necessary at this point to follow the course of education among the Jews, who honored God at least in a measure, as the Gentiles in general did not. Education is not, however, an activity over which any people have a monopoly. Very soon after the beginning of any people education appears. Because the main characteristics of primitive education shed light on the nature of Christian education, these characteristics will be considered. Also, the nature of religious education among non-Christian peoples prior to the development of Jewish education will come in for consideration.

Characteristics of Primitive Education

In every primitive society is found the essential characteristic of education, the fitting of the individual to his environment through utilization of the accumulated experience of previous generations. Always, the environment of man has these three aspects: the physical, that of objects and events; the social, that of people; and the spiritual, that of spirits or mysterious beings, actual and imagined.

Man's first relation is to the physical environment, for he must have food, clothing, and shelter. However, these must be obtained without offending the spirit or "double" dwelling in every plant, animal, and object having to do with the satisfaction of physical need. So there is a most real connection between the primitive man's physical existence and his religion. For him there is no separation into the secular and the sacred; all of his life—and therefore his education—is religious in nature.

There is also a close connection between the satisfying of physical needs and the social organization. The family is the basic social institution. Whatever its form, it is always a group consisting of a married couple and their children. There are economic as well as biological reasons for its existence. Above the family stands the clan, an aggregation of families who are typically concerned with economic matters. The tribe is a group of clans, each much like the other in language and manner of living. Many ties bind together the members of a tribe, but the need for food, clothing, and shelter demands a common struggle and serves as a strong unifying force.

Education in the tribe is basically practical, involving training in the activities of obtaining food, shelter, and clothing. The first learning of the child is natural—without design or intent on the part of anyone, without planning or organization for learning. Much that the primitive child learns of life as he must live it he learns through play. The second stage of his learning is informal: he is required to participate in the activities of adults, and he learns through participating. For the most part this learning is not consciously directed, that is, it does not have for a purpose the training of the individual but the accomplishing of the work.

From birth to death the individual in the primitive tribe lives in what is to him the actuality of a spirit world as real as the material world. He believes that each object in the material world possesses consciousness. Through its "double" it has the power to feel and think and will as he himself has. The world of spirits is a counterpart of the world of material objects. The spirits are worshiped and placated when crises occur in the life of either the tribe or of individuals. Before any event of significance, the aid of the spirits is sought. Gratitude is expressed to them for rain, for crops and herds, for freedom from disease, for deliverance from attacks by wild animals, for victory in war. Sacrifice is made to them, both for placating and for expressing gratitude.

Through religious and social ceremonies founded upon these beliefs and practices there develops in the course of time among primitive peoples an education definitely formal in character. Before any important activity involving the members of the tribe, such as a hunt, the planting of crops, a harvest, or a military expedition, a ceremonial performance is held. Because they contain explanations of the beliefs, religious teachings, or historical traditions of the tribe, such ceremonials have an educational function. Thus the young are continually instructed in the spiritual and intellectual life of their people.

For the most part the youth's formal education is given through the rites of ceremonies of initiation which begin at the age of puberty and mark entry into tribal membership. Those conducted by the women for girls are much less elaborate than those for boys conducted by the men. There is great variation in these ceremonies from tribe to tribe, as is attested in the voluminous descriptions given by many writers. But, whatever the form, initiation ceremonies have a number of educational values, the most significant of which is the religious value. Through them the young man becomes a full-fledged member of the tribe; to him all the sacred beliefs and secrets concerning the world of spirits have been made known.

Initiation ceremonies are the culmination of an educative process preparing the young for life in the group. The primitive child is educated by living and acting in his physical environment. Later, by actual participation in the activities of adults, boys and girls learn how to perform the duties of life. Then through formal training the boys become prepared to transmit to succeeding generations the ideas and beliefs of their people. The whole atmosphere in which primitive people live is one of continuous recognition, through ceremonial, of the actuality of the spirit world. Men engage in ceremonial rites throughout their lives. Thus these rites constitute a lifelong education especially for the men but also to some extent for the women and children, who for religious reasons are not allowed to participate in them.

So, "a belief in Spiritual Beings" permeates not only every phase of the lives of primitive people but as well every aspect of their education. What most interests the student of the history of Christian education in the study of the education of primitive pagans is this fact: even people who in opposition to God develop a godless religion do not in their education any more than in their religion get away from the idea of God.

The family and the tribe are the schools of primitive man. Parents direct the practical education of their children, and tribal leaders have charge of the formal initiation ceremonies. The method is essentially imitation; in physical, social, and religious activities, each generation learns by imitating the ways of the older generation. The chief feature of primitive education, therefore, is its static character.

However, as time moves on, advance is made gradually. The tribal elders who direct the ceremonial activities to placate unfriendly spirits or to win the favor of friendly ones develop into a priest class. This priesthood becomes a special teaching class for all the people, not only in primitive times but for centuries to come. As the interpretation of life becomes more complex with accompanying complication of the ceremonies, written language is invented to give the interpretation permanent form. Written language is the chief mark of the beginning of civilization. The priestly class then has special subject matter for study—a religious literature, for all early literature is of a religious nature. With the forming of a special priesthood and the development of a written language and a literature, the necessity arises for teaching prospective priests what to do and how to do it, hence the first school emerges.

Education Among Ancient Oriental Peoples

The education based upon written language and a clearly differentiated teaching class, stressing formal instruction as well as practical training, is a higher type of education than that of primitive peoples. The earliest forms of this level of education are to be found among ancient Oriental peoples—the Chinese, the Hindus, the Egyptians, the Babylonians, and the Hebrews. To the education of some of these peoples attention is now directed, because noting religious aspects of these heightens appreciation of the nature of Christian education.

Very early the Chinese developed a most elaborate system of

education. Nine sacred books constitute the foundation on which it is founded. These are the productions of Confucius and his followers. Confucius strengthened the native Chinese religion but actually Confucianism is not a full-fledged religion on a par with the other Chinese religions, Taoism and Buddhism. The former is concerned with charms, fasting, alchemy, astrology, ritual and sacrifices, divination, and the search for the elixir of life. The latter emphasizes meditation and trance. Both Taoism and Buddhism stress ethics, so Confucius found in them a congenial atmosphere for his teachings.

In essence, his system is a delineation of the Chinese social order, defining the relationships within the kinship structure of the clan. As such, it is concerned with ethics more than it is with religion. It endeavors to regulate the five relationships of life: of prince and subject, of parent and child, of brother and brother, of husband and wife, of friend and friend.

Confucianism absolutely dominated Chinese education. In its formal aspect, this centered in the mastery of language and literature. Since the language consisted of many thousands of characters, each having a meaning for the eye but not for the ear, this was a stupendous task. First, the pupil was required to master these language forms; second, he was obliged to commit to memory the sacred texts; and, third, he had to study a host of commentaries on these texts so that he might develop a literary style similar to that of the sacred writings. All the way through, the work was memorization and imitation. Even his writing was in slavish imitation of the formal literary style. For the Chinese, this imitation was the end, not a means to something else.

Ancient India, like other Oriental nations, was priest-dominated, with religious interests in ascendance over secular activities. The religion taught the immortality of the soul, also its transmigration through successive incarnations, each dependent on the preceding manner of living and all subject to the tragedies of earthly existence. The ideal was to escape the sufferings of life, to terminate the process of reincarnation, by the absorption of the individual soul into the world soul. The basic sacred books were the Vedas, four in number, enlarged by priestly commentaries, mystical sections, philosophical additions, and the wisdom and teachings of the basic literature. Beneath the Vedas were several less sacred books. In Hinduism there is one unknowable God who is the only reality. There are multiplied thousands of other gods—personified nature gods and mere local godlings, such as spirits of trees, streams, and other material objects.

This mystic religion and a dreamy philosophy were combined closely. Also, there were four major castes besides the outcastes. These two factors determined the nature of education. Since it was only for the priests, teachers, and rulers, about 95 percent of the population was deprived almost entirely of educational opportunity. For the upper classes education was based upon this combination of religion and philosophy. Education was connected with every phase of an eternal scheme. Emphasis was upon the attainment of a shadowy goal in an other-world future. The basic purpose of education was to instruct the individual concerning the divine social order and his place in it.

The Hindu did not lose sight entirely of practical realities. The aim of education was cultural but at the same time social. The ideal of duty was stressed, and the individual's first duty was to the social order. Yet the Hindu looked beyond the social goal to the attainment of spiritual harmony between himself, society, and the divine cosmic order. Always, practical training was made subordinate to the training of the soul.

Education consisted largely in memorization of the Vedas. Any inquiry as to meaning had to be kept within the boundary of assumptions that were unquestionable. Education was an intellectual and moral discipline, with its beginning marked by the ceremony of initiation. It was open only to members of the higher castes. The student led an austere life, subjecting body, mind, and will to rigorous discipline. This discipline was an end, not a means to an end. It meant the separating of desires from things in the natural world with a view to attaining spiritual perfection.

Ancient Egypt had a religion in which there was much nature worship. Gods were numerous; the greatest, Osiris, undoubtedly evolved from primitive animism and spirit worship. There was a sun-god, an earth-god, an ocean-god, a Nile-god, animal gods, and human gods. The sacred bull was prominent among the divinities. Belief in the immortality of the soul was an important tenet; with it was connected belief in the judgment of the dead.

Religious practices were magical and heavily burdened with ceremonial.

The idea of death was central in the culture of Egypt, hence the prevalence of mummification of bodies and the building of tombs. The religion was permeated with traces of primitive traditions and expressions relating to economic need. The Nile and the sun were worshiped because of their relation to the fertility of the soil and to the supplying of food. Every living person possessed a spirit "double" which left him at death. This belief was, of course, a relic of animism, but for the Egyptians the "double" was identified with the individual's inner mental states, being akin to the Greek and the Christian concept of the soul. It was believed that the "double" would eventually return to the body and restore it to life.

The formal education of Egypt was essentially cultural in that its primary purpose was to teach the language, literature, and ideas of the Egyptians. Priests were the teachers, as a matter of course; because of the relationship between culture and the technical subjects, the arts, crafts, sciences, and professional activities of the people were also under the direction of the priests, though these were not taught formally. Thus vocational pursuits were by religious requirement connected with the cultural, and their techniques were controlled by the priests. The many specialized arts and crafts were directed mostly by the middle and lower levels of priests. Above the artisans were professional groups, one of which was made up of priests who taught and wrote commentaries on the scriptures. Medical practice was carried on mostly by a special class of priests. High administrators of the Pharaoh, who was a god, composed the legal class. Thus educational purpose was very practical or vocational, though the real purpose was to preserve Egyptian civilization by preserving its traditional culture.

The pupil learned by imitating traditional forms of writing and of thought. Drill and memorization were strongly emphasized. Entire portions of the sacred books and many magical formulas were committed to memory. It was considered essential that men know the exact words of the gods. The priests were the national custodians of religious literature, and their control of the education of the upper classes seems to have been complete. The right to instruct boys for official or professional life was vested in political and ecclesiastical officials, who also controlled indirectly the apprenticeship training of artisans.

Thus the culture of Egypt was built upon a literature thought to be divine in origin. Education was under the guidance of an official and religious orthodoxy which had originated in tradition, in limited knowledge, and in fear of the unknown. By means of education this orthodoxy was to be perpetuated. It was thought that Egyptian society was the creation of the gods and, therefore, the perfect society. With this creation man was not to meddle.

In the life of the ancient Babylonians religion played an important part so their education was essentially and fundamentally religious. The religion was polytheistic; thousands of deities were worshiped. There was an aristocracy of gods, consisting of a heaven god and a heaven goddess, an earth god and his consort, a mother goddess thought to be the supreme goddess and known as "Queen of the gods," a moon god, and a sun god. Beneath these were nearly four thousand deities associated with aspects of culture, patrons of individuals, etc. A very complex theological system existed. The "Queen of the gods" ever interceded for men when they sinned. The male gods punished with extreme vengeance. The gods lived in the temples, which were centers of widely extended influence. Outstanding characteristics of Babylonian religion were the elaborate systems of magical practices, or incantations, and the interpretation of omens, or divinations, particularly the movements and position of the heavenly bodies, the actions of animals, and the meanings given to the entrails of sacrificial victims. Incantations against the devils consisted of endless descriptions of the demons and magical rituals and curses in the names of the gods.

Education was religious and under the direction of priests. According to legend, all human knowledge had been written upon tablets which were buried before the flood. The priests who could divine future events were the possessors of all wisdom, therefore only they could impart to others what could be known. Many devils brought upon men diseases, plagues, and other afflictions; these devils troubled sinners only, so anyone who was afflicted had sinned. His salvation depended upon the intervention of a powerful priesthood. For their service they had to be trained; this training constituted the greater portion of the education. For the masses there was little opportunity to become educated.

Readings

BOWER, WILLIAM CLAYTON, and HAYWARD, PERCY ROY. *Protestantism Faces Its Educational Task Together.* New York: National Council of Churches of Christ, n. d.

CUBBERLEY, ELLWOOD P. *The History of Education.* Boston: Houghton Mifflin Company, 1920.

GRAVES, FRANK PIERREPONT. *A Student's History of Education.* New York: The Macmillan Company, 1915; rev. ed.; 1936.

JAARSMA, CORNELIUS. *Fundamentals in Christian Education.* Grand Rapids: Wm. B. Eerdmans Publishing Company, 1953.

MARIQUE, PIERRE J. *A History of Christian Education.* 3 vols. New York: Fordham University Press, 1924-1932.

MONROE, PAUL. *A Brief Course in the History of Education.* New York: The Macmillan Company, 1907.

MULHERN, JAMES. *A History of Education.* New York: The Ronald Press Co., 1946.

MURCH, JAMES DEFOREST. *Christian Education and the Local Church.* Cincinnati: Standard Publishing Company, 1943.

PERSON, PETER P. *An Introduction to Christian Education.* Grand Rapids: Baker Book House, 1958.

SAUER, ERICH. *The Dawn of World Redemption.* Grand Rapids: Wm. B. Eerdmans Publishing Company, 1952.

SAUER, ERICH. *From Eternity to Eternity.* Grand Rapids: Wm. B. Eerdmans Publishing Company, 1954.

The New Schaff-Herzog Encyclopedia of Religious Knowledge. New York and London: Funk and Wagnalls Company, 1908-1914.

Articles on:

"China," Arthur H. Smith, III, 29-30.

"Comparative Religion," George W. Gilmore, III, 194-196.

"Egypt," Charles Ripley Gillett, IV, 86-91.

"India," Justin E. Abbott, V, 473.

At the center of Jewish education for more than 2,000 years has been the synagogue. While the superstructure of this synagogue at Biblical Capernaum probably dates to the third century, the floor may be as early as the time of Christ.

(Courtesy of the Consulate General of Israel)

2

Jewish Education

GOD, who created the world and all things in it, is the God of the whole human race. He "hath made of one blood all nations of men for to dwell on all the face of the earth, and hath determined the times before appointed, and the bounds of their habitation; that they should seek the Lord, if haply they might feel after him, though he be not far from every one of us; for in him we live, and move, and have our being" (Acts 17:26-28). Through all time, however much men spurn Him, He remains in personal relation to the whole human race. He decides the destinies of nations, which to Him "are as a drop of a bucket, and are counted as the small dust of the balance" (Isa. 40:15).

God is the center of all history, general and sacred. Within the limits of the history of the world, He directs a special history, the history of revelation, in which He makes Himself known personally to man. He works in world history, though men perceive Him not. Even in the heathen world there is found much high and noble thought which can be explained only as an outcome of the activity of God producing knowledge in human minds. Thinkers and poets, as was the case with the pagan ones quoted by Paul (Acts 17:28), give expression to truth that could have had its origin only in God. In addition to what God gave man by creation there survive among the peoples remnants from the revelation made to previous generations before they departed from God.

In the history of revelation God works as the God who reveals Himself. During the period of time from the creation of man to the call of Abraham, the revelation He made of Himself was not confined to any certain group but was to all men as members of the human race. Man failed in all that God sought to do for him through direct command, through conscience, and through human government. He set himself in self-will against the first, abused the freedom of the second by turning to all kinds of wickedness, and became rebellious and vain under the third.

Therefore, God changed His method of revelation. Because the race in its united strength tried rebelliously to withstand Him and to rob Him of His glory, God destroyed the unity of the race. Thereafter He confined His revelation to an individual and his physical and spiritual descendants.

In so doing God did not cast away the nations. He is still their God, though they refuse to honor Him. He is not in covenant relation with them, nor does He reveal Himself directly to them. But He orders world conditions, sets national boundaries, raises up one nation and puts down another, overrules historical events, and acts in the cultural and spiritual life of peoples to exert influence upon their outlook, customs, and morals. Though He found it needful to set aside the peoples, God yet loves them and yearns for them to turn to Him. After He has completed His program for man, He will stand justified in having done away with human sufficiency and having appointed a way of redemption through grace in Christ Jesus. Then, on the new earth there will be nations, for the heavenly city of God will be on the new earth, and "the nations of them which are saved shall walk in the light of it; and the kings of the earth do bring their glory and honor into it" (Rev. 21:24).

It is through Abraham and the nation that descends from him that this is brought to pass. God, in calling him out, revealed the final end: "in thee shall all the families of the earth be blessed" (Gen. 12:3). Through the people that sprang from Abraham God makes Himself and His ways known to all nations, then in the fullness of time brings forth the Redeemer of all mankind.

Education of the Patriarchal Period

God intended the education He would have had this chosen people carry on to be an important means of achieving His plan for them and for all men. Just as within the limits of the history of the world God directs a special history of revelation, so within the limits of the history of education in general He directs an education centering in the revelation He is making to mankind.

Data concerning the nature of this education during the period of the patriarchs are few and meager. The family of Abraham was a branch of the descendants of Shem. Abraham came from Chaldea, part of Babylonia whose people early in world history developed a civilization of high order, as archaeological discoveries attest. One of these discoveries is the Code of Hammurabi, the greatest king of the Old Babylonian dynasty. Though he lived two or three centuries after Abraham, numerous provisions of this code date back to the time of Abraham and show the interest of the people of that day in moral, social, and economic matters.

Abraham, then, the one chosen of God to be the channel for bringing to mankind the revelation of redemption through faith, was no primitive man. Instead he came from an environment of superior culture. Josephus says of him, "He was a person of great sagacity, both for understanding all things and persuading his hearers, and not mistaken in his opinions."[1] These are marks of an educated man. Josephus quotes another historian as saying of Abraham that he was "skilful in the celestial science."[2]

Furthermore, Josephus reports that Abraham, when he visited Egypt, confuted "the reasonings they made use of every one for their own practices, demonstrating that such reasonings were vain and void of truth; whereupon he was admired by them in these conferences as a very wise man, and one of great sagacity, when he discoursed on any subject he undertook; and this not only in understanding it, but in persuading other men also to assent to him. He communicated to them arithmetic, and delivered to them the science of astronomy; for, before Abraham came into Egypt, they were unacquainted with these parts of learning."[3]

This man, learned in the knowledge of the Chaldeans, Josephus says, "was the first that ventured to publish this notion, 'That there was but one God, the creator of the universe; and that, as to other [gods], if they contributed any thing to the happiness of men, that each of them afforded it only according to His appointment, and

[1]*The Complete Works of Flavius Josephus*. Translated from the original Greek by William Whiston (Philadelphia: David McKay), p. 49.
[2]*Ibid.*, p. 50.
[3]*Ibid.*

not by their own power.' "[4] Abraham said that the things of nature and of heaven, which the Babylonians worshiped as gods, were under the control of God, the Creator of the universe, who alone ought to be worshiped by men. These things he taught in Chaldea until he left that land.

If doubt arises about his continuing to teach the pure worship of God after he entered Canaan, such doubt is dispelled by the Scripture. In the first place, the Lord Himself paid high tribute to Abraham's steadfastness in teaching His ways when He said, "For I know him, that he will command his children and his household after him, and they shall keep the way of the LORD, to do justice and judgment" (Gen. 18:19). The meaning of this verse, according to modern versions, is: God chose Abraham that he might charge his children and his household after him to keep God's ways.

In no manner other than by teaching could the revelation of God have been made known to others. When Abraham, with his recognition of God and the memory of the glorious promises He had made to him, looked at the stars of heaven and the sands on the seashore, he most certainly would have talked of these promises and the One who made them. Thus his children and other people around him would have learned of his faith and hope in God. One who taught Egyptians arithmetic and astronomy would have been far more ready to teach his children and the members of his household about a revelation with far more precious meaning than anything temporal.

This implies, of course, that the education of this period was natural and informal instead of formal. The nomadic life of the patriarchs did not permit of the founding of schools. As their children and others saw Abraham and Isaac and Jacob building altars and offering sacrifices to God, they naturally learned both the obligation to worship Him and acceptable ways of doing so. Then as those to whom God had spoken talked with others informally about the revelation, they were instructed further in the things of God.

That Abraham taught the truth of God is, in the second place, borne out in the case of Isaac, his son, and in the case of Abraham's descendants during the several centuries intervening between his call and the exodus of the children of Israel from Egypt. Particularly in connection with the offering of Isaac upon Mount Moriah

[4]*Ibid.*, p. 49.

do evidences of the effectiveness of Abraham's teaching of his son stand out. Isaac understood the need for and the circumstances attendant upon the making of an acceptable offering to God. Also, the complete obedience of Isaac to the will of God, even if it meant death, shows right response to what he had been taught.

Throughout their lives, both Isaac and Jacob were mostly obedient to the teachings of Abraham and presumably continued to transmit them. Each received from God confirmation of the Abrahamic covenant, something that undoubtedly would not have been given had they been untrue to these teachings. Their descendants, during their sojourn in Egypt, where they had more permanent dwelling places, were prevailingly in accord with the will of God. From the Exodus narrative one would gather that the Hebrews had effectively preserved the teachings of God during the intervening centuries. At least, God heard and answered their cry for deliverance from bondage.

The Law and Education

This deliverance God effected through Moses of the seventh generation of Abraham's descendants. Because of his immediate family's faithfulness to God, Moses' life was preserved in infancy, and he was given, in addition to that family's instruction concerning God and His ways, a thorough education in Egyptian schools. "Moses was learned in all the wisdom of the Egyptians, and was mighty in words and deeds" (Acts 7:22). He has been called "the greatest of all schoolmasters."

"By faith Moses, when he was come to years, refused to be called the son of Pharaoh's daughter" (Heb. 11:24). At some point Moses made a choice for God against the earthly attractions of a high place in the nation of Egypt. No one knows all the factors which entered into the choice he made. Undoubtedly, he had been impressed early in life by the faith he had seen in others. The years he spent with his parents, by the direction of Pharaoh's daughter, must have been years during which he was taught much about the things of God. The faith he possessed apparently had its origin in the instruction given by his parents. From them he undoubtedly learned of the promises made to Abraham which, by faith, were kept alive among the Israelites. It would seem that he had received instruction concerning the Messianic hope, for his choice was "to suffer affliction with the people of God" because he esteemed "the reproach of Christ greater riches than the treasures of Egypt."

At any rate, Moses was the man chosen by God to be the deliverer of His people from Egyptian bondage. That deliverance, attended by signs and wonders, taught both Israelites and Egyptians—and all the world, for that matter—the omnipotence of God and His judgment upon those who oppose Him. In connection with the deliverance God instituted the Passover, which was to the Israelites of that day—and has been to all Jews ever since—an important means of educating. For this purpose God commanded His people to keep it "a feast by an ordinance forever" and to instruct their children, whenever it was observed, as to its meaning. This meaning was twofold: historical, pointing backward to deliverance from Egyptian bondage, and prophetical, pointing forward to deliverance from bondage to sin through Christ.

Once His people were free from bondage to the Egyptians, God gave them the Law. This was the fifth step in His program of educating the human race. From the call of Abraham until the giving of the Law at Mount Sinai, He was testing mankind as to faith in, and willingness to act upon, the promises He made. Unbelief prevailed more and more, even in connection with events related to God's mighty deliverance and subsequent events. The culmination of Israel's unbelief was expressed in the decision to do instead of to continue to believe (Exod. 19:8).

The Bible says the Law "was our schoolmaster to bring us unto Christ, that we might be justified by faith" (Gal. 3:24), thus indicating that a main purpose of the giving of the Law was instruction. The Law sets the standards for right conduct. The definite rules the Law gives are difficult for man to argue against or explain away when he tries to deceive himself about what is right or wrong. It makes known to man the nature of sin, showing him that it is missing the mark, disobedience, transgression, and rebellion against, God. By declaring man guilty of sin, the Law makes manifest the guilt of the sinner. The demands of the Law are holiness and righteousness; its very basis is the holiness of God. Over against this, the weakness, the sinfulness, and the lack of man stand out clearly. When man sees sin dwelling in him to be the source of his evil deeds, his pride and self-sufficiency are shattered. Thus the manifestation of the holiness of God expressed in His Law induces in man the realization of his lost state, impels him to acknowledge his need of grace, and causes him to turn to Christ.

The Mosaic Law is one law, an indivisible unit binding on all men in every one of its provisions (Deut. 27:26; Matt. 5:18; Gal. 3:10; James 2:10). It consists of three parts: the commandments, setting forth the holy will of God (Exod. 20:1-26); the judgments, or the rules governing social life (Exod. 21:1—24:11); and the ordinances, or the rules having to do with worship (Exod. 24:12—31:18). The commandments and the ordinances are related to each other; the breaking of any commandment necessitated the bringing by the sinner of an offering, as specified in the ordinances, to make atonement for his sin. From the time it was given to Israel at Sinai, the Law has been the central core of Jewish education. The Law was far more than a ritualistic code; it regulated every aspect of life—home, dress, food, work, conduct, property, politics, civil life, and religious life. In that the Law contained within itself a plan for instruction in its provisions, it regulated education also. Had Israel fully adhered to that plan, the nation would not have failed as it did. Even with their failure as a nation, the Jews have remained a distinct people through the centuries. This distinctiveness is to no inconsiderable degree the result of their emphasis upon instruction in the Law given them by God.

Hebrew educational ideals are the glory of Israel because they make God central. Ancient China, India, and Persia had high-grade education, but it left little impress upon the world. Babylon and Egypt, more highly civilized than Israel, gave the world the beginnings of science but nothing spiritual and no lofty ethical concepts. Jewish education trained servants of God who knew how to be obedient to His Law. The chief end of their education was to make the boy a good son, one who feared the Lord. God was high and exalted, yet very near to His people. The comprehensive aim of education was *righteousness,* which consisted of three subsidiary overlapping aims: happiness, good character, and fellowship with God.

Drazin quotes Josephus as saying, "Our principal care of all is this, to educate our children well; and we think it to be the most necessary business of our whole life to observe the laws that have been given to us, and to keep those rules of piety that have been delivered down to us. Our legislator [Moses] carefully joined two methods of instruction together; for he neither left the practical exercises to go without verbal instruction, nor did he permit the hearing of the law to proceed without the exercises for practice."[5]

Through the entire history of the Jewish race, God has been the center of their education, which has the Law for its foundation. Had not God told them at the time of the giving of the Law, "Now therefore, if ye will obey my voice indeed, and keep my covenant, then ye shall be a peculiar treasure unto me above all people: for all the earth is mine: and ye shall be unto me a kingdom of priests, and a holy nation" (Exod. 19:5-6)? Their ideal was "holiness to the Lord"; to them God was to be always first, though, in human weakness, they neither continually lived up to the ideal nor completely succeeded in always giving God the first place.

These words of Drazin are pertinent at this point: "Jewish education was never something extraneous to life or merely an instrument that served to prepare for life and that could later be discarded when its utility was exhausted. Jewish education was rather synonymous with life. It unfolded life, giving it direction and meaning. In fact a modern Hebrew term for education, *Hinuk,* from a root found twice in the Bible in the sense of 'to train,' etymologically means dedication or initiation, and hence may refer to the fact that the child on receiving Jewish education was dedicating his life to the service of God and to the observance of all His laws. This has been the characteristic essence of Jewish education from the earliest times."[6]

The Educational Work of Parents

As was said above, within the Law provision was made for the teaching of the Law. Parents were commanded to teach their children the history of the people and the commandments and the ordinances of the Law (Exod. 12:26-27; Deut. 4:9-10; 6:6-7; 11:19). Moses was appointed to teach (Exod. 18:20; 24:12; Deut. 4:14; 6:1;

[5]Nathan Drazin, *History of Jewish Education from 515* B.C.E. *to 220* C.E. (Baltimore: Johns Hopkins Press, 1940), p. 11.

[6]*Ibid.,* p. 12.

31:19). The priests were commanded to teach (Lev. 10:11; Deut. 24:8; 31:9-13; 33:8-10). God had a plan for educating His chosen people. As a consequence, this people have always regarded education as the most important activity of life, next to doing God's will. To Jews, religion and education are words so nearly synonymous in meaning as not to admit of clear distinction between them. They use the single word "Torah" to refer to what is common to both religion and education. This word, appearing many times in the Old Testament and commonly translated "The Law" really means "The Teaching."

Teaching in the home was basic in the plan God had for the education of His people. Children were a gift from God, and parents were responsible to God for teaching them. In accord with the principle being stressed today, that religious education is the concern of the family, parents were the child's first teachers and the home the fundamental educational institution throughout most of Jewish history.

There were no schools, in the modern sense of the word, among the Jews until after their return from captivity. The family was the first school; the home, where life begins, was the place where teaching began. In the family the will of God was to be made known to the child and reduced to practice in his living. Each father among the people chosen of God to be His peculiar treasure was to cherish His words and to instill them in the hearts of his children. "And these words, which I command thee this day, shall be in thine heart: and thou shalt teach them diligently unto thy children, and thou shalt talk of them when thou sittest in thine house, and when thou walkest in the way, and when thou liest down, and when thou risest up" (Deut. 6:6-7).

The Jews were to hand down from generation to generation the knowledge of the Law of God as something precious for its own sake. "For he established a testimony in Jacob, and appointed a law in Israel, which he commanded our fathers, that they should make them known to their children: That the generation to come might know them, even the children which should be born; who should arise and declare them to their children: that they might set their hope in God, and not forget the works of God, but keep his commandments" (Ps. 78:5-7).

Both the father and the mother taught the child (Prov. 1:8). His education began at a tender age; just when, it is impossible to determine. Philo says that the Jews "were from their swaddling clothes, even before being taught either the sacred laws or the unwritten customs, trained by their parents, teachers, and instructors to recognise God as Father and as the Maker of the world" and that, "having been taught the knowledge (of the laws) from earliest youth, they bore in their souls the image of the commandments."[7] Josephus says that "from their earliest consciousness" they had "learned the laws, so as to have them, as it were, engraven upon the soul."[8]

God's chosen people were not only to have His words in their hearts and bound for a sign upon their hands but they were commanded to write them also upon the doorposts of their houses. So, even while the child was yet carried in arms, his attention would be drawn to the parchment containing the words of God fastened to the doorpost, and he would be influenced by the reverent attitude toward this sacred object manifested by his elders as they went in and out of the house. Furthermore, he would receive indelible impressions from the hallowed atmosphere that pervaded the life of the family. Prayer was made to God morning and evening and before and after each meal. The ritual of the household included things such as the putting on of the phylacteries each day, the lighting of the Sabbath lamp each week, the partaking of the Sabbath meal, the replacing of the ordinary bread by unleavened bread, and the family's leaving home to attend one of the national feasts. Thus was the soul of the child continually molded almost from birth by a reverent family life.

As soon as he was able to speak, his parents began to teach him words and sentences. The first memory tasks were mainly blessings, especially those that formed part of the daily prayers. The child rose from bed with one of these upon his lips and went to bed reciting words proclaiming belief in the one God. Much stress was placed upon memorization. As he grew older, he was required to memorize portions of the Scriptures. The mother had a large part in the training of the earliest years, but it was considered the duty

[7]Alfred Edersheim, *In the Days of Christ: Sketches of Jewish Social Life* (Boston: Bradley and Woodruff, 1876) , p. 111.

[8]*Ibid.*, p. 112.

of the father to assume responsibility for directing this more advanced phase of the child's education.

When the child was old enough to do so, he was required to participate in the work which provided the family with means of subsistence. Thus much of the family education was vocational. This did not mean, however, that learning was for merely temporal or secular purposes. What was done for sustenance of the body was part of one great whole, a whole in which the will of God was the supreme consideration. Therefore, vocational training was not without spiritual meaning.

All the festivals and ceremonies were to be utilized as means for the instruction of children. The Law ordained a number of religious times: the weekly Sabbath, the Feast of Trumpets, the Feast of Tabernacles, the Passover, the Sabbatical Year, the Year of Jubilee, the Feast of Pentecost, and the Day of Atonement. These were to be used as bases for teaching the young about the goodness and mercies of God. The works of God commemorated in the ceremonies connected with these religious observances were to be a topic of informal conversation. As the children asked questions about the meaning of the ceremonies, the parents' answers were to be informative and instructive.

Jewish family life and education required obedience on the part of the child. Above all else, the child was to respect and honor his parents. Discipline was severe. Inasmuch as obedience would not likely come of itself, parents were to develop it by the use of rigorous measures. In the Jewish family there was neither a "sparing of the rod" nor "soft pedagogy." The Law taught loving consideration of parents and visited severe penalty for crimes against them. The authority of the father was absolute in the home, and obedience to him was its foundation stone. With such a basis, it was relatively easy for the child to learn the fear of the Lord, which is "the beginning of wisdom."

The education which so basically vested instructional activity in the parent made the content constantly more meaningful to the instructor. No Jew—nor any other human being—can teach children what he himself has never learned. The Law was no simple code of regulations; he who sincerely desired to obey it fully was confronted first, last, and always by an intellectual as well as a spiritual challenge. Hillel said, "An empty-headed man cannot be a sin-fearing man, nor can an ignorant person be pious."[9] And the obligation to teach what they had learned for themselves was a constant challenge to parents to relearn the meaning of what they were to teach their children. Thus the provision God made for children to be taught by their parents constituted an admirable means not only for education of children but also for ever-continuing education of adults.

The history of Jewish education in Old Testament times falls naturally into three periods. The first extends from the exodus out of Egypt to the setting up of the kingdom under Saul. The second covers the time between the beginning of the kingdom until 538 B.C., the date of the return from the Babylonian captivity. The third extends from 538 B.C. to the birth of Christ. In all this time the family was considered the fundamenal educational institution. Parents were responsibile both for the instruction and the conduct of their children. Not always did they fulfill their educational responsibility. Upon entering Canaan the people became so engrossed with temporal affairs that they neglected the teaching of their children. Because of this neglect there arose after Joshua's time a generation that knew not God. The result was confusion, for every man did as he pleased instead of obeying the Law of God.

Nevertheless, the educational ideal remained. In the course of time, thirteen was set as the age at which the boy became personally responsible for knowing and keeping the Law. Up to this age, responsibility rested upon the father for his son's instruction and conduct. As Swift says, "Even the rise of a system of elementary schools devoted to the task of daily religious instruction did not free the home of this, its most important responsibility."[10]

Educational Work of the Priests

However, in none of the three periods between the exodus and the birth of Christ was education carried on by the home alone. Even in the first period when its influence, or the lack thereof,

[9]Drazin, *History of Jewish Education . . .*, p. 18.

[10]Fletcher H. Swift, *Education in Ancient Israel from Earliest Times to 70* A.D. (Chicago: The Open Court Publishing Co., 1919) , p. 50.

loomed proportionately large, other factors played a part in the education of both children and adults. Most potent among these was the direct and the indirect educational work of the priests. "Moses wrote this law, and delivered it unto the priests the sons of Levi, which bare the ark of the covenant of the Lord, and unto all the elders of Israel" (Deut. 31:9). The command to these was: "At the end of every seven years, . . . thou shalt read this law before all Israel in their hearing. Gather the people together, men, and women, and children, and thy stranger that is within thy gates, that they may hear, and that they may learn, and fear the LORD your God, and observe to do all the words of this law: and that their children, which have not known any thing, may hear, and learn to fear the LORD your God, as long as ye live in the land whither ye go over Jordan to possess it" (Deut. 31:10-13).

The priests performed various duties as set forth in Deuteronomy 33:8-10. That instruction was important among them is shown by the words: "They shall teach Jacob thy judgments and Israel thy law." The priests were responsible for acquainting the people with the teachings of the law which had been delivered into their hands. Moreover, the priests had the duty of transmitting to generations of priests to come knowledge concerning the rituals and ceremonies of the Law. Also, the priests were to teach the people how to worship, to instruct them in the law of sacrifices, in ritual, and in religious duties. Every place a priest functioned was a place of instruction in law and in religious observances.

And every sacrifice, symbol, and ceremony was a basis for a feeling and an attitude toward God and an effective means of teaching some belief, conception, or law. By the procedures connected with the tabernacle worship especially, the people were taught the holiness of God, the importance of faithfulness to Him, the way He regarded sin, and the need for repentance. Every sacrifice offered in the tabernacle or elsewhere powerfully, if indirectly, proclaimed the nature of God, impressing this upon young and old far more vividly than words alone could have.

It was also the duty of the priests to teach the people how to live in relation to one another. They gave advice to them and made decisions on questions they brought. That is, they instructed the people in respect to their ethical and civil duties. interpreting for them God's ways in terms of practical living and helping them to deal with their personal problems. For God's chosen people ethical rules, civil law, and duty to God were all bound into one. The priests were those set by God to "handle the law" and on the priests the people were to depend for instruction and guidance in every phase of their living.

Until the time of the exile the priests were the main public instructors of the people. The men of the tribe of Levi were set apart to be priests; they were not required to enter military service, and they were allotted no land for agricultural purposes. Being supported from the tithe, their whole time was devoted to the handling of the Law and related matters. Naturally, the people believed in the divine authority of the priests and relied upon them. These circumstances afforded them large opportunity to guide and instruct.

Education by the Wise Men

Another class of teachers found among the Israelites in the first period of their educational history, as well as later, was the wise men. Every nation of the ancient East had its wise men, whose functions had to do with education along with other matters. Little is said of wise men in Old Testament history. The only traces of them before the time of Saul are found in the book of Job, which treats of life as it was lived in the patriarchal age, and in the riddles of Samson (Judges 14:12-18). While they were somewhat more prominent after the exile, the wise men, often referred to as elders, did teach in earlier times. Because of their age, insight, understanding, and experience, they were accepted as teachers and looked up to as such.

In Israel, where it was recognized that "the fear of the Lord is the beginning of knowledge," wise men had a function different from that of wise men in other nations. A few centuries beyond Saul's time the people of Jeremiah's day placed the wise men on a par with priest and prophet in respect to the revelation of God, saying, "for the law shall not perish from the priest, nor counsel from the wise, nor the word from the prophet" (Jer. 18:18). The book of Proverbs is a collection of sayings which applied divine wisdom to the earthly life of the people of God. These probably represent the teachings of a number of God-fearing wise men who lived over a considerable period. Solomon, in addition to composing proverbs and answering "hard sayings," gathered into orderly arrangement teachings which were current among the people and perhaps had been for centuries (Eccl. 12:9).

The aim of the teaching of men wise in the ways of God is quite fully expressed in Proverbs 1:2-6: "To know wisdom and instruction; to perceive the words of understanding; to receive the instruction of wisdom, justice, and judgment, and equity; to give subtility to the simple, to the young man knowledge and discretion. A wise man will hear, and will increase learning; and a man of understanding shall attain unto wise counsels: to understand a proverb and the interpretation; the words of the wise, and their dark sayings."

These words indicate that the purpose of the wise men of Israel was to teach wisdom that was not simply intellectual but which involved the whole man—wisdom which had its origin in the fear of God, a wisdom that was God-given, not the product of the thinking of man apart from God. Along with wisdom, spiritual education was to be given, that is, instruction in wise, just, and fair dealing. These were features of the rule of God; those taught were to receive knowledge to guide their practice. This wisdom and knowledge was available to all, even to the simplest and the youngest; yet those who were wise and good could always learn to become wiser and better. The purpose of the instruction given was to inculcate understanding of moral and spiritual principles previously taught by men of God to the end that learners might practice godly living.

The wise men stressed the harm and evil of impurity, falsehood, pride, dishonoring parents, unjust practices, cruelty, intemperance, and irreverence. They highly exalted such virtues as truth, honesty, fairness, patience, courage, humility, charity, and godliness. The instruction they gave was individual and personal. While they by no means neglected adults, the wise men gave special instruction to the young as those who, if they would but take heed to their ways when they could learn readily, would be able to live soberly, righteously, and godly when they came to maturity.

The Failure of Israel

During the second period of Jewish education, extending from the coronation of Saul to the return from exile, parents, priests, and wise men theoretically continued to be the teachers. But the history of Israel is a story of failure to follow God's plan. Parents became lax in the performance of their duty to instruct their children diligently in the Law. Priests failed in their duties as teachers. The wisest of the wise men, Solomon, put in writing, along with the sayings of wise men of previous generations, many teachings of his own. However, in his life he did not exemplify very well the truths he taught. Beyond what is said of Solomon, there is virtually nothing on record concerning the activity of wise men in the second period.

Teaching through public institutions continued to some extent. At least some of the feasts were kept. With the building of the temple, larger opportunity was afforded for emphasis on the worship of God. Here the priests offered the national sacrifices, provided lessons in worship, and did some teaching of the Law. The various national feasts were connected with the temple and made it more important as a teaching institution. Instruction in public assembly, commanded by Moses, got a bit of attention. Jehoshaphat sent out a corps of princes and Levites to teach in all the cities of Judah (II Chron. 17:7-9). Josiah reinstituted the reading of the Law in an assembly of all the people (II Chron. 34:29-30). A public event such as the coronation of a king or the dedication of the temple afforded occasion for reiteration of the teachings of the Law and for expression of renewed devotion to God.

But, on the whole, instruction in the ways of God was not prevalent. There were no real schools; it seems that the people in general were given no formal instruction other than that based on oral tradition. During the latter part of this second period, writing developed, and reading became rather widespread. Undoubtedly the priests were the first to use writing, and they made historical records. Decisions made by the priests on questions of law were preserved. The priesthood became the depositary of an increasing body of judicial and historical literature, and they studied the civil law more and more. Scribes, who ordinarily were Levites or priests, grew in importance as a class. At first they devoted themselves chiefly to the making of transcriptions. As time went on, the scribes acquired knowledge of the Law; of this they became eventually the preservers and the teachers while the priests came to function mostly in the temple services. Only after the exile, however, does it seem that priests and scribes were clearly differentiated.

Educational Work of the Prophets

As a substitute for the agencies that had failed to function, God raised up the prophets. Their rise was the most outstanding development of the second period of Jewish educational history. Of them Swift says, "Probably no nation has ever produced a group of religious and moral teachers comparable with the prophets of ancient Israel. Through their spoken public addresses and writings they became creators of national religious and social ideals, critics and inspirers of public policies, denunciators of social wrongs, preachers of individual and social righteousness, and the source and channel of an ever loftier conception of God and of the mission of Israel. In fulfilling each of these capacities they were acting as public teachers. In every national crisis they were at hand to denounce, to encourage, to comfort and always to instruct. They were the public conscience of Israel, the soul of its religion, the creators of its public opinion, its most conspicuous, its most revered, its most convincing teachers."[11]

The prophets were raised up by God; theirs was not a mere profession but a divine calling. God chose each and gave him a message He wanted the people to have. They spoke to the people for God, while the priest spoke to God for the people. They proclaimed a truly spiritual faith. Those of the eighth century were not the first to be called prophets. Abraham was a prophet, and Moses was one. There were many prophets before Jonah; he was the first of the prophets in point of time whose message is recorded as part of the Bible. Ezekiel and Daniel prophesied during the exile; Haggai, Zechariah, and Malachi, after the exile. All the other prophets whose names are given to books of the Bible were preexilic. Though

[11]*Ibid.*, p. 38.

Jeremiah was in the latter class, his teachings extended into the exile. The prophets represent in their teachings the highest education, an education that centered in God. Their messages were based upon the truth revealed in the past, especially in the teachings of Moses, on which foundation they all built. They were not against the ritual and ceremonies of the Law but they pleaded for a spiritual worship of God instead of the mere outward form.

More specifically, their teachings may be summarized thus: they redirected attention to and brought more fully into view the true nature and character of God. This was needed because God's people, influenced by the survivors of the idolatrous population of Canaan and not knowing the Law of God, either forsook the worship of the only God or came to think of Him as but one among many gods. The prophets taught that the God of Israel is the Creator, the Sustainer, and the Ruler of the universe. All things in earth below and in the heavens above do His bidding. His power controls and overrules in the events of human history. Nothing takes place without His notice; all is in accord with either His directive or His permissive will.

God is holy, righteous, just, and merciful. All men are accountable to Him; He knows man altogether, not only in what he does but in what he thinks, even before man himself is aware of his own thoughts. This God, all-powerful, all-knowing, holy, just, loving, and merciful, is Israel's God. He has chosen Israel from all the peoples of the earth to be His own people. He bears long and patiently with them, He trains them, He ever seeks their good, He punishes them when they refuse to do His will, He desires that they return to Him. Never will He utterly abandon them, nor will their failure frustrate the purpose He had in making them His people.

The prophets fearlessly taught against sin in all its forms and continually called upon the people, high and low, to repent, telling them the consequences if they did not turn from their evil ways and make their peace with God. Their merciful God, in lovingkindness, ever stood ready to pardon abundantly the penitent sinner. Their highest good was righteousness in the sight of God; that which hindered in seeking and attaining the highest good was sin. It separated them from God, making vain their worship of Him. There was only one way that was right, and that was the way appointed by God. He who departed from this way, whether king, priest, prophet, or other, was guilty of sin. Repentance, to which the prophets ever invited men, meant acknowledgment of sin and sorrow for it, a wholehearted turning to God, choosing the good way, and departing from iniquity.

The prophets taught that goodness of character was obtained through repentance, faith, and obedience to God. Trust in God was the source of strength for duty, of help in meeting aright the issues of life, and of the soul's highest welfare. In respect to duty, the teaching of all of the prophets may be summed up in the words of God through the last of their number: "Remember ye the law of Moses my servant, which I commanded unto him in Horeb for all Israel, with the statutes and judgments" (Mal. 4:4).

Not the least important aspect of the teachings of the prophets had to do with the future. There was coming a "day of the Lord" in which He would reveal Himself. To a disobedient people this would be a day of darkness and fearful judgment for wrongdoing. To the righteous this would be a day when God would vindicate His holy character by visiting terrible punishment upon all, whether chosen people or heathen, who refused to follow His ways. The chosen people, because they possessed higher privileges, would suffer severer punishment. But the prophets also taught about a glorious future for God's chosen people. Because of sin the nation was to undergo great suffering and loss, but the time would come when they would be restored. Then would they be enabled to instruct the peoples of the earth in the knowledge of the Lord and to guide them into paths of righteousness and peace.

This glorious future will be realized through the Messiah of whom various prophecies have been made, beginning in the Garden of Eden (Gen. 3:15). In the writings of the prophets of the eighth and succeeding centuries, this One is presented as the ideal Prophet, Priest, and King. Triumphing through suffering, rejection, and death, He will, not by physical might or force, gain possession of His kingdom, which shall be universal and everlasting. He will judge and reprove not by sight of His eyes nor after the hearing of His ears but by insight into the eternal moral law. Righteousness, equity, and justice will characterize His rule, and under it physical force and moral evil will vanish. Then the knowledge of the Lord will fill the earth as the waters cover the sea.

In connection with the educational work of the prophets, mention must be made of the so-called "schools of the prophets." It seems that these existed at various places throughout the land. They are mentioned only in connection with the times of Elijah and Elisha (II Kings 2:3-5; 4:38; 6:1), though it is reasonable to suppose that the companies of prophets in the time of Samuel (I Sam. 10:10; 19:20) were of the same type. Seemingly, small bands of prophets lived together and had a common table. The Bible refers to them as "sons of the prophets," not as "schools." The nature of these bands is not clear, but it seems that they were groups of young men who, under leadership, held religious meetings in which there were manifestations of enthusiasm and prophetic ecstasy.

While it is possible that some instruction in prophetic vision as an art may have been given in these groups, there is no warrant for attributing to them any great educative influence. Though a considerable number of young men were at times in these groups, nothing in the record indicates that the inspired prophets were trained in such societies. From what is said of them in the Bible, these so-called "schools" seem to have been under the direction of Samuel, Elijah, and Elisha. It may well be that their chief importance was the spreading of the messages of these three.

Jewish Education Made National and Universal

The third period of the history of Jewish education in Old Testament times began with the return from captivity in 538 B.C. and ended with the birth of Christ. The Jews learned from the captivity the danger of losing their identity as a people. Accordingly, upon returning to Palestine, the leaders determined to bring the people back to the true worship of God that they might be preserved as a nation. Universal education was recognized as a means for achieving this end. So, the Law, and with it the sum total of eternal truth about God's justice and love, the teachings of the prophets as well as those of Moses—the whole of the revelation to man of God's will—became the interest of the Jewish people. To them this constituted the Torah, the chief study at home and in school, of children and of adults, and the motivating force in private and public life.

The synagogue was the central place of instruction as well as of worship. During the fifth century B.C. the books of the Mosaic Law in written form were made the foundation unit of instruction, the essential core of teaching and learning. Boys were required to memorize large portions of these books, thus making education very much a matter of instruction in the Law. In the fourth century, Aramaic instead of Hebrew became the spoken language of the Jews, leaving Hebrew as the written language of religious law. Since knowledge of Hebrew was necessary as a means of preserving the religious and national identity of the Jews, Hebrew became the major subject of instruction for those older boys who were to become priests, scribes, and scholars.

In the third century Greek influence began to affect Jewish life. The result was a tendency to develop a culture suitable to all men everywhere. It seems that Jewish education emphasized for a time the moral values and social teachings set forth in the wisdom literature of Job, Proverbs, and Ecclesiastes rather than centering only on the Mosaic Law and the teachings of the prophets. In the second century, however, Jewish nationalism again came to the fore and educational effort was once more directed toward the teaching of the Mosaic Law. During the first century B.C. elementary schools were rather widely established outside the synagogues to give instruction in reading and writing to younger children. These elementary schools were called "Houses of the Book." Older boys went on to study more of the Book, oral as well as written. Those who could afford to spend the time would often continue further in their study with the purpose of becoming scribes, the name and function of which was open to all.

So much for an overview of the education of this third period. More specifically it is to be noted that under Ezra and Nehemiah at the very beginning of the period was started a work which set the pattern for later education. Out of the teaching given then grew at least in part the synagogue methods used later.

They assembled the people together, "all that could hear with understanding," and "read in the book in the law of God distinctly, and gave the sense, and caused them to understand the reading" (Neh. 8:2, 8). They gathered together the "chief of the fathers of all the people, the priests, and the Levites, unto Ezra the scribe, even to understand the words of the law" (Neh. 8:13). That is, teachers were taught so that they in turn could teach the people the words of the Law. The result was that the people as a whole found their duty to God and set about diligently to perform it, confessing their sins, restoring what was missing in worship, entering into a covenant with God, separating themselves from ungodly peoples, and providing for keeping holy the Sabbath day.

The educational institution that served to make Jewish education what it was in the third period was the synagogue. It is not known with certainty if there was anything corresponding to the synagogue prior to the exile, but from the time of Ezra synagogues were instituted throughout the land of Palestine and were found in other places wherever there were Jews in any number. The services of the synagogue were intended not to supplant but to supplement the temple worship. With the introduction of synagogue worship, religion became much more a matter of teaching and learning. In the synagogues the Law was read weekly and expounded to the people. The whole Law was read consecutively so as to be completed within a given period of time. The writings of the prophets were read, as second lessons, in a corresponding order. Thus all the people were students of the Scriptures. It is impossible to estimate the educational influence of the system of teaching thus developed.

It was in the synagogue that the Jewish elementary school developed. The attendant of the synagogue taught the children during the week. The Jewish child studied in these schools from about five years of age onward. In time attendance was made compulsory, and it was required that every community with as many as ten families maintain such a school for the children. No teacher was to have more than twenty-five pupils; if there were more, he was required to have an assistant. These teachers served without pay and, in common with the attitude toward teachers in general, they were highly honored. Thus, through the development of the elementary school, the synagogue became a place of education for the young as well as the old.

Reading, writing, and arithmetic were taught in these schools, but the main objective was the teaching of the Hebrew Scriptures. As soon as the pupil had learned the alphabet, he began to memorize "the Book"—the Pentateuch. His study began with the book of Leviticus so as to acquaint him with the laws of purification and holiness. Large portions of the Scriptures were memorized. The synagogues played a large and very important part in Jewish education, bringing to all Jews everywhere the central teachings of the revelation of God. The synagogue schools were considered to be the life of the nation and their teaching the very life of the Jewish people. Under the influence of the synagogue and the scribes all Jews became students of the teachings of God. These were to them the most reverenced of all studies and the center not only of spiritual and intellectual interest but of political interest as well.

The development of a learned teaching order side by side with the priesthood is another significant fact of this period of Jewish education. Wise men may have continued to teach, but now the scribes came to be in a special sense the teachers and they exercised a far-reaching influence during all subsequent Jewish history. The scribes had been gaining prominence before the exile, but now they assumed the most important place. Ezra is called "the priest, the scribe, even a scribe of the words of the commandments of the LORD, and of his statutes to Israel" (Ezra 7:11). After the return from captivity, scribes gradually increased in number. By the beginning of the second century B.C. they were indistinguishable from the wise men, that is, the two were one. A priest or Levite or one of no order at all might be a scribe. The scribes became the learned and legal class and as such the leaders among them were teachers of the Law. They were trained in and obedient to the Law. Such obedience implied total consecration to God, with the forsaking of all duties and activities not related to the worship and service of God. In addition to teaching the Law, the scribes interpreted its meaning.

The scribes regarded their work as holy, for to them had been entrusted the sacred task of transmitting the laws God Himself had given. Schools of the scribes were centers of disputation where difficult matters were settled. These came to be known by the time of Christ as the "rabbinical schools"; they gradually gained complete control over religious thought and education. The heads of these schools were first called "rabbis" about the time of Christ. In the centuries immediately preceding the birth of Christ, the growing influence of these rabbinical schools weakened that of the priesthood more and more. During the first century of the Christian era, the teaching scribes, or rabbis, finally superseded the priesthood. In their schools all learning was concentrated, but the priesthood and the higher laity benefited from instruction given in them.

Drazin shows that three ideals or goals prevailed in Jewish education during this third period.[12] The first was the nationalistic ideal. This sought to make education of a religious nature the goal of Jewish nationality. It was felt by the Jews of that time that a complete return to all the teachings of the Mosaic Law and the customs of their fathers originating in these teachings and the spread of their education would result in the preservation of the nation and also give it a high position among the nations of the world. The religious ideal was inherent in the nationalistic one. In theory at least, God was always the center of Jewish education. The ideal of devotion to Him had two aspects: a full knowledge of the Law and in practice a strict obedience to the Law. This ideal made education sacred and of great importance. The command, "Ye shall teach them to your children" was interpreted to mean that every male adult had the obligation to study the Torah and to teach it to his sons. To keep this command necessitated a high level of education. The nationalistic and religious ideals gave rise to a third goal, to universalize Jewish education. If this wish existed at all in earlier times, it was not nearly so keen as it was in the later centuries of the Old Testament period. Then, instead of seeking to have the full knowledge of the Torah confined to the chosen few, it was the prevailing wish that every Jew might become a channel through which knowledge of God and His will could be transmitted to others.

The Torah taught the duty of man to God and the duty of man to man. Above all else, man was to believe in one God, the Creator of all things. It was considered that this conception of God had been fully made known by Moses. This one God had been revealed as a God of righteousness who required of those who worship Him pure hearts and upright lives. The people were commanded to love God, to fear Him, and to develop in their lives the holy characteristics of His nature, made known to them by the prophets. Duties to man were concerned with all that man does, including his thinking. In everything he does he is responsible to God, who sees all and knows all. Because a sound body is necessary to perform God's service, the individual has the duty to maintain good health. Therefore, many hygienic and sanitary instructions are given in the literature, though athletic activity for its own sake is discouraged. The

[12]Drazin, *History of Jewish Education . . .*, pp. 15-23.

fundamental rule of Jewish ethics was that every activity was to be done as in the presence of God and to be guided by His will.

The good life was one lived in the realization of the presence of God. Through performing religious duties, the individual remained continually in communion with God. The child was required from early years to observe religious practices. The life of every member of the family involved frequent prayer. Prayers were offered three times a day, morning, afternoon, and evening. Before and after meals a prayer of thanksgiving for the food was made. Hands were washed before and after eating a meal, every morning on arising and always after attending to physical wants. When reciting the morning prayers, one had to wear the phylacteries, which served to bring to mind the one God and the sacred duty of keeping all His commandments.

Portions of the Pentateuch were read four times a week at the synagogue services, twice on the Sabbath and once each Monday and Thursday morning. Numerous benedictions were memorized and recited on various kinds of special occasions. It was required that the Sabbath and all the festivals be strictly observed in all their details. The individual was expected to have a fixed period morning and evening, and to utilize any other available opportunity, for the study of the Torah.

With awareness of the failure of their fathers to instruct their children and the dire consequences of such failure, the Jews attached new importance to the home after the return from captivity. Parents were to teach the Law diligently. In the first few years of his life the boy learned in the home many passages of Scripture, some prayers, and many customs and traditions. Also, he saw and took part in many festivals. In postexilic times, more than thirty days of each year were given over to ceremonial observances of one kind or another. These had great educational significance. Through them, as explanations were given of the origin and meaning of each act, the child learned God's ways. Religious instruction was definitely connected with most of the festivals.

Once schools came into existence, there was some change in the boy's environment and activities. However, school instruction centered in the Torah, for the school work consisted mostly of memorization of the content of the Torah. The chief school texts were books of Scripture, especially those constituting the Pentateuch.

Likely the Psalms, because of the place they had in worship, received much attention. Proverbs and the apocryphal book, Ecclesiasticus, also had a prominent place. The aim of the elementary school was to give every boy mastery of the Torah so that he would be prepared in adult years to teach it. Thus the Jews of this period were "a people of the Book." The boy who completed the program of the elementary school probably knew by heart most of the Pentateuch and in addition portions of many other books of the Scriptures. He was prepared to explain the origin and meaning of the sacred rites and customs, public and private, which were a vital part of the daily life of his people.

History gives little information about the education of adolescents. From tradition and from what is known of the practice of peoples in general, it is reasonable to infer that even from times much earlier than postexilic days, adolescence was recognized as a stage of deep religious and social significance and that training was given adolescents in preparation for assuming the responsibilities of adulthood. Thirteen was the age at which a Jewish youth became responsible for the Law. In preparation for this he entered upon a period of religious instruction shortly before his thirteenth birthday. On the first Sabbath after his birthday, his father went with him to the synagogue and in the presence of the congregation formally renounced responsibility before God for his son's conduct. Henceforth, the boy was regarded as an adult member of the congregation.

Education did not cease when the Jew became an adult. A wise man of this later period, referring to the Torah, made the following statement: "Turn it and turn it over again, for everything is in it, and contemplate it and grow grey and old over it and stir not from it, for thou canst have no better rule than it."[13] Its depth and scope were a constant challenge to adults to seek out its truths and to become better acquainted with those they already knew. Never did they feel that they had learned all that could be learned of the Torah. Adults were expected to review constantly what they had learned lest they forget some teaching and become guilty of sin.

Vocational and industrial training was fundamentally the same after the exile as it had been before. Every boy, seemingly, learned some handicraft, usually the trade of his father. Every father, whatever his position, was directed to teach his son a trade. All arts and

[13]Quoted by Drazin in *History of Jewish Education* . . ., p. 14.

crafts were regulated according to the requirements of the Law. An educational ideal of the period found expression in these words: "Excellent is the study of the law combined with some worldly occupation, for toil in them both puts sin out of mind." As in preceding periods, there was, therefore, no sharp line of demarcation between vocational and religious life.

It seems that when schools arose, they were not open to girls. Their education remained almost entirely in the family; the training of the ideal Jewish wife did not stress the learning of the schools. Woman's duties and her education were for life in the home, so it sufficed that girls be given no education beyond the rudiments. Woman's chief duties were to honor God, manage her home, train her children, and serve her husband. Consequently, the aim of the girl's education was to develop a God-fearing, efficient, industrious, obedient woman. Institutions other than the home which had some educational effect upon girls were the synagogue, the temple, and the festivals.

God's Education of the Jews

God chose the people of Israel and set them apart for the purpose of carrying out through them the plan He has for all mankind. They developed an education with three interrelated goals: They taught the Law God gave them in order to preserve their nation and give it a high position among the nations of the world, and in order to make this Law known to other peoples. While the people of Israel developed their education, God was educating them to bring them and all mankind to realization of the total insufficiency of man and the abundant sufficiency of God through grace.

First, God educated Israel for separation. From the day He commanded Abraham to leave his country and his kindred until the time the nation went into captivity, He dealt with them as He did with no other people, training them for separation unto Himself. He spoke to them as He did to no other nation, giving them His Law to keep that they might be unto Him "a peculiar treasure . . . above all people" (Exod. 19:5). He planned to have them live alone in a land where He would rule them directly (Exod. 15:18; I Sam. 8:7). He made provision for a temple in which they were to worship

Him (Exod. 15:17; I Chron. 22:10, 19). But when they disobeyed His Law, rejected His rule, and turned away from worshiping Him, He adopted a different method of dealing with them.

After a thousand years of patient endurance of their unwillingness to learn what He wanted to teach them, He sentenced them to captivity in Babylon. Upon termination of this sentence, God educated them for service as His messengers to the heathen world. The means He used for training them to render this missionary service were the scattering of them among other peoples and the establishing of centers of Jewish life in all cities and lands, the development, alongside the temple, of synagogues where the Scriptures were taught, and the translation into Greek of the Hebrew Old Testament, making available to Gentiles as well as Jews the message of God.

The Jews failed miserably in their response to all God sought to do for them and through them. In all the time He sought to train them for separation from other peoples they persisted in a contrary course. God wanted them to be a people who worshiped Him; they worshiped the idols of heathen nations from Aaron's time until He sent them into captivity. God wished them to live holy lives; they ceased not to go after the unholy practices of the peoples of the world. God forbade them to enter into league with heathen nations; they made alliance after alliance with peoples opposed to Him and His ways.

In Babylon, however, the Jews were cured of their chief sin, idolatry. Chastened by their captivity experiences, they learned that there is one God who is to be feared and worshiped. So they returned from captivity with new aims and goals.

Second, God sought to prepare Israel for carrying His truth to all other nations. However, they again took a contrary course, showing themselves to be always perverse in their attitudes toward Him. In self-righteous pride they despised the Gentiles. They so exalted nationalism as to make ineffective God's purpose to use them to show other nations His ways. They so perverted His Law by their additions and interpretations as to make it an obnoxious burden both to their own nation and to other nations. Instead of associating with the world, they haughtily withdrew themselves from the world. Just as when God wished separation they practiced association, so now, when God wished association, they practiced separation. Always, they were a people of a straying heart who refused to respond aright to what God wanted to teach them.

This contrary course led the Jews eventually to the rejection of the Messiah and to God's judgment for that rejection. For two thousand years, from Abraham to Christ, God gave them an education in faith. For fifteen hundred years, from Sinai to Christ, He gave them an education in repentance. These two belong together. "Repent" and "believe the gospel" was what Christ taught when He came "preaching the gospel of the kingdom of God" (Mark 1:14-15), thus joining the two in redemption. In their postexilic zeal for the Law, the Jews had lost sight of the pure law of God. They had so encrusted the Mosaic Law with human opinions and ideas that they no longer perceived its spiritual meaning. For its true teachings they had substituted a host of outward observances. They had added to the Law a vast number of rabbinical evasions and restrictions.

They had reduced the righteousness required by the Law to mere ceremonialism, and the Old Testament teaching of the kingdom to a mere matter of outward splendor and power. So, when Christ came proclaiming the kingdom, they rejected both the kingdom and its king. Consequently, for another nineteen hundred years, from the destruction of Jerusalem to the present, they have been under the judgment of God for the sin of sins, the rejection of the Messiah. This period of judgment will continue until the setting up of the kingdom upon the return of Christ.

But in spite of their lack of right response the Jews are God's chosen people. In the annals of a history not yet transpired, it shall be recorded of them that they finally learned this lesson: it is not of works but "of God that sheweth mercy"; also that they attained unto right standing with God through faith. God will fulfill all the promises He has made concerning them. This people who have been for centuries a curse among the nations will in the end be a blessing. As in the course of history all races are having a part in their judgment, so will they all, when "the earth shall be filled with the knowledge of the Lord," be blessed along with the Jews in the kingdom of glory. Small wonder that Paul, in contemplation of that wonderful future, bursts out in this paean of adoration: "O the depth of the riches both of the wisdom and knowledge of God! how unsearchable are his judgments, and his ways past finding out" (Rom. 11:33).

The Law of which the Jews made so much in their national life and to which they gave the chief place in their education is God's means of educating them and all mankind in developing expectation of the Redeemer by revealing human sinfulness and insufficiency. The Law gives to sin the character of personal guilt, proving absolutely the chronic sinfulness of man's nature. The Law awakens in the sinner recognition of the need for redemption and thereby becomes a tutor to direct men to Christ that they may be justified by faith (Gal. 3:24). The Law brings the sinner into the depths of despair in the realization that he is dead but thereby leads him to lay hold of life in Christ.

The Law was given to the Jewish people, not to other nations. Nevertheless, the Jews and the Law given them are "an object-lesson in the grandest style upon the stage of world history (I Cor. 10:11) so that all peoples of all centuries can read it as they pass by."

Readings

Benson, Clarence H. *A Popular History of Christian Education.* Chicago: Moody Press, 1943.

Butts, Robert Freeman, *A Cultural History of Western Educatino.* 2nd ed.; New York: McGraw-Hill Book Company, 1955.

Cornill, Carl Heinrich. *The Culture of Ancient Israel.* Chicago: The Open Court Publishing Company, 1914.

Drazin, Nathan. *History of Jewish Education from 515 B.C.E. to 220 C.E.* Baltimore: Johns Hopkins Press, 1940.

Edersheim, Alfred. *In the Days of Christ or Sketches of Jewish Social Life.* Boston: Bradley and Woodruff, 1876; New York: F. H. Revell Co., 1904.

Ginzberg, Louis. *Students, Scholars and Saints.* Philadelphia: The Jewish Publication Society of America, 1928.

Hastings, James (ed.). *Encyclopaedia of Religion and Ethics.* New York: Charles Scribner's Sons, 1956.

Josephus, Flavius. *Complete Works.* Translated from original Greek by William Whiston. Philadelphia: David McKay, n.d.

Laurie, Simon S. *Historical Survey of Pre-Christian Education.* New York: Longmans Green and Company, 1915.

Lotz, Philip Henry. *Orientation in Religious Education.* Nashville and New York: Abingdon-Cokesbury Press, 1950.

Maynard, John A. *A Survey of Hebrew Education.* Milwaukee: Morehouse Publishing Company, 1924.

Murch, James DeForest. *Christian Education and the Local Church.* Cincinnati: Standard Publishing Company, 1943.

Person, Peter P. *An Introduction to Christian Education.* Grand Rapids: Baker Book House, 1958.

Price, J. M., Carpenter, L. L., and Chapman, J. H. *Introduction to Religious Education.* New York: The Macmillan Company, 1932.

Sauer, Erich. *The Dawn of World Redemption.* Grand Rapids: Wm. B. Eerdmans Publishing Company, 1952.

Sauer, Erich. *From Eternity to Eternity.* Grand Rapids: Wm. B. Eerdmans Publishing Company, 1954.

Sherrill, Lewis J. *The Rise of Christian Education.* New York: The Macmillan Company, 1944.

Swift, Fletcher H. *Education in Ancient Israel from Earliest Times to 70* A.D. Chicago: The Open Court Publishing Company, 1919.

The Encyclopedia of Sunday Schools and Religious Education. New York: Thomas Nelson and Sons, 1915.

Articles on:

"Religious Education among the Jews," E. H. Lehman, pp. 587-593.

"The Bible as a Sourcebook of Religious Education," W. T. Whitley, pp. 94-96.

Most famous of the catechetical schools of the second and third centuries (designed for the training of clergy) was the one at Alexandria. This city continued to be a prominent center of Christian thought until the seventh century. Here is the Sidi Bishr Beach with the skyline of Alexandria in the background.

(Courtesy of the Consulate General of the U.A.R.)

3

Early Christian Education

CHRISTIANITY came into history related to the past. It had close connections with the revelation God had made in the Old Testament preparatory to redemption through Christ. Jesus based His teachings upon the Old Testament and said emphatically that He had not come to destroy the Law but to complete and fulfill it.

The two parts of the Old Testament closely connected with the Gospel are the Law and the Prophets. The Mosaic Law revealed clearly the will of the holy God, especially in the two tables of the Decalogue. These show the essence of true godliness and morality to be supreme love to God and true love to man. The Law set forth the ideal of righteousness, thus awakening in man the realization of his utter lack of it and the sense of sin and guilt. The awareness of guilt and of need for reconciliation was kept alive by daily sacrifices and by the ceremonial law which, by type and shadow, pointed forward to atonement through a Redeemer. Thus in the Law was the promise of a future ideal righteousness in living form, which would make it possible for repentant sinners to meet the demands of the Law and become perfectly righteous.

Thus the Jews had a hope. It is true that at this time they had turned away from the spiritual and social teachings of the prophets. For these, they had substituted a narrow nationalism and a formal legalistic religion. Nevertheless, everything in their history, their religion, and their institutions pointed to a glorious future to be realized in the coming of the Messiah and the establishing of His kingdom on earth. This promise of hope had its beginning before the Law was given; therefore prophecy is actually older than law. Prophecy began in the Garden of Eden and was prominent in the patriarchal age, especially in Abraham. Moses was a prophet who pointed the people to One greater than himself (Deut. 18:15). Apart from the hope of the coming of this One, the Law wrought only despair.

For eleven hundred years before Christ came, prophecy had organized form in a prophetical order. "In this form it accompanied the Levitical priesthood and the Davidic dynasty down to the Babylonish captivity, survived this catastrophe, and directed the return of the people and the rebuilding of the temple; interpreting and applying the law, reproving abuses in church and state, predicting the terrible judgments and the redeeming grace of God, warning and punishing, comforting and encouraging, with an ever plainer reference to the coming of the Messiah, who should redeem Israel and the world from sin and misery, and establish a kingdom of peace and righteousness on earth."[1]

Judaism, therefore, had much influence on Christianity. Jesus and the apostles reverenced the teachings of the Old Testament though they spoke out forcefully against the ideas and opinions of men that had corrupted God's revelation. In harmony with the practice and the example of Jesus and His apostles, Christian preaching and worship quietly built upon Judaistic teaching and worship in many of the synagogues.

Judaism exerted influence upon Christianity in the sphere of education also. From the education that had developed among the Jews much was taken over into the theory and practice of Christian education. The teaching of children was stressed very early in the Christian church. Presumably, in a Jewish household which had become Christian, parental responsibility toward the children therein would be carried out much as it had been under Judaism. It would be logical to assume that more, rather than less, emphasis was put on the use of the Scriptures, though one would naturally suppose that household ritual did not long continue to have a place among Jewish Christians.

Soon after churches were founded, teaching was given concerning the duty of parents to train and instruct their children. Beginning near the end of the first century, church fathers (whose writings have been preserved for us) urged upon parents certain aspects of their responsibility toward their children and stressed the impor-

[1]Philip Schaff, *History of the Christian Church* (New York: Charles Scribner's Sons, 1882-1910), I, 68.

tance of educating them. It is evident that as soon as Christian communities developed, it was recognized that children born into them should be taught Christian truth.

All through the New Testament, teaching is emphasized. From the beginning it was seen to be essential to the life of the church and was so linked with worship as to make it impossible to consider one without thinking of the other. Teaching was needed, along with preaching, to present the Gospel of the suffering, death, and resurrection of Christ. Teaching was needed to complement and supplement the evangelizing work carried on by means of preaching. Jews acquainted with the Old Testament had to have its teachings reinterpreted in the light of the Christian faith. Men not familiar with Judaism had to have much more instruction. Teaching was necessary to convey to believers the meaning of the Christian confession of faith. It was needful for all who believed to become more familiar with what Jesus taught and to be instructed in the Christian way of living.

The Work of Jesus as a Teacher

Christian education in the early church had its beginning in the teaching done by Jesus. When He founded His Church, He made the teaching of the Scriptures its basis. While all that Jesus taught was perfectly suited to the conditions and the needs of the time and related to the Old Testament message, what He taught was not the outcome of anything that existed then or before. His teachings had no human source. Even the officers among His enemies said of Him, "Never man spake like this man." He came from God and He taught God's message, showing that God's work among and in behalf of men is an ever continuing work. He was of God and He taught as God, "as one having authority." Everything He taught He exemplified in His actions. "Jesus was before He did, He lived what He taught, and lived it before He taught it." He has no peer in loftiness of teaching and holiness of character. Witness to this is given not only by disciples and followers who view Him from the standpoint of faith but also by rationalists and skeptics who look at Him from the standpoint of reason. None ever taught as effectively as He.

Jesus was a teacher, whatever else He was. He was not primarily a preacher, an orator, a reformer, a propagandist, an organizer, or a ruler. He used teaching as the chief means of accomplishing what He had come into the world to do. That was to show men the way to God and to shape their attitudes, ideals, and conduct to conform to God's will. Teaching was His chief business. He was often a healer, sometimes a worker of miracles, frequently a preacher, but always a teacher.

Not only did Jesus do much teaching of His message but He also devoted a goodly portion of His ministry to teaching and training a small group of disciples. He sent forth His disciples to teach others that these might in turn teach still others, thus reaching out until the purpose for which He came might finally be realized. He began His public ministry with preaching or proclaiming the Gospel. However, after He had gained some followers, He changed from preaching to teaching. It was with teaching rather than with preaching that the middle and the later portions of His ministry were chiefly occupied. For the most part, His teaching was concerned with instructing His followers about the nature of the kingdom of God, its laws, and His relation to it. He said that His Father had "taught" Him (John 8:28).

Jesus regarded Himself as a teacher. He spoke of Himself as such, He permitted others to address Him thus, and He was generally recognized by others as a teacher. The term "Master," so frequently used in the Gospels, is a translation of the Greek word, *didaskalos,* "teacher." The disciples often spoke to Him and referred to Him as teacher; rarely did they use any other title. His addresses contained so much of the teaching element that people always thought of Him as a teacher. The disciples and others could not help recognizing the teaching function of His parables because they were so didactic in nature. People other than the disciples gave Jesus the title of teacher. Nicodemus addressed Him thus, and then went on to say, "We know that thou art a teacher come from God." Even His opponents among the Pharisees, the Sadducees, the Herodians, and others called Him "the teacher."

Again and again Jesus is spoken of as teaching in the synagogues. According to Jewish custom, two services were held in a synagogue each Sabbath day. One was the morning service of worship and preaching; the other was an afternoon service devoted primarily to teaching. The natural inference, then, is that the synagogue services mentioned in the Gospels in connection with Jesus' ministry (in which teaching predominated) were largely afternoon services.

Moreover, He is seen in all four Gospels as engaging in the work of teaching wherever He was. The words descriptive of much of the activity of Jesus are "walked" and "talked." As He moved among people, it was his habit to talk in a natural, friendly and intimate way of the things pertaining to the kingdom of God. That is to say, His teaching was of the informal type rather than the formal; He talked about the things of God as He walked, and in talking, He taught. This He did by the wayside, on the seashore, in a desert place, on a mountain, in a home, by a well, or in the temple court, as well as in the synagogue.

Wherever He might be, He was, as Paul enjoined a later disciple to be, "apt to teach." Jesus as teacher was occupied with a simple world of people, nature, objects connected with everyday living, and commonplace activities. In this natural human environment, He walked among people, observing them in their daily living. He concerned Himself with their spiritual interests and problems, and talked with them about God and their relation to Him.

It is not likely that Jesus devoted conscious study to methods of teaching. However, He was a master in the use of methods. Probably these were natural to Him instead of being deliberately studied and planned. He used in essence practically all the methods common in teaching since His day and He used them most effectively, teaching as no other has ever taught. As a master-teacher, He made it a practice to adapt Himself to the situation and to the state and need of the one or ones taught. Thus, while He used methods, He was above method in the formal sense of the word.

Jesus did not teach as one who does not know where he is going and whether or not he has arrived. He never taught merely for the sake of teaching; when He taught He always had a purpose and He always had definite aims. He had clearly in mind what He wanted, and He moved so as to attain a previously conceived purpose. He was not so much concerned with imparting knowledge as He was with stimulating to action in terms of what was already known. His basic, all-consuming purpose was to relate hearers properly to God first of all, then to others. Upon right relationship as a foundation, He sought to develop right attitudes, to form proper ideals, to prepare for effective meeting of life problems, to grow mature character, and to train for service.

As already mentioned, the manner in which Jesus carried on instruction was natural and informal instead of formal. Typically, it was conversational, consisting of question and answer, dialogue and discussion, and storytelling. Little did He try to instruct passive hearers by using a continuous discourse. He knew, as did contemporaneous Jewish educators, that in order for the learner to come to know he must listen attentively and participate in discussion, asking and answering questions. He made frequent use of the question, especially in beginning instruction, both asking questions and encouraging questions from others.

Jesus' way of teaching was to begin with the living person where he was in his experience, then turn to Scripture for the help and understanding it could give him in living. He took persons as they were and sought to bring them to where they ought to be. Always He dealt with vital issues pertaining to spiritual living, not with secondary or incidental matters. History, geography, theology, even the memorization of Scripture, He never emphasized.

The world of Jesus was essentially a world of persons, divine, human, and demoniac. He saw the unlimited possibilities inherent in each person He taught. For Him, life as it was being lived in relation to this world came first, then came the application of the truth of God to life's experiences. To Him, there was something far more important than for the person merely to know truth. It was important for him to see the bearing truth had upon every phase of his life and to reduce truth to practice in his living. Once Jesus had led the learner to see truth in its relation to himself, Jesus' word to him was, "Go, and do thou likewise."

For Jesus, the individual was the primary consideration; He stressed the personal touch, not mass following. Each soul stood alone, had eternal value, and was worthy of the teacher's supreme attention. Each person had to have specific instruction in the truth of God. Over and over He talked with individuals, drawing out the best in them, working on their conscience, teaching them the requirements of God, and showing them how to become children of God. Even when He talked to a group, it seemed as if He directed His teaching first to one, then to another, with a view to meeting the needs of individuals. Much of what is recorded of His teachings would not be in the Gospels had He not given primary attention to the individual.

After Jesus had finished His work on earth and just prior to His ascension, He gave a teaching commission to His disciples: "Go ye therefore, and teach all nations, baptizing them in the name of the Father, and of the Son, and of the Holy Ghost: teaching them to observe all things whatsoever I have commanded you: and, lo, I am with you alway, even unto the end of the world" (Matt. 28:19-20). Thus He gave a twofold teaching task: to teach in order to bring men into fellowship with God; to teach the ways of God to those brought into fellowship. This charge meant three things: the recognition of teaching as essential to the building of the kingdom; the necessity of teaching in the building of Christian character; and the continual presence of Christ in the person of the Holy Spirit with those who obey His command to teach. In the light of educational practice among the Jews at that time it seems that Jesus was commanding the starting of schools for teaching the Gospel. Gathering people—children and older ones willing to be taught—into classes, under skilled teachers, for group study of the Word of God was the starting point of the Christian church, as Christ likely intended it to be.

At any rate, Christ commanded His followers to teach. They are to teach all nations; teaching is to be for all people, irrespective of race, color, or any other mark of distinctiveness. They are to teach, then to baptize; teaching is to secure avowed recognition of Christ as Saviour and Lord. Finally, they are to teach men to observe all things commanded by Christ. Teaching is to stress everything about duty to God and to man, and to lead men to act in the light of known duty.

The Apostolic Period of Christian Education

The apostles hastened to render obedience to the Great Commission. On the Day of Pentecost they first put it into action. What is usually called Peter's sermon represented teaching the apostles gave concerning Jesus, prophecies fulfilled in Him, and His works as Lord and Christ. Of those who received his word, it is said that they "continued stedfastly" in the apostles' teaching. Every day in the temple and in houses, the apostles "ceased not to teach and preach Jesus Christ" (Acts 5:42). The apostles were Jews as well as Christians; as Jews they had learned well the Scriptures and how to teach.

The early Christians recognized a difference between teaching and preaching, for there is frequent use in the New Testament of the one term over against the other. As was true of Jesus, the teaching ministry had ascendance over the preaching ministry among early Christians. When they did preach, their sermons—notably those of Peter, Stephen, and Paul—were saturated with the teaching elements.

The truth taught by apostolic teachers was not the same as the truth they had learned under Judaism, but the method of teaching seems to have been essentially the same. As people were converted, groups were formed for purposes of instruction, fellowship, and worship. All centered in Christ, and it was of Him the teachers taught. Their subject matter was the Word of God, but their theme was the Christ of God who rose from the dead in order that men might have life through believing on Him.

The outstanding teacher of the early church was the Apostle Paul, who called himself a teacher as well as an apostle. Unlike the other apostles, he did not have the privilege of being taught by Jesus. He had, however, been a pupil in the school of Gamaliel, a renowned Jewish teacher; therefore he was skilled in the best Jewish teaching procedures. When he became a Christian, he turned his skill to good account for Christ and His cause. From the time that Barnabas sought him out and brought him to Antioch (where the two of them taught a whole year) until his death, Paul engaged in teaching.

While Barnabas and Saul carried on their teaching ministry at Antioch, the Holy Spirit directed that they be commissioned to launch a greater and more widespread ministry. Far from being flying evangelistic campaigns from city to city, the great missionary journeys thus instituted were teaching missions. Everywhere Paul went, to everyone he met, he taught of the Christ whom God had raised from the dead, according to the Scriptures, that men who believed on Him might become right with God. He taught in the synagogue, by the riverside, in prison, on Mars' hill, in the school, in the market place, in the theater, in homes, on board ship, on courthouse steps, in public, and in private. He taught Jews, Gentiles, Greeks, Romans, friends, enemies, philosophers, governors, and kings. In some cities he spent days teaching, weeks in others, months and even years in still others.

He taught individuals, small groups, and great assemblies. On those occasions when he made public addresses, he saw to it that what he said was instructive in content and in manner of presentation. He devoted the greater part of his ministry to instructing small groups rather than speaking to crowds. Typically, he used the discussion method. Even his discourses and his epistles, especially the one to the Romans, are examples of teaching carried on by the discussion method.

His primary purpose in writing an epistle was to teach. Each epistle was written to give knowledge and understanding of some truth or truths. In the two epistles to the Thessalonians Paul corrects wrong views and teaches the truth about the second coming of Christ. He wrote the Corinthian letters to correct wrong ethical conditions and to set forth spiritual standards for social living. In the Epistle to the Galatians he teaches that justification and right living are by faith and by the power of the Holy Spirit. In Romans he teaches that all men have sinned and come short of God's requirements, that all may be justified by faith in Christ, and that those saved should live above sin in dedication to God, serving and loving one another, as loyal citizens and as those who have respect for the views of others. In Ephesians Paul teaches the nature of the true Church. He wrote Philippians to show that Christian experience is inner and not dependent on outward circumstances. Colossians was written to correct two forms of error: legality, in the form of asceticism, and false mysticism. He wrote the epistles to Timothy and to Titus to show the order that should prevail in the churches and how to secure and maintain it.

Thus this foremost of all workers in the church, who was at the same time its greatest thinker, left on the world the impress of his teaching. Educated, as the other apostles were not, he had learned in the rabbinical school how to arrange and state and defend his ideas. So both by word of mouth and by pen he brought to men the truth of the Gospel of Christ. He had undergone a long and peculiar course of instruction to become a rabbi, a course consisting of the study of the Scriptures and the comments of sages and masters upon them. He had committed to memory both Scriptures and the sayings of the wise; he had engaged in discussions about disputed points; and he had participated in the asking and the answering of questions.

The result was such grounding in the Scriptures that he could be used of God to commit effectively to others what he had learned. It is impossible to estimate how much God accomplished through the oral messages of this teacher who met untold difficulties victoriously and bore most intense sufferings cheerfully for the sake of Christ. Through the teachings he put into writing he gave the world its best explanation of Christian truth. If his epistles were to perish, the loss would be inestimable. They have brought to the minds and the hearts of men the truths of God's grace as no other writings have done.

Catechumenal Schools

The original members of the Christian church were Jews who had no reason to turn from the religious customs of their nation. Thorough instruction in the Scriptures was given in the synagogue schools. The Messianic hope was emphasized in Judaism. On this Jewish foundation the apostles and their successors could build by teaching that the crucified and resurrected Jesus was the Messiah. The development of the organization of the Christian churches was gradual. Jewish forms of training constituted the starting point of that development.

These forms sufficed so long as the church was concerned with Jews only. But when its ministry was extended to non-Jewish people who had not received the training the Jews enjoyed, change in its system of instruction became necessary. These people were not familiar with the Scriptures and the teachings of Judaism, so they had to be given background. The Old Testament, which had been translated into Greek in the third century before Christ, was used for this purpose, for Greek was the language most people used. Since the Jews lived under Roman rule, it was natural for Christian education eventually to take on the Roman pattern.

Centuries elapsed, however, before Christianity had one land and people where it could enforce a formal religious education such as

Judaism had. But individual Christians were zealous in their efforts to reach and teach the young whenever and wherever there was opportunity. Thus Christianity spread, not by a system of formal education but by Christians reaching and teaching others naturally and informally, as Jesus Himself had done. As a result, in less than three hundred years from the death of the Apostle John the whole population of the Roman empire was nominally Christianized.

The first formal education by the early church was through its catechumenal schools. Such schools were established in the first and second centuries and were designed to train converts, both young and old, for church membership. Such trainees, called catechumens, included children of believers, adult Jews, and Gentile converts. The words "catechism" and "catechumen" are derived from a Greek word meaning "instruct," literally "to din into the ear." It occurs seven times in the New Testament (Luke 1:4; Acts 18:25; 21:21, 24; Rom. 2:18; I Cor. 14:19; Gal. 6:6). These passages show its use as it applies to the giving of systematic and thorough instruction in the teachings of the church to converts preparatory to admitting them into fellowship.

The period of preparation covered two or three years. There were three grades or classes of catechumens. When first admitted, they were called *hearers,* because they were permitted to listen to the reading of the Scriptures and the sermons in the church. They received elementary instruction in the fundamental doctrines and practices of the church, and had to show by their conduct that they were worthy of promotion into a second grade or class. This second grade was that of *kneelers,* those who remained for prayers after the hearers withdrew. They received more advanced instruction and had to prove by their manner of living that they were worthy of entering upon the last stage of their probationary period. Those in this third grade were called *the chosen* and were given intensive doctrinal, liturgical, and ascetical training in preparation for baptism.

Teachers in the catechumenal schools at first were the bishops and the priests or the deacons. Later the catechist or instructor often happened to be a minor cleric or even some able layman.

It was not the aim of the catechumenal schools to give any intellectual training. It is true that the doctrinal and liturgical instruction afforded catechumens some intellectual training, but this was secondary, not primary. The definite purpose was to train morally and spiritually candidates for church membership. The church was fundamentally interested in teaching people how to live as Christians. In times of persecution such as Christians met in those days, it was not easy to live a consistent Christian life. The church was compelled to be careful in the preparation of those who professed conversion to Christianity, because of the possibility that members of the church under stress of persecution might not stand true.

Moreover, the conditions of the times required of Christians separation from many social and moral evils. The church taught catechumens, and Christians in general, that they were duty bound to shun the impurities of pagan shows and festivities, to regard marriage as a sacred contract entered into for life, to look upon children as a blessing and a trust for which they were responsible to God, to deal justly with all men, and to practice every one of the precepts Christ proclaimed in the Sermon on the Mount.

The method of teaching in catechumenal schools was basically catechetical, i.e., by question and answer. No more than the Jewish rabbis before them did the early Christian teachers try to teach passive hearers by continuous discourse. And their instruction was not mere questioning with response by rote answers. It savored more of the nature of dialogue in that pupils as well as teachers both asked and answered questions. Often it was the pupil who asked the question, and it was the teacher who answered it. Each pupil was handled according to his individual needs; the catechist might ascertain these needs by preliminary questioning and thus make the pupil's error or lack the starting point for his special instruction. The individual was to be caused to *know* for himself the truth, not merely to *hear* it. In the instruction of catechumens, it was the individual pupil who was taught, not an assembly of pupils which was sprayed with content the teacher had learned.

Catechumenal teaching originated during the first and second centuries. It was practiced in perfected form between 325 and 450. After 450 the teaching deteriorated. The growth of the practice of infant baptism accounted in large part for this deterioration. Infant baptism made for a change of the time of systematic instruction in basic Christian truth from before until after baptism. The church created no special agency for teaching those born in the church and baptized in infancy or childhood. It was deemed that the Christian home ought to perform this task. Many sermons and tracts admonished parents concerning this duty. Some church fathers went so far as to advise parents to have their children educated in convents. Along with the change resulting from infant baptism, the difficulty of teaching adult converts increased as an outcome of the alliance between state and church.

But catechumenal teaching has continued all through the centuries even to this day. In heathen countries at the present time it is found needful to have converts undergo a period of training in doctrine and Christian living before they are received into full membership in the church. In the case of some church bodies in Christian lands, instruction comes mostly before confirmation, which is separated by a considerable interval from baptism, allowing those who are baptized to reach the age of discretion. In other church bodies preparation of converts for membership is provided for by means of the Sunday school or by church membership classes. Thus, in various ways the practice of the early church of properly instructing in the faith those who are to be admitted to full fellowship is still retained.

Catechetical, Episcopal, and Cathedral Schools

The early Christians were from the lower classes and had little interest in the learning of the Greeks and Romans. Furthermore, the moral character of the educated people of the time was not in harmony with Christian standards. Accordingly, parents were loath to send their children to Roman schools where they would be exposed to pagan literature and be subjected to the influence of pagan ideals.

But as the church grew and as Christians came into contact with Greek and Roman culture, people from the educated classes became members. These, seeking intellectual understanding of the truths of Christianity, asked leaders and ministers difficult questions. Furthermore, the inquiries of pagan philosophers and the attacks of heretics made it imperative for the clergy to have such preparation as would enable them to deal effectively with those inquiries and attacks. Then too by the end of the second century there were in the church men who thought that pagan literature and philosophy could be very useful to Christians if objectionable features were eliminated.

Thus there evolved out of catechumenal schools in the last half of the second century and during the third a new type of Christian school known as the catechetical. The purpose of these was to equip the clergy with intellectual training similar to that of learned people of the day. In the course of time these schools produced Christian scholars who could think and reason like other educated men and had a knowledge comparable to that possessed by teachers of Greco-Roman culture.

The most famous of the catechetical schools was the one at Alexandria. It probably started as a catechumenal school. Tradition says that Mark founded the church in Alexandria and gathered converts together for instruction. In 179 Pantaenus, a converted Stoic philosopher, became head of the school. He developed it on a wider basis, combining in his teaching the exposition of the Scriptures with that of philosophy. Under Clement, who succeeded Pantaenus, the curriculum was further extended to include Greek literature, history, dialectic, and the sciences. Clement's teaching is known through his writings, which make Greek learning and culture the handmaidens of Christianity. After Clement fled from Alexandria, Origen came into charge of the school. Under him it rose to its highest point, attracting many pagans and Gnostics as well as Christians. Alexandria continued to be a prominent center of Christian thought until the seventh century.

Similar schools were opened in other cities; the most famous were those at Jerusalem, Edessa, Nisibis, Constantinople, and the one founded at Caesarea by Origen after he left Alexandria. Though not originally intended for the instruction of the clergy only, these schools supplied the early church with some of its greatest leaders and may be considered the forerunners of the episcopal and cathedral schools.

These cathedral schools were a further development of Christian education in the early church. As Christianity spread, bishoprics were established, with the tendency to an episcopal hierarchy in which the bishops wielded power over local churches. The particular church over which the bishop presided was known as the cathedral. The catechetical school located there came to be known as the episcopal or cathedral school. It had higher cultural standards than other schools; in it the clergy were trained under the direct supervision of the bishop. These schools were highly organized under rules or canons of the church as early as the latter half of the fourth century.

The cathedral schools came to dominate all education. During the fifth and sixth centuries, church councils decreed that all children destined for the priesthood should early be placed in these training schools. Thus in time their teachings changed and colored the doctrines of the church, including even the apostolic doctrines. Conflicting theological opinions of men in these schools rocked the church and destroyed the unity of its fellowship.

Greek influence had entered the Roman world before Christ came. During the early Christian period it maintained a strong hold wherever Christianity had not come. The chief difference between Hellenism and Christianity was that the Greeks sought to find truth through reason, while Christians believed the truth had been revealed in Christ. So Greek culture emphasized reason and cultivated the intellect, and Christians emphasized faith and cultivated the soul. Pantaenus and others who first combined Greek culture and Christianity had a good motive in trying to meet the former by using it to serve the latter, but they opened the gates to a subtle influence which undermined Christianity.

With the catechetical and cathedral schools are connected the names of some of the great leaders of the early church and the first theological controversy within the church. Origen went farther than Pantaenus and maintained that Greek culture was necessary to training for Christian leadership. The school he founded at Caesarea was essentially a Greek school, though he tried to teach Greek culture from a Christian point of view. Justin Martyr, teacher in the school in Rome, taught that Christianity was already contained in Greek philosophy and that Plato and Socrates were Christians before Christ came into the world.

But among the leaders of the church, especially in the West, were those who were opposed to pagan learning. By the close of the third century hostility to the pagan schools and to Greek learning had become pronounced. Many leaders who had been teachers in pagan schools before their conversion advised against including Greek learning in Christian schools. Tertullian branded the wisdom of the

Greeks as foolish and dangerous. Jerome tried to create a Christian literature, but all his life he loved the pagan classics and was disturbed by that love. He tells of dreaming that he had died and was condemned before the bar of Heaven for being a classicist rather than a Christian.

The attitude of the church on the question af pagan learning was negative. It was felt that the Bible contained all that man needed and that he should have nothing to do with the writings of non-Christian authors. Finally, in 401, largely at the instigation of Augustine, the Council of Carthage forbade the clergy to read any pagan author.

Consequently, after the overthrow of Roman culture by the barbarians, when the church had come into complete control of education, Greek learning gradually died out in the West and was largely forgotten until the Renaissance. In the meantime, the episcopal, cathedral, and monastic schools were almost the only ones in the West.

The episcopal and cathedral schools intensified the tendency begun in the catechetical schools to take less and less interest in the instruction of all Christians and to form a special priestly class. In time, the result was an intellectual aristocracy in the church, with much ignorance among the masses. As the church grew in worldly prominence, it lost in spiritual life through failure to continue to perform the duty imposed upon it by its Lord in the Great Commission. Man does not live by truth he discovers through his own thinking but by truth he learns through coming to know the Scriptures. As Greek learning came in, the Bible went out; as the Bible went out, spiritual life declined. When thorough instruction in the Word of God ceased, vital piety was replaced by church orthodoxy and barren formalism.

The Church Fathers

In the early centuries of its history the church numbered among its members many learned men, doctors, teachers, writers called the "church fathers." Allusion has already been made to some of these who had a part in the work of the schools. Because of the influence of the church fathers on education, it may be well to give further consideration to several of these, some in the East and some in the West, who lived during the first three or four hundred years of the Christian era. Many of these men had been Greek philosophers before their conversion, and all of them had been pupils in Greek schools.

Among the first and the best known of the early Christian teachers and writers was Justin Martyr (100-165), the most famous of the second-century apologists. He was brought up in paganism and became an enthusiastic student of philosophy, especially that of Plato. In his writings as a Christian, he drew from different systems, especially Stoicism and Platoism, and tried to trace a real bond between pagan philosophy and Christianity. Much of his *Apology* seems to be rewritten catechetical material.

Clement of Alexandria (150-215) came to Christianity from the ranks of the Greek philosophers. He had a thorough knowledge of Biblical and Christian literature and was familiar with the works of pagan poets and philosophers. He was one of the first Christian teachers who sought to bring philosophy to the support of faith. He compared the influence of philosophy on the Greeks to the educative power exercised on the Jews by the Law, and he taught that pagan philosophy was "a pedagogue to bring the world to Christ." His *Miscellanies* are an attempt at reconciliation between science and religion in which he expresses many ideas on education. More educational in tone is the *Paedagogus*. The great Pedagogue is Christ, who first calls man to Himself and then fashions his whole life and character according to His own. Clement places emphasis on faith and, in a later work, sets forth the steps by which the Christian should advance to knowledge or understanding. To him knowledge is not opposed to faith but consists rather in a fuller comprehension of what is already in faith. He sought to convince Christians who were hostile to pagan learning that it was possible for an orthodox Christian to acquire a knowledge of dialectic and the best philosophical thought and also a proper understanding of the physical universe. Such knowledge, he maintained, would serve to strengthen one's grasp of the truth of Christianity, not harm his faith.

Origen (185-254) was probably the most influential of the early writers and teachers and has been called the most learned of all the Christian fathers. He was a voluminous writer. Unfortunately most of his works have been lost, though some have been found in recent years among the papyri. A man of rare intelligence, he devoted himself so diligently and so effectively to reconciliation of pagan and Christian thought that he was pronounced a heretic. He was not only a great teacher but a great scholar. He sought to compare the doctrines of Christianity by the teachings of the philosophers, and did not hesitate to set aside passages of Scripture that seemed to conflict with reason.

Cyril of Jerusalem (c. 315-386) was an instructor of the catechumens at Jerusalem before he became bishop of that city. He wrote a series of twenty-three addresses instructing catechumens. These addresses include lectures to candidates for baptism and instructions to the same persons after they were baptized. His work gives insight into the creedal forms and the ceremonies of baptism of the early church.

Basil the Great (331-379) received a good literary education in the schools of Caesarea and Constantinople and at the University of Athens. After teaching for some time, he retired from the world and became the founder of monastic life in the East. He was deeply interested in the education of the poor. Though recognizing the value of pagan literature, he warned against its unlimited use. The young Christian, he said, can derive profit from the study of some of the pagan poets and writers provided he is always on guard against what is morally base.

Gregory of Nyssa (331-396), brother of Basil the Great, was originally completely devoted to pagan culture, toward which he always remained tolerant. Even after he had entered the priesthood he retained his interest in teaching, as is shown in his *Oratio Catechetica,* which gives many practical directions to teachers concerning the methods of instructing converts to Christianity. He explains how the teacher's purpose must be to adapt teaching to the needs of each convert according to the religious beliefs he held before conversion. The work strikingly illustrates the heavy obligation which rested on the Christian teacher of the fourth century to convince well-educated converts to Christianity that the religious tenets they had held were found on error.

Chrysostom (347-407), the most prominent doctor of the Greek Church, was one of the greatest preachers Christianity ever had. He received his literary education in the best schools of his native city, Antioch, under teachers devoted to pagan culture. However, he withdrew from profane studies to devote himself to a religious life and the study of the Scriptures. He conceded the value of pagan schools but did not give full approval to pagan education, and he derides pagan philosophers frequently. He stressed that the moral purpose of education is more important than anything else.

Chrysostom has an assured place in the history of Christian education by virtue of his address, *On Vainglory and the Right Way for Parents to Bring Up Their Children.* In the central part of this he sketches a catechetical method adapted to youthful minds. He bases his system on the psychology of the child, using the love of stories all normal children have, as well as their curiosity and their tendency to rivalry. He takes two narratives from the Old Testament and shows how these can be told to the child, partly in the words of the Bible, partly in simpler language. He explains and illustrates his method so that parents may apply it to the teaching of other parts of the Old Testament. The New Testament narratives, he maintains, involve fundamentals of the Christian faith which, however simply stated, can be grasped only by a person of mature understanding.

In the West as well as in the East the church won converts from the higher classes of pagans—public men, professional men, men educated in Roman learning, Roman government, and Roman education. Among the most famous of these, from the standpoint of their influence on Christian thought and education, were Tertullian, Gregory Thaumaturgus, Arnobius, Jerome, Ambrose, and Augustine.

Tertullian (150-230) was a man of great learning and strong intellect who had been a lawyer before his conversion. He felt that there were dangers to faith and morals in pagan poetry and philosophy; therefore the study of pagan learning by Christians should be concerned only with detecting and refuting errors. He was opposed to all attempts to combine philosophy and Christianity. In a writing *On Schoolmasters and Their Difficulties* he states that a Christian could not be a teacher of pagan learning. His *Apologeticus* is a splendid defense of Christians against their pagan adversaries. He wrote several tracts dealing with the needs of catechumens, emphasizing warning and instruction as the main duties of the catechist.

Gregory Thaumaturgus was a pupil of Origen in Caesarea. He stressed the need for utilizing in the curriculum the best the liberal arts could offer, to form a solid ground for later instruction. Teaching began with language, which was followed by the sciences and a study of ethics. Lastly, came the study and interpretation of the Scriptures. The pupil was urged to read all kinds of writings except those written by atheists. No subject, pagan or spiritual, divine or human, was forbidden the pupil.

Arnobius (325) was a teacher of rhetoric in Africa before his conversion. As a pagan he so vigorously opposed Christianity that his conversion was viewed with suspicion. To prove his sincerity he wrote *Against the Pagans,* a seven-volume defense of the Christian faith. In this he attacks philosophy, principally Platonic idealism, exposes pagan myths, and shows the hollowness of the ceremonies of the cults.

Jerome (340-420) was probably the most learned of the Latin fathers. He studied in various schools and knew Greek and Hebrew in addition to his native Latin. He was much influenced by the writings of Origen. Though very fond of the ancient classics, he turned to the Scriptures after being warned in a dream of the danger of excessive devotion to pagan learning. The most widely known of his many writings is the *Vulgate,* his Latin translation of the Bible from the Hebrew and Greek versions. Among his writings are his letters to Laeta and Gaudentius concerning the education of girls. These letters are important in the history of early Christian education. In his second letter to Paulinus of Nola he sets forth principles for the study of the Scriptures. The zeal for learning manifested by many pagans, he says, has its spiritual counterpart in the Apostles Paul, Peter, and John, whose wisdom was from God. Not everyone can interpret the Bible; Biblical exegesis, the same as all other human knowledge, must be learned. Learning involves three things: teaching, method, and practice. Jerome censures mere verbal dexterity and ingenuity in argument, and demands a sound education based on intelligent considerations.

Ambrose (340-399) was a lawyer who held office under the emperor when the people of Milan elected him bishop of that city. Above all else, he was an ecclesiastical teacher whose absorbing concern was to win men for Christ. The conversion of Augustine was due to the influence of Ambrose. In his writings he always follows some practical purpose; he has no liking for philosophical speculations. Often he draws from the ideas of an earlier writer, Christian or pagan. He was much influenced by the writings of Philo, the Jewish philosopher, who sought to fuse into a unity the truth revealed in the Old Testament and the wisdom of the Greeks. His chief work, *De Officiis Ministrorum,* is a manual of Christian ethics, intended primarily for the use of ecclesiastics. Among his writings are at least two works addressed specifically to catechumens.

Augustine (354-430) is the most illustrious of all the fathers of the church. Born of a pagan father and a Christian mother, he received a good literary education in various schools and became a professor of rhetoric, teaching first in the schools of his native African province, then in Rome and in Milan. His conversion, for which his saintly mother had long prayed, took place when he was thirty-three. From this time on he gave himself wholly to Christian service. For thirty-three years he was the center of ecclesiastical life in Africa, where he was bishop of Hippo.

Perhaps no man has ever exerted greater influence on the thought of his own and later centuries than Augustine. He is acknowledged by all to be in the foremost rank of theologians; he is the equal of the great philosophers of all the centuries; he was the founder of the Christian philosophy of history; and he made outstanding contributions to the field of education. Of him it has been said, "He so moulded the Latin world that it is really he who has shaped the education of modern minds."

His voluminous writings include treatises on education, many passages bearing on the purpose of education, its content, and the methods of instruction to be used. Augustine prepared a guide for the use of teachers in the catechetical schools. In it he stresses the necessity of treating each pupil according to his individual needs. To this end the catechist should ascertain through preliminary questioning the pupil's motives and his present state of knowledge so that he can make the pupil's present state a starting point for instructing him personally. The teacher, all through his teaching, is thus to watch, to question, and to deal carefully with the pupil individually. The aim of the teacher is to cause the pupil to know, not merely to hear, the truth. To this end the teacher is to obtain from the pupil at every point all the reaction he can to the content taught.

Augustine said that pagan writings can be of value if rightly used and their dangers avoided. In his later life, he did not have so much sympathy for classical learning. He discountenanced its use and is supposed to have been responsible for the action of the Council of Carthage in prohibiting reading of pagan literature. But that prohibition had no meaning and little effect in the light of the fusion of philosophy and Christian truth that had already taken place.

Augustine himself found in Plato all the Christian doctrines with the exception of the incarnation. It has been said of Augustine, "In philosophy he had the merit of being the first to synthesize the best elements of pagan inquiries into a coherent system of Christian thought."[2] Inherent in his teaching was the dictum that knowledge is the basis of faith, a dictum that overwhelmingly influenced Scholasticism. Augustine insisted that reason is given to man by God so that man may comprehend all things, including God Himself. Reason is a faculty of the soul by which man is able to see truth directly without the use of the senses. Both religion and philosophy strive for the same eternal truth. In the course of a few centuries Augustinianism was established as official church dogma. His thought governed religious faith through the medieval period and has come down to the modern world through the Renaissance and the Reformation.

To understand clearly the situation of the church fathers and their use of pagan learning to support Christian truth in spite of its disturbing effect on them, one must consider the nature of education during these early centuries. Essentially it was still the system that had been evolved in Athens in the fourth century B.C. and had spread over the entire Mediterranean world. It was definitely Hellenistic and pagan, an education emphasizing human development apart from God. It was education founded upon opposition to the truth revealed by God—opposition that had its origin many generations back in the history of the people who evolved it. Into the pagan world Christianity came. For the first two centuries the instruction Christians received was Biblical, but as Christianity spread it drew into the church many who were interested in intellectual training such as the pagan schools of the day afforded.

Objections to this were obvious and valid. Pagan literature was

[2]Pierre J. Marique, *History of Christian Education* (New York: Fordham University Press, 1926), I, 51.

filled with references to polytheism and, in many of its aspects, was anything but uplifting. Even pagan writers expressed criticism of the lack of moral regard that characterized their own literature. Christians had the choice between being pious and unlearned on the one hand or becoming educated under ungodly influences on the other hand.

The church had no schools for the masses except as the monastic schools served that need. There were plenty of Christians who saw the dangers to children in pagan education—an education which exposed the Christian child, the same as the child of the non-Christian, to teachings about many gods and to the influence of wrong ideals. But the old pagan education went on essentially unchanged after Christianity became the state religion, though Christians knew that this education was opposed to Christian truth. Before Constantine, they were unable to do anything about it, but when they came to power, Christians made no provision for the education of children.

Why should church leaders have looked to an education founded upon human wisdom when God's revelation of truth was theirs? To begin with, many leaders had been philosophers or were philosophically oriented. One who might expect them to return to Jewish educational practices needs to be aware that, however strong the Jewish influence on Christian thought and practice, after A.D. 70 there were few contacts of Christianity with Judaism except hostile ones. One who might draw the seemingly obvious conclusion that a true Christian education would naturally accompany Christianity's marvelous missionary spread fails to remember what all human history shows as to man's tendency to put his own puny insufficiency in the place of God's boundless sufficiency.

As was said in the Foreword, Eve was but the first of a long line of human beings who have yielded to the attractions of knowledge gained by one's own efforts. As she did, so man always does, taking his own way—that of indulging in the delights of intellectual exercise, of enjoying the power and satisfaction of using his own reason, and of seeking to have a greater breadth and depth of intellectual understanding. Following the way of Eve and "the way of Cain," men forsake God's way—that of unwavering reliance upon the truth God reveals, of wholehearted acceptance of God's Word, and of complete dependence upon God as the one and the only source of knowledge and wisdom.

These church fathers were responsible for shepherding churches in a world hostile to Christian faith. Upon them rested also the obligation to interpret the teachings of Christ to a body of converts largely uninformed in spiritual matters and in considerable proportion illiterate. These fathers recognized the necessity of guarding Christianity against the attractively developed human ideas of Greek wisdom and of showing that Christianity, having come from God, was the answer to man's need and longing. They reasoned that they, being Christians who had been trained in Greek philosophy, could, of all men, meet Greek argument on its own ground. Hence they undertook the task of defending the faith.

The results of the attempts at defense by men of such training were disastrous to Christianity and to education founded thereupon. They sought to appeal to the reason of man and to represent Christian teaching as being in accord with reason. In so doing, they did not proclaim Christianity for what it was, "something as different from Greek thinking as God's thoughts are different from man's thoughts." Rather "the gospel was Hellenized." They attempted to make the message of the Gospel consistent with Greek philosophy and to put Christian meanings into this most appealing man-made system. However worthy their motives may have been, the church fathers under deceptive allurements thus started the process of introducing human philosophy into the doctrines and education of the church. That this process of infiltration did not stop with the edict of the Council of Carthage in 401 is abundantly manifest in succeeding centuries as other men have again and again done just as these church fathers did.

Readings

BENSON, CLARENCE H. *A Popular History of Christian Education*. Chicago: Moody Press, 1943.

BOWER, WILLIAM CLAYTON. *Christ and Christian Education*. New York: Abingdon-Cokesbury Press, 1943.

COOKE, ROBERT L. *Philosophy, Education and Certainty*. Grand Rapids: Zondervan Publishing House, 1940.

CUBBERLEY, ELLWOOD P. *The History of Education.* Boston: Houghton Mifflin Company, 1920.

EAVEY, C. B. *Principles of Teaching for Christian Teachers.* Grand Rapids: Zondervan Publishing House, 1940.

EBY, FREDERICK, and ARROWOOD, CHARLES FLINN. *The History and Philosophy of Education, Ancient and Medieval.* New York: Prentice-Hall, Inc., 1940.

EMME, E. E., and STEVICK, P. R. *Introduction to the Principles of Religious Education.* New York: The Macmillan Company, 1926.

ENSLIN, MORTON SCOTT. *Christian Beginnings.* New York: Harper & Brothers, 1938.

HASTINGS, JAMES (editor) *Encyclopaedia of Religion and Ethics.* New York: Charles Scribner's Sons, 1956.

Articles on:

"Catechumen, Catechumenate," C. L. Feltoe, III, 256-258.

"Education (Jewish)," Morris Joseph, V, 194-198.

HORNE, HERMAN HARRELL. *The Philosophy of Christian Education.* New York: Fleming H. Revell Company, 1937.

LAISTNER, M. L. W. *Christianity and Pagan Culture in the Later Roman Empire.* Ithaca: Cornell University Press, 1951.

MARIQUE, PIERRE J. *A History of Christian Education.* New York: Fordham University Press, 1926, Vol. I.

MONROE, PAUL. *A Brief Course in the History of Education.* New York: The Macmillan Company, 1907.

MULHERN, JAMES. *A History of Education.* New York: The Ronald Press Co., 1946.

MURCH, JAMES DEFOREST. *Christian Education and the Local Church.* Cincinnati: Standard Publishing Company, 1943.

NEWMAN, ALBERT HENRY. *A Manual of Church History.* Rev. and enlarged ed., Philadelphia: The Judson Press, 1932, Vol. I.

PERSON, PETER P. *An Introduction to Christian Education.* Grand Rapids: Baker Book House, 1958.

PRICE, J. M., CARPENTER, L. L., and CHAPMAN, J. H. *Introduction to Religious Education.* New York: The Macmillan Company, 1932; reprint, Grand Rapids: Wm. B. Eerdmans Publishing Co., 1940-1950.

SCHAFF, PHILIP. *History of the Christian Church.* New York: Charles Scribner's Sons, 1882-1910, Vol. I.

SHERRILL, LEWIS J. *The Rise of Christian Education.* New York: The Macmillan Company, 1944.

TRUMBULL, H. C., *Yale Lectures on the Sunday-school.* Philadelphia: John D. Wattles, 1888.

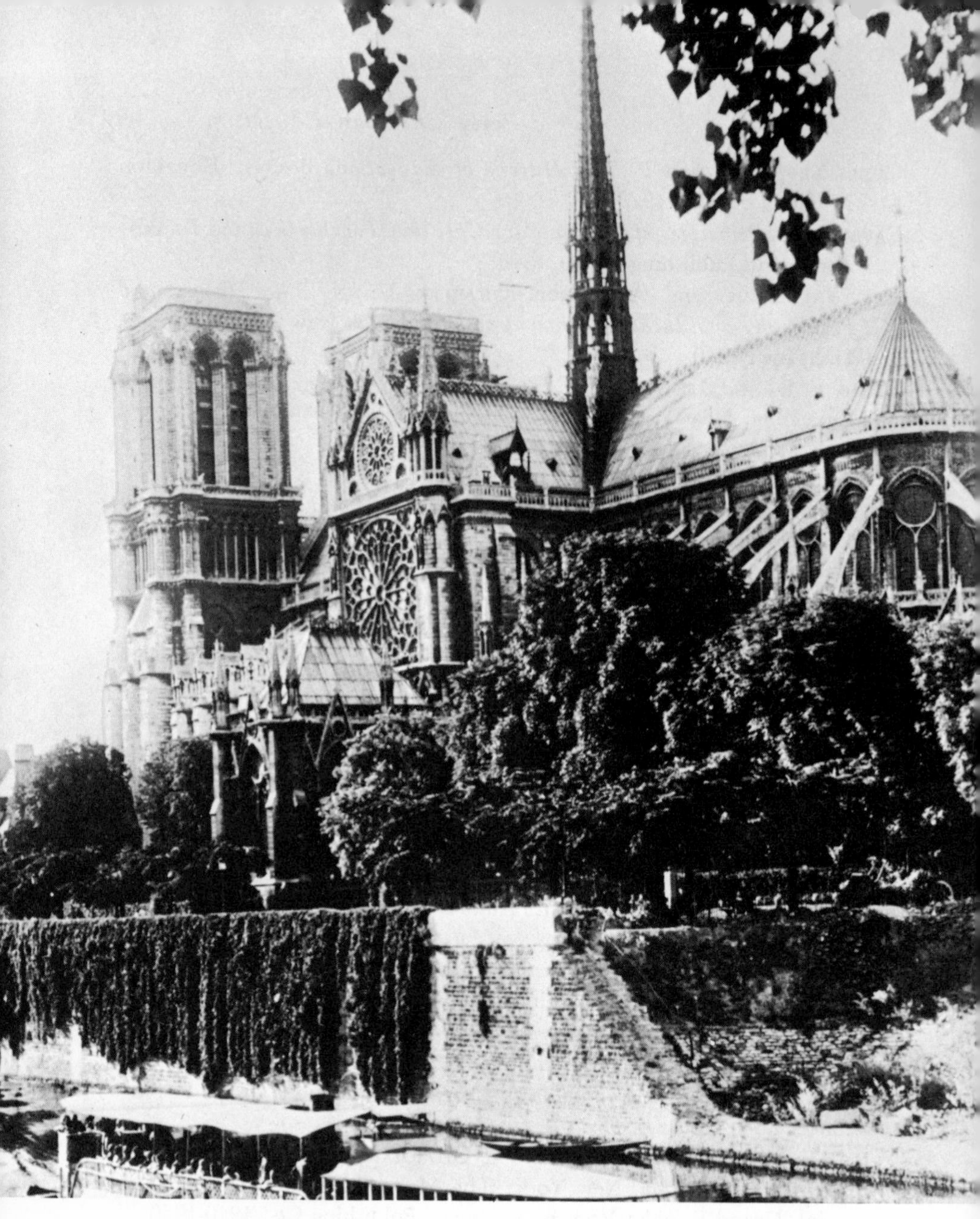

The first university in northern Europe developed from the cathedral school of Notre Dame at Paris. A university before the end of the twelfth century, the University of Paris had lecture rooms in the shadow of the great cathedral. By the thirteenth century all the left bank of the Seine was covered with quarters for students and rooms where the masters lectured. Here the proud old cathedral is viewed from the Seine.

(Courtesy of the French Government Tourist Office)

4

Christian Education in the Middle Ages

For a long time indecision on the issue of revealed truth versus philosophic truth marked the official attitude of the church. Ultimately, however, the position of the church fathers was approved and Augustinianism was established as official church dogma. The teachings of philosophy were deemed essential in the winning of educated pagans and in settling problems met in the Christian church. In its educational work the church rarely any longer declared the facts of the Gospel but substituted for these mere human intellectual speculations. Thus in contact with the world Christianity became a system of philosophical thought instead of a religion of faith.

The Council of Nicaea in 325 met when the trend was definitely away from simple vital Christian truth. The Council might have reversed the trend or at least slowed it, but philosophical teachings had become so intermixed with Christian doctrine as to confuse even the church leaders in their thinking. If the Council had taken a stand for the Bible and the simple teachings of the apostles unspoiled by Greek pagan thought, the medieval church might have been able to fill the place God intended it to fill and the course of history would have been different. Instead, the Council yielded to the influence of Greek philosophy and strengthened the tendency toward its progress. From this union of philosophy and Christianity developed a worldly-minded and apostate church which carried on an education that was religious but not Christian—an education that had in it plenty of church but little of God.

As the Roman empire, weakened within, disintegrated under the onslaughts of the barbarians from without, the church gradually assumed the role of major educator and introduced its own type of education. Between the fourth and sixth centuries, Roman schools declined in number almost to the vanishing point, and the church had little to offer in place of them. With the widespread destruction of Roman culture by the barbarians, the lack of culture among the conquerors, and the passing away of need for training in law and government, there was little use for learning outside the service of the church. Hence education narrowed to preparation for such service and to the few who needed it. Even the education of the clergy, during some three centuries prior to Charlemagne, was very much neglected. By the beginning of the seventh century education was largely in the hands of bishops, priests, and monks, many of whom were themselves illiterate.

Since education was virtually denied to people, ignorance and vice began to flourish. During the seventh and eighth centuries, conditions grew worse. The church itself suffered from the prevailing ignorance, and introduced into its government and worship harmful heathenish customs and practices. Ignorance and superstition so prevailed among clergy and laity, worship was so given over to veneration of saints and relics and shrines, the church had so developed appeal to the senses, that Christianity savored more of the nature of a crude polytheism than it did of simple faith in God.

Church Schools

These deplorable conditions were characteristic of the Early Middle Ages, roughly from 500 to 1000, and a social and intellectual restoration took place in the Later Middle Ages from about 1000 to 1200 or 1300. During the entire period the church played a large part in nearly all phases of life. Having grown rapidly in the later centuries of the Roman Empire, after the Empire fell, the church was a source of stability and security in the midst of the great change and flux of the times. It continued to grow in power and influence throughout the Middle Ages until it reached its peak in the thirteenth century.

During the Early Middle Ages some secular authorities sponsored education, but they generally operated through the clergy. When secular rulers wanted schools established, these schools with few exceptions were set up in churches or cathedrals or monasteries. Kings and emperors sometimes stimulated educational activity among the clergy and in the church. The agency of control of most schools was the church. As the political power of the emperors declined during the ninth and tenth centuries, the pope and the church councils took more and more independent action in educational matters. Lay teachers were tolerated, but the cleric was officially the teacher prior to the Reformation. The most learned among the clergy taught the more advanced subjects, leaving the rudiments to be taught by the junior clergy or by priests who had little learning. There was no teaching profession, as distinguished from the clerical, until near the end of the Middle Ages.

The activity of the church in education continued to increase throughout the Middle Ages. Cathedral schools existed at the beginning of the period. Church councils early in the period prescribed that boys destined for the clergy should be instructed in the cathedral schools. The most important of the schools established by the church during the Middle Ages were the monastic schools.

When worldliness crept into the church, men conceived the idea of separating themselves from material things and going into seclusion. While Scripture had something to say about separation from the world, the main bases of monasticism were found in oriental asceticism and especially in Greek philosophical dualism. In Plato, for instance, reality was found to exist in the world of ideas or the immaterial world; matter was looked upon as being something inferior. This emphasis on two levels of existence (carried to the extent of a desire for release from the material world into the immaterial) was further developed in Neoplatonism. Monasticism first arose in the East. Thus monasticism was a continuation of the effect on Christianity of Greek thought. And in the education developing from monasticism there was a continuation of the alliance of these two which had found expression in the church fathers.

Monastic regulations imposed reading and study as part of the daily duty of every monk. These regulations made at first for the purpose of educating and disciplining the monks, led to the establishing of schools and the development of a system of monastic education. Youths received into the monasteries at an early age had to be taught to read since they were later to use the sacred books. This necessitated the instructing of novices, so the teaching of reading was begun in the monasteries. Since books were scarce and available only through the handwritten process, the novices had to be instructed in writing as well as in reading. The services of worship of the church made necessary some instruction of the novices in music, and the calculating of the church calendar called for elementary knowledge of numbers and calculation.

Out of these needs arose the monastery school, the copying of manuscripts, and the preservation of books. In an age when lawlessness and disorder prevailed, monasteries offered the one opportunity for a quiet scholarly life, so they became the leading educational and literary institutions of the Early Middle Ages. Monasteries came to have schools as a regular part of their organizations. From the ninth century on, monasteries provided instruction for nonclerics as well as for those who were destined to become monks. Consequently two types of monastic schools developed, one for those entering monastic life and one for outsiders. Monastic schools were dominant in the education of Europe from the sixth to the eleventh centuries.

The need for the copying of books led incidentally to the preservation of ancient literature. Under the lack of cultural influences and the general ignorance of the period, Latin, the language of all education of the church and of the monasteries, was rapidly corrupted. There was need for good models of Latin prose and verse and these were found in the classical authors, especially Caesar, Cicero, and Vergil. To have classical works it was necessary to copy them, for there had been a great destruction of old books during the centuries of barbarian invasion. So the monasteries began to preserve and to use as models the ancient Roman books. From using them an interest in their contents was awakened. Many monasteries accumulated libraries and became noted for literary and educational activity. In all this the Bible had only a small part. While the monasteries contributed comparatively little to pure Christianity or to true Christian education, they were, nevertheless, conservatories of learning and centers of missionary and philanthropic work. The monks were the writers, preachers, philosophers, and theologians of the age.

Along with the monastic schools, the cathedral or episcopal schools played a large part in the education of the Middle Ages. From these two types of schools came practically all medieval church leaders. Moreover, from the impetus given to advanced study by the most outstanding of the cathedral schools arose the universities of later times.

The curriculum of the cathedral schools was a survival of the pagan past, coming down from Plato through Roman education. It consisted of what came to be known as the *seven liberal arts.* These schools passed this liberal arts curriculum on to the medieval university. Martianus Capella, an African pagan, wrote early in the fifth century a treatise entitled, *The Marriage of Philology and Mercury.* In it the seven liberal arts are introduced as nuptial presents from Mercury to his bride and are described in some detail. Throughout the first half of the Middle Ages this was the most widely used textbook of the ancient learning and helped definitely to fix the content of the medieval liberal arts.

These seven arts were grammar, rhetoric, dialectic (or logic), arithmetic, geometry, music, and astronomy. In church schools the first three, the literary arts known as the *Trivium,* were regarded as lower studies and the last four, the mathematical arts known as the *Quadrivium,* were the higher studies. Cassiodorus (490-585) also wrote an educational treatise on the seven liberal arts as well as commentaries and textbooks for the monks. A third writer was Isidore (c. 560-636), who composed for monks and clergy an encyclopedia, called *Etymologies,* which was supposed to be a summary of all knowledge worth knowing. Boethius (480-524), sometimes said to be the most influential of all the learned men of the Middle Ages, wrote on at least five of the seven arts, treatises that were much used as textbooks. Moreover, he gave to several succeeding centuries knowledge of the Greek writers, especially of Plato and Aristotle. Besides these the Venerable Bede (673-735), Alcuin (735-804), and Rabanus Maurus (776-856) wrote compendiums of the liberal arts that were used in the medieval schools.

The seven liberal arts were thought to contain virtually all that medieval clerics needed to know. For them, these studies were prerequisite to the study of theology, the one professional study of the period. Not all of the liberal arts were taught in every monastic or cathedral school. During the Dark Ages many of the lesser schools gave six of the liberal arts scant attention. Even later, interest in them was not always the same, either in time or in place. But the study of grammar, which included literature, was always stressed quite generally. Some schools emphasized the *Trivium* and taught little of the *Quadrivium*. Only a few, the great schools of the times, taught the entire range of medieval learning.

Beyond the liberal arts came ethics or metaphysics, the canon and civil law, the Scriptures and, most important of all, theology. Interest in theology increased from the time of Erigena (815?-?877), who used philosophical arguments to support theology, teaching that philosophy and religion are one, that theology must agree with philosophy, and that authority is derived from reason. Theology had chief place in the work of the scholastics, becoming after 1100 the most important of all studies, more important even than the Scriptures themselves.

The cathedral school was the mother of the grammar school. Grammar schools, for elementary education, first appeared in the sixth century. The meager instruction of these schools included teaching in reading, writing, music, simple calculating, religious observances, and rules of conduct. Other elementary schools were conducted by parish priests for both boys and girls and thus were known as parish schools.

In the cathedrals and in the larger churches, singing was an important part of the service. To secure boys for the choir and for other church services, song schools were established. The song school was typically for poor boys who were boarded and taught free in return for the services they rendered the church. In addition to singing, they learned elementary Latin and, in some cases, arithmetic. Some of the pupils of song schools became priests and later received more advanced instruction. In the latter part of the medieval period, boys not serving the church were admitted to song schools. These schools, along with parish schools, came in time to be the chief elementary schools of the church.

Prior to those of Charlemagne's time, it seems that few parishes other than episcopal towns had schools. That church councils, popes, and bishops frequently issued orders for establishing schools indicates neglect of previous injunctions and need for exerting new pressure upon the local clergy. In the Later Middle Ages, there was increase in the number of parish schools.

In the Middle Ages there were schools other than those conducted by the church. Among these were lay schools of grammar, rhetoric, and law, royal schools, palace schools, schools of chivalry, and private and city vernacular schools. In most of these, the church had a part. But though there were schools in considerable number, the masses were illiterate. There was no school system and no compulsory education. Usually pupils had no textbooks and teachers were poorly qualified, hence instruction was inefficient.

In spite of many prohibitions on the part of the church, people lived on a very low moral level. Of the Bible and its teachings the masses were almost totally ignorant. Even many of the clergy did not understand the meaning of the services they conducted and the prayers they recited. The church did much along educational lines but it did not do enough. Rulers such as Charlemagne and Alfred the Great sought to better conditions, but their efforts accomplished little so far as the masses were concerned. Probably 90 percent of the population belonged to the peasant laboring class. These were born in squalor, lived in poverty and ignorance, and died as wretchedly as they had lived.

A modern educational institution that also grew out of the cathedral school is the university. The eleventh and the twelfth centuries were characterized by a new movement toward association, that is, the forming of guilds, or collections of like-minded men united for mutual benefit, protection, advancement, and self-government within the limits of their city, business, trade, or occupation. Also, there was at this time a revival of interest in learning, with the realization that the old schools were inadequate to meet the needs of a changing world. Certain of the cathedral schools enriched their program and attracted many students. The actual teaching function and the direct control of the school were often delegated by the bishop to a church official known as the "chancellor." The pope had authority over the bishop and the bishop over the chancellor. In course of time the chancellor gained the power of issuing a teaching license to qualified students within the diocese. Then when some of the cathedral schools became still more prominent, the pope often conferred on the chancellor through the bishop the right to issue a license to teach anywhere.

A teacher of some reputation drew around him a constantly increasing number of students. Other teachers, finding a student body at hand, came along and began to teach at the same place. Still other teachers and more students came. In this way certain of the cathedral schools acquired the name *studium generale,* thus called because their students came from a wide area and their teachers were licensed to teach beyond the limits of the diocese. By the beginning of the thirteenth century a number of these *studia generalia* began to adopt the characteristic medieval practice of organizing into associations, or guilds. The term applied to all chartered guilds was *universitas.* Gradually, this term began to be applied specifically more and more to universities of faculties and students. Thus, as teachers and students organized themselves into guilds, a cathedral school became a university. The development of a university out of a cathedral school was a long local evolution.

The influence of the universities, direct and indirect, was marked. Organized on a purely democratic basis, freedom of discussion of political, ecclesiastical, and theological matters characterized them. On the masses of the people they, of course, had little direct influence. Yet they often became the mouthpiece of the common people in opposition to a church leader or secular ruler. From them evolved a new type of members of society, ranking with church, state, and nobility. And these new members soon began to express themselves definitely on matters concerning both church and state. Perhaps their greatest work was the training of leaders of the future in church and state. As they became common, they drew as students many clerics, though it did not follow that the clergy in general now had a university education. Developing rapidly after 1200, universities were responsible for the diffusion of what little learning there was in those days. The first great result of their work in training leaders was manifest in the Renaissance movement of the fourteenth and fifteenth centuries. Out of the universities came such men as Roger Bacon, Dante, Petrarch, Wycliffe, Huss, Copernicus, Luther—men unafraid of taking a stand for truth as they saw it.

Scholasticism

Scholasticism, a system of philosophy and type of intellectual life—and hence of education—prevailed from the ninth to the fifteenth centuries. Scholasticism was closely connected with the rise of the universities. In the higher schools, as already noted, the seven liberal arts were taught. Of these, grammar and rhetoric were at first the leading subjects; but gradually dialectic, or logic, was elevated to the place of highest importance, both in the arts and in theology. Dialectic was essentially a logical inquiry into the nature of reality, an attempt to get at what lay beneath the symbolism which had come to prevail everywhere in life and especially in religion. Out of this teaching of dialectic, around which there gathered also in time questions of psychology and metaphysics, Scholasticism gradually developed. Usually, the head of the school, *scholasticus,* was the teacher of this growing system of philosophy, so it took its name from the title of the person who taught it.

Based upon the teachings of the church fathers and the logical works of Aristotle, scholastic philosophy's fundamental tenet was that there is no antagonism between faith and reason. Scholasticism's purpose was to bring reason to the support of faith and was to overcome all doubts and to answer all questions by argument, disputation, and logical analysis. From the ninth to the thirteenth century, Scholasticism was influenced by Platonism coming through the church fathers. From the thirteenth century on it was influenced more and more by the philosophy of Aristotle.

Educationally, the purpose of Scholasticism was to develop the ability to organize beliefs into a logical system and the power to set forth and defend such systems against all arguments brought up in opposition to them. Along with this, there was avoidance of developing an attitude critical of the basic principles established by recognized authority. Thus, scholastic education aimed at systematization of knowledge, thereby giving it, incidentally, scientific form. However, to Scholasticism, knowledge was almost entirely theological and philosophical in nature, so its prized form was deductive, not inductive, logic. A third phase of the educational purpose of Scholasticism was to give to the individual mastery of this knowledge systematized into a logical whole in the form of propositions and syllogisms.

Scholasticism may be regarded as beginning with Erigena, who has been mentioned in connection with the development of theology during the Middle Ages. Maintaining that true religion and true philosophy are identical in content and object, differing only in form, he, and those who followed in his train, made philosophy the means for the understanding of and their demonstration of the truth of church dogma. In actuality, the purpose of Scholasticism was to bring reason to the support of faith. This meant the bringing of reason to the support of church dogma, because faith or revelation had been made identical with "authority," that is, church dogma as formulated by the church fathers—the combination of Greek philosophy and Scripture they developed, not the plain and direct revelation of the Bible. All church dogmas, Erigena said, must, since they are true, be in harmony with reason which, being supreme and invariable, is the only safe guide to the interpretation of truth.

Anselm (1033-1109) was called the first great Scholastic. He held that faith must precede reason and that reason is incapable of understanding the revelation of God. However, to him the dogmas of the church were identical with revelation itself. His one desire in life was to add knowledge to faith, or church dogma, by means of reason. His interest had for its center the teachings of the church fathers; he has been called "the last of the Fathers."

In developing his position Anselm revived the problem of the relation of universal conceptions to particular experiences. What had been a central problem to the Greeks after Socrates now became the center of controversy of the Age of Scholasticism—the controversy between realism and nominalism. The thinkers of the age were called realists or nominalists or even conceptualists, depending upon their interpretation of reality. The first maintained that the general idea—the universal—had reality and that the particular is only a copy of it. The second held that the universal is only a name (*nomen*), an abstraction, and that individual things perceived by the senses are the only reality. The conceptualists in their effort to mediate between the realists and the nominalists held that the universal had no reality apart from a particular object or person.

The controversy was of much practical importance to the church. In that day when churchmen were trying to establish the primacy of Rome, it was a vital matter whether the universal church was real or whether particular churches were. If the first was real, then its dogma was authoritative; if particular churches were the reality, then general church dogma was without authority. This controversy was entirely between theologians, and it involved the method of discovering and knowing reality and truth as well as the question of their nature.

Anselm, a realist, held that faith is the basis of intellectual belief. Opposed to him was Roscellinus (1050-1121), a nominalist, who argued that truth can be arrived at only through reason, that dogmas must be demonstrable by reason. He applied his nominalism to the Godhead and declared that the one nature of the three divine Persons is universal, therefore a mere name applying to no reality. He was condemned by the church as a heretic and obliged to recant. From this controversy it can be seen that the debate over realism had doctrinal as well as organizational overtones.

Abelard (1079-1142) attempted to find in conceptualism a middle ground between realism and nominalism. He maintained that the universal has no reality apart from the particular object or person; outside the individual it exists only as a concept. He was critical of faith, condemning as credulity the acceptance of any doctrine without first subjecting it to examination by reasoning. One was to believe a doctrine not because God said it but because reason showed it to be true. Abelard found all the essential teachings of Christianity in the works of the classical writers and considered the difference between paganism and the Gospel not so great as the difference between the Old and the New Testament. He held that men have the right to question all dogmas and all teachings of the church fathers.

In his treatise *Sic et Non,* after formulating the main theses of theology, he gives the teachings of the Scriptures and the opinions of the church fathers to support both sides of the questions. This method of appealing to private judgment as the deciding factor in questions of faith became one of the recognized methods of teaching in the thirteenth century.

The second period of Scholasticism extended from the beginning of the thirteenth century to the early fifteenth century. It began with the introduction of the works of Aristotle into western Europe through the activities of Arab and Jewish scholars. By the middle of the thirteenth century the church had good translations of Aristotle's scientific works on biology, physics, astronomy, metaphysics, ethics, politics, and poetics. Because this gave a tremendous amount of new material to digest, absorb, and argue over, the scholastic controversy became more acute and more divergent in its outcomes. The church became concerned about the contradictions between church dogma and the outcomes of reason as represented by Aristotelian science.

Thomas Aquinas (1225-1274) set himself to the task of reconciling Aristotelian thought and the teachings of the church. His life purpose was to bring Christianity into harmonious relation with civilization and science. This was to him the same as bringing the dogmas of the church and the teachings of Aristotle together, because Christianity meant to him church dogma and Aristotle stood for the entire product of ancient civilization. His reconciliation is presented in his greatest work, *Summa Theologica,* which became the authoritative exposition of Roman Catholic theology.

To Aquinas, Aristotle's philosophy was the ideal estimate of things. He took from Aristotle the frame for his theological system, then filled this in with the dogmas of the church or of revelation. He held that philosophy and theology are separate subjects, the former dealing with the natural and the latter with the supernatural order, but, though separate, they are not contradictory. God is the author of all truth, so there can be no contradiction between revealed truth and the human reason. Instead of making, as Augustine did, a sharp cleavage between the knowledge of nature, with which reason deals, and the knowledge of supernatural things, with which faith deals, Aquinas attempted to make the two allies. Reason must function where it can. Its results are science, and men experience these results as knowledge, not faith. But where truth is revealed, reason does not intrude; faith, not knowledge, is man's part there. Aquinas built his system squarely upon Aristotle's teachings wherever he could. Thus he fixed the position of the church, making reason the interpreter of revealed truth and the formulator of doctrine and following Aristotle, a pagan, who did not teach the Trinity, the creation of the world by the word of God, the immortality of the soul, the resurrection of the dead, and other fundamental truths of the Christian faith.

In Aquinas, Scholasticism reached its highest point. After him it began to decline. As soon as he had reconciled the teachings of the church and Aristotelian philosophy, Duns Scotus (1270-1308) began to show that in matters of faith reason has no part, because revelation, being absolute truth, compels faith. Theology is a science with high aims it can never attain, for the revelation of God is beyond the reach of human reason.

Duns Scotus, an extreme realist, was followed by William of Occam (1300-1349), a nominalist and the last great medieval Schoolman. In him the skepticism of the period found clear expression. He taught that reason can prove nothing about God and that all dogmas of theology should be handed over to faith. None of its doctrines can be demonstrated by reason, for real truth is not dependent on reason but on what God reveals. He said that the two spheres of reason and authority are so different each from the other that they have no common principles. The church, he taught, should give up speculation and stress faith; it ought to return to the simplicity of the apostles. Thus Occam paved the way for Luther's rejection of Scholasticism, for Luther also represents a turning from controversial theology to the simple teaching of the Scriptures.

Probably no education has been subjected to more criticism than has Scholasticism. Undeniably, it had defects. One of these was such overemphasis on the importance of intellect or reason that it did not meet human needs. The ends it reached possessed only formal, not practical, value; these ends affected only thought life, and quite indirectly and very remotely the conduct of people. Another defect was the fact that much of the discussion was pointless, having to do with words and terms. Not only had it no reality in the world of everyday life but it also had no validity in thought. Moreover, it sharpened the logical faculties without furnishing fresh content for thought; it made the outward form of theology supremely important but lost sight of the stimulating truths of Christianity. Again, it made the church the final and absolute judge; the teachings of the church had to be accepted without regard to the dictates of conscience. In so doing it became a great bulwark of the papacy and erected a chief obstacle to the reformation of the Catholic Church.

On the credit side, Scholastic education dealt with content of the greatest importance—the reality of the existence of God, the attributes of God, and the relation of man to God. It gave an impetus to the study of theology and raised it to the dignity of a science. It kept alive and quickened interest in things intellectual, and it gave to many great minds a vigorous and thorough intellectual training. It led, at least in northern Europe, to the rise of the universities.

God-centered Education

As observed in Chapter 1, from the time of Cain and Abel two "ways" run through human history. One is the way of man in the pride of self-sufficiency, inclining him to trust himself for knowledge, apprehension of truth, and deliverance from sin. The other is the way of humble dependence upon God, leading man to rely simply upon God for knowledge, for understanding, for wisdom, and for redemption, accepting as truth what He has revealed. In the same chapter it was pointed out also that from Japheth descended the peoples characterized by superior achievements in the realm of human knowledge and human culture—the Greeks and the Romans—while from Shem came the people through whom God purposed to bring spiritual life to mankind.

Out of their reasoning, with supreme confidence in the sufficiency of man and virtually no recognition of God, the Greeks developed a marvelous system of thought. Their three greatest men agreed in giving human reason the central place. Socrates taught that reason is the key to the good life; Plato held that reason is the only way to truth; Aristotle declared that reason is not only the source of happiness and virtue but also the crowning achievement of man. Thus these, with other Greeks, under the dominion of man's common disease, sin, built an intellectual world and an education centering in man.

The Jews to whom God revealed Himself and truth in a special manner for the purpose of bringing about the redemption of man, under the power of the same common and pervading disease, sin, likewise built an education that left God out of the picture. However, Judaism did serve to keep alive some knowledge of the revelation God had made. Into this milieu composed of Greek and Jewish elements—of reason and legalism—Christ came and proclaimed the Gospel, the remedy for man's sin. Then on the cross He made atonement for sin.

In the preceding chapter something was said about how man responded to the teachings of the Gospel—how he received them with reservations, taking what was acceptable to his intellect, and modifying what did not satisfy it to meet the criteria of his reason. From the efforts of the early church fathers issued a mixture of revealed truth and human reasoning. The purpose of this chapter thus far has been to trace the process of further compromise of revealed truth. This process ended in the fixing of a body of church dogma so distorted in contrast to the plain teachings of the Gospel as to be impossible of acceptance even by the human reason which developed it. Familiarity with the history of this process is necessary as a background to understanding later developments in the history of Christian education.

While the majority of men were following the way of human wisdom and strength, there were a few who followed another way, the way of reliance on the power and authority of God. These few honored God not only in their faith and practice in general but also in their education. These were, for the most part, sects persecuted by the church, many of which were small evangelical groups that withdrew to inaccessible places where they could continue their worship and instruction as they believed Christians had received them from the apostles. Due to their fewness in number, their place of retirement, and the fact of the church's ignoring them except to persecute them, historical records of both their doctrines and their education are scarce.

However, it is known that among them was no insignificant amount of learning. Their children could read and write, their preachers and leaders possessed portions of the Gospels, and every member received instruction in the Scriptures. Not infrequently they learned the Gospels by heart and it was not uncommon for some of them to be able to repeat from memory other long passages. Even the ignorant among them had a better knowledge of the Scriptures than the scholars of the church. In general, the training of the leaders of these sects was confined to the vernacular, but some of them were familiar with the Greek and Latin classics, as well as with the writings of the church fathers. What counted for most in terms of God-centered education was the fact that the evangelically-minded, both in the church and in the case of these heretical sects, sought for all people a knowledge of reading so that every individual might know the Scriptures for himself.

The education of the group to be treated first here is that of the mystics. In the Middle Ages mysticism was characteristic of no special group of people. There was an element of mysticism in the teaching of the church from Augustine onward. Scholastics were often mystics but not all mystics were Scholastics. Mysticism is not easy to define, but essentially it involves direct communion with God on the part of the individual—a subjective, individualistic process in which the church may play little part. In the last period of Scholasticism there were many independent mystics representing the tendency to individualistic religion which was to result in the Reformation.

There had been a pagan mysticism before Christianity ever came on the scene. The most systematic presentation of mysticism in early Christian literature was made by the pseudo Dionysius whose works, translated into Latin by Erigena, had a deep influence on medieval thought. But it was not until the twelfth century that Christian mystics became numerous. Among these were Bernard of Clairvaux, Hugo, Richard, and Walter of St. Victor. Bonaventura came in the thirteenth century and in the fourteenth Eckhart, Tauler, Ruysbroeck, Groot, Thomas a Kempis, and Gerson.

Scholasticism emphasized reason at the expense of the emotions and will. The mystics stressed the latter, believing that the human soul comes into union with God through contemplation and love. The method of mysticism involves the discipline of the mind for the sake of attaining this spiritual union. The first step is purification of the outer life. This brings mysticism into possible, but not necessary, relation to asceticism. A mystic need not be an ascetic, but he is likely to find mortification and self-denial helpful to contemplation of divine truth. The second step is illumination of the inner life through concentration on spiritual truths and the doing of good works in imitation of Christ. The third step is contemplation of the higher life, or perfection in union with God. Knowledge is helpful as a stepping-stone toward mystical union, which progresses through thought, meditation, and contemplation. Thought seeks God in the outer world, meditation finds Him in the inner life, and contemplation unites the soul with Him.

The education of the mystics was a protest against the narrow educational views of the dialecticians of the Middle Ages. Education in general had been definitely intellectual and aristocratic—a narrow education for the few to the neglect of the many. Instead of placing undue emphasis on logic, the mystics stressed the unity of all knowledge and the study of other branches of learning prior to the study of philosophy and theology. Basically, they believed study of the revelation God made of Himself in His Word constitutes content for education, leading to union with God in mystical fellowship.

The group most prominent in religious life and in education was the Brethren of the Common Life, who represent one of the most successful of the many efforts made during the Middle Ages to revive the pure teaching of the Gospel. Because they were a strong factor in pre-Reformation religion and because their influence on education extended beyond the limits of the Middle Ages, their services in these fields will be considered in the following chapter.

A third group that put God at the center of education was the Waldenses. Against a worldly, secularized church with Rome for its authority, a body of witnesses in the Alpine valleys of Piedmont silently protested and continued through the centuries to preach and teach the Bible, uninfluenced by the relations existing between the church and the state. Always they were persecuted, but always they survived. In the thirteenth century Innocent III made a desperate attempt to annihilate them. Persecution gave them new strength and their doctrines passed to Wycliffe and Huss, through whom they became a factor in producing the Reformation. Surviving to the twentieth century, they have been regarded as the most ancient and the most evangelical of the medieval sects.

Not a great deal is known of their doctrine. They considered the Scriptures to be binding for all time and not rendered obsolete by change of circumstances. They were well versed in Scripture, and maintained its supremacy over the traditions of men. Their whole life in thought and action seemed to be devoted to the task of holding fast the character of original Christian teaching. They were against indulgences, purgatory, and masses for the dead, and they denied the efficacy of sacraments administered by corrupt priests. The content of their preaching involved as its chief theme the literal teachings of Christ. For the most part, they were simple people without any theological training. Always and everywhere they observed the practice of regular individual reading of the Bible, regular daily family worship, and regular instruction of children in Bible truth.

They were earnest teachers of the Word of God, going about by twos from house to house, teaching whole families the Word. Laymen among them did the work of teachers and preachers. Trumbull[1] quotes as the testimony of one of their enemies that "he who has been a disciple for seven days looks out for someone whom he may teach in his turn, so that there is a continual increase" of them. Furthermore, this same enemy said, "I have heard one of these poor peasants repeat the whole Book of Job by heart, without missing a single word; and there are others who have the whole of the New Testament by heart, and much of the Old; nor . . . will they listen to anything else, saying that all sermons which are not proved by Scripture are unworthy of belief." Even Pope Innocent III said that the Waldenses would only listen to a man who had God in him.

John Wycliffe (1324-1384) was the leader of the Lollards, called also the Wycliffites, another group which held to the purity of the Gospel. They based everything on the absolute will of God. The church militant, they taught, is the whole number of the elect; the pope is not necessarily the head of the true church, for it is not certain that he is even a member of it. The Lollards were against prayers for the dead, absolution, and the worship of saints. They held the Bible to be the unconditional and absolute authority and entirely sufficient for every need. They differentiated between the Bible and the teaching of the church and asserted the right of every man to examine the Bible for himself. They did not accept the tradition of the church as the standard of interpretation of Bible truth. Wycliffe and his followers carried on their educational work through writing and distributing popular tracts and by organizing bands of traveling teachers and preachers.

The Hussites were much like the Lollards, although current scholarship recognizes that the views of their great leader, John Huss (1371-1415), were not so dependent on Wycliffe's works as commonly has been thought. Before the time of Luther, the Hussites had printed the Scriptures in the vernacular. They had a good system of schools and an outstanding university. The supreme aim of the Hussites was to promote practical Christianity. They stressed purity of conduct, self-denying love to one's neighbor, and made the Scriptures the one standard in matters of faith. For them, as for the Lollards, the church was not the hierarchy at Rome but the body

[1]H. C. Trumbull, *Yale Lectures on the Sunday-school* (Philadelphia: John D. Wattles, 1888) , p. 66.

of the elect. They were severely persecuted in Bohemia and Moravia but maintained their faith wherever they could.

The Moravians, descendants of the Hussites, never ceased to carry on their method of working. They gave primary place to the Bible, and their first care was to instruct children in Christian ways. Count Zinzendorf, a Moravian worker, concentrated on children, gathering them into the church in large numbers and arranging for training them individually by dividing them into small classes under well-trained teachers.

The Albigenses were neighbors to the Waldenses; the latter occupied the southern and Italian valleys of the mountains on the northern and French side of which the former lived. But there was little intercommunication between the two. Both were possessed, however, by a common spirit of resistance to the dominance of Rome in matters doctrinal and ecclesiastical and both sought to realize a more spiritual type of worship than prevailed in the medieval church. What little is known of their doctrines has come down through the suspicious channel of their enemies' accounts of confession which was made under torture. However, these people were able to maintain their faith through Bible instruction by parent and teacher and later, though scattered by persecution, helped to bring on the Reformation.

Readings

BENSON, CLARENCE H. *A Popular History of Christian Education.* Chicago: Moody Press, 1943.

BUTTS, R. FREEMAN, *A Cultural History of Western Education.* 2nd ed.; New York: McGraw-Hill Book Company, 1955.

COOKE, ROBERT L. *Philosophy, Education and Certainty.* Grand Rapids: Zondervan Publishing House, 1940.

CUBBERLEY, ELLWOOD P. *The History of Education.* Boston: Houghton Mifflin Company, 1920.

HASTINGS, JAMES (ed.). *Encyclopaedia of Religion and Ethics.* New York: Charles Scribner's Sons, 1955-1958.

Articles on:

"Education" (Introductory), J. Adams, V. 166-200.

"Monasticism," F. Cabrol, VIII, 781-797.

"Scholasticism," S. H. Mellone, XI, 239-249.

"Mysticism"
(Christian, N. T.), Rufus M. Jones, IX, 89-103.
"Brethren of the Common Life," S. Harvey Gem, II, 839-842.
"Waldenses," Walter F. Adeney, XII, 633-643.

HYMA, ALBERT. *Renaissance to Reformation.* Grand Rapids: Wm. B. Eerdmans Publishing Company, 1951.

LOTZ, PHILIP HENRY. *Orientation in Religious Education.* New York: Abingdon-Cokesbury Press, 1950.

MARIQUE, PIERRE J. *A History of Christian Education.* Vol. II. New York: Fordham University Press, 1926.

MONROE, PAUL. *A Brief Course in the History of Education.* New York: The Macmillan Company, 1913.

MULHERN, JAMES. *A History of Education.* New York: The Ronald Press, 1959.

MURCH, JAMES DEFOREST. *Christian Education and the Local Church.* Cincinnati: Standard Publishing Company, 1943.

NEWMAN, ALBERT HENRY. *A Manual of Church History.* Vol. I. Philadelphia: The Judson Press, 1933.

SHERRILL, LEWIS J. *The Rise of Christian Education.* New York: The Macmillan Company, 1944.

TRUMBULL, H. C. *Yale Lectures on the Sunday-school.* Philadelphia: John D. Wattles, 1888.

The New Schaff-Herzog Encyclopaedia of Religious Knowledge. New York and London: Funk and Wagnalls Company, 1908-1914.

Articles on:
"Church and School," C. Geyer, III, 103-105.
"Brethren of the Common Life," L. Schulze, III, 172-177.
"Universities," William H. Allison, XII, 98-104.
"Monasticism," G. Grützmacher, VII, 466 (see paragraph on "The Rules").
"Scholasticism," R. Seeberg, X, 262-269 (see especially paragraphs on Thomas Aquinas, pp. 262-263, Duns Scotus, pp. 264-265, and Anselm and Abelard, p. 260).
"Mysticism," S. M. Deutsch and C. A. Beckwith, VIII, 68-73.
"New Manicheans," O. Zöckler, VIII, 145-146 (see paragraphs on Albigenses, pp. 145-146).
"Menno Simons," Johns Horsch, X, 422-427.

John Calvin was one of the greatest educators of the Reformation period. His best-known achievement was the founding of the University of Geneva, which became the center of literary and theological education for Protestants of western Europe.

(Courtesy of Presbyterian Historical Society)

5

Christian Education in Early Modern Times

ALWAYS man seeks truth. There are only two possible ways for him to obtain it. One is through his own capacity for reason and insight; the other is through divine revelation. Man must either depend upon what comes from beyond him or accept what originates with some human thinker, past or present. Being proud and self-sufficient, man is not generally willing to receive as true that which comes from a source other than himself.

The Greeks, in fullness of human pride and self-confidence, built a truly marvelous structure from the products of human thinking. In the later centuries of Grecian history, however, there was much dissatisfaction with the findings of man's reasoning. Men everywhere felt a heart need for some better authority, for a more reliable source of knowledge and happiness than finite man's understanding and insight. The shaken confidence in the power of intellect resulted in the rise of a demand for authority higher than man. Greek and Roman religions, and even the mystery religions, did not satisfy. Moreover, man, still clinging to human reason, was unwilling to reject entirely the teachings of great thinkers of the past. So in the centuries just before and following the birth of Christ, attempts were made to reconcile the message of the Old Testament with the wisdom of the Greeks and to explain in the light of Greek philosophy the revelation made by God.

The effect of these attempts, as was true of many succeeding ones of like nature, was to blunt the power of God's revelation upon man. Always the enemy of God sees to it, when statements from revelation come into conflict with man's ideas, that it is not the latter which lose their appeal to the human mind and heart. So attempts made to construct a satisfying synthesis from the best offerings of Greek thought and the Old Testament resulted only in the placing of the results of Greek reasoning above the revelation of God.

Into the midst of these human gropings after truth came Christianity. Never should it be forgotten that Christianity is of God, that in it there is always the supernatural element. It is the final and complete answer given by God Himself to the riddle of life and the problems of existence man finds insoluble. In Christianity God made to man the great offer of truth, freely answering the questions for which he has no answer. But the truth thus revealed must be accepted in humble faith and in complete dependence on God.

Christianity is Christ, who is the truth as well as the way and the life. Jesus proclaimed Himself to be the Christ, the Saviour of men, God's final revelation to man. A small group of people accepted Him as such during His days on earth. Their faith was vindicated by His bodily resurrection from the dead three days after He had died on the cross to make atonement for the sin of mankind. His resurrection proved Him to be the Son of God with power to satisfy every need of the hungry soul of man. Within a hundred years after the death of Christ, the whole of the New Testament, inspired of God, appeared, making completely and perfectly clear the glorious purpose of God for man, intimations of which had been presented repeatedly in the Old Testament, likewise inspired of God.

Thus Christianity began in an obscure corner of the Roman Empire with a small group of followers of Christ. So long as these followers in simple faith trustfully obeyed Christ's commission to teach, the church grew rapidly. Each new convert, under the impulsion of faith untrammeled by human speculations, felt it his God-given duty to pass to others the good news of the Gospel. Persecutions designed to stamp out the new religion only served to scatter abroad disciples who proclaimed the truth wherever they went. So by the end of the first century Christian communities existed in practically every province of the Empire, and by the fourth century Christianity was established as the state religion.

At the time of the coming of Christ a movement to revive pagan philosophy was under way, so for about three hundred years there was antagonism between secular systems of thought and Christianity. By the time pure Greek philosophy died out, the opposition to true Christianity assumed another form, the blending of truth and error at the hands of the early church fathers into a doctrine so distorted that it had slight appeal, even to human reason. Christianity really suffered more from this dressing up of its truths in the garb of reasoning pleasing to man than it did from direct attack by its enemies.

Then came Scholasticism, which was no new development of human thought but a clever way by which man sought to justify himself in his chosen course of pursuit of knowledge and wisdom for himself. Scholasticism but continued the tendency to place dependence on the results of human reasoning instead of accepting in simple faith the truth revealed by God. In spite of the warnings of the Word of God, in spite of the stand of a faithful few who were true to the teachings of this Word, medieval man persisted in building more and more into his philosophy, his dogma, and his education the products of human thinking, continually taking man instead of God as his guide.

Background of the Reformation

Beginning as early as the close of the twelfth century many influences were combining to bring about the decay of the structure built up during the Middle Ages and to effect great changes in philosophy, dogma, and education. The Catholic Church, which had reached its height of domination during the thirteenth century, thereafter declined. It had had abundant opportunity to make use of its great power to help solve the tremendous problems confronting mankind. However, it had turned away from both spiritual and intellectual light and had permitted a deep darkness to come upon the understandings of men.

Internal factors contributing to the decline of the Roman Church. One cause of decay was that, instead of keeping their minds open to fresh ideas inductively arrived at, the Scholastics, who were the intellectual leaders of medieval times, employed only *the deductive method of establishing truth.* This form of reasoning inevitably became an end in itself, degenerating into quibbling, meaningless discussions and the frittering away of time on unimportant verbal questions—a kind of intellectual activity carrying within itself its own sentence of death.

A second cause of decay was *a double standard of truth;* on this no system can long exist. It was assumed that the truth or the falsity of things was judged by infallible church dogma; but actually during the later Middle Ages reason, based on the logic of Aristotle as well as dogma, was used as the test of truth. At first dogma was considered the supreme criterion for all thinking, and reason was used only to explain dogma. However, the explaining of dogma by logic, the defending of faith by argument, means the supporting of revealed truth by reason. "It was a defense of the infallible and the revealed by the fallible and secular."[1] That is, reason questioned what was considered perfect. Thus there were two realms of truth, each with its particular standard. What was true for dogma might not be true for reason; what was true for reason might not be true for dogma. Once reason, thus separated from revelation, got the help of experimental investigation, medieval life was ready to give way to modern life.

The *development of mysticism* was a third factor which helped to bring to an end the medieval system. Mysticism is essentially individualistic, for it is direct communion with God by the individual and therefore has no need of a church to function between man and God. From the twlefth century on, mystics arose in ever-increasing numbers as representatives of the tendency toward a personal religion which was to culminate finally in Protestantism.

A fourth factor operating to bring about the end of the Middle Ages was *nominalism.* That particulars alone have objective existence is the view of nominalism, which appeared in the eleventh century as a mere theory. In the course of time nominalists went further and maintained that universals are nothing more than "names." When science developed, nominalism allied itself with empiricism. So long as nominalism had been mere theory, the church could cope with it. But with increase in the knowledge of nature during the later Middle Ages, it became too strong to suppress. Nominalism emphasized individual opinion, opposed tradition, stressed the value of practical experience, made science more impor-

[1]Cushman, H. E., *A Beginner's History of Philosophy* (Boston: Houghton Mifflin Co., 1920), II, 3.

tant than spiritual actualities, and turned man away from the things of the spirit. Hence it struck at the very roots of the authority of the church, the ascendant institution of medieval times.

External factors contributing to the decline of the Roman Church. Besides these defects within the structure of life and education of the Middle Ages that had a part in bringing the period to an end, there were outer factors which contributed to the process of decay and helped to introduce the many-sided transformation—in religion usually called the Reformation—that marks the beginning of the modern period. Among the external factors assisting in the uprooting of conceptions that had become a part of church tradition were inventions, discoveries, social and institutional changes, political unrest, economic dissatisfaction, and religious conditions.

In the area of *invention or rediscovery* came the magnetic needle, which made possible geographical discoveries; the production of gunpowder, which was an important factor in the passing of the feudal system; inventions in the process of manufacturing paper, which greatly increased and made more certain the supply; and the invention of printing, which vastly increased the amount of literature, made for widespread knowledge, imparted a strong desire for learning and contributed to a profound intellectual awakening.

Discoveries were many and varied. Columbus discovered America, and Vasco da Gama the all-sea route to India. Magellan circumnavigated the globe. Such geographical feats fired the imagination of men, awakened the suspicion that information and knowledge they had hitherto accepted as authentic might be wrong, and challenged them to highest achievement. The discovery[2] that caused the greatest upheaval was that of Copernicus: the conception that the earth moves around the sun and is not the center of the universe. Kepler, Galileo, Descartes, and Newton contributed to the construction of a theory of a world system run by natural laws. Paracelsus (1493-1541) rebelled against the medieval medical tradition, introducing chemical drugs. Andreas Vesalius (1514-1564) won recognition as the founder of modern anatomy, and Ambroise Paré (1517-1590), as the father of modern surgery. The new conceptions of the universe, of the world, of nature and of man made for new conceptions of life and of the meaning and the purpose of education.

[2]This view was not original with Copernicus, but was effectively set forth by him in his *Revolution of the Heavenly Orbs*, 1543.

Social and institutional life was transformed within a short space of time about the beginning of the sixteenth century. Many institutions and customs ceased altogether while others were changed in varying degrees. Chiefly as a result of the invention of gunpowder, knighthood became a thing of the past, for neither the knight's coat of armor nor his moated castle was adequate to protect him against assaults by gun or cannon. Monastic life, because of its corruption and the wealth gathered into monasteries, became suspect. The civil power of the priesthood came to be resented more and more. The great foundations, the source of support of a number of priests, were liquidated. Because the mendicant orders had grown in strength, Europe was filled with beggars of all kinds. The many free towns of northern Europe were places of social and industrial progress as well as the chief factor in the establishing of popular schools.

Politically, conditions were explosive. The church was arrogantly dominant, not only in the spiritual sphere but also in politics and civil affairs. A large part of the territory of Germany had come under the temporal rule of the church. Because of the sovereignty of the church and increasing power of the great nobles, the Holy Roman Empire had so declined that it possessed only a shadow of authority. Not only was the Church of Rome a symbol of tyranny; it was also regarded as a foreign power. As feudalism declined in western Europe, able leaders formulated nation states in such countries as Portugal, Spain, France, England, and Sweden. Kings engaged in power politics and empire building. Nationalism and patriotism became strong. The Lutheran Church was used as a tool of the state in Scandinavia and some parts of Germany for the consolidation of national power and the defeat of Rome. A national church (the Anglican) was established in England for the same reason. Calvinism became involved in the nationalistic fervor displayed in Scotland. Even in France and Spain princes won from the Pope the right to exert considerable power over the Roman Church in their realms. Princes, free cities, and the minor nobility were ready to support Luther when he took his stand against the church. Civil powers everywhere were eager to destroy the monasteries and abolish the temporal rule of Rome.

Economic dissatisfaction was an important factor in the revolt. Conditions of the social and religious life of the age had brought great wealth into the hands of the church. It taught the earning of salvation by doing charitable works, the absolution of sins by payment of money, and the shortening of purgatory by endowing a living for a priest to celebrate mass. Consequently gifts, payments for indulgences, endowments, and tithes had filled the treasuries of the church until much of the wealth was in ecclesiastical foundations. Besides, money was continually drained directly to the papal court at Rome. Everywhere the lot of the peasantry had become deplorable. Oppressed by overlords, the common man, densely ignorant and intensely superstitious, was an easy prey to the extortions of an unscrupulous priesthood. Everywhere in the northern countries people were ready to rebel against the demands of the church, which they had come to regard as an agent of financial corruption, seeking its own glory at the expense of those whose interests it pretended to serve.

Religiously, the Reformation was no sudden transformation. From the end of the thirteenth century on, there were many who protested against the domination of the Roman Catholic Church, the increasing corruption within it, and its low level of spiritual life. Those who thus protested were persecuted by church authorities and generally treated as heretics. As time passed, their number grew, and various sects developed, named according to the place where the adherents lived or the leader they followed. Little unity existed among these sects, but they all strongly opposed the evils which corrupted the church. Everything the church did to them by way of persecution, torture, and even putting members to death, served only to make more bitter the opposition of these sects to the Roman hierarchy. The evils they stood against were not unrecognized by the church itself. Church councils and church leaders made numerous efforts to bring about reform. However, the corruption was so deep-seated that it could be eradicated only by a violent revolutionary reorganization of society on a new and different basis.

The factor counting for most in spiritual life and in Christian education immediately preceding the Reformation was the work of the Brethren of the Common Life. How far the effects of their work reached both at the time and later is impossible to determine.

Gerhard Groote (1340-1384), the founder of the group, intended it to be closely connected with the church. A native of Holland who graduated from the University of Paris, he longed to serve God by serving others. He saw the need for true Christian charity, for knowledge of the Scriptures, for science instead of formal Scholasticism, and for a more effective command of Latin and the vernacular. After his conversion, Groote was grounded in faith through meditation, self-discipline, and the influence of the saintly Ruysbroeck, "the father of practical mysticism." Then he set out as an evangelizing preacher, full of zeal for the revival of truly spiritual religion among the people in general, and eager to work for the reform of monks and clergy. As he went about the Netherlands preaching the simple Gospel, he drew many lay men and women, priests and monks, and people of all classes out of sin and worldliness and influenced them for holiness of life. These he organized into brotherhoods and sisterhoods in which they might have places of refuge from the world.

Though the Brethren took no vows and practiced no rule, Groote organized them into communities called houses, with all levels of society together—nobles, priests, scholars, students, artisans, and common laborers. These houses served as a means of help to the members of the brotherhoods and sisterhoods and also as a model for the reform of the monasteries. Members lived a common life, worked for their maintenance, gave to the poor and the sick what they could save, and devoted themselves to the teaching of the young. The purpose of their work was to emphasize primitive Christian living. Their simplicity, their sincerity, and their love for the poor and the distressed exerted widespread and wholesome influence.

It is difficult to determine what were the specific doctrines of the Brethren. One book, the *Imitation of Christ,* attributed to Thomas a Kempis, who was educated by the Brethren and lived in one of their houses, reflected the spirit of the group. Groote held firmly to the dogmas of the Roman Church. He opposed Ruysbroeck on the subject of mysticism, yet mysticism is prominent in much of Groote's teaching as well as in that of other Brethren, in that personal and inward realization of spiritual truth imparted by God is contrasted with a mere outward and formal religion.

The Brethren of the Common Life were not reformers in the sense of advocating a break with the Roman Church. However, they were reformers in other senses, such as emphasis upon the pure, unadulterated teachings of the Scriptures and the stand they took for encouraging the laity to read and study the Scriptures in the vernacular. Their reform which reached farthest was the introduction of the use of the mother tongue in preaching and teaching. For the first time Christianity in its original purity and purpose was brought to the people of northern Europe. Great preachers trained by the Brethren spoke with spiritual power and feeling, placing stress upon practical Christian living. Multitudes flocked to hear them. Thus at the very time the Italian Renaissance was emphasizing a return to ancient paganism the Brethren were succeeding in their attempt to reinstate the plain, simple teachings of apostolic Christianity.

The only enduring reforms originating prior to Luther's time were those introduced by the Brethren. They corrected the Vulgate, translated most of the Bible into the mother tongue, circulated thousands of portions of the Bible and of other religious literature, reformed education and textbooks, helped the afflicted, fed the poor, housed needy students, and inspired the writing of some of the best literature of the times. The reforms of no other group before the Reformation itself were comparable to theirs in extent. They denounced the evils existing in the Roman Church. In returning to the simplicity of the presentation of the Gospel and the expression of genuine love characteristic of the first Christians they showed the way to true spiritual reformation. Their emphasis upon the study of Latin and Greek encouraged scholarship. Their contribution to Christian education was tremendous, as will be seen later.

A second religious condition playing an important part in bringing on the Reformation was the spiritual awakening in England led by John Wycliffe. In essence it was much like that in the Netherlands under the Brethren of the Common Life. Wycliffe, like Groote and his followers, was dissatisfied with the low ebb of spiritual life, the many lacks among priests and monks, and the evils he saw in the Roman Church. First he preached at Oxford, standing for reform within the Church; but in 1378 he took a definite stand against the Church, adopting the principle of the supreme authority of the Scriptures. From this principle he deduced that the pope is the head of the Roman Church, not of the true Church, which is the totality of those predestinated to salvation. This was revolt in that it denied the claim of the Roman

Church to be the representative of Christ on earth and the sole agency for administering God's grace to men. Wycliffe now began to bring about change; he preached to the masses of the people, and he translated the Bible into English.

After 1380, Wycliffe reached the conclusion that the pope is the Antichrist, since his deeds are opposed to those of Christ. In his later writings, he advocated the abolition of the papacy. The conclusion, regarded as most heretical by his contemporaries, was Wycliffe's denial of the doctrine of transubstantiation. He also condemned monasticism and taught that all authority, ecclesiastical and secular, is derived from God and is forfeited by one who lives in mortal sin. So great was his influence in the direction of revolt that he has been called "The Morning Star of the Reformation."

Another condition of a religious nature at the bottom of the revolt was doctrinal controversy. Nearly all of the doctrines of the Christian faith were involved, but the chief one at issue was the doctrine of salvation. The Roman Church made good works the basis of salvation, whereas those inclined toward Protestantism recognized faith in the atoning merit of a crucified Redeemer as the one and only essential. Along with this they contended that the only mediator between men and God is Christ, through Whom every person has direct and free access to God; the Roman Church maintained that the priest mediates between God and men and has power to forgive sins. The question of authority was a point of controversy. The Roman Church contended that the Church through the pope and the rulings of church councils was the final authority, while those of the Protestant persuasion maintained that ultimate authority is lodged in the Scriptures. The Lord's Supper and the form of worship were also subjects of much controversy.

The Renaissance and Humanistic Education

The revolution of the sixteenth century affected every phase of life, involving political, economic, moral, philosophical, literary, and institutional as well as religious life. On its economic side, this great movement is called the Industrial Revolution; on its political side, the Nationalization of Europe; on its religious side, the Reformation, and on its intellectual side, the Renaissance.

The Renaissance was, among other things, a revival of secular learning, another instance of man's endless search for true knowledge. In many ways this revival was a radical departure from medieval views of the world, of life, and of culture—views developed under the domination of the church. Men had become tired of this domination, both in the spiritual realm and, more especially, in the intellectual. When men were turning away from the church, why were their minds not drawn to the authority of the Word of God, the real source of truth and life? The basic answer to this question is that man is forever disposed to seek knowledge and truth in man instead of in God. The question also has an answer in the fact that, to men of that time in general, revelation meant not the pure revelation of God but a body of lifeless dogma set forth in the decrees of a church. This church they did not respect because they knew it was false and corrupt. Vast numbers of men wanted nothing more to do with it.

With the truth God had offered darkened by human and ecclesiastical wisdom and despised, men in rebellion against church bondage chose to go to the original writings of the ancient Greeks and Romans for enlightenment. So the majority of men went back to early philosophy to grope for truth. In this groping they were guided only by man's mind and were concerned with those efforts to find truth which in the ages before Christ had failed to satisfy human cravings. During the Middle Ages the writings of the ancient Greeks and Romans had been considered a storehouse of an immense amount of learning which could be used as a tool for intellectual work and as a starting point for advancement in knowledge. During the Renaissance, these writings were regarded as the admirable expression of a perfect humanity of a bygone age. It was held that though the ancient world was dead, its marvelous achievements in all areas of life, which made for a many-sided humanity, should be studied anew and be the model of the prseent.

This revival of the classics originated in Italy in the fourteenth century; it reached its height in the sixteenth and died out in the seventeenth after its effects had been felt in every European nation. In Italy the movement meant a return to the classical writings of the Greeks and Romans, while in the north it resulted largely in a return to the Scriptures in the original. The Renaissance in the north was therefore to a great extent a reformation; it was the most important step toward the Protestant Reformation, if not the Reformation itself, and is distinguishable from it only in spirit and outcome.

Various tendencies were present in the many interests and activities of the Renaissance, but the one of concern here is the literary, artistic tendency commonly referred to as humanism. Basically the term means that which is characteristically human, that which belongs peculiarly to man, that which elevates man or at least satisfies him. Historically it stands for the admiration and love of the writings of the ancients. Those possessed by this regard for the classics claimed that the best portrayal of the perfection and development of human nature was that man, in the fullness of his nature and achievements, should be sought for, studied and imitated in the wonderful civilization of Greece and Rome. In time men became aware of a difference between the pagan and the Christian concept of human nature and human life. As the result of this awareness humanism took two forms which are today as far apart as they ever were: a pagan humanism and a Christian humanism.

The former has nothing for Christianity; it adheres not only to the standards of perfection set forth in the classics but appropriates the very spirit of ancient paganism found in classical literature and thought. It teaches that human nature is essentially good, therefore it should be allowed to develop free from the restrictions Christianity places upon it. Antiquity, not the Middle Ages, sets forth the ideals man should seek to attain; reason alone is the criterion of truth; and the principles which man needs for guiding conduct should be sought not in the Word of God but in ancient philosophy, the storehouse of human wisdom.

Christian humanism, like pagan humanism, is founded upon admiration for ancient classical writings. The Christian is a human being, therefore he appreciates the grand beauty of the masterpieces of literary artists, the exalted ideas of great thinkers and the lofty teachings of outstanding philosophers. The Christian humanist is interested in and enthusiastic for all that is worthy in ancient works of art and classical learning. But he does not substitute that which man originated for the revelation God has given concerning life and its purpose. The marvels and the glories which issue from the finite creature do not dim for him the loftier and truer manifestation of truth that came from the infinite Creator. Yet the Christian humanist does seek to reconcile the teachings of Christ and the ideals of ancient philosophy as did the church fathers.

One man in whom Christian humanism appeared at its best was Vittorino da Feltre (1378-1446), the most famous of the early Italian educators. An able and well-trained scholar, a devoted Christian, he was also a practical teacher who taught at the university of Padua before organizing a court school at Mantua which was the means of his great influence. He called his school the "Pleasant House" because it had agreeable surroundings and because of the spirit he intended should prevail there. He dwelt with his pupils, acting as a father, looking out for their food, clothing, and health, and taking part in their games, pleasures, and interests, always supervising closely their conduct. Above all, he strongly emphasized spiritual and moral influences. The atmosphere of his school was Christian. By precept and still more through example he sought to develop in his pupils piety, reverence, and the practice of all duties commanded by the Bible. Every day there were services of worship and spiritual instruction which all pupils were required to attend.

Vittorino believed that truth and appreciation of moral values could be derived not only from Christian authors but also from classical writings, if portions of the latter were expurgated. While the curriculum of his school retained the seven liberal arts, literature dominated, with dialectic and grammar wholly subordinated. Physical training received as full attention as intellectual education, for Vittorino considered such training an integral part of a complete education.

The aim and general method of Vittorino's work were noteworthy. His ultimate goal was the forming of the complete citizen through developing harmoniously the mind, body, and character of the pupil. All school activities—physical training, studies, and spiritual instruction—had a single purpose: to educate young men who would serve God and the state in any position they might occupy. Vittorino manifested complete dedication to his work and the welfare of his pupils. He carefully studied their character, interests, abilities, and their intended career, and shaped each pupil's course of study accordingly. Very definitely he reconciled the new conception of education current among the humanists of his time with the traditions and spirit of Christian education. His practices were often in harmony with present-day educational views, as, for example, his insistence on consideration of the personality of the child. In his school were trained many men who became prominent as statesmen, church leaders, scholars, and teachers, thus extending beyond limits that can be fully known the effects of the type of education he developed.

Vittorino was not the only humanistic educator of Italy, although he probably deserved the title "Christian humanist" more than most of the others. Toward the close of the fifteenth century, however, the liberal education of the humanists—Christian and pagan—in Italy degenerated into a fixed and formal discipline called "Ciceronianism." This consisted simply in a slavish imitation of style with Cicero as a model. But the humanistic training could not be confined to Italy. With the invention of printing, the writings of classic authors were rapidly reproduced and spread everywhere. Thus the Renaissance and the classic literature made their way into the northern countries of Europe.

The character and effects of the Renaissance and humanistic education in northern Europe differed greatly from those in Italy. With the peoples of the North, especially those of Germanic origin, the Renaissance led less to a desire for personal development and individual achievement and more to a social and moral emphasis. The chief purpose of humanism became the moral and religious improvement of society, and the revival of the study of the classics pointed the way to obtaining a new and better meaning from the Scriptures. Through the revival of Greek, northern scholars, especially German and English ones, attempted to escape from church doctrines and traditional practices and get back to the teachings of true Christianity by studying the New Testament in the original. This led naturally to a similar desire in respect to the Old Testament and an arousal of interest in Hebrew. Consequently, to people of the north, renewed study of the Bible was as important a feature of humanism as appreciation of the classics.

Humanism was introduced into northern Europe by the Brethren of the Common Life. John Wessel (1420-1489) was among the first to sponsor increasing interest in the revival of classical Latin and the study of New Testament and Patristic Greek. Rudolph Agricola (1443-1485), like Vittorino da Feltre, tried to harmonize Christian principles and pagan culture. One of his pupils, Alexander Hegius (1433-1498), headmaster of the Brethren school at Deventer, trained some of the leading humanists, including Erasmus. John Reuchlin (1455-1522), who with Agricola transplanted humanism to Western Germany, made Hebrew one of the languages of learning, with the primary object of emphasizing the study of the Old Testament and the secondary one of appealing to Mohammedans through interest in languages cognate to Hebrew. A noteworthy teacher was Jacob Wimpfeling (1450-1528), who shared with Melanchthon the title "Preceptor of Germany." He lectured upon the classical authors and the church fathers and wrote treatises on education in which he urged the study of the classics for spiritual and moral purposes.

The most famous of all humanists and one of the most influential men of all time was Erasmus (1467-1536). Though not as profound a scholar as some other Renaissance leaders, he was the most effective humanist and educator of the entire period and did much to bring about a new emphasis in Christian education. All his work was primarily educational, for it was designed to reform the many abuses in society that were the outcome of ignorance.

Most of Erasmus' preuniversity education was obtained in schools conducted under the auspices of the Brethren of the Common Life. Through the influence of Hegius and Agricola especially, he developed enthusiasm for classical learning. Then, in Paris, at Oxford, and in Italy, he perfected his knowledge of languages and of the literature of ancient times. All his life he was a tireless student; for many years he traveled from place to place in Europe, studying at centers of learning.

Through teaching, through personal contacts and correspondence, by means of publications written for the enlightenment of the people, through editions of many Latin and Greek classics, by preparing Latin and Greek grammars and textbooks, and through direct discussion of educational matters, Erasmus sought to reform the many conditions in society which had developed because of ignorance. His Greek edition of the New Testament and his editions of the works of the church fathers had no little effect upon the religious revival of the time. His aim seemed to be the popularization of the original sources of Christian theology; the same tendency appeared also in many other humanists.

The educational views of Erasmus were intensely humanistic. He would give the mother tongue no place in school or in everyday life. The writings of the classical authors, the church fathers, and the Scriptures contain all that is needed for guidance in this life and for the correction of the numerous existing abuses. He ridiculed scholastic methods, the silly disputations of the schoolmen, vulgar Latin, and allegorical interpretations of the Scriptures. The task of education is to promote study of a wide selection of the works of classical authors, the church fathers, and the Scriptures in the original and in their uncorrupted form that the spirit of these writings may be thoroughly imbibed. Mere mastery of form is insufficient, as is also a limited selection of authors. Instead of formal distinctions, rhetorical analysis and appreciation are to be emphasized. Grammar is necessary but it should be an intelligent approach to literature. Nature, history, and present-day content are to illumine literary study, as it in turn is to reform society.

He made piety primary in his aim of education and thorough learning of the liberal arts secondary. Preparation for performing satisfactorily the duties of life was also included in his stated aim. Education must be open to every child with ability, regardless of wealth, or birth, or sex. Education should be started in the home in infancy by the mother, the child's first teacher, from whom the child receives his first training in good habits, his first lessons in language, and his early knowledge of surroundings. This early instruction should be informal and should be made interesting. Systematic instruction begins at the age of six, or seven, at home if possible, otherwise in a day school.

Erasmus advised a study of the child and insisted upon personal care and direction of his studies. He recognized the importance of play and of physical exercise and the necessity of keeping education vitally in touch with the life of the times. All subjects, whether sacred literature, the classics, or other subjects, were to be studied chiefly for their content, for the light they throw on life, its meaning, and its duties and responsibilities. He set forth in his writings many details of sound method. He did not hesitate to combat educators of the humanistic persuasion who made of their education a mere formalism no more productive of worthwhile results than the old which it replaced.

Among Christian humanists other than Erasmus who were educators were men such as Melanchthon of Germany, Budé of France, Vives of Spain, and Elyot, Ascham, and Milton of England, to mention only a few. Though called "Christian" their main outlook often was secular, and the secular emphasis increased as time passed. The aims of humanistic education were to produce a broadly educated person of well-rounded personality capable of assuming leadership in church or state. He should be at home in the field of classical knowledge and yet be an effective man of action in the world. He should be able to express himself in poetry, song, and dance; manifest good health and physical dexterity; and be a Christian gentleman with all the social graces. The humanistic educators drew much from the ideals of classical writers, then added their own ideas about the varied accomplishments appropriate to a scholar, a gentleman, and a citizen of Renaissance times.

In spite of their secular emphasis, the Christian humanists greatly strengthened the spirit of reform in the church. Also, they prepared the way for Bible study, which opened the eyes of men to the authority of the Scriptures rather than that of the church. The Renaissance movement, through the effect it had in making men think for themselves and causing them to cast off old ideas and enter into new paths, was a tremendous influence in bringing on the Reformation. Erasmus, though he never broke with the Roman Church, was such a bitter critic of it that he was later called by the reformers themselves "the precursor of the Reformation."

The Brethren of the Common Life and Christian Education

While the Christian humanists were attempting to combine an interest in what originated among men of the past with a desire to remain in the church and to hold to its teachings, there were groups which had long been inclined more toward simple faith. That is, they were disposed to take the Bible as the book of faith leading to truth, and to regard knowledge, not as something "spun out of the human self" but as the outcome of faith acting upon faith. These evangelical groups, somewhat less prone to the error of assuming that human effort working independently of God can arrive at truth, made a greater and a more enduring contribution to Christian education than did the humanists.

Among these groups were evangelical Catholics and heretical sects such as those discussed in the last section of the preceding chapter. Belonging to the former were the Brethren of the Common Life, who launched a movement of far-reaching consequence in educational history.

Gerhard Groote, the founder, early recognized the value of Christian education. He saw the need of better education for all classes but more especially for the clergy. Finding it difficult to make much impression on adults, particularly those members of the clergy who led lives of vice and neglected their parishes, he became interested in boys. He saw in their training a means of bringing about reform in the church through filling the ranks of the clergy with young men who had been not only properly educated but also trained to imitate Christ. Accordingly, he encouraged such of his followers as had the ability to teach in the schools. This teaching became the most effective instrument used by the Brethren for realizing their purposes.

Before the year 1450 few Brethren actually taught school. Most members made the copying of books their chief occupation; what teaching they engaged in was done mostly in the "houses." With the invention of printing, the Brethren turned to that mode of supplying religious reading matter. The materials they published included the Scriptures, books of devotion, and texts for use in the schools, making it possible for even the poor to possess these works, which were for the most part printed in the everyday language of the people.

After 1450, many Brethren became teachers in the public schools. People in general had great respect for the Brethren because of their devoted work, hence they experienced no difficulty in becoming teachers in the town schools of the Netherlands, which schools had existed from about the year 1200. Thus the spiritual message and influence of the Brethren became blended with secular education. There was no opposition to religious education in those days; on the contrary, school authorities in the Netherlands and Western Germany invited Brethren to help them, induced individual members to settle in their midst, and even built houses for them to live in. In the beginning of their educational work the Brethren founded no schools of their own; they taught in, supervised, and reformed the public schools.

The first of the Brethren to become a teacher was John Cele (d. 1417), an intimate friend of Gerhard Groote. He wanted to become a monk, but Groote persuaded him to accept the principalship of the town school at Zwolle, a post he held until his death more than forty years later. Pupils flocked to Zwolle from many countries. Cele improved the curriculum in various ways. He retained grammar, rhetoric, logic, ethics, and philosophy, but adopted a definite practical aim in teaching these branches. He believed that future priests and even laymen could profit from these studies.

His greatest change was in the field of Christian education. It was his conviction that "the Bible should be studied by everyone in order to regain the image of God in which man was made."[3] Cele had the desire, common among the Brethren, to lead people to become imitators of Christ. Up to his time religious education had been a matter of learning the Lord's Prayer, the Ten Commandments, and the Apostles' Creed, attending services of formal worship, and engaging in singing—all in the Latin language.

Cele introduced the teaching of the Bible not only on Sunday but also on weekdays. He substituted the teaching of the New Testament for that of scholastic formalism. Three times daily he presented the Scriptures, using in the morning the Epistles, in the afternoon the Gospels, and in the evening other books. He taught his pupils to pray both in the vernacular and in Latin. From the New Testament he chose verses which he dictated to the whole school, instructing pupils to memorize them and to put their truths into practice. A devout imitator of Christ, he taught by example as well as by precept. Good conduct and godly living were the goals he sought to achieve.

Alexander Hegius (1433-1498) was another educator of note among the Brethren. He was principal of their school at Deventer which at its height had some two thousand pupils. Hegius had definite leanings toward humanism. Late in life he learned Greek from the humanistic scholar, Agricola, and he strongly favored the study of Greek authors. However, he never diverged from the spiritual purpose of the Brethren. His love for the classics did not keep him from declaring that "all learning is pernicious if acquired at the expense of piety"[4] or from carrying on his educational work in accordance with this principle.

[3]Quoted by Frederick Eby, *The Development of Modern Education* (Englewood Cliffs, N. J.: Prentice-Hall, Inc., 1952), p. 18.

[4]*Ibid.,* p. 25.

The Brethren were strongly opposed to the practice of begging, which was common during the later Middle Ages, especially among students. Following Groote's example, the Brethren developed ways to help students. They persuaded kindhearted widows to take them into their homes and treat them as their own sons. They made provision for many in the "houses" of the Brethren. In some instances they built near the schools dormitories, which were under the control of the brotherhood. They furnished many boys with books and other necessities and also gave many employment, first in the copying of manuscripts and, after the invention of printing, in the publishing of a great quantity of evangelical literature.

The earnest educational purpose of the Brethren was to have their students unite learning and practical Christian living. They selected the subjects of the curriculum with this objective definitely in view. Contrary to the practice of using only the Latin language in all learning, they began the teaching of religion in the everyday language of the people, which made possible to each individual a knowledge of the Scriptures.

The Brethren used their influence wherever they could to reform church and city schools already in existence and, wherever invited to do so, established new schools. Before the end of the fifteenth century they had founded or reorganized schools in Germany, the Netherlands, and northern France. Through the scholars they trained, their influence penetrated everywhere, reaching into Switzerland, Belgium, and farther into Germany. Their schools, particularly in their strong religious and moral element, became the models for the reorganization and reform of all the large institutions of western Germany. Most of the great scholars and the educational leaders of this period were the direct products of the schools of the Brethren. John Wessel had a part in founding the University of Paris. Erasmus owed much to the training he received in the schools of the Brethren, though he later criticized their methods. John Sturm, founder of the famous gymnasium at Strasbourg, made that school a continuation of their work. Rudolph Agricola was a potent force for Christian education. Pope Adrian VI was trained under Brethren influences. Even the Jesuits profited much from the practices of the Brethren.

The Reformation and Christian Education

No one knows how great a part the spiritual influence and the educational activities of those who maintained simple faith in the revelation of truth given by God played in bringing about the Reformation. Always God carries on through a remnant His education of mankind. In every fresh beginning He makes in history, the godly few are the agents He uses to lead straying men on the way to His goal of final redemption. These, the insignificant among men, are the human foundation for the achievement of His ultimate purpose. Ignored, despised, persecuted, and cast aside by their fellows, the few who rely upon God are the ones through whom He works out His plan for the eternal redemption of mankind.

During the centuries when the many were compromising by mixing the human with the divine, there were a few whose faith in revealed truth never wavered. The groups to which these belonged carried on educational activities of which historians of education have recorded little or nothing. Yet the leaven of their single-hearted devotion was working—often to an extent and in ways imperceptible to men. No one knows how far the influence of the Brethren of the Common Life reached. No one has ever been able to measure the strength of the evangelical impact of the activities of the Waldenses. Christian education was emphasized in Bohemia long before the reaction against the church took place in Germany. There John Huss studied and taught doctrines of Protestant nature. The Hussites issued many publications, including the Scriptures, in the vernacular—publications which unquestionably had a great effect on minds and hearts. Among other small groups which exerted immeasurable spiritual and educational influence at that time as well as later were the Anabaptists in Switzerland and the Mennonites in Holland.

The reaction against the dogma of the church and the demand for a return to the simple teachings of Christ grew gradually and became stronger with the passing of time. The demand did not break out all at once and with Luther, as is often thought. No one man—Luther or any other—could have brought on a revolution such as the Reformation. For at least two centuries dissatisfaction with the church had been increasing, and various efforts at reform had been attempted. By the close of the fifteenth century persons who wished to reform the church fell into two main groups. The one used the methods and content of Renaissance learning; the other, the approach of piety in the conviction that God teaches individuals through His Word by the Holy Spirit. Although their programs differed greatly in origin and character, these groups were alike in two respects. Each demanded a return to the teaching and practices of the early Christians, as derived from study of the Bible and of the writings of the early church fathers. Each group insisted also that Christians should have the privilege of studying the Bible for themselves in order to reach their own conclusions as to Christian duty.

Humanly speaking, it happened that the first largely successful revolt broke out in Germany and centered in Martin Luther (1483-1546). Had it not started with him, it would have come about through someone else; had it not taken place in Germany, it would have come in some other land. The spirit of free searching for truth was in conflict with the spirit of dogmatic and repressive authority; the eventual clash of two such forces was inevitable.

Luther at first only protested against the practices of the church, not intending revolt from it. However, one step followed another until he was in open rebellion and finally, in 1520, found himself under a sentence of excommunication. He took his stand on the authority of the Scriptures, so the battle became one between the forces representing the authority of the church and those standing for the authority of the Bible, between those who stood for salvation through the church and those who emphasized salvation through personal faith. Luther's battle cry, so to speak, was "The just shall live by faith." He also forced the issue for freedom of thought in spiritual matters, asserting in religious affairs what the educators and scholars had stood for in intellectual matters.

The Roman Catholic church, which had been for centuries the one unifying force in Europe, was permanently split by the revolt. Much of Germany followed Luther, and the outbreak there soon spread to other lands. Lutheranism was adopted as the religion for all the Scandinavian nations. A reform movement much like Lutheranism, led by Zwingli, made much headway in German Switzerland during the time Luther was carrying on his work in Germany. In 1534 the Act of Supremacy severed England from Rome. By this act the king instead of the pope was made head of a new national church, which became known as the English or Anglican Church. John Calvin, the third great reformer, made Geneva a little religious republic, transforming it into the "Rome of Protestantism."

From Geneva as a center, Calvinistic doctrines dominated church reform in France, Scotland, Holland, and portions of England. In France Calvinists became known as Huguenots, in Scotland they were known as Scotch Presbyterians, in Holland they became the Dutch Reformed Church, and in England they were called Puritans. Calvinism was carried to America by the Puritans who settled New England, by the Huguenots who came to the Carolinas, by the Scotch Presbyterians who settled in the central colonies, and by the Dutch who came to New York. For a long time it was the dominant religious belief, and it had profound effect on early American education. Lutheranism was brought to America by Swedish people who settled along the Delaware and by Germans who came to Pennsylvania. Members of the Anglican Church, known in America as the Episcopalian, brought that faith to Virginia and, in later years, to New York.

Luther, as well as Wycliffe, Huss, Zwingli, and Calvin, revolted against the human authority of the church and the pope and against the collective judgment of the church. They substituted for these the authority of the Bible and the right of individual conscience and judgment. They were against church responsibility for salvation, holding that the individual is personally responsible for his salvation. Collective responsibility for salvation, or the judgment of the church, required the education of only a few. The new theory of individual judgment and responsibility made it important that every person be able to read the Word of God, be enlightened in respect to church services, and order his life in accordance with real understanding of what God required of him. This made necessary the education of all. Furthermore, the natural consequence of freedom of judgment and personal responsibility in religious matters was the development of the concept of individual participation in and personal responsibility in other phases of life, including government. Hence the rise of democratic governments and the provision of universal education were logical outcomes of the Protestant views concerning the interpretation of the Scriptures and the place and authority of the church.

Though not a humanist himself, Luther did rely upon the humanistic and individualistic atmosphere of the times. Like the humanists, he was in revolt against the existing order of things. At first he strongly upheld the supremacy of reason, claiming that anything opposed to reason is much more in opposition to God. In his vigorous attack upon Aristotle and Scholasticism and in the struggle for the right of free thought and an enlightened Christianity, he identified himself in spirit with the humanists. He himself had studied the classics, and he advocated for others the study of the great works of classical writers.

Before the close of his life, however, he fiercely attacked reason, which earlier he had praised. His later view was that reason is "the Devil's bride or harlot" who "should be trampled underfoot or have dirt thrown in her face to make her more hateful."[5] Evidently he had awakened to the realization of the insufficiency of the human and had become aware of the dangers involved in placing dependence upon what originates alone in man.

Luther was well aware of the importance of education. Once he had revolted, he devoted much of his time to promoting the education of the masses. All his writings, religious and pedagogical, had clearly the purpose of being, in a broad sense, educational. To awaken the minds and hearts of the common people, he translated the Bible. This contributed greatly to education by stimulating the masses to read and reflect. He issued two catechisms, one for adults and the other for children. He wrote many tracts, addresses, and letters containing allusions to education, its organization, and its methods.

Luther recognized the need for educating young people for service in the church, the state, and society in general. He laid upon those in authority the responsibility for the necessary instruction of youth. Schools should, therefore, be maintained at public expense for rich and poor, high and low, boys and girls, and attendance should be compulsory. He posed and answered a question: "Though there were no soul, nor heaven, nor hell, but only the civil government, would not this require good schools and learned men more than do our spiritual interests? . . . For the establishment of the best schools everywhere, both for boys and girls, this consideration is of itself sufficient, namely, that society, for the

[5]*Ibid.,* p. 77.

maintenance of civil order and the proper regulation of the household needs accomplished and well-trained men and women."[6]

Luther's views of education, as well as his views of doctrine, were derived chiefly from the Scriptures. He regarded the commandment, "Honor thy father and thy mother," as the foundation of all institutional existence and all social order. He maintained that home training and obedience produced sound family life, and that sound family life is the foundation of good government on all levels. He contended that no one ought to become a father unless he could teach his children Bible truth. He declared also that we must be taught from birth if God's kingdom is to grow. He strongly censured laxity in parents and wrong methods of training.

Just as definitely he frowned upon undue severity. Education, he held, should be basically Christian. He declared that the Scriptures should be the chief content of instruction in all schools and that parents should not send their children to schools where these are not taught. In his catechisms he simplified the truths of the Bible to adapt them to the understanding of pupils. He instructed teachers to see that pupils knew not only the answers but understood what was meant by them.

Luther held that pupils should be taught, in addition to the Scriptures, the languages and history, singing, instrumental music, and mathematics. He strongly advocated the study, in the higher schools, of the ancient languages, Latin, Greek, and Hebrew, but only for the aid they would be to an undertsanding of the Scriptures. On the whole he did not exert much influence for secular culture and the study of science. He was especially interested in the study of history, which he claimed was a means of understanding human nature, morals, and institutions, and contained many evidences of God's providences not found in the Bible. He also placed a high educational value on Aesop's fables, ranking them next to the Scriptures for moral instruction. He encouraged the study of music and singing on all levels of instruction, for he believed that music was next to theology with respect to spiritual values. He wrote many hymns, and the first German hymnal was printed under his direction.

Luther exalted the position of the teacher, saying that no calling

[6]F. V. N. Painter, *Luther on Education* (St. Louis: Concordia Publishing House, 1928), pp. 194-196.

except that of the minister is more important. He held that teachers should be trained for their work and that ministers should have had previous experience as teachers.

Side by side with Luther stood Philip Melanchthon (1497-1560), who made concrete in schools the ideas of Luther that had bearing on general education. He was the greatest scholar of the German Reformation, being second only to Erasmus in breadth of learning. Like Erasmus, he was through all his life an enthusiastic humanist. He did much to introduce the humanistic studies in the secondary schools and the universities. In his textbooks in grammar, rhetoric, logic, ethics, physics, and history he emphasized humanistic pedagogical principles. The influence of Melanchthon was spread throughout Germany by the students whom he taught. Through his Saxon plan for elementary instruction, revised and approved by Luther, he became the founder of the modern state school system.

Melanchthon saw the need for an intermediate school between the Latin schools brought into existence by his Saxon plan and the universities. Such a school, stressing both Latin and Greek literature, he deemed necessary to train young Germans in matters important to the nation and the Protestant faith. It was from the municipal Latin schools, when the course had been modified and expanded, that the gymnasium developed. The most famous of these classical secondary schools was the one organized at Strasbourg by John Sturm (1507-1589), perhaps under the inspiration of Melanchthon. Sturm took the old Latin school of the city, gave it a humanistic purpose, and changed it into a gymnasium. He made piety, knowledge, and eloquence the aim of his training. By the first he meant knowledge of the Scriptures, catechism, and creed, with reverence for religion and participation in church services. To him knowledge meant the Latin language and literature and eloquence the ability to use that language in practical life.

His school was most successful. Its pupils became the headmasters of all the outstanding schools, and the course of study formulated by Sturm became a model not only for Germany but, to a considerable degree, for all of Europe. Most of the existing secondary schools in Germany, as well as those founded later, became gymnasiums. These embodied the purpose of teaching classical literature for the sake of liberal training and the preparing of church and civil leaders. Thus, following Luther's views, the education of such leaders continued to be a purpose of secondary education throughout the sixteenth century.

Ulrich Zwingli (1484-1531), a priest of Zurich, led a revolt against the church at the very time Luther was active in Germany. His revolt sprang from northern humanism. He was a zealous supporter of humanism, which he had studied at several universities. Under the influence of Erasmus and others he had become convinced that traditional theology had no Biblical basis, and he carefully read the Scriptures in the original Greek and Hebrew. In charge of the cathedral at Zurich, he attacked the dogmas and traditions of the church and, supported by the town, gradually dropped one church form after another. He made the extension of education a part of his work of reform, fostering humanistic learning and founding a number of humanistic institutions. He introduced elementary schools into Switzerland and also published an educational treatise recommending a course of studies similar to that of Luther.

The Anabaptist movement had its origin among the followers of Zwingli in 1524-25. Anabaptists were dissenters who sought to reform both Lutheranism and Calvinism by returning Christians to the simple faith and moral life of the teachings of Jesus. They stressed the need for restoration of primitive Christianity as revealed in the Scriptures and as manifested in the lives of martyrs. State religions, they held, are not truly Christian, for the state cannot be Christianized. The Christian, like Jesus, must always expect persecution and death. They stressed and practiced a strict morality but maintained that the church should always be separate from the state, to which the Christian should pay no allegiance whatever.

The Anabaptists opposed war and oaths and abstained rigidly from worldly affairs. In spite of persecutions by Lutherans and Catholics, the Anabaptists clung tenaciously to their beliefs, and thousands of them accepted martyrdom until they were largely exterminated in Germany. Remnants of their number found refuge in Holland, Switzerland, and then in America. Menno Simons, the founder of the Mennonites, had a leading part in developing their present doctrines and ways of life. Today Mennonites and Amish in America remain as descendants of the Anabaptists and have stood by the principles of simple Christian living and the right of man to be different. The influence of the Amish in Christian education has been negative, for their abstention from worldly affairs leads them to oppose education. The Mennonites have in recent years been taking active interest in education; the nature and extent of their contribution to Christian education has not been insignificant.

John Calvin (1509-1564), like Zwingli, broke with the church through the influence of northern humanism and the study of the Greek Testament. He did not merely attack Catholic doctrine, but he formulated a system of theology. He was the first among Protestants to do this. Called upon to reorganize the government of the city of Geneva, he founded schools and promoted education. Like Luther, he deemed it the duty of the church to instruct the young, holding that learning was "a public necessity to secure good political administration, sustain the Church unharmed, and maintain humanity among men." He said that reason had been given by God to everyone in order that he might discover and understand truth.

He wrote catechetical helps or guides for the instruction of small children. He believed that children should be carefully trained in the home by parents and that they should attend Sunday catechetical classes. Also he urged that children be taught to sing the songs of the church. He insisted that they be trained not only in sound learning and doctrine but also in manners, morals, and common sense. His catechetical helps were widely used and became the basis of the Heidelberg Catechism and the Westminster Catechism.

His plan for elementary instruction in the schools of Geneva called for the instruction of every pupil in the Bible, reading, writing, grammar, and arithmetic, all in the vernacular. Calvin considered the Scriptures the foundation of all learning. As Luther had done, he upheld the principle that instruction in the liberal arts is essential. He therefore organized secondary schools to prepare men for the ministry and for service to the State. The ideal for these schools was the "learned piety" of Melanchthon, Sturm, and other northern humanists and Protestants. The usual humanistic curriculum was combined with intensive religious instruction. Psalms were sung, public prayers offered, and selections from the Bible repeated each day. In the seven classes of a secondary school in Geneva the pupils learned reading and grammar from the Latin catechism and then studied Latin classics and Latin composition. Later in the course, Greek was studied, with the reading of writings of classical Greek authors and the Gospels and Epistles.

As in other Reformation schools, logic and rhetoric were studied in the higher classes. The University of Geneva, founded by Calvin about 1559, became the center of literary and theological education for Protestants of western Europe. Students were required to subscribe to the Christian theology before they entered upon their studies, whether classical or religious.

From Geneva, Calvinism exerted tremendous effect upon education wherever the religion went. In England its influence penetrated Oxford and Cambridge through the Puritans. Graduates of Cambridge carried Calvinism to colonial New England, where it set the pattern for and determined the practices of early American education, making it center definitely in the Bible. In France the Huguenots founded many elementary and secondary schools and eight universities. In Holland the national synod required that parents, teachers, and ministers instruct all children in Christian doctrine. John Knox (1505-1572), the Scottish Reformation leader, a personal friend of Calvin, introduced the Genevan ideal of education into Scotland. He formulated a plan for a national church and the establishment of schools in which Christian instruction would be given. His plan provided that the church compel all parents to rear their children in "learning and virtue" and he made the church directly responsible for providing and supporting schools for all classes and both sexes.

Protestant revolt brought Catholic reaction, marked by both violent and peaceful methods. Before and after the revolt, there were, inside the Roman Catholic Church, those who sought to improve its practices. Now Catholics in general felt it their duty to crush the Protestant heresy and recover lost ground. The result was severe persecution and a number of religious wars. Thousands of people were killed, some by Catholics, some by Protestants, for the two groups were about equally fanatical, bitter, cruel, and forgetful of the teachings of Christ when they ostensibly for the sake of His kingdom heaped upon each other hatred, persecution, and bloodshed.

One of the peaceful methods of dealing with the situation was the convening of the Council of Trent by the pope in 1543, to effect reforms. It did much to eliminate abuses from the church, reform the practices and outward lives of the clergy, and initiate a program of education. Seemingly, the Catholics gave no thought to consideration of church dogma to ascertain if they might by a spiritual regeneration effectively combat the Protestant movement but instead prepared to fight human success with human weapons. An important element in Protestant success had been their educational program. The history of general education shows great achievements of Protestants in secular instruction. The idea of education for every person advanced by them appealed mightily to people, with the result that whole states became school systems under the influence of Protestantism.

Now a new movement of education was launched within the frame of the church. This took place through the organization of new orders, chief among which was the Society of Jesus, usually called the Jesuit Order, founded by Ignatius of Loyola (1491-1556). The purposes of the order were to combat heresy and to strengthen the authority of the pope. The means to be employed to accomplish these ends were the pulpit, the confessional, missions, and education. Of these, the last was taken as the chief mode of operation. It was realized that the chief cause of the Reformation had been the ignorance and the licentiousness of so many of the clergy and the abuses practiced by the church. Therefore, the order took as its first principle upright and industrious living on the part of its members and the effort to reach and train those who might become future leaders in Church and state.

The means of moral training in the Jesuit schools were example, careful supervision, moral instruction, and the sacraments of the Church. The Jesuits held that imitation is the most important and most subtle of all influences, hence every teacher was prepared so as to be what it was considered the pupils should be. And every Jesuit teacher deemed it his sacred duty to watch over the conduct of pupils with the purpose of guarding them from dangers which surrounded them. Much ethical instruction and advice were given pupils in private conversation with their teachers and in connection with their studies. But the great means of education, Jesuits asserted, was religion and its associated practices. They considered it the duty of the school to implant in the hearts of the young reverence and love for their Creator and Lord.

Pupils lived in a thoroughly religious atmosphere. Every Jesuit school had its church or chapel, every classroom its crucifix and religious pictures. The school session began and ended with prayer, and all pupils were advised to participate daily in religious exercises. The catechism was explained in all classes; in the higher classes religious instruction was given as a course in apologetics. More important than formal religious instruction, however, was the permeation of all instruction from beginning to end with religious principles. The first and the most sacred duty of the teacher was so to teach all subjects that the students would come to the knowledge and love of their Creator and Redeemer.

Jesuit training, which combined humanism with religion, was long, thorough, and effective. One secret of its effectiveness was its splendid organization of the content taught. Teachers used the best methods known at the time. Teacher and pupil were in such close personal contact that Jesuit schools had great molding power. Next to this personal interest was the principle of thoroughness underlying their work. Much stress was placed upon memorizing, reviews were frequent and systematic, and interest was maintained by means of prizes, ranks, and the definite and careful use of rivalry. Teachers made instruction interesting and pleasant. Any teacher of today, whether his interest is in general or in Christian education, may well consider studiously and carefully the methods and practices of Jesuit education.

Outstanding features of Jesuit education are worthy of imitation. One which contributed greatly to its marked success was the care exercised in the selection of teachers and the thoroughness with which they were prepared for their work. From the members of the order, every one of which was a picked man to begin with, only those best adapted to teaching were selected for this permanent service. Those chosen were given a preliminary course of carefully supervised training, then assigned to teach in the lower courses of some college. Here they might remain, but if qualified for higher work, they taught there for two or three years, after which they took more advanced courses in a university. The training was in scholarship, religion, theology, and apprenticeship teaching. Jesuit teachers were therefore far superior to their contemporaries and wielded an influence quite out of proportion to their number. Catholic and Protestant historians agree in saying that it was the educational work of the Jesuit Order that checked the advance of Protestantism and saved much of Europe for Catholicism.

The Foundation of Modern Christian Education

Thus from about 1400 to 1600 two interrelated movements called the Renaissance and the Reformation transformed life in all its phases. Through these movements, the power of the Catholic, or universal, church was broken. They brought about growth of nationalism in politics. Through them the use of reason and scientific investigation as the way for arriving at knowledge was substituted for unquestioning acceptance of dogmatic authority. They promoted the development of individualism in thought and in life. And the outcome of the movements was the appearance of numerous churches, or denominations, within Christianity.

The two movements left a permanent mark on education in general and on Christian education in particular. The Renaissance emphasized reason, exalted the individual, stressed the right of private judgment, and turned men to the study of the ancient classics of Greece and Rome to develop familiarity with the sources of supposedly true knowledge. Thus the Renaissance brought into education the humanistic studies and laid the foundation for the humanistic emphasis in Christian education—the emphasis that Christian education is properly concerned with knowledge developed through human reason as well as with knowledge given by revelation.

The Reformation was concerned with moral and theological matters. It exalted the use of individual judgment. The natural outcome was the division of the church into denominations because of the fundamental differences in the attitudes of men toward spiritual truth. Inherent in the Reformation position were two principles having the greatest bearing on education. The first was the authority of the Bible, instead of the authority of the church, in faith and morals. The second was justification by faith, which meant that the individual is accepted of God on the basis of his faith in Jesus Christ without the mediation of priest or church and with no interpreter of truth other than the Holy Spirit.

In opposition to Catholic insistence upon an infallible church and denial of direct access to divine truth by people in general, Protestants claimed an infallible Book and for every individual the right to seek truth from that Book. Thus every Protestant was provided with a safeguard against the tendencies of church leaders, including early Reformation ones, to combine human knowledge and divine revelation. Making the Bible the sole authority also prevented the mixing of human reason with revealed truth in the formulation of Protestant doctrine. The result, in spiritual matters, as expressed in the creeds of the various Protestant churches, was a remarkably faithful body of doctrine characterized by essential agreement. Without the faithfulness of certain men to the truth God revealed, He could not have given the spiritual victories that are recorded in history. It is true, of course, that this has not been an uncheckered history, for there have been defections from the faith and heresies in theological matters.

The principle of the authority of the Bible required that all persons should know the Bible, for only through such knowledge could they come to understand God's will. The principle of justification by faith required that the individual should be appealed to through his reason as the avenue to an understanding of the Word of God. The Christian attitude on the subject of reason, as expressed by Protestants, was not to do away with reason but to use it, not to doubt God's revelation or to make additions to it from the products of reason but to appreciate the fact of man's need for redemption and of God's wonderful offer of redemption through grace. These two principles, taken together, necessitated universal Christian education. To the development of the idea of such education, Protestants set themselves. Although the goal has never been reached, although it has been obscured again and again, it has never been entirely lost to sight.

Early Protestants sought in several general ways to achieve the goal of universal Christian education. The first was the translation of the Bible into the language of the people, followed by as wide a distribution as possible. Since then, wherever Protestantism has gone, it has translated the Bible into the mother tongue of the people, practiced the reading of it in that language during the services of worship, put it into the hands of the people, and encouraged them to read and study it for themselves. Early Protestantism was characterized also by a revival of Biblical and doctrinal preaching. Always, preaching with Biblical content as the core of the message has been the instrument used by God in great revivals to the cleansing of national life and the salvation of thousands of souls. The preaching of the pure Gospel is an inseparable part of Christian education and can by no means be divorced from it.

A third means of seeking to make Christian education universal was the teaching of the Bible in the family. Through systematic formulations of doctrine for use in the home, the reformers made an immeasurable contribution to Christian education. Luther prepared two manuals of doctrine which had wide circulation. After thirteen years of strenuous labor he brought forth his *Small Catechism* which is said to be, next to the Bible, the most widely circulated and translated book ever published. Calvin wrote a catechism which was used extensively. The Anglican catechism was first published in 1549; its outstanding characteristic is its simplicity. The *Heidelberg Cathechism* appeared in 1563. It has been used in many lands, having been translated into almost every European language and into some dialects of other continents. Both Luther and Calvin, as well as other Protestant leaders, urged upon parents the solemn duty of instructing their children in Bible truth. Among the Dutch and the Scotch, family teaching was much practiced.

Christian schools were established for all the youth of the community. Lutheranism and Calvinism were especially strong in their emphasis upon Christian education for all youth irrespective of sex or level in society. Both Luther and Calvin wrote on education, established schools, and encouraged in every way possible the Christian training of children in schools as well as in the family. In the Netherlands, in France, in Scotland, in England, in America—everywhere Protestantism went—Christian schools were founded.

Finally, Protestants, with the purpose of reaching the goal of universal Christian education, adopted the view that all education is or should be a unity. This was not a peculiarly Protestant view, for Catholics had long held it. Now Protestants who promoted education took it for granted and blended together humanistic and religious content. Virtually all of the reformers were humanists or at least had been trained in humanistic schools and were altogether willing to borrow from humanistic sources. Luther advocated the study of the Greek and Latin classics. Melanchthon, who made concrete in practice the educational ideas of Luther, was definitely a humanist and emphasized humanism in education. Calvin was strongly humanistic and made humanistic studies basic in his educational planning. Zwingli was a humanist rather than a theologian and to the end of his life had a high regard for the heroes of classical antiquity.

Consequently, official Protestantism from its very beginning failed "in spite of the spiritual heights achieved, to do for the world of mind what it did for the world of spirit."[7] Thus, once more, when men were given the opportunity to accept as true knowledge the revelation coming from God, they chose instead, though in education now rather than in religion, to weaken the truth of God by means of an admixture of human wisdom which would in the future, just as the human had done in the past, fail to satisfy the yearning of men for truth. And it was by the choice then made that there was introduced into modern education, general and Christian, the leaven of wordly intellectual paganism.

Readings

BENSON, CLARENCE H. *A Popular History of Christian Education.* Chicago: Moody Press, 1943.

BUTTS, R. FREEMAN. *A Cultural History of Western Education.* New York: McGraw-Hill Book Company, 1955.

CAIRNS, EARLE E. "A Blueprint for Christian Higher Education." Faculty bulletin of Wheaton College, Wheaton, Illinois (unpublished).

COOKE, ROBERT L. *Philosophy, Education and Certainty.* Grand Rapids: Zondervan Publishing House, 1940.

CUBBERLEY, ELLWOOD P. *The History of Education.* Boston: Houghton Mifflin Company, 1920.

———*Readings in the History of Education.* Boston: Houghton Mifflin Company, 1926.

CUSHMAN, HERBERT ERNEST. *A Beginner's History of Philosophy.* Boston: Houghton Mifflin Company, 1918.

EBY, FREDERICK. *The Development of Modern Education.* New York: Prentice-Hall, Inc., 1952.

———and ARROWOOD, CHARLES FLINN. *The History and Philosophy of Education, Ancient and Medieval.* New York: Prentice-Hall, Inc., 1940.

GRAVES, FRANK PIERREPONT. *A Student's History of Education.* New York: The Macmillan Company, 1921.

[7]Robert L. Cooke, *Philosophy, Education and Certainty* (Grand Rapids: Zondervan Publishing House, 1940), p. 114.

GRIMM, HAROLD J. *The Reformation Era.* New York: The Macmillan Company, 1954.

LOTZ, PHILIP HENRY. *Orientation in Religious Education.* Nashville and New York: Abingdon-Cokesbury Press, 1950.

MARIQUE, PIERRE J. *A History of Christian Education.* Vol. III. New York: Fordham University Press, 1926.

MONROE, PAUL (ed.). *Cyclopedia of Education.* 5 vols. New York: The MacMillan Company, 1911-1913.

Articles on:

"Brethren of the Common Life," I, 446-447.

"Mysticism," IV, 362-364.

"Humanism and Naturalism," III, 338-340.

———*A Textbook in the History of Education.* New York: The Macmillan Company, 1916 (reissue, 1948).

PAINTER, F. V. N. *Luther on Education.* St. Louis: Concordia Publishing House, 1928.

PRAY, L. G. *History of Sunday Schools and of Religious Education.*

PRICE, J. M., CARPENTER, L. L., and CHAPMAN, J. H. *Introduction to Religious Education.* New York: The Macmillan Company, 1944.

QUALBEN, LARS P. *A History of the Christian Church.* New York: Thomas Nelson and Sons, 1933.

SCHAFF, PHILIP. *History of the Christian Church.* Vol. VI. New York: Charles Scribner's Sons, 1888.

John Amos Comenius (1592-1670) has frequently been called the "father of modern education" by secular educators. But he was a Christian educator par excellence.

(Courtesy of National Union of Czechoslovak Protestants)

6

Christian Education in Post-Reformation Centuries

FOR ORIENTATION to the content of this book, four kinds of education were described in the Foreword: general education, religious education, education called Christian, and true Christian education, or education centering in God instead of man. Also it was stated that the purpose of the book is to trace through time the development of the last of these four. The critical reader may feel at this point that more on general education and so-called Christian education has been included than is ideal in terms of the stated purpose. Justification for including at least some of such content lies in the fact that full understanding of the history of true Christian education requires familiarity with the historical development of other forms of education.

Now that the beginnings of modern Christian education have been traced, attention will be centered more on the educational work done by evangelicals either within other movements or through organizations they founded for the purpose of carrying on true Christian education. Always it is those known as evangelicals in the Biblical and historical sense of this abused word who do the work of God in Christian education. As has been seen, it was evangelicals who made God central in this field prior to the Reformation. Through Reformation times, in spite of the all too general acceptance of the mixture of man's wisdom with God's revealed truth, there were evangelicals who maintained a firm stand for education founded upon the Bible. Since Reformation days, evangelicals have grown in number, though they always have been and still are in the minority.

Nevertheless, evangelicals under the blessing of God wield influence which cannot be measured by man. As always, so at present, they are not confined to membership in any particular church; they are to be found in virtually all denominations. Many who do not express themselves vociferously carry on quiet but effective witness to the truth of God. Evangelicals have always accepted the Bible as God's revelation to man; always they have been in essential agreement among themselves as to the means by which growth in the knowledge of this revelation can be promoted. From the eighteenth century on, and especially in the present century, they have been manifesting concern about Christian education and developing activities for advancing the cause of true Christian education.

Before turning to consideration of these activities, some influences operating during the century or two following the Reformation need to be treated because of the bearing they had on Christian education not only in those times but also in later centuries. Chief among these are Calvinism as an educational force, the work of Comenius, and the Christian education of the German Pietists. These are treated in the present chapter. In the chapter following, Christian education in early America is considered.

Calvinism and Christian Education

The Reformation strengthened the tendency to depart from Catholic orthodoxy, but it did not result immediately in marked theological changes. Both Protestant and Catholic churches retained on a dogmatic basis the main beliefs of Christianity such as the trinity, the incarnation, redemption, the resurrection, miracles, and prophecies. In fact, the creeds of all leading Protestant churches founded as an outcome of the Reformation are in essential agreement on basic theological matters.

While Germany is considered the land of the Reformation and Luther the Reformer, the revolt began neither in Germany nor with Luther. Nor did it end in the acceptance of Lutheranism by all who were dissatisfied with the Catholic Church and its abuses. Calvin led a revolt which eventually left upon Christendom a deeper mark than did Lutheranism. In a sense, Calvinism was a reformation of Lutheranism. The Reformed Church, a protest against

Lutheranism, is Calvinist. And there were those, such as the Anabaptists, who sought to reform both Lutheranism and Calvinism by bringing Christians back to simple faith in Christ and humble obedience to His teachings.

Calvinism was a mental and a spiritual revolution; it was no mere theology but an ideology which neither knew state boundaries nor respected traditions. Its basic tenets were expressed in Calvin's *Institutes of the Christian Religion.* His conceptions, which determined in large part the educational theories and practices of Calvinism, are the following: the absolute sovereignty of God; the predestination of man at birth to eternal salvation or everlasting damnation; the obligation of man to submit to the will of God; redemption by the grace of God through Christ; the total depravity of man, meaning that all his natural inclinations are perverted and can but lead him astray; the necessity, for moral and spiritual life, of suppressing these natural tendencies and engrafting in their place good habits and holy thoughts.

The absolute sovereignty of God required, for Calvin, the welding of church, state, and family into a combined institution with one objective, the fulfilling of the will of God on earth. Thus the perfect society is a theocracy designed solely for the glory of God; in this theocracy the political power is the servant of the ecclesiastical. Pastors are to control every activity of man and government, including education; the entire citizenship is to be subject to pastors and instructed, disciplined, and trained by them to do God's will. This kind of government Calvin instituted in Geneva.

In the home, parents were required to teach their children the catechism and to train them in Christian living. The ruling body of pastors closely supervised not only this work of teaching and training children but also the daily conduct of the parents. At least once each year every home was inspected to see that the rules made by the governing body of pastors were carried out. The church building was used both as a place of worship and as a school in which young and old were instructed in the catechism. It was the function of the state to make laws for putting into effect the ideas of the church leaders, to organize and support schools, and to see that the regulations of the church were enforced.

For the moral and spiritual discipline of all the people, Calvin established the Academy of Geneva as the capstone of the ecclesiastical organization of the city. While the curriculum was humanistic, no other school of the period placed more emphasis on religious training. Every class began the day with prayers and ended it with the reciting of the Lord's Prayer and the giving of thanks. An hour at midday was devoted to singing psalms. At four in the afternoon the school assembled to recite the Lord's Prayer, the confession of faith, and the Ten Commandments. On Wednesday morning, students and teachers heard a sermon; on Saturday afternoon, all studied the catechism; on Sunday, students attended a service of worship and spent the rest of the day meditating on the sermon.

This academy became the nursery of Protestant preachers and teachers for other lands. It was taken as the model for the organization of the University of Leyden in Holland, Edinburgh in Scotland, and Emmanuel College at Cambridge in England, which in turn set the model for Harvard in Massachusetts. The effect of Calvin's work in Geneva was notable because by the teaching of Christian truth both grosser sins and lesser moral evils were eliminated and the city stood as a testimony to the power of the Gospel. John Knox declared that Geneva was a perfect school for Christian training.

Whereas Lutheranism favored national governments, Calvinism led to the founding of the Reformed Church, for which there were no state boundaries. From Switzerland and France it spread into Germany, with Heidelberg University as its center, and into Holland, where it became especially strong. Here, for some time, the Mennonites had been the evangelizing sect of greatest influence. To escape persecution, many Calvinists fled from England to Holland and helped to strengthen the influence of the Reformed Church. Calvinism was established in Scotland by John Knox, who induced the Scottish Parliament to abolish Romanism and accept Calvinism. In Holland, which attained the leading role in European civilization, the University of Leyden, founded in 1575, became the most outstanding center of learning in northern Europe and a meeting place and refuge for learned men from every country. Most of the teachers became Protestant; many of them were from among the Brethren of the Common Life, who had long been evangelical in faith.

Though Calvinism was established as the official religion of Holland, the Reformed Church did not have complete control of education. Nevertheless, it made religious instruction universal; girls as well as boys were admitted to the elementary schools where these practices were followed: the reading of the Scriptures, singing of psalms, instruction in the catechism, training in moral habits, and attendance upon the services of the church. Thousands of Englishmen emigrated to Holland, where many of them attended the universities and their children were taught in the schools. Among these were some who later came to America. Also, after conditions changed, many more thousands emigrated from the Netherlands to England and there exerted influence on life and education. Thus, in at least two ways the influence of Dutch education was brought to bear upon colonial America.

In practice, Calvinism exemplified the application of one of several theories of the relation of church and state. The church had existed for centuries before national governments ever arose. Church and empire had not always been in harmony, but no one seriously questioned their connection or denied to the church the preeminence in religion and education. Emperors and kings bowed to the church, which under the medieval form of organization had complete control of education. After the separation from the Roman Church, the question of the relation of church and state in education and in other matters became a subject of great controversy.

The Catholic position remained as always: the Roman Church was Christ's representative on earth, so it had authority over all civil powers and the exclusive right to control education. Luther acknowledged the civil power as the supreme authority divinely instituted to govern in all temporal affairs. Education, therefore, though closely connected with the interests of the church, was the function of the state. Calvin viewed church and state as separate institutions having the same purpose—to realize the will of God on earth—yet functioning in different fields. Though they functioned as two separate organs, church and state together formed a united organism. Accordingly, they cooperated in education and constituted one agency which combined family, church, and school into a single functional organization. The state supported the school but the church controlled the aim, the methods, the curriculum, and the organization of education, even the teachers.

Another point of view was that of the Anabaptists, who held that church and state are entirely separate. They contended that religion is purely a private affair, a personal concern, with which the state has nothing whatever to do. Since every European state of that time adhered to a particular established faith, this theory could not be put into practice. Having no connection with schools administered under joint state-church action, Anabaptists flourished only in Holland, where education was controlled by the state.

By the beginning of the seventeenth century Calvinistic doctrine and practice had been accepted in Scotland, by the dominant party in Holland, by the Huguenots in France, by the Puritans in England, and by groups of zealous followers in other lands. Lutheranism prevailed in most of Germany, in the Scandinavian countries, and had scattered groups of adherents in other lands. The Moravian Brethren, the Anabaptists, and the Mennonites did not markedly affect education in Europe, but were to become important in America.

While these developments had been taking place in the realm of Protestant Christian education, human thinking was beginning to supplant the doctrines of both Catholicism and Protestantism in general education. The Reformation has given rise to doubt, skepticism, and inquiry about ideas which up to that time had been accepted. The terrible destruction of the religious wars following the Reformation caused many people to ask whether all religious doctrines could be wrong and if some new way to truth might be found. The effect of geographical discoveries which gave knowledge of how other people lived led many to wonder if their own cultures were the best. Developments in anatomy and medicine gave rise to changes in conceptions about human nature.

During the seventeenth century the interest in nature found in the Renaissance of the fifteenth and sixteenth centuries was given philosophical and scientific formulation. The movement known as realism marks the beginning of modern science and modern philosophy. Realism existed in three forms: humanistic, social, and sense. Sense realism was the beginning of the modern scientific movement in education, but it contained within itself also the germs of the psychological and the sociological movements. Realism also marked the start of the reign of rationalistic philosophy, which branched out into materialism and idealism.

Francis Bacon (1561-1626), a materialist, demanded the observation of nature and the use of experimentation and inductive reasoning, which he claimed could answer all questions. Hobbes (1588-1679), more materialistic than Bacon, scorned supernatural religion and completely rejected Christian and humanistic moral values; to him everything was mechanistic. Descartes (1596-1650), an idealist, propounded theories which had a most decided influence on future education. He taught that man could advance from matter to the supreme Mind by starting with doubt. Rejecting revealed truth, he became the parent of much modern materialism and unbelief. Spinoza (1632-1677) denied revelation and the personality of God, making mind and matter elements in one and the same universe united in one Being, which is God. Thus he merged the finite and the Infinite into a transcendental pantheism. Leibnitz (1646-1716) developed a doctrine of monads, or "spiritual atoms," which exist in different forms and manifestations in animate and inanimate things. God is the Monad of monads and there is a mystical evolution from the lowest monad of matter to the highest Monad, God.

Locke (1632-1704) represented a return to a materialistic rationalism. He maintained that the one guide to truth was reason, and he applied this principle to education so effectively as to exert on leaders in education who followed him an influence that is clearly seen and generally acknowledged. "A sound mind in a sound body" was his description of education. He did not neglect morals and religion, for he stated that the foundation of morality is a knowledge of God. This knowledge, he said, comes alone through revelation. However, he made reason the final guide, maintaining that revelation is not to be accepted when it contradicts knowledge derived from experience coming either by sensation or by reflection. Man's individual consciousness is both the source and the criterion of all truth. Thus did Locke, the greatest of all rationalists, turn education to a materialistic rationalism which was the more readily received for being presented in the language of religion. The consequence was the exaltation in general education of intellect above all else.

But the deep interest of Calvinists in an education based upon the principles of Christianity did not flag with the quite general casting aside of everything except human reason and the beginning of that series of speculations about education which continues even in the present. In Holland their interest found expression in a general system of education of their own devising. The outlines of their plan are set forth in the resolutions adopted by a great council of Reformed churches held at Dort in 1618 and 1619. Their system provided for religious instruction in the home and the church and for the establishment of schools under civil authority. Religious instruction was the chief concern of those who originated the plan. To the end that the young might be trained in piety, three modes of catechizing were employed: in the home by parents; in the schools by teachers; and in the churches by ministers, elders, and catechists appointed especially for the purpose. Civil officers were requested to use their authority to promote this work, and all leaders in schools and churches were required to give special heed to religious instruction.

Parents were to instruct their children and their entire household diligently in Christian truth, to admonish them faithfully to cultivate true piety, and to take them to church services regularly. In order that all parents might be brought to perform their duty, any parent who was negligent along these lines was to be admonished by the ministers and, if not responsive, to be censured by the consistory. Schools for the instruction of the young in Christian doctrine were conducted in cities, towns, and rural areas. These schools were open to all children and were in charge of well-trained teachers who were required to be members of the Reformed Church, strong in faith, upright in conduct, and pious. Every teacher had to sign a statement indicating his acceptance of the Confession of Faith and the Heidelberg Catechism and promising to instruct his pupils in the principles of Christian truth set forth in these.

To make sure that teachers would perform their duties well and that pupils would profit from the instruction given, ministers, elders, and, if necessary, a civil officer visited frequently all schools, private and public. The purpose of these visits was to stimulate teachers to earnestness, to encourage them, to advise them in respect to the duty of catechizing, and to set them an example by questioning them. All this was done in a spirit of helpfulness, with a view to inciting them to diligent spiritual activity. Any teacher who proved negligent was admonished by the ministers and, if necessary, by the consistory.

The standard set up by the Reformed Church in Holland became the standard for Calvinistic education in all countries in the measure permitted by local conditions. This church gave leadership in Christian education to the people of Holland, and its influence led to similar practices among Calvinists in England, Scotland, France, and America. Christian emphases in education among the Germans were inspired by Calvinists. Some of the principles advocated by Comenius had their origin in Calvinistic education.

Comenius and Christian Education

John Amos Comenius (1592-1670) has such an outstanding place in the history of general education that secular educators have called him the "father of modern education." His writings contain in germ almost all educational theory of later centuries. He wrote more than a hundred treatises and textbooks. These were summed up in his large theoretical work, *The Great Didactic,* a truly remarkable educational treatise. He also dealt with educational problems in a most practical manner. His textbooks, which stressed modern principles of method, were extraordinarily popular. His recommendations concerning content to be studied are in accord with modern trends of reform in subject matter. He devised a plan for the organization of schools that is essentially like the one in vogue today. He introduced and dominates the whole modern movement in the field of elementary and secondary education especially.

To list the principles stressed by Comenius is to show the specific elements of modern education that found expression in him. He advocated the following: a free and universal system of education open to all children of both sexes and compulsory for all; preschool home training; instruction in the mother tongue prior to the teaching of Latin; the grading of material to adapt it to the level of the pupil's development; study of the mind of the child and the suiting of teaching to his present needs; gentle, understanding discipline; making school work interesting and enjoyable through dramatization and play; adaptation of the curriculum to the child's needs and capacities, with correlation and coordination of different subjects throughout the entire period of education; close connection of thought with things; and the extreme importance of developing the whole personality of the pupil instead of training him only for some particular career.

Comenius was famous as an educator during his lifetime. Great scholars were his friends, and rulers had confidence in him. The governments of several countries invited him to reconstruct their educational systems. A number of his many books were translated into most of the languages of Europe and into several Asiatic languages.

Though he was a great educator both in his day and in the influence he left on general education, the service he rendered Christian education is even more important. He advocated the Christian education of all youth. At the time he lived, new and strong forces were at work and these inevitably influenced education. Comenius was in part a product of the environment in which modern education, which is naturalistic and humanistic, had its origin. Because he saw defects in education, he devoted his life to efforts to make it what it ought to be. He realized keenly the necessity of having education center in Christian principles. He stands as a transition figure between those who subordinated everything in education to religion and later educators who made religion but one element in a secularized education. Though Comenius was preeminently an educator, the work of God always had first place in his thinking. He believed that the Bible was the basic source of knowledge. For him education was a means of bringing individuals to accept Christ as Saviour, of teaching them how to live the Christian life, and of training them for service to God.

While Comenius was in part a product of the environment in which modern education originated, he was also influenced strongly by the Bohemian Brethren, or the Moravian Church—two terms which are used interchangeably. His people were Brethren who were followers of John Huss. In doctrine they were related to the Wycliffites and the Waldensians. The Brethren placed chief stress on practical Christian living, giving little heed to doctrinal matters. Protestant writers in general are agreed that no other church since the days of the apostles so fully observed the ethical teachings of Christ and that none has evidenced a more missionary spirit. The beginning of the modern missionary movement can be traced to them. Martin Luther gave their church the highest praise for closeness to apostolic doctrine and practice.

Simple faith in God, warm love, deep personal piety, self-sacrifice, humble dependence on God, devotion to His cause, and interest in education were outstanding characteristics of these people.

Comenius was a Moravian, a minister among them, and one of their bishops. He exemplified, therefore, in his teachings and in his life their beliefs and their spirit. Holiness of life meant much to him; he held it a necessity that Christians be filled with the Holy Spirit, and he possessed missionary vision.

In his times education was passing from extreme dependence upon reflection and reason to extreme reliance on sense and observation. Francis Bacon had held that things should be taught instead of words because man learns inductively. Wolfgang Ratich had declared that education should be realistic instead of humanistic and had emphasized seeking the method of nature. Descartes had taught that all primary ideas are innate and that growth of knowledge consists merely in drawing out their implications, so learning is fundamentally rational thinking. Comenius shared both the Baconian principle of sense perception as the origin of knowledge and the Cartesian theory of innate ideas. However, they were not for him the final word; he believed that absolute truth is apprehended by faith, therefore these antagonistic principles were to him nothing more than methods of study. He was greatly influenced by the ideas of Ratich on following the method of nature in teaching.

Comenius held that a Christian puts primary dependence on God's revelation, then uses reason to arrive at understanding of that revelation. Reason does not give man truth but enables him to know and understand truth which God, its one and only source, reveals. God's supreme revelation of truth is found in the Scriptures, but He reveals it also in nature. Science and the Scriptures throw light upon each other as the Holy Spirit aids man in his search for truth, but the Bible is the final standard, because, being the revelation of the infinite God, it is more trustworthy than finite man's conclusions from nature. Sense, reason, and the Bible are all needed for gaining knowledge of truth. Man learns through the senses the truth imprinted in or on things; defects of sense and correction of errors of sense are supplied by reason; and things he cannot obtain through either the senses or his reason man learns through faith in what God reveals.

Comenius was definitely evangelical. The Moravian Brethren held in common with other evangelical groups all essential teachings. When Comenius referred to evangelicals in his writings he always meant those who accepted the doctrine of salvation by faith alone, including the Calvinists, the Lutherans, and especially his own denomination. Thus he was fully in accord with the original statements of belief of all leading Protestant denominations as formulated in later years.

To him the Bible was God's inerrant Word. He maintained that his theology was what was written in the Bible. He considered the Bible to be the basic and the most important source of knowledge. However, he taught that men must make use also of knowledge they gain from men. All men seek eternal truth, therefore all men must be taught about things of eternity; every person during his sojourn on earth has certain duties to perform among his fellows, therefore all must be taught things relating to human beings. That things of nature as well as spiritual truth are to be taught is shown, he said, by the example of Christ, who often drew upon nature to illustrate divine truth.

Comenius believed that God, who exists in three Persons, created and sustains the universe. He taught that Jesus Christ as God manifest in the flesh died on the Cross for man's sins. He said that our salvation was consummated on the Cross, where Christ died that men might live. To him education was the means for bringing men to the place where they would accept Christ and by accepting become able to fulfill God's purposes for their lives; education is not a direct agent in conversion; it is only a means whereby conversion may be brought about. He believed that the Holy Spirit was sent to draw men to God, to indwell, to teach, and to guide believers, and that He usually works through parents, teachers, and ministers as natural agents.

He taught that man, created good and upright, chose to do evil and thereby became totally depraved in his nature. Salvation is provided in Christ, the sinlessly perfect Son of God, whom man must personally receive by repentance and faith. Those who in unbelief and impenitence reject Him will spend eternity in Hell while those who believe will be resurrected from the dead to eternal life.

He believed in the reality of Satan and taught that whoever Satan finds entirely unemployed he will occupy first with evil thoughts and afterwards with wrong deeds; he advocated therefore that none, even early in life, should be idle. Education is not a means of ridding the pupil of natural tendencies but of bringing him to Christ in salvation, then of training him mentally, morally, and spiritually to live the Christian life. The purpose of education is to enable the pupil to become truly Christian through the establishing of right habits, which are formed and guided by means of adequate knowledge.

The aim and purpose of education Comenius sets forth as follows in the titles of the first seven of the thirty-three chapters of *The Great Didactic:*

1. Man is the highest, the most absolute, and the most excellent of things created.
2. The ultimate end of man is beyond this life.
3. This life is but a preparation for eternity.
4. There are three stages in the preparation for eternity: to know oneself (and with oneself all things), to rule oneself, and to direct oneself to God.
5. The seeds of these three (learning, virtue, religion) are naturally implanted in us.
6. If a man is to be produced, it is necessary that he be formed by education.
7. A man can most easily be formed in early youth, and cannot be formed properly except at this age.

Comenius held that Christian education must be universal. It was his belief that such education would lead children to accept Christ as Saviour early in life. Therefore, all—high and low, rich and poor, boys and girls—should receive Christian education. It should be a process based upon man's nature and destiny. Its primary agency is the Christian home. He held that man should early in life be molded as he ought to be in later years. This molding should be done in the home while the child is most impressionable. The school should continue the Christian education begun in the home. To Comenius, if home and school functioned properly, little instruction would need to be given by the church.

He gave only one aim for education—to prepare each individual for life with God. He said that "the chief end of man is to attain eternal happiness in and with God." To him this was the fundamental principle of education. Thus he put God at the center. Life on earth is only a preparation for eternity. The aim of every home and every school should therefore be spiritual and eternal—to bring its work and methods into harmony with God's purpose of restoring through Christ the image of God which man lost by sinning. This ultimate goal is to be achieved through specific objectives. These are that man must know all things, including himself; be master over all things, including himself; and direct all things, including himself, to God. These objectives—and the ultimate goal—are to be attained in three ways: by instruction and learning, by virtue and morality, and by piety. The work of Christian education, then, is to develop the pupil in knowledge and understanding, in moral insight and action, and in reverence to God and in true spiritual living. These three, Comenius taught, are the main concerns of life; all other things, however good, are subsidiary.

He did not limit Christian education to a narrow content. He held that it should not lag behind the cultural advances of the times but that it should comprehend all knowledge. True education, he maintained, is basically spiritual, yet it is necessary to prepare pupils to live on earth in relations with fellowmen. So he would include many subjects in the curriculum. However, all centered around the Bible which, he asserted, contains the beginning and end of all learning. He said that in every Christian school the Bible should rank above all other books and that every youth should be taught its truths from childhood. It was his contention that the Scriptures are equally suitable to all, that they contain truth comprehensible even to little children.

Comenius believed that what the child is taught during the first six years is the foundation for all he will learn in later life. Accordingly, he outlined an inclusive curriculum for the Mother School as a broad basis upon which to build all later learning. This included simple lessons on natural objects, knowledge of the members of the pupil's body, other information in connection with his immediate environment, training in fundamental moral habits, and the memorizing of the Lord's Prayer. During these six years, he said, the child should learn faith, virtue, wisdom, knowledge, reverence, and obedience—things that come only through teaching, not as a matter of course. Parents are the child's teachers for the first six years, and it is their duty to teach these things. He placed much stress upon obedience, saying that youth ought to learn to obey because submission of the will is the foundation of all virtues.

Comenius held that the child should have very definite ideas about

God and His ways. He said a child of six should know (1) that God is; (2) that He is everywhere present; (3) that He gives all good things to those who obey Him; (4) that He punishes the disobedient; (5) that He is to be reverentially feared and loved; and (6) He takes to Heaven those who are good and righteous.

Christian education is basically the responsibility of the child's parents, Comenius said. He said that parents do not adequately perform their duty when they teach their children how to care for their body, but neglect to instruct them in spiritual truth. He urged parents not to leave to teachers in the school and to ministers in the church the entire instruction of their children but to talk with their children about the things of God and His eternal kingdom. Only when parents were unable, incapable, or unwilling to do their Christian duty by their children were they to be turned over to others for instruction.

Comenius believed, however, that the teacher has a position of dignity and tremendous importance. He stressed the necessity of every teacher's being a model in every way so that children, who learn much by imitating, might be influenced aright. The teacher should continually pray for his pupils and be cheerful and gentle in dealing with them. The chief work of the teacher, so far as learning is concerned, is to stimulate and guide, not to dominate and to pass out knowledge. The teacher should aim to do his part in developing each pupil's potentialities for the service of God and for eternal happiness with Him in His everlasting kingdom.

To Comenius, teaching was a matter of studying and following the "method of nature." He showed how Nature does things "with certainty, ease, and thoroughness" and that teachers must realize above all else that a pupil's being always moves in the direction nature impels it to move, feeling pleasure in so doing and experiencing pain if held back. He therefore enunciated nine fundamental principles of learning and teaching from which he drew practical inferences that along with the principles may profitably be pondered by every teacher—Christian and other.

These principles are as follows:

1. Nature observes a suitable time.
2. Nature prepares the material before she begins to give it form.

3. Nature chooses a fit subject to act upon, or first submits one to a suitable treatment in order to make it fit.
4. Nature is not confused in its operations, but in its forward progress advances distinctly from one point to another.
5. In all the operations of nature, development is from within.
6. Nature, in its formative processes, begins with the universal and ends with the particular.
7. Nature makes no leaps, but proceeds step by step.
8. If nature commences anything, it does not leave off until the operation is completed.
9. Nature carefully avoids obstacles and things likely to cause hurt.

Comenius' specific ideas on method were the outcome of his views as to how man obtains knowledge. He maintained, as was said earlier, that there are three sources of knowledge—the senses, the intellect, and revelation. Pupils should be taught to use their senses. Accurate observation of facts must always come first, then these should be collected, analyzed, and arranged. Only then can explanation be given and principles established. This is the method to be followed in all fields of learning. When the method of observation is found inadequate, then reason is to be used. When observation and reason together prove inadequate, divine revelation contained in Scripture, the final criterion, must be taken as the ultimate source of knowledge.

In a special chapter of *The Great Didactic* Comenius sets forth his views on the method of teaching the child about God and Christian living. He says that piety is the gift of God given to man by the Holy Spirit. To him, piety is what one has after he has come to know thoroughly the conceptions of faith and of religion, when the heart has learned to seek God everywhere, has found Him, and is following and enjoying Him. The sources of piety, he states, are three: the Bible, which is the Word of God; the world, which is God's handiwork; and man's self, which is inspired by God. Piety is drawn from these sources by meditation, prayer, and examination.

Comenius puts special stress on the Bible in training for piety. Anything not found in the Scriptures is to be avoided; teachers can speak where the Scriptures speak but must be silent where the Scriptures do not speak. Information concerning the Scriptures is to be obtained firsthand. Faith is to be founded upon what God says, not upon man's wisdom, and the Bible is to be all in all to man. Training in piety is to be started as soon as children begin to talk and use their eyes and feet, for it is early in life that best and most lasting impressions are made. Training is to be intensified as the child grows, with parents watchful lest anything minimizing piety reach the eyes and ears of their children.

To Comenius children were potentialities. He was a careful student of child nature. He saw children as impressionable, pliable, active, growing beings who are great imitators. He stressed the necessity of parents and teachers being good examples, saying that, if they always were, the need for teaching in words would be less, as also would be the need for punishment. However, he recognized that children have limitations which require the giving of timely and prudent instruction beyond accompanying example. He also thought of each pupil as a unit of spirit, soul, and body to which Christian education must minister physically as well as spiritually and mentally. Because children are active they must have time for play and physical exercise; since it is their nature to play, they must have opportunity to do so. He laid much stress upon the importance of play.

If there be a weakness in the work of Comenius as a Christian educator, it probably lay in overemphasis on education according to the "method of nature." He might be thought of as holding that, since God was the Creator of nature, one who followed nature would be led back to God. It might seem that he thought of the child as an unfolding plant which, when given the nurture of a plant, would arrive at the goal of Christian education—"eternal happiness with God." This would mean the substitution of the power of education for the regenerating work of God in the human heart.

Sin is an alien factor in the life of man, making for a corrupt nature that needs more than education. The only nature that can really be followed in true Christian education is a new nature implanted in man by the regenerating power of God through faith in a crucified Redeemer. It is likely that Comenius, writing as an educator, took the need of regeneration for granted as he would not have done had he been writing as a theologian. From what he said on the subject of Christian experience, it can hardly be concluded that he would have denied the necessity of the new birth, a factor so essential to education that is truly Christian.

German Pietism and Christian Education

The latter part of the seventeenth century and the first half of the eighteenth saw the beginnings of modern general education. Men had found humanism insufficient, and they were weary of the deadening effects of dogmatic theology. So they were turning more and more to nature, with the result that education was becoming naturalistic in its outlook and tendencies. Into this state of change was introduced about the middle of the seventeenth century an element which has not received much attention in the history of education. This was Pietism, a devout religious movement which originated in western Germany and which exerted immeasurable influence on German life, literature, philosophy, and education. It also put into Christian education an emphasis of far-reaching effect.

Essentially, Pietism was a protest against changes that had been made in connection with the Lutheran Church. The Thirty Years' War had wrought political, economic, and spiritual conditions affecting the Church in many ways. The Lutheran Church was ruled from without by civil authorities. Within it there were a number of theologians, each with his own official clergy, who were as autocratic as the papacy had been. These theologians were at odds with one another; the result was an immense amount of quibbling on questions of doctrine. In the midst of the struggle over doctrine, a religious formalism had developed. The clergy were not unmindful of their functions, but they had become enamored with the idea that if doctrine were sound everything else would be all right. For Luther's emphasis on faith they had substituted intellectual reasoning, holding that if knowledge were properly imparted the will would be directed aright as a natural consequence. Instead of placing the Bible above dogma as Luther had done, they reversed the order, with the result that the church neglected the Bible in home and in school. Christian living and the practicing of Christian virtues were at a low ebb because pastors did not teach them.

In reality, Pietism was but another instance of man's turning to

God in his endless search for knowledge of truth. Persistently, from Eve's time throughout all history, men have sought this knowledge in the dry cisterns of human efforts to understand. Not finding in these what they long for, they come for a time to the Fountain of living waters. Then, led astray once more by a cunning enemy whose avowed purpose is to keep men from drinking at this Fountain, they are induced to go back to continue in human ways their unavailing search.

Pietism was a reaction of the spirit against the letter, a relegating of doctrine to a minor place and the exalting of the pure, simple teaching of the Bible. It stood for a return to the Bible as a whole, with freedom from creed. It emphasized an acute realization of one's sinfulness, a personal spiritual experience, and a holy life. It stressed self-examination, honest study of the Bible, and complete reliance upon God. It made much of the work of the Holy Spirit in illuminating the Bible, giving the knowledge of Christ, producing a sense of forgiveness and peace, and effecting in the Christian good works, love, and sacrifice for others. It required the separation of the individual from the world and his avoidance of carnal pleasures. Pietism opposed dancing, attendance at the theater, ostentation in dress, joking, and the reading of literature appealing to the flesh. Pietists combined Luther's emphasis on the study of the Scriptures, prayer, and faith with the Calvinistic stress on puritanical conduct. However, they went further than either of these in insistence upon the experience of the new birth and the work of the Holy Spirit in the life of the Christian.

It seems that Pietists owed their evangelical outlook to the writings of John Bunyan and Richard Baxter. They taught no new doctrines but simply sought to express orthodox teachings in genuine spiritual living in everyday practice. Pietism did not advocate separation, but remained within the bounds of existing Protestant Christianity. It was in harmony with Luther's original evangelical views and it willingly cooperated with the Church of England, the Reformed Church, and the persecuted sects. Some of the latter were revived through contact with Pietism.

As has been seen earlier, there were forerunners of the spirit of Pietism long before it existed as a system. The history of Pietism proper is mostly bound up in the life, work, and influence of Philip Spener (1635-1705) and August Hermann Francke (1663-

1727). Within the span of their lives the movement arose, grew, and began to decline, though its influence extended far beyond their times.

In 1670 Spener, a pastor in Frankfurt, instituted his famous *Collegia Pietatis,* first in his home, later in the church. His object was to make theological knowledge popular and practical through promoting Christian fellowship and Bible study. At his meetings people were permitted to engage in prayer, to ask questions, and to participate in discussion. By these means, by the instruction he gave, and especially by the spirit in which he gave it, Spener hoped to correct their spiritual and moral faults, to comfort them, and to stimulate them to godly living. From these efforts, supported by Spener's friends and pupils, Pietism developed, placing emphasis upon spiritual living rather than upon learning, and making kindness and love of more value than adherence to mere doctrines or systems of theology.

Five years after he began this school, Spener published a work in which he advocated the following: earnest Bible study; a lay share in church government as the logical consequence of the Christian doctrine of the priesthood of believers; that Christian knowledge is practical, not merely doctrinal and theoretical, and is shown in charity, forgiveness, and sincere devotion; that, instead of taking unbelievers to task for wrongdoing, they should be given sympathetic treatment to win them, if possible, to truth; that theological training should be reorganized, with emphasis on devotion rather than doctrine; and that preaching should be more practical and less rhetorical.

Later, while a preacher at the court of Dresden, Spener occupied himself much with the Christian education of youth. By his teaching and example he revived catechetical instruction, which had gone out of practice. More important even than this, he made his teaching spiritual, emphasizing the vital truth that in the work of instruction the spirit is to be regarded as far better than the letter. In 1694 the University of Halle was founded, and Spener had a voice in nominating its professors.

Spener was severely critical of the education of his time. He maintained that too much attention was given to secular knowledge and entirely too little to cultivation of a vital Christian faith and the fruits thereof, that teachers should be concerned about the godly living of their pupils as well as the acquisition of knowledge. He thought that too much time was given to the learning of Latin and too little to the study of Hebrew and Greek, the languages of the Scriptures, and that too little attention was placed on the Scriptures and too much on memorizing church doctrine. Moreover, he deemed it wrong to have the study of the pagan ethics of Aristotle take the place of the teaching of practical Christian morals.

From the standpoint of education, however, August Hermann Francke was the most important of the Pietists. Of him Eby says, "He was the noblest example of the practical Christian educator of Germany. It may well be doubted if there ever has been in the history of education a more efficient representative of the Christian spirit."[1] Through him Pietism exerted a powerful influence on education. He, along with Spener, held that the chief faults of the age were due to lack of Christian training in home and school and to poor teaching. Both saw the evil of stressing memory instead of intelligent understanding and of placing emphasis upon verbalism to the neglect of the real and the practical.

Francke, who was very intelligent, received a good education under private instruction prior to his entering the advanced class of the gymnasium at Gotha. Here he came under the influence of the principles taught by Ratich and Comenius. At the age of fourteen he entered the University of Erfurt. Here and at the universities of Kiel and Leipzig he studied philosophy, theology, general and church history, physics and natural history, rhetoric and the languages, especially Greek and Hebrew. After he took his degree and had become an instructor at Leipzig, he had an experience which transformed him in heart and life. From his early days he had been pious in spirit, but he was also self-centered and ambitious by nature and troubled by doubts of the truth of the Bible and the Christian religion. While praying for light on an evangelical text on which he was obliged to preach, he experienced a sudden conversion. Shortly thereafter he became connected with Spener, who had already brought the evangelical spirit into the religion of Germany.

Francke was driven from the University of Leipzig and from a

[1]Frederick Eby, *The Development of Modern Education* (Englewood Cliffs, N.J.: Prentice-Hall, Inc., 1952), p. 247.

pastorate at Erfurt by enemies of Pietism. Through Spener's influence he was appointed to the chair of Greek and Hebrew at the newly founded University of Halle; later he was transferred to the professorship of theology, his favorite subject. As pastor of a church in a suburban village, he catechized children and was shocked at their ignorance, poverty, and immorality. So he assumed the task of raising them from their degradation by means of Christian education. The outcome of his efforts in their behalf was the establishment of many orphanages and schools and the extending of an influence throughout Germany which had definite effect on education in Germany, America, and elsewhere.

The motivation of Francke originated in his conversion, which put into his being a consuming love for God and for fellowmen. From the time he was converted, his absorbing purpose was to show the power of true Christian education in the home and in the school. He claimed that he got his educational ideas from God, not from reading the views of other men. He held strongly that the supreme aim of life is to honor God and that all conduct and thought are to be directed to this end. Far from denying the evil tendencies of the human heart, he fully recognized them and stressed the necessity for guarding against them and controlling them. He equally acknowledged the presence in human nature of good tendencies and maintained that they should be called out, fostered, trained, and wisely directed.

In his *Brief and Simple Treatise on Christian Education* he says that godliness is the chief end of education. Thus he did not make knowledge as such the end; it was for him instead the means whereby the individual might be brought to godliness through faith and be made wise unto salvation. He said, "One dram of living faith is more to be valued than one hundred weight of mere historic knowledge; and one drop of true love, than a whole sea of learning in all mysteries."[2] For Francke as for other Pietists, learning that did not have love for God and man as its foundation was worthless.

Thus Francke and the Pietists in general sought to make knowledge an adjunct to godliness; they felt that learning must always be subordinate to practical Christian living, that knowledge apart from love to God and man is worse than useless. They believed that

[2]Henry Barnard, *German Teachers and Educators* (Hartford: Brown & Gross, 1876), p. 413.

true knowledge is of God and attained by man through divine illumination. They deemed study to be necessary but that discernment of the truth is a matter of inspiration. Spener insisted that the Christian student prays as earnestly for divine illumination as if he had no need to study, then studies as zealously as if it were necessary for him to learn everything by his own efforts. Pietists realized that intellectual knowledge of Christian truth does not produce Christian living, that godliness is a matter of the heart instead of the head. And it was Francke who applied these principles to education.

He advocated no narrow, impractical education but an enlarged, enlightened work conducted on Christian principles. Physical, mental, and spiritual development were all regarded as necessary; in the courses of study he outlined he emphasized the spiritual, the useful, and the realistic. Everything was to contribute to the honor of God and the good of fellowmen. The intellect and the reason received much care and attention; the purpose was to train them in view of the occupation the pupil would enter in afterlife. The spiritual was central in every course of study; secular subjects were secondary, deemed to have value only as they could contribute to spiritual life. Every means was employed to keep children from developing evil tendencies and to nurture good ones.

Francke held that the essentials for training in spiritual living are good example and a vital personal acquaintance with the living Christ. In his view, the means of Christian education were the example of godly living, avoidance of evil, the catechism, prayer, and the daily study of the Bible for light and direction in everyday living. In elementary instruction, four of seven hours each day were devoted to Bible study, catechism, prayer, and spiritual practices, and reading and writing were based upon the Bible. In secondary instruction, the spiritual was the chief study; Greek and Hebrew were taught mainly for the sake of exegesis, compositions were written on Bible subjects, and French was learned through the study of the New Testament in that language. Francke was not content with mere formal inculcation of Christian teachings; he appealed directly to experience, seeking to make spirituality a reality, a genuine personal experience of each pupil.

Good teaching was strongly emphasized by Francke. Teachers were directed to study each pupil as an individual and to train each to observe, concentrate, reason, and think for himself. He stressed memory work, but "children were not permitted to prattle words without understanding them." Early in his educational career, he started a group which developed into the *Teacher's Seminar* for the training of common school teachers and the *Select Seminar* for the training of teachers in secondary schools.

Francke's own experience of conversion had so gripped his life as to awaken in him an eager desire to grasp every possible opportunity to help needy people, especially poor and ignorant children. He went without food to provide funds for instructing neglected, unprincipled children; he established schools for needy children; he employed university students to teach in these schools; he provided free tables for feeding needy students and poor children; he developed training classes for teachers and thus initiated teacher training in Germany; he set up the Canstein Bible Institute, which printed and sold tracts, sermons, and copies of the Scriptures; he established an apothecary shop to furnish medicines free to needy people. His achievements were so enormous that at the time of his death, he left as a monument hundreds of institutions to advance the cause of Christian education.

Francke's influence was tremendous and extensive. The Prussian elementary school system was established according to the principles he advocated. Through Hecker, one of his pupils, he became the father of the Realschule, which was to have an outstanding place in German education. Numerous orphanages on the model of his institutions were established throughout Germany. Men trained in his schools were eagerly sought as pastors, teachers, school supervisors, orphanage workers, and as missionaries. Francke's influence extended to lands other than Germany. The king of Denmark, interested in missionary work in East India, called upon Francke for missionaries among his students. He was a corresponding member of the English Society for the Propagation of Christian Knowledge and of the Society for the Propagation of the Gospel.

Through his followers, who came to America in considerable number, he exerted direct effect on education in Georgia and Pennsylvania. Among the various sects which migrated to America in the early part of the eighteenth century for the purpose of obtaining religious liberty were small colonies of Salzburgers and Moravians who settled in Georgia. Evangelical in faith, these had pastors and other leaders who had been trained in Francke's institutions. These colonists founded orphanages and schools which had considerable influence. Moravians and bodies of Lutherans settled in Pennsylvania, where they established churches, orphanages, and schools modeled on those of Francke. Among the settlers in Pennsylvania were some who had served as instructors and supervisors in his schools; the most prominent of these were Count Zinzendorf, Henry Melchior Muhlenberg, and John Christopher Kunze.

Count Zinzendorf (1700-1760), a Saxon nobleman, lived in Francke's home while a student. A man of deeply spiritual nature, he adopted both the Christian convictions and the educational principles of Francke. He set up on his estate a religious community of Moravian Brethren. Through him and his devoted followers, the message of the Gospel has been carried to almost every part of the world and has deeply influenced the thinking of churchmen in various lands. Following the example of Francke, Count Zinzendorf established a number of orphanages and schools in Saxony.

His most important work, however, was the founding of Moravian colonies and schools in Pennsylvania, all of which show the influence of Francke. Colonies were begun in Bethlehem, Nazareth, Lititz, and elsewhere. Moravian schools were not merely places of instruction but institutions where godly living was emphasized. In Europe, Count Zinzendorf had organized small classes for purposes of instruction, testimony, and fellowship. Such groups were made up of children and the unlearned and met twice a week under a good instructor. These classes spread throughout Europe and became forerunners of the modern Sunday school. The Moravians in America, as elsewhere, were zealous in educating the young, and they spared no pains in the spiritual training of their children. Wherever a Moravian group existed, certain of its members were appointed overseers of the young. These overseers were to visit the children in their homes, to take special interest in them, and to win them for Christ. The Moravians extended to the schools they founded this same care for the spiritual welfare of children.

Through followers of Francke, especially Henry Melchior Muhlenberg, a system of schools was organized among the Lutherans in Pennsylvania. In accord with the practice in Germany, Muhlenberg, who was in charge of the Lutheran churches in the vicinity of Philadelphia, led each congregation to establish a parish school in connection with the church. Thus he created a uniform system of parochial schools, employing teachers, encouraging the people to support them, visiting the schools, and supervising their work. Though the work was encouraged by various organizations in America and England and had the cooperation of the churches, it did not flourish long due to opposition on the part of smaller denominations and to the financial problems involved in carrying it on.

One of a number of leaders from Francke's schools who assisted Muhlenberg was John Christopher Kunze. As a pastor in Philadelphia, he founded a secondary school for the purpose of giving better training to future pastors and teachers. He served on the faculty of the University of Pennsylvania and later, as a pastor in New York City, on the staff of Columbia College. Into both of these institutions he introduced the German language, literature, and philosophy.

Unfortunately, the spread of the evangelical faith of the Pietists was arrested by the rise of Rationalism and the development of Deism. The direct influence of Pietism ceased by the middle of the eighteenth century, though the legacy it left has been inherited by many later forms of evangelical activity. Pietism itself, though originally a protest against bondage to dogma and spiritual lifelessness, lost in later years much of its vital power and deteriorated into a formalism in religious life and thought. Later Pietism transformed insignificant daily deeds into acts of spiritual devotion and grew artificial and insincere. Its effect on education then became merely formal with the result that its hold on real living was lost.

But while Pietism lasted, it exerted highly important direct effects on life and education. Pietism showed afresh the reality of spiritual experience; it revealed the value of practical Bible study for Christian living; it gave birth to a powerful new interest in philanthropy and missionary work; it led to a new emphasis upon Christian education, making it a realistic training for practical life; and it directed attention to the need of all children for such education. Its indirect influence was to awaken men to a truer conception of God's revelation and to a better idea concerning the form of worship. In Christian education it served to emphasize the fact that God should be at the center of all instruction.

Readings

BENSON, CLARENCE H. *A Popular History of Christian Education.* Chicago: Moody Press, 1943.

BUTTS, R. FREEMAN. *A Cultural History of Western Education.* New York: McGraw-Hill Book Company, 1955.

CAIRNS, EARLE E., "A Blueprint for Christian Higher Education." Faculty Bulletin of Wheaton College, Wheaton, Illinois (unpublished).

COOKE, ROBERT L. *Philosophy, Education and Certainty.* Grand Rapids: Zondervan Publishing House, 1940.

EBY, FREDERICK. *The Development of Modern Education.* New York: Prentice-Hall, Inc., 1952.

GRAVES, FRANK PIERREPONT. *Great Educators of Three Centuries.* New York: The Macmillan Company, 1912.

HASTINGS, JAMES (ed.). *Encyclopaedia of Religion and Ethics.* New York: Charles Scribner's Sons, 1955-1958.
Articles on:
"Jesuits," Herbert Thurston, VII, 500-505.
"Pietism," E. S. Waterhouse, X, 6-9.

JANTZEN, ARNOLD ALEXANDER. "The Reliability of John Amos Comenius as a Christian Educator." Unpublished Master's thesis, Wheaton College, Wheaton, Illinois, 1947.

KIK, JACOB MARCELLUS. *Ecumenism and the Evangelical.* Philadelphia: The Presbyterian and Reformed Publishing Company, 1958.

LOWE, ISABEL RAMOTH. "John Amos Comenius as a Religious Educator." Unpublished Master's thesis, Wheaton College, Wheaton, Illinois.

MONROE, PAUL (ed.). *A Cyclopedia of Education.* 5 vols. New York: The Macmillan Company, 1911-1913.
Articles on:
"Idealism and Realism in Education," III, 373-375.
"Calvinists and Education," I, 491-499.
"Comenius, John Amos," II, 135-141.
"Francke, August Hermann," II, 684-685.

———*A Textbook in the History of Education.* New York: The Macmillan Company, 1916 (reissue, 1948).

MULHERN, JAMES. *A History of Education.* New York: The Ronald Press, 1946.

MURCH, JAMES DEFOREST. *Christian Education and the Local Church.* Cincinnati: Standard Publishing Company, 1943.

PRAY, L. G. *History of Sunday Schools and of Religious Education.*

RENWICK, ALEXANDER M. *The Story of the Church.* Grand Rapids: Wm. B. Eerdmans Publishing Company, 1958.

VAN DUSEN, HENRY PITNEY. *God in Education.* New York: Charles Scribner's Sons, 1951.

Nassau Hall at Princeton was the largest academic building in the American colonies when it was completed in 1756. Designed by Robert Smith, architect of Independence Hall in Philadelphia, it was a severely plain stone edifice 176 feet long and 54 feet deep. Here in 1783 George Washington received the formal thanks of the United States Congress for his conduct of the Revolutionary War.

(From an engraving by Amos Doolittle)

7

Early Christian Education in America

THE HISTORY of Christian education in colonial America is the history of the development of general education. The two were inseparably united because the first settlers were mostly of the Protestant faith and a large percentage of them held the firm conviction that the Gospel was the means to personal salvation. Logically, this required teaching each child to read, else he could not become acquainted with the Scriptures to gain the knowledge necessary for salvation and the living of the Christian life. Not being allowed to worship and to rear their children as they wished in their homelands, many Christian congregations left Europe and came to settle in America. Here they built their social, political and ecclesiastical institutions on the firm foundation of a general education that was fundamentally Christian.

This was especially true of the Puritans, Calvinistic dissenters from the Church of England. They settled the New England colonies and, more than any other people, set the course of the future in educational development. But there were others whose influence on American education was Christian. The Huguenots, to escape persecution in France, fled to America and settled in the Carolinas; the Calvinistic Dutch and the Walloons settled in and about New Amsterdam; the Scotch and the Scotch-Irish Presbyterians came first to New Jersey and later spread along the back country of most of the colonies; the English Quakers and a few English Baptists and Methodists settled in eastern Pennsylvania; the Swedish Lutherans took up their abode along the Delaware; and the German Lutherans, the Moravians, the Mennonites, the Dunkers, and the Reformed

Church Germans came in large numbers to the mountain valleys of Pennsylvania. Adherents of the Church of England also settled in Virginia and other southern colonies and later in New York and New Jersey. While Maryland was founded as a Catholic colony by a group of persecuted English Catholics, Puritans and Presbyterians were soon in the majority there.

A great many of the colonists (especially in the northern and middle colonies) came in congregations, bringing with them their ministers and leaders. Wherever such groups settled, they set up a government for the purpose of perpetuating the Christian principles for which they stood. The Bible was their supreme authority for everything, and the aim was to establish a code of civil law based upon Biblical moral codes. The church and worship were central in life; the sermon was the chief means of popular Christian education. Sermons had great effect even on political developments throughout the colonial period. At first the education of children was carried on informally in the family, where the young were taught to read and to participate in worship both in the home and in the church. Practical moral and spiritual training was also afforded through the apprentice system, with the master giving instruction. But the pioneer settlers early gave serious attention to formal education of the young for membership in the church and for the training of ministers to carry on the work of the church, establishing schools for accomplishing these ends.

Christian Education in New England

The Calvinistic Puritans of Massachusetts made prompt provision for educating their children. As soon as they settled in New England, they set up a combined civil and religious form of government on the order of that of Calvin in Geneva. Each town had its own independent government, and all were loosely bound together in a federation. The General Court, a representative body made up of the governor, the council, and two delegates from each town had authority to deal with matters pertaining to the welfare of the entire colony. Since they had come to America to obtain religious freedom, it was but natural for them to direct their attention to education as the means for perpetuating their faith once they had built their homes, assured themselves of a livelihood, erected houses of worship, and established a civil government.

Everything the Puritans did was for Christian purposes. They had come to this land by the direction of God. For the sake of His cause they had endured persecution in Europe and terrible hardships in America. In organizing their government they recognized God as supreme; the political and economic functions of their colonies were means of regulating a community for God. In 1631 they decreed that only members of churches should have political rights and privileges. To the civil authority was ascribed the right and the obligation to promote the cause of God through the churches, to preserve order in the churches, and to protect orthodox doctrine against heresies. In their homes they gave the things of God first place. Therefore, when they instituted educational activity, they did this also as unto God.

Their first efforts along educational lines were patterned on what they had known and done in England. They began in the home, as was the practice in England among those devoted to God. Parents who cared only for the bodies of their children were considered by Puritans to be neglectful of what was most important. Every home was required to maintain family religion. Every day the Bible was read and God was worshiped. No child or servant or apprentice was to be allowed to grow up without instruction in the truth of God, without being taught to reverence Him, His Word, and His day. Puritans deemed families to be the nurseries of the church and the state, maintaining that neither of these could survive the ruin of the family. Parental obligations to children were enforced by law; if, after being warned, parents did not provide instruction in the home, their children might be taken from them and placed under such masters as the civil officials thought suitable.

Instruction in the home was not limited to spiritual content; children were to be taught civil laws as well so that no child would grow up in ignorance of either Biblical truth or the civil laws he should obey. Not only did the civil government punish parents who failed to do their duty in the home but the clergy also warned of greater punishments that would be meted out to unfaithful parents on the Day of Judgment.

Puritans began to instruct their children in Bible truth at a very early age—as soon as they were able to understand anything. They believed that when the child is young he can receive little by little what is given him. Their practice for the first three years was to speak often with the child of good things, laying precept upon precept, line upon line, here a little and there a little, following the Mosaic injunction to talk of the ways of God "when thou sittest in thine house, and when thou walkest by the way, and when thou liest down, and when thou risest up."

Such natural instruction was considered satisfactory for little children. Those over three years of age were to be instructed more formally and systematically. Once a week, the head of the family taught his children from a shorter catechism or from some other work designed for instructing the young. Such books were available to all. Children were supposed to study them and to memorize answers to questions contained in them. Then parents were to test the children to determine not only how well they had memorized but also how well they understood what they had memorized. Moreover, it was emphasized that even understanding was not enough; it was necessary for parents to teach their children so effectively that they would put into practice the truths they understood.

Instruction from the catechism was only one part of the spiritual emphasis in homes. Accounts of the practice of leading Puritan fathers indicate that parents spent much time with their children to show them the ways of God, how to worship Him, and how to serve Him acceptably. Fathers prayed for their children, guided them, and encouraged them in spiritual living. Parents were also careful to set before their children a proper example, realizing that precept apart from right example counts for little in bringing children into right relation with God.

Puritan parents followed English practice not only in home instruction but also in regard to apprenticeship. To give their children practical education, parents frequently bound them out to skilled workmen for a period of years. The indenture agreement obligated masters not only to teach such young people the trade agreed upon but also to provide for their physical, moral, and spiritual welfare.

It was not long until Puritans began to establish schools in order to advance knowledge of the Scriptures among the citizens. In 1635, the people of Boston voted in a town meeting to request a schoolmaster for their children. In 1636, Harvard College was started for the preparation of ministers. The grammar school at Charlestown dates from this same year as also does the one at Ipswich. The school at Salem was begun in 1637.

Thus within a few years after America was settled a plan of education was established to serve as a bulwark of church and state. The system was typically English, providing for elementary instruction in reading and spiritual truth by parents in the home and by masters of apprentices, and later by a town schoolmaster, for secondary instruction in a grammar school to prepare boys for college and for higher education, to train them for the ministry. All schools were children of the church, established by the civil government of the towns, which was usually in partnership with or subordinate to the church. Moreover, all education was voluntary, under the assumption that interest in the things of God which had brought the people to America would be sufficient incentive to insure everything necessary by way of education and inculcation of Christian truth.

However, this incentive lost much of its appeal in the strong competition between the temporal and the eternal resulting from hard pioneer conditions. Some parents and masters failed to perform faithfully their educational and spiritual duties. Accordingly, the Puritan church sought the help of the state for assistance in seeing that these responsibilities were not shirked. The Massachusetts law of 1642 ordered the officials of each town to ascertain from time to time whether parents and masters were faithful, whether all the children were being trained properly and were being taught the principles of religion and the laws of their country. Town officials were given authority to assess fines on those who did not respond when required to give account of their educational activity on behalf of their children.

The law of 1642 governed education in the home and under the master but contained no provisions applicable to schools or the employment of schoolmasters. Results not proving satisfactory, the General Court enacted five years later the law of 1647 directing that every town having fifty householders must employ a teacher, paying him the salary the town fixed and that every town of one hundred householders must provide a grammar school to fit youth for college. The preamble of this law leaves no doubt whatever that the purpose of Puritan education was definitely Christian: "It being one chief project of that old deluder, Satan, to keep men from the knowledge of the Scriptures, as in former times by keeping them in an unknown tongue, so in these later times by persuading from the use of tongues, that so at least the true sense and meaning of the original might be clouded by false glosses of saints seeming deceivers, that learning may not be buried in the grave of our fathers in the church and commonwealth, the Lord assisting our endeavore. . . ."[1]

Connecticut followed Massachusetts in its legislation on education. In its law of 1650, it combined the spirit of the law of 1642 and stated, word for word, the law of 1647. In 1701, Yale was founded to give preparation for the ministry in Connecticut, and grammar schools were established to prepare young men for the new college. Massachusetts laws applied to Maine, New Hampshire, and Vermont, because these were then a part of Massachusetts. Of all the New England colonies, it was only in Rhode Island that Massachusetts procedures had little influence.

The first step in elementary instruction in the early days was for parents to teach their own children to read and write. Soon, however, parents began to use the Dame School which had arisen in England after the Reformation. This was a school conducted by some woman willing, for a small sum of money, to take children into her home and teach them reading, writing, and arithmetic—the three R's. After 1647, elementary instruction was given in town schools under a teacher employed for the purpose.

It was required of this teacher that he be capable of catechizing and of leading pupils in the worship of God. Religious faith was deemed more important than academic training. Before a teacher was employed, he was carefully examined as to his spiritual experience. Every teacher was required to adhere closely to the teachings of the church and to attend regularly its services. Local pastors sometimes served as school teachers, since their duty was to give spiritual instruction. When others taught, pastors frequently visited schools to examine pupils on their knowledge of the catechism and the Bible. Memorization was the method most used. Pupils were expected to memorize in detail the lessons assigned so as to be able to repeat them when called upon by the teacher. The work of the teacher was to assign lessons, to discipline pupils to get them to

[1]Quoted by James Mulhern, *A History of Education* (New York: The Ronald Press Co., 1959) , p. 390.

study, and to test their memories by calling them for recitation, sometimes in classes, sometimes one at a time.

Books were scarce, consisting mostly of those the colonists had brought from England. The Catechism, the Psalter, the New Testament, and the Bible were the only books to be found in the majority of New England homes, and these constituted the main sources of the content of instruction. The earliest book used in the schools was not a book at all but a paddle-shaped piece of wood having on the smooth side a printed sheet of paper two or three inches wide and three or four inches long over which was a covering of transparent horn. This covering gave the object its name—the *Hornbook.* The printing consisted of the alphabet in large and small letters, the Lord's Prayer, and the apostolic benediction. The *Hornbook* was used to teach children the rudiments of reading to enable them to study the catechism and the Bible.

During the colonial period the book exerting greatest influence, next to the Bible, was *The New England Primer,* which superseded the *Hornbook* as a beginner's textbook. Appearing about 1690, the *Primer* was for a century and a quarter the chief school and reading book used in all the colonies except those under the control of the Church of England. It went through many editions, being changed from time to time in details to accord with the particular views of its users. It had only eighty-eight pages three and a quarter by four and one half inches in size, but packed within was a vast amount of content of deep spiritual meaning; most of this was made up of selections from the Bible. Included were proverbs and poems calculated to impress spiritual truth upon the minds of the young, poems inciting to diligence and earnestness in learning about God and His ways, the Lord's Prayer, the Apostles' Creed, an illustrated alphabet, a rhymed alphabet, pictures of animals with a rhyme under each, an alphabet of "Lessons for Youth," rhymed admonitions, prayers for children, including grace before and after meals, "Advice to Children" written by John Rogers, a martyr of the sixteenth century, "Instructive Questions and Answers," the Shorter Westminster Catechism, "Spiritual Milk for American Babes," and a dialogue between Christ, a youth, and the devil, showing the woeful end of one who persists in sinful ways.

The New England Primer was found in every home and was sold in all bookstores. It has been estimated that its total sales were at least three million copies. It was used both in school and in church, the schoolmaster drilling children on the catechism in the schools and the people reciting it annually in the churches. Some city schools used it as late as the beginning of the nineteenth century, and rural schools used it well into that century. Cities gave it up first to use readers with secular content that gradually came into use everywhere. Compared with these new readers, *The New England Primer* seems limited in content and crude in format, but no textbook of later days had over children and adults so great influence for God and Christian education. Of this reader it has been said that "it taught millions to read, and not one to sin." It led naturally to the Psalter, the New Testament, and the Bible, which were the basis of practically all of the reading matter in colonial schools until about 1750.

While the New England elementary school performed its function of carrying on effective Christian education, the grammar school was set up to prepare young men for entering college. Grammar schools placed stress on careful study of the Bible in the original languages and the reading of the works of ancient writers. Teachers were usually college graduates and candidates for the ministry employed until they obtained churches. They were selected on the basis of moral and spiritual as well as academic qualifications. None were continued in the office of teacher who were found unsound in the faith or who did not live upright lives.

Teachers not only supervised study preparatory to college entrance but also helped to train students in Christian living. The following from the rules and regulations for the government of the grammar school at New Haven indicate the purpose and describe the instruction in these secondary schools:

> That the scholars being called together the Master shall every morning begin his work with a short prayer for a blessing on his labors and their learning. . . .
>
> That the scholars behave themselves at all times, especially in school time, with due reverence to their Master, and with sobriety and quietness among themselves, without fighting, quarreling, or calling one another or any others, bad names, or using bad words in cursing, taking the name of God in vain, or other profane, obscene, or corrupt speeches which if any do, that the Master forthwith give them due correction. . . .

> That if any of the school boys be observed to play, sleep, or behave themselves rudely, or irreverently, or be in any way disorderly at meeting on the Sabbath Day, or at any time of the public worships of God that upon information or complaint thereof to the due conviction of the offender or offenders, the Master shall give them due corrections to the degree of the offense. . . .

> That all the Latin scholars, and all other of the boys of competent age and capacity give the Master an account of one passage or sentence at least of the sermons of the foregoing Sabbath on the second day morning. And that from 1 to 3 in the afternoon of every last day of the week be improved by the Masters in catechizing of his scholars that are capable.[2]

In the grammar school Latin was given special prominence, but other cultural subjects were also taught by way of preparation for college. From this school evolved, in the middle of the eighteenth century, the American academy which maintained the Christian emphasis but added new subjects of practical value. Academies marked a transition from the Latin grammar school of colonial days to the most typical American educational institution, the public high school. This arose in the second quarter of the nineteenth century and, like the elementary school, became predominantly secular in its emphasis.

Puritan education included provision for higher as well as elementary and secondary institutions. Harvard College was founded in 1636 to advance and perpetuate learning, to supply the church with ministers and the colony with teachers and civil officers. Over its entrance was carved the inscription, *Pro Christo et Ecclesia* ("for Christ and the Church"). The rules and precepts for the government of the college show how firmly it stood for Christian education: Every student was to be instructed that the chief purpose in life is to know God reconciled in Jesus Christ. All were exhorted to engage much in secret prayer, asking God for wisdom. Also, all were commanded to read the Scriptures twice each day and to be ready to show upon questioning by tutors that they had profited from such reading. Furthermore, each was to hold God's name in reverence and to honor His truth, worship, and cause, not to associate with men who lived dissolute lives, and to be present in his tutor's room

[2]Adapted from Barnard's *American Journal of Education,* IV, 710.

at a stated hour in the morning and at another in the evening for Scripture reading and prayer.

The course of study covered three years and was designed to give broad and comprehensive training for the ministry. For sixty years Harvard was a training school for ministers, having Christian training as its basis and its chief object. All of its earlier presidents were ministers. The Bible was studied systematically for the entire three years. A year was devoted to catechetical divinity. Early leaders were aware that to direct students in the pursuit of knowledge was only a part of their work. Genuine effort was made by the professors to guide each student in his personal life. It was the purpose of president and faculty that each graduate have knowledge of the Bible, be equipped with skills for its continuing study, and be trained in habits of godly living.

The Puritans provided a second college, Yale, in Connecticut in 1701. Its purpose as expressed in the charter was to instruct young men for service in church and state. It was established by conservative theologians to be a bulwark to Christian faith. As a safeguard against impiety, the governing body of the institution consisted of eleven ministers. Many streams of missionary and evangelistic influence went out through the land from Yale. Other New England colleges of the colonial period which had the Christian aim and were brought into being largely by ministers to serve the church were Brown, founded by the Baptists in 1765, and Dartmouth, founded by the Congregational Church in 1769.

Christian Education in the Middle Colonies

The story of early education in New York, Pennsylvania, New Jersey, Delaware, and Maryland is the story of Christian education in parochial schools instead of common schools like those of New England. These middle colonies were settled by German Reformed, Dutch Reformed, Quakers, Anglicans, Presbyterians, Scotch Presbyterians, Baptists, Methodists, German Lutherans, Moravians, Mennonites, and other sects. Most of these came to America to obtain religious liberty, all were Protestant, all recognized the need of learning to read the Bible as a means to personal salvation, and all were committed to promoting education under church control and direction. However, since there were so many sects, a common school for all was out of the question. The parochial system they had known in their homelands was the one most satisfactory to them. That education in this type of school would be fundamentally Christian was only natural.

The West India Company, conducting the settlement of New Netherlands, which became New York after the English occupation, bound itself to provide settlers with preachers and schoolmasters. The Dutch government required that a pastor and a schoolmaster accompany each group of colonists coming to America. The latter had to be a member of the Reformed Church of Holland and qualified in Christian character and in education to take charge of the instruction of the young, and to conduct church services in the absence of the pastor.

The Dutch settlers established a school in connection with every church. This was in accord with the Calvinistic conception of universal education under church auspices which various synods in Holland, especially the great one of Dort, had set as the practice of the Dutch Reformed Church. The Dutch in New Netherlands, therefore, followed essentially the scheme of Christian education that had been adopted long before they came to America. This, as was seen in an earlier chapter, provided for spiritual instruction in the home by parents, in the schools by schoolmasters, and in the churches by ministers, elders, and catechists appointed for the purpose.

Agreements with schoolmasters stipulated the reading of the morning prayer from the catechism at the beginning of each morning and each afternoon session of the school. Each such session was to end with prayer while the evening session was to begin with the Lord's Prayer and to close with the singing of a psalm. The schoolmaster was required to instruct his pupils every Wednesday and Saturday in the common prayers and the questions and answers in the catechism, so that they might be better able to report them before the congregation in connection with the church service Sunday afternoon, or on Monday. Only orthodox Christians might teach in the schools. The church examined teachers, enforced adherence to the creed, and, in the case of elementary schools at least, largely determined the appointment of teachers and managed the schools, though the legal support and control of education were vested in the civil authorities.

In 1656, the colonies of New Amsterdam took steps to secure an academy or classical school to give secondary education. Provision was made in New York for higher education when King's College, now Columbia University, was founded in 1754 by the Anglican Church. The purpose of the College was thus set forth by its first president, Samuel Johnson: "The chief thing that is aimed at in this college is to teach the children to know God in Jesus Christ and to love and serve him, in all sobriety, godliness, and righteousness of life, with a perfect heart, and a willing mind."[3]

Pennsylvania developed church school education similar to that of New Netherlands. Differences were: it was carried on in connection with a number of different sects, and the civil government seldom had anything to do with it. Pennsylvania had more religious groups, and each was devoted to its own educational work. Early in the eighteenth century all Protestant groups were authorized by law to conduct schools and to receive bequests and hold land for their support. Ministers were usually the teachers in the parochial schools, and the instruction was limited to reading, writing, and the catechism.

The Pennsylvania Law of 1683 made it mandatory that all persons in charge of children—their own or others—should see that they were so instructed as to be able to read the Scriptures. The Friends provided elementary and, to some extent, secondary schools near all meeting houses in the colony for educating their youth in spiritual life and upright living under the tutelage of religiously qualified teachers. Lutheran congregations each set up a school alongside the church, as was mentioned in the preceding chapter. The work of the Moravian Church in education in Pennsylvania was also discussed in the preceding chapter. Like the Friends, they made some attempt at secondary as well as elementary education. The Mennonites included within their system of education the schools of Christopher Dock, who in 1750 produced America's first educational treatise of note. Thus parochial schools, with their Christian emphasis, exerted the greatest influence on education in the Middle Colonies.

For higher education the Presbyterians founded first the Log College in 1729 and in 1746, Princeton University, which bore much

[3]Quoted by Edwin H. Rian, *Christianity and American Education* (San Antonio, Texas: The Naylor Co., 1949), p. 189.

missionary and evangelistic fruit far and wide. In 1755 the University of Pennsylvania had its beginning—the first institution of higher learning in America without definite denominational connection. However, its ablest teachers were ministers, and most of its students entered the ministry. Moreover, it gave the senior minister of each denomination a seat on its board of trustees, and the city churches contributed regularly to its support. Rutgers College was founded in New Jersey by the Dutch Reformed Church in 1766. In all colleges of colonial days, Christian teaching was the aim. The Scriptures and theology were taught, daily worship was observed, and moral habits were inculcated with the purpose of forming Christian character.

Christian Education in the South

As the parochial education in Pennsylvania was typical of the middle colonies, so the *laissez faire* form in Virginia was representative of the education current in the southern colonies. Unlike most other colonists, those of the South came to America not for religious freedom but to gain wealth. These colonists believed in the English practice of providing no education for the poor except as apprentices and of letting the rich educate their children through private tutors, grammar schools, and colleges without assistance by church or state. The conception was that any kind of public education planned for orphans and children of the poor was philanthropic and the state was not obligated to render it support.

The apprenticeship system was an important agency of training not only in the southern but in other colonies as well, until the nineteenth century. Virginia laws of 1643, 1646, and 1672 had to do with the apprenticeship of orphans and children of the poor. They required overseers and guardians of these to train them in knowledge of Christian truth.

As early as 1618 colonists began to try to establish an educational system in Virginia. Land and money were contributed for the undertaking, but the revocation of the Virginia Company's charter in 1624 ended these early efforts. From 1634 onward, bequests and contributions were made for endowing schools in accordance with the practice these upper-class people had known in England. Parish schools thus established were regarded as agencies of the Church of England and were subject to joint control of church and civil officers. Instruction offered on the elementary level included reading, writing, and particularly the catechism. On the secondary level, it was a common practice for learned ministers to teach small groups of more advanced students in order to prepare them for college.

From the beginning Virginian colonists directed much of their educational energy toward establishing an institution of higher learning. Failing in this, they chartered during the first half century of the colony's life a number of secondary schools, endowed with bequests of land, money, slaves, horses, cows, or other property. In 1660, another unsuccessful attempt was made to found by subscription a college and a free secondary school to educate youth in the principles of piety and to provide for a supply of ministers. By the latter part of the seventeenth century the necessity for a college was more strongly felt than ever. Up to this time, wealthy citizens sent their sons to England or to Harvard for college training. However, this was too expensive for most people. Moreover, ministers were needed for the churches, and leaders were needed for service in various other callings.

Finally, in 1693, James Blair, the missionary representative of the Bishop of London, was instrumental in obtaining a charter for the College of William and Mary. Blair used in his request for funds the plea that the people needed salvation. The purpose of this second college to be founded in America, was, as stated in its charter, to provide a seminary for the training of ministers and to make possible the right training of the young that the cause of the Gospel might be advanced.

Transition from Christian to Secular Education

Christianity was the mother of education in America. The settlers gave to Christianity in the educating of their children the ascendant place it held in their lives. Whatever their nationality or sect, they established in their adopted land the forms of church and school they had known in their homelands. Though insistence on the Christian element was stronger in New England than in other colonies, the Christian purpose dominated everywhere. Elementary education, whether carried on in the common schools of New England, the parochial schools of the Middle Colonies, or the private schools of the South, was conducted in close alliance with the churches. Children were educated that they might be able to read the catechism and the Bible in order to learn the will of God.

Secondary education was provided in grammar schools and academies taught by ministers and operated under Christian auspices. These schools prepared boys for colleges existing mainly to supply learned ministers for the churches. Every student in college was to be instructed plainly that the chief end of life and study is to know God and Jesus Christ, His Son. Most American colleges were founded by churchmen to advance the cause of God as represented by their respective churches. In short, Christianity played in early American education the role it had played from the beginning of the Christian church. Always the church had been prevailingly the originator and the sponsor of education; always it had recognized at least in theory that God is the source of truth and therefore to be kept at the center of the educational process.

In colonial days children were kept in a Christian atmosphere weekdays and Sundays under the oversight of masters, pastors, and elders charged with the duty of instilling the doctrines and practices of the church they served. Schoolmasters were chosen in the light of Christian character and were required to instruct and lead children to live Christian lives, suiting example to instruction. They were to teach pupils to read the Bible and other good books and to give them thorough instruction in the catechism. It was the duty of the schoolmaster to pray with and for his pupils morning and evening. Also he was to see that they attended church on Sundays, both morning and afternoon, and on other days of worship. He was to show them how to behave during the service and afterward to examine them as to what they had heard and learned. Schoolmasters were to confer frequently with the minister about the manner in which the work of the school was to be carried on.

In the schools the Bible was read and explained, and the catechism was taught. Luther's *Smaller Catechism* or the later pious and very personal *Heidelberg Catechism* was used among German-speaking people. European Calvinists commonly used the catechism of Calvin, but in early America the *Westminster Catechism,* recognized as the ablest of all catechisms, had first place in Calvinistic circles. The earlier Anglican Catechism, which had been publishd as a part of its official *Book of Prayer,* was basic in instruction in schools under the control of the Church of England.

Catechetical instruction had a large place in colonial education. Sunday schools did not yet exist, so catechization was the chief means for instructing people, especially children, in the things of God. The church being in control of education, these things were central. Teachers were required to drill pupils in the catechism even more thoroughly than in any other subject. Sentences from the catechism were included in writing books as examples to be copied. Pupils were required to memorize the answers to questions in the catechism. The doctrines contained in the catechism were stressed by teachers and ministers, hence children were brought under the influence of the teachings set forth therein. No other book except the Bible had a larger place in education. Catechetical instruction was much used even after the Revolution. Until the rise of Sunday schools, it was the one important means of Christian education possessed by churches. And nothing was more potent in building Christian character and grounding children in Christian truth than this form of instruction.

But the Christian emphasis in education soon gave way under the onslaughts of human reason against the truth of God. What happened in America by way of the withdrawal of Christian content from education was but part of the movement that has characterized man since the Fall—the human in opposition to the revelation of the divine will. Also, it was only part of a whole which started in the sixteenth century with the beginning of modern scientific inquiry. The rise of early scientific realism headed up in the seventeenth century in the Enlightenment with its revolt against almost everything, including Christianity. The movement of which the Enlightenment was the center resulted in a long series of intellectual speculations, ending finally in divorcing the Christian element from the intellectual and the ushering in of the modern period.

After 1650 the advance of science with its emphasis on human reason was rapid. By the middle of the seventeenth century the spirit of inquiry had extended to most of Europe. The characteristics developing from such inquiry had their origin in presuppositions and habits of thought traceable to early thinkers of the modern period, especially Descartes and Kant. The major characteristics of what is called the Modern Mind are individualism, intellectualism, modernism, "scientism," and dualism. Through the Enlightenment, which had tremendous influence in America, these played a large part in bringing about two interrelated, far-reaching effects: the separation of church and state; the taking of education from the church and secularizing it. These five forms of modern thought, separately and collectively, tend to emphasize the human and to deemphasize the acknowledgment of God and His revelation of truth.

Of the three sources from which it is possible to acquire knowledge—the senses, reason, and faith—men now were coming to believe in the insufficiency of the third and the importance of the first two. Leaders of the Enlightenment era combined emphases on reason and the senses for which Descartes and John Locke, respectively, had stood. The result of this combination was abandonment of belief in revelation in favor of dependence on sense perception and reason. The outstanding achievements in the sciences during the sixteenth and the seventeenth centuries seemed to justify the confidence thinkers now placed in the power of science. The results of the work of Copernicus, Galileo, Leibnitz, and Newton gave an assurance of certainty lacking in the uncertainty and obscure thinking of leaders in the realm of human social, political, and spiritual matters.

Since reason had accomplished so much in discovering the laws of the physical universe, could it not do as well in connection with the laws of human nature? If reason could so effectively bring to light the secrets of the macrocosm, surely it could also cope effectively with the nature of the microcosm, man. Thus developed the objective of studying man himself. Leading thinkers and students of law, political life, society, education, religion, and human relations in general set themselves to the task of discovering a science of human nature. Regarding man as merely a part of nature, nothing more than a physical being, they assumed him to be subject to the laws of nature and therefore explainable by reason.

It was assumed furthermore that a knowledge of the nature of man would become the basis of a science of society. If the laws of human society were known, then it would be possible to control society for its own good, for the knowledge of man's nature could be used to mold his life and improve his lot. In this way scientific knowledge would put an end to man's benighted condition, because progress would come through natural law. What had been done in outer nature was equally possible in the realm of the human. A science known and applied to the life of man and society would elevate human nature to its highest state of perfection. The one means for bringing about such perfection was the spread of knowledge gained by man through reason.

Exponents of these views rejected knowledge coming by revelation. They ridiculed Christianity as a superstition, maintaining that all who believed in supernatural revelation were victims of deception. They said the Bible, being full of errors, could not have been inspired, so it was entirely without basis for confidence. Miracles they held to be impossible, because they would violate natural law. Providence is contrary both to reason and to common sense. The only religion of any worth, they held, was one derived from nature, one founded upon human reason.

Formal education during the colonial period had been marked by a union of Christian and general education under the direction of church and state working together. The opposite extreme was the complete separation of all religious education and church schools from general education and state schools. The causes underlying the transition from the one to the other extreme had long been developing. The basic cause was the spread of the rationalistic and secular view of life described in the six preceding paragraphs. The infiltration into the thinking of the colonists of ideas related to this view led near the close of the period to notable waning of the original interest in spiritual matters and the definite tendency to do away with Christian instruction in the schools. By 1750 the change in Christian thinking in America had become quite marked, and even before the Revolution broke out, church control of education had begun to weaken.

Another cause was the tremendous influx of European people beginning about 1697. Freedom from family loyalties, church connections, and from the influences and restraints of the community life in the homeland resulted in their engaging in loose ways of living in a land where liberty of action was the rule. The outcome was the presence in America by the end of the first third of the eighteenth century of a large percentage of unchurched people who had little or no interest in Christian education. Closely related to this was the effect of colonial revivals with their emphasis on the equality of all men in the sight of God, an emphasis which became fundamental not only in connection with the founding of the Republic but also in relation to the setting up of a system of public education. These revivals had a great leveling effect on colonial society, influencing it markedly for democracy.

In the fourth place, rude frontier conditions tended to make men self-reliant individualists, inclined to go their own way, paying little heed to established courses of procedure. Typically, the pioneer believed in complete social equality. Moreover, he held rather firmly the idea that all men are free from dominion by anyone in matters such as religion. Other causes of declining interest in general education with church participation were the conflict between sects, preventing Christians from taking a united stand in community and state; the failure of the old church-town governments to function effectively; and the development of new economic and civic interests.

Out of these causes grew wholly new principles for the establishment of a government and a way of life, including religion and education. A basic principle was that human life can be greatly improved. A corollary to this was the principle that it is the function of government to bring about such improvement by exalting the rights of the individual and by restricting the operation of government. A third important principle was that life, liberty, and the pursuit of happiness are inalienable rights belonging to every person simply because he is a human being. And it was firmly believed that education was the indispensable means for promoting the general welfare. Moreover, it was even more firmly believed that God governs in the affairs of men and that a nation could not be founded apart from faith in Him.

To understand how church and state came to be separated in America, one must consider that subject in the light of church history. Almost from the time the church began, there have been two phases of Christianity, one stressing the outer and more formal aspect of religion, the church as an institution, and creeds and sacraments, the other laying stress upon the inner, personal character of religion, not much concerned about its institutional nature and having slight interest in creeds and sacraments. From the Reformation emerged two types of Protestantism characterized by differences such as these. In the first class were included those Protestant churches established by law in European countries where

Protestantism gained ascendancy—Lutheran, Reformed, Presbyterian, and Anglican. These churches formulated elaborate creeds or confessions of faith into which was incorporated much of the theology that had developed from the time of the beginning of Christianity.

To the second class of churches belong those groups, beginning with the Anabaptists, which have received less attention in history. In contrast to churches of the first class, these smaller, little-known bodies opposed all union between church and state and denied the right of the civil government to interfere in any way with matters of religion and conscience. In short, they did away with all in church-state relationships that had developed since the Council of Nicaea. This type of individualistic Protestantism was bound to thrive in an environment where the rights and privileges of the common man were recognized. All the great concepts of American democracy—individual rights, freedom of conscience, freedom of speech, self-government, and complete religious liberty—were espoused by these groups.

While the common people were being influenced by the groups in favor of religious freedom and the separation of church and state, many leaders in the colonies were being led in another way to acceptance of the same views. John Locke, whose writings were widely read and highly favored in eighteenth-century America, was in large measure responsible for this development of opinion. Locke clearly and convincingly argued for the separation of church and state, insisting that the church is a completely voluntary organization, one that men join of their own accord for worshiping God. He maintained that no religious body has dominion over men in matters of religion, for no authority on earth can say the doctrines of any church are the right ones. Locke agreed entirely with the dissenters in their position that religion is a personal concern and that liberty of conscience is every man's right. Leaders such as Madison and Jefferson were much influenced by Locke's writing.

Thus not only the majority of people but also many of the leaders of the Revolution had come to believe in the principles of freedom of conscience and separation of church and state. When the first settlers came to America, no Christian nation was without an established church and it was generally thought that to be safe and united, a state had to have one religion. Nine of the thirteen colonies had established churches. But by the time of the Revolu- separation of church and state were inevitable. The expressing of these two principles in the Constitution of the United States was only a matter of putting into written form a preponderating public opinion.

The Constitution makes no mention of public education, but upon the religious question the framers of the Constitution took action which had far-reaching effect on education. The First Amendment forbade Congress to make any law respecting the establishment of religion. This fundamental principle of separation of church and state guaranteed freedom of worship to all. Undoubtedly the authors of this amendment were not envisioning a nation without faith in God or a system of education for the nation's youth without recognition of His revelation of truth.

As someone has said, they were seeking to provide freedom *of* religion, not freedom *from* religion. What they wanted to rule out was sectarianism—not faith—and special advantage for any one religion—not God. Though all men did not have the same views, they were not asking that public-supported education be wholly secular, having no religious content, but that no governmental authority should give preference to any religion or any denomination. Yet the unforeseen result of this amendment was the complete secularization of public education. The amendment also brought on the scene a dual system of education—one fostered by the state, the other by the church.

The Tenth Amendment gave to the states, or the people, the powers not delegated to the nation by the Constitution. The purpose of this amendment was to safeguard the right of self-government and the liberty of the individual. As an outcome, responsibility for education was left to the states, with support and control coming from state and local government and private agencies. Congress early showed its concern for religion in connection with public education. This is evident from the content of the Northwest Ordinance of 1787, which incorporated the Northwest Territory. It reads thus: "Religion, morality and knowledge being necessary to good government and the happiness of mankind, schools and the means of education shall forever be encouraged."

The concern of Congress for religion in education was shared by the framers of the constitutions of many of the States, for they expressed in these the need for education that acknowledged God. All through our history it has been recognized that education and religion belong together. In our laws, institutions, and practices, faith in God has been expressed. But always, in view of religious differences among men, it has been considered that the principle of separation of church and state is a guarantee of our liberties. Never in the past has this principle been so construed as to make the state nonreligious or atheistic.

In harmony with this are the words of Luther Weigle, who thus sets forth the true American tradition: "Here in America we believe in the separation of church and state. It is a sound principle, but one that is much misunderstood. It means just what the phrase implies—that church and state are mutually free. It means a separation of control, so that neither church nor state will attempt to control the other. But it does not mean that the state acknowledges no God. . . . The American government favors no sect and fosters no sectarianism, but it is founded upon faith in God and it protects religion. . . . There is nothing in the status of the public school as an institution of the state, therefore, to render it godless. There is nothing in the principle of religious freedom or the separation of church and state to hinder the school's acknowledgment of the power and goodness of God. The common religious faith of the American people, as distinguished from the secular forms in which it is organized, may rightfully be assumed and find appropriate expression in the life and work of the public schools."[4]

Theoretically, then, general or public education could have been kept Christian, as it had been in colonial times. Actually, after about a century of national life, the American people established a system of public education in which the teaching of Christian truth received scant consideration. This secular development was not sudden. Even after the nation had been founded, the church continued to lend support to Christian emphasis in public education. But in the nineteenth century the radical, almost imperceptible, unpurposed secularization of education began. It came about in connection with the general recognition of the value of and the need for the enlightenment and the development of the individual citizen.

[4]American Council on Education Studies, *Religion and Public Education,* Series I, Reports of Committees and Conferences, Number 22, Vol. IX (February, 1945), 32-34.

The movement toward elimination of the Christian element from public education had many causes. One of the most basic of these and one with very far-reaching consequences was the scientific tendency. After the middle of the nineteenth century, the biological and the physical sciences took precedence over humanistic culture. As an outcome of the contributions of Charles Darwin, Herbert Spencer, and Thomas Huxley, there developed a new scientific point of view that radically affected education. Biological investigation took first place in human interest after 1860, making for change in every field of study. New theories of psychology and of education were an outcome of a different conception of the nature of mind and its place in the universe than had prevailed hitherto.

Champions of scientific evolutionalism strongly opposed humanism and idealism. Herbert Spencer (1820-1903) developed a theory of evolution that applied to mental and social as well as to physical life. Upon this he built an instrumentalist or utilitarian philosophy of education. His work *Education* was universally popular and exerted strong influence in the direction of a materialistic emphasis on life in general and on education in particular. Thomas Huxley (1825-1895) by means of addresses, lectures, sermons, publication of textbooks, and writings on education influenced education through the popularizing of scientific knowledge. His most important book was *Science and Education*. He was a strong exponent of Darwin's theory.

This theory wrought universal disturbance in all of human thinking. It led to a drive to give science a more prominent role in education—a drive that was highly successful in its results. The physical and biological sciences were given a place in schools, and laboratories were set up. Scientific experiment and observation came to be considered as the only method of reaching truth. The scientific tendency merged with the sociological since both stood for the democratization or the liberalization of education. Both agreed also in considering the function of education to be the general dissemination of knowledge. Practically, education was viewed as one form of social control. Moreover, it was interpreted as the process of the social mind and the chief means of social evolution—the means by which man can be brought to perfection. Such man-devised conceptions have no place for God and revealed truth.

Secularization was caused to no small extent by the sectarianism of the churches. Christian people did much to eliminate religion from the public school by their controversies over what should or should not be taught in the schools. Controversies of this kind were bitter. Adherents of particular faiths were more concerned that nothing objectionable to them be in public education than they were about the teaching of Christian truth. Other factors contributing to the secularizing of education have been the general secularizing of life and loss of concern about eternal values, the development of liberal theological teachings, the quite general acceptance of the pragmatic point of view in education, and the resulting confusion concerning the aims of education.

The separation of church and state in America is a political separation. Christianity is not the state religion, though its influence permeates the life of the people. The nation, from its beginning to the present, has honored and now honors the name of God in many ways. That public education should not be carried on under sectarian control is necessary. The elimination of the Bible and all other Christian content from public education is not necessary. The result of doing this has been to make defective an education that has otherwise been effective. It meant that the teaching of the truth of God had to be left to the churches to handle as they saw fit. It was at this juncture that the Sunday school came to America.

Readings

Benson, C. H. *A Popular History of Christian Education.* Chicago: Moody Press, 1943.

Brewer, Clifton Hartwell. *A History of Religious Education in the Episcopal Church to 1835.* New Haven: Yale University Press, 1924.

Brown, Arlo A. *A History of Religious Education in Recent Times.* New York: Abingdon Press, 1923.

Cooke, Robert L. *Philosophy, Education and Certainty.* Grand Rapids: Zondervan Publishing House, 1940.

Cubberley, Ellwood P. *A Brief History of Education.* New York: Houghton Mifflin Company, 1922.

———. *Readings in the History of Education.* New York: Houghton Mifflin Company, 1926.

Eby, Frederick. *The Development of Modern Education.* New York: Prentice-Hall, Inc., 1952.

GRAVES, FRANK PIERREPONT. *A Student's History of Education.* New York: The Macmillan Company, 1921.

HASTINGS, JAMES, (ed.). *Encyclopaedia of Religion and Ethics.* New York: Charles Scribner's Sons, 1955-1958.

Article on "American Education," A. F. Chamberlain, V, 174-177.

LOTZ, PHILIP HENRY. *Orientation in Religious Education.* Nashville and New York: Abingdon-Cokesbury Press, 1950.

OSBORN, RONALD E. *The Spirit of American Christianity.* New York: Harper & Brothers, 1958.

PITCHER, CALVIN SHERMAN. "Positive Aspects of Puritan Christian Education in New England." Unpublished Master's thesis, Wheaton College, 1951.

PRICE, J. M., CHAPMAN, J. H., CARPENTER, L. L., and YARBOROUGH, W. FORBES. *A Survey of Religious Education.* New York: The Ronald Press, 1959.

RENWICK, ALEXANDER M. *The Story of the Church.* Grand Rapids: Wm. B. Eerdmans Publishing Company, 1958.

RIAN, EDWIN H. *Christianity and American Education.* San Antonio, Texas: The Naylor Company, 1949.

SWEET, WILLIAM WARREN. *The American Churches.* Nashville and New York: Abingdon-Cokesbury Press, 1948.

———. *The Story of Religion in America.* New York: Harper and Brothers, 1942.

SWEETS, HENRY H. (compiler). *Source Book on Christian Education.* Louisville: Executive Committee of Christian Education of the Presbyterian Church in the U.S.A., 1942.

VAN DUSEN, HENRY PITNEY. *God in Education.* New York: Charles Scribner's Sons, 1951.

WILLIAMS, JOHN PAUL. *The New Education and Religion.* New York: Association Press, 1945.

To Robert Raikes (1735-1811) goes credit for founding the modern Sunday school movement. His first school met in Gloucester, England, in 1780.

(Courtesy of the National Sunday School Association)

8

The Sunday School—Its Early History

THE HISTORY of modern Christian education is to a great extent the history of the development of the Sunday school, for Sunday schools were the forerunners of all later activities in the field. The modern Sunday school movement was the continuation of the work of instructing others in the knowledge of revealed truth by those who recognized God as the source of truth. Basically, the Sunday school was a reaction of Protestants against the damaging effects of rationalism and secularism in education. All Protestant denominations have made Sunday schools a leading agency in their teaching ministry. As the name suggests, it is a school which functions on Sunday. It has been called the Sabbath school, the Bible school, and, to differentiate it from the vacation church school and the weekday church school, the Sunday church school. However, the term that persists is "Sunday school."

Through schools operating one hour each Sunday, churches have endeavored to provide instruction to suffice for the spiritual needs of people. Obviously, these schools do not reach all people, not even all of the young. Moreover, one hour a week, only a portion of which is devoted to instruction, is too short a time to do thorough work. And when it is recognized that inadequately trained teachers often serve under poor physical conditions, inefficient administrative arrangements, and with content not well adapted to the needs of pupils, the marvel is that so much good has been accomplished by the Sunday school. So great has been its contribution to the world that it has been called "the university of the people."

Historically, the modern Sunday school comes on the scene at the time of separation between religious education and secular education. Before its arrival, all education, religious and secular, had been in the hands of the church and was conducted almost entirely by church teachers. The church's failure to give children thorough education in Christian truth brought the Sunday school into being. It originated in various efforts of men and women earnestly concerned with giving elementary instruction neglected by the church. Thus the Sunday school was started apart from the church, and it has carried on much of its work independently of the church. In fact, church leaders were for a long time opposed to the Sunday school movement. Nevertheless it grew, extending its area of activities and improving its forces very rapidly.

When the modern Sunday school began, it stressed general education along with religious education. Through the one hundred eighty years since Sunday schools began, education in the Sunday school has been varied in nature, depending on where it was administered and by whom. Thus, some of it has been secular instead of religious, some of it religious instead of Christian, and some of it Christian in name but not in actuality. In this chapter and the two following, the history of the Sunday school will be traced, with particular heed being given, in accord with the purpose of this book, to truly Christian education.

The Sunday School Idea Prior to 1780

The ideas basic to the development of the modern Sunday school were ideas with a long history. They are almost as old as the human race, for from the earliest history of mankind, responsibility for giving religious education to the young and untaught has been recognized. At first such instruction was imparted informally in the family, with the father serving as teacher and priest of the household. But early in human history religion assumed organized form, which made impossible the transmission of its truths only in a loose, unplanned manner. After the rise of general recognition of the need of training for the work of imparting such truths effectively, religious instruction to supplement that given in the home became a matter of formal education characterized by the use of educational methods. So two age-old ideas found expression in the modern Sunday school: the duty of imparting spiritual truth and recognition of the necessity of imparting it in a school through the use of educational methods.

The origin of the Sunday school is not fixed definitely in history, but it seems to have existed in its basic characteristics before the time of Abraham. Traditions of a religious agency such as the Sunday school extend far back, long before authentic records. Though tradition is not history, tradition does have value in that it constitutes evidence of the early existence of that upon which it is founded. Hence the many traditions of the work of a school in which the truth of God was taught very early in the world's history, which are recorded in the Talmud and the Targums, give to the Sunday school the distinction of antiquity when first it appears in history. Explorations show unmistakably that well-equipped schools existed in Chaldea and Babylonia among the ancestors of Abraham. Tablets have been found giving knowledge of methods of these schools which carried on religious instruction before Abraham's time.

The Old Testament record indicates that Abraham taught those for whom he was responsible—servants as well as children (Genesis 14:14; 18:19; 22:7). The Mosaic law required all the people, old and young, to come together at certain seasons to hear the Law read and explained. The prophets, from Samuel to Elisha, promoted instruction, teaching the people God's will. When Jehoshaphat was instituting reforms in the nation, he sent educational leaders to all the cities of Judah to teach the people the Law of the Lord (II Chronicles 17:7-9). Josiah made a similar effort (II Kings 23:1-3). The most important educational event recorded in the Old Testament is the one mentioned in Nehemiah 8, telling about Ezra's national Bible school. In this, teachers trained in the law of God taught and explained its meaning in a manner similar to modern methods of school procedure.

Where the Old Testament is lacking in fullness of detail, there are other records to show that the Jews were not slack in their duty of teaching the law of God in schools as well as in homes. Philo states that the synagogues were really "houses of instruction" where Jews were thoroughly taught the knowledge of the law "from their earliest youth."[1] Josephus claims that from the days of Moses it was customary for the Jews to come together every Sabbath to hear the law and "to learn it accurately."[2] And he maintains that the young learned it so well in these weekly gatherings for Bible study that they could repeat all of it more easily than they could their own names. The Talmud and other rabbinical writings also contain many items of information bearing upon educational work.

So, from historical evidence and from incidental proofs found in the earliest records of the Talmud, it is known that there were Bible schools in connection with the synagogues at the beginning of the Christian era. And it is known also that these Bible schools were essentially like the modern Sunday school. Their main object was not to stress general education but to inculcate knowledge of Scripture. Bible study was esteemed as highly as, if not more highly than, public worship in its stricter sense. Thus, among the Jews a synagogue presupposed a Bible school just as now a Protestant church implies a Sunday school. The methods of these Bible schools were not unlike those of the Sunday school. Questions were freely asked and answered. Opinions were stated and discussed, and ideas were exchanged. Memory work had a place, but the pupil was not left to study by himself; the teacher saw to it that he gained understanding of what he memorized.

Jesus, on His human side, was apparently a product of this Jewish educational procedure, for as early as twelve years of age, He was well versed in the law. Throughout His ministry, which was one of teaching rather than preaching, He showed evidence many times of effective learning of the Scriptures. Just before He ascended to Heaven, He gave the Great Commission which, whatever else it meant, must have included the charge to organize groups for teaching the Bible, first to win men, then, to build them up in the faith. It would seem that this was the way the Great Commission was understood by the apostles and the early Christians in general, for little is said about worship and preaching in the Book of Acts and the Epistles, but much about teaching. There is the best of evidence for supposing that the basic methods practiced among the Jews, the command of Christ concerning the church's care of chil-

[1]H. C. Trumbull, *Yale Lectures on the Sunday School* (Philadelphia: John D. Wattles, 1888), p. 7.

[2]*Ibid.*

dren, and the systematic study of the Scriptures through the process of instruction typical of Sunday school teaching were kept in mind and put into practice in the apostolic church.

As the Christian church gained in power and as it spread geographically, it reached out to evangelize new peoples. For accomplishing this, it recognized officially the value of the Bible school. Thus, in the fourth century, Gregory the Illuminator founded Bible schools for the children of Armenia. By means of these that land was built up for Christianity. The sixth general council of Constantinople, in 680, promoted the establishing of schools in all country churches on the order of the Sunday school—schools in which the Bible was the primary subject of teaching and learning.

So long as the church continued this practice of teaching the Bible it thrived, but when it neglected its teaching function it declined in spiritual life. Wherever the Bible school idea was adhered to most closely as a means of instruction and training, there the light shone most brightly. This was the case with the Waldenses, the Albigenses, the Wycliffites, and the Bohemian Brethren. It was through the teaching work of these peoples that they were preserved in the midst of the very general defection of the Dark Ages.

During the Reformation era the Bible school was accorded a place of great importance. Every Reformation leader, including Luther in Germany, Calvin in France and Switzerland, Zwingli and Beza in Switzerland, Knox in Scotland, Cranmer and Ridley in England, and Ussher in Ireland, recognized the need for stressing the church school idea as the basis for the growth of the church. Insofar as this method of religious training prevailed, the results of the Reformation were preserved and transmitted, and where there was lack along this line that influence was diminished or lost entirely.

Even the Roman Catholic Church adopted the church school idea as a means of preserving its existence. Never has that church forgotten the lesson it learned in this connection. It was in consequence of this lesson that Carlo Borromeo, Archbishop of Milan, alarmed at the spread of the Reformation, gave himself largely to gathering and teaching children. The result was the establishing of a number of Sunday schools in which thousands of children were taught. Cardinal Bellarmine, Archbishop of Capua, a bit later than Borromeo's time, set an example to pastors of his diocese by going personally into the parishes and gathering about him the children for the teaching of simple catechisms. These efforts were typical of the Catholic practice of assigning importance to the imparting of instruction to children for the purpose of saving them for the church.

All the Protestant churches were in the beginning alive to the need for such instruction. The Heidelberg Catechism set forth as a requirement of the fourth commandment "that the ministry of the gospels and the schools be maintained." The General Assembly of the Church of Scotland stipulated in 1560 that the second of two public services on every Sabbath be given to worship and the catechizing of the young and ignorant. As early as 1603 the Church of England required "every parson, vicar, or curate, upon every Sunday and holiday, for half an hour and more," to instruct the youth and the unlearned of his parish "in the Ten Commandments, the Articles of the Belief, and in the Lord's Prayer" and to "diligently hear, instruct, and teach them the Catechism."[3]

The early Protestant settlers of America considered it the duty of the church and state to maintain schools in which the Bible was taught. Moreover, Puritans met on Saturday afternoons for catechetical instruction. About this time many schools met on Sunday for doctrinal instruction. There are authentic records of what may properly be called Sunday schools in many places in America and England long before 1780.

Nevertheless, for various reasons, there was a general decline in spiritual life in the seventeenth and eighteenth centuries. One cause of such decline was the perversion of instruction—the degeneration of the catechetical method into a purely mechanical process of drawing from pupils memorized rote answers to questions. This procedure eliminated interchange of thought between teacher and pupil and thus made for lack of development of the knowledge of the pupil. Along with this misuse of method, greater emphasis was placed upon proclaiming and preaching than upon the simple teaching of the truth of the Gospel. The consequence was that spiritual life suffered.

Great and godly men saw and regretted their mistakes in this respect. Bishop Joseph Hall, near the close of his life, said he

[3]*Ibid.*, p. 74.

repented much for not having given more time to catechizing and less to sermonizing. Henry More assigned to catechizing the place of first importance for effectively presenting the Gospel to men. George Herbert did likewise; he said, "At sermons and at prayers men may sleep or wander, but when one is asked a question, he must disclose what he is." John Owen asserted that "more knowledge is ordinarily diffused, especially among the young and ignorant, by one hour's catechetical exercise than by many hours' continual discourse." And Robert South, an old English preacher, declared that young minds cannot be impressed with the principles of truth through preaching but that a foundation has to be built through teaching before preaching can have effect.[4]

Into the midst of the decline in spiritual life, which was general throughout Europe and America, there came remarkable revivals near the middle of the eighteenth century. These centered much in the work of Count Zinzendorf in Germany, of Wesley and Whitefield in England, and of Whitefield and Edwards in America. These men, especially Count Zinzendorf and Wesley, recognized that no revival could be permanent in its results except as the young were systematically taught the ways of God. It was in the light of the recognition of this fact that they carried on their evangelizing and grounding of believers in the truth.

Count Zinzendorf and his fellow workers dealt directly with children, gathering numbers of them into the church and arranging for their instruction in small groups by trained teachers. Wesley likewise stressed work among children and the class instruction of converts. He declared that, unless children were taken care of, the revival of religion "will last only the age of a man." He maintained that "God begins his work in children."[5] From the beginning of his labors, Wesley insisted upon the gathering into groups or "classes" for personal training all who were won through his efforts. Thus the Wesleyan movement contained in itself important elements of the Sunday school.

However, the methods used by Wesley and Count Zinzendorf were limited to the Methodists and the Moravians. Also, their efforts were occasional, not systematically directed toward large and inclusive goals, and the training they gave their converts was mostly in the

[4]*Ibid.*, pp. 90-92.
[5]*Ibid.*, pp. 107-108.

sphere of Christian experience. The need was for a church school which could be used alike by every branch of the Christian church for the continued and systematic training of all children and adults in the truth of God's revelation to man. It was the founding of the modern Sunday school which provided the means for meeting this need.

That the idea of the Sunday school was no sudden inspiration giving rise spontaneously to a system of Bible training institutions is evident from even a cursory consideration of history. Schools of its character, with all its essential features, had been organized centuries before the modern Sunday school was founded. Through all of the history of the Christian church, more or less successful attempts had been made repeatedly to establish such an agency of Biblical instruction. From as far back as 1560 there had been such definite anticipations of the modern Sunday school as to lead to claims of its having begun in various places other than Gloucester, England.

One of the earlier experiments with a Sunday school was that of Joseph Alleine, a Puritan divine, in Bath, England. In 1660, he catechized pupils weekly in a day school, made friends with young people, invited them to his dwelling, and started a Sunday school in which he taught sixty or seventy children. During the seventeenth and eighteenth centuries, many such attempts were made in England, Ireland, Scotland, Wales, and America.

However, most of these experiments were individual and fitful. General conviction of the value of Bible teaching was lacking. For the most part, the essential features of the Sunday school did not have a place in these sporadic attempts; in nearly all of them the work was catechizing by the minister instead of Sunday school teaching. To Robert Raikes, beyond all doubt, belongs the credit for founding the modern Sunday school, and side by side with his name must be placed that of William Fox, founder of the Sunday School Society, who did more than any other man to spread knowledge of the methods used by Raikes.

The Beginning of the Modern Sunday School Movement

Robert Raikes (1735-1811) was a benevolent man to whom the

sight of pain, poverty, misery, and vice was very distressing. So active was he in developing schemes and carrying out plans for putting into practice benevolent ideas that those among whom he lived in Gloucester gave him the nickname "Bobby Wild Goose." He was a man who caught at principles slowly, but once he grasped them, he held to them tenaciously. A prosperous man, vain by nature in bearing and dress, he allowed nothing to deter him in carrying out his convictions. Neither wealth nor social position nor innate vanity kept him from contacting degraded adults or young ragamuffins if he thought he might be able to help them. Moreover, he was a steady, methodical man, willing to work patiently and silently toward an end without calling attention to what he was doing until he felt confident of the success of his efforts.

The physical, intellectual, and moral conditions of the masses in Raikes's day were deplorable. People lived in dwellings rudely put together, often with geese, chickens, and pigs. They wore coarse clothing, existed on a very poor diet, and slept on straw. In industrial cities like Gloucester conditions were especially bad. There was no system of public education. Few common people had the privilege of attending even an elementary school; it was not easy to find a poor man who could read. Ignorance and vice, dissipation and ungodliness prevailed, especially among the lower classes. The ruling class attempted to control vice and crime by means of drastic laws and severe penalties. As a result, prisons were filled with people of all types, from confirmed criminals to respectable persons who were imprisoned because they could not pay their debts.

Robert Raikes's father was a man who pitied unfortunate people and tried to relieve distress wherever he could. When he died, Robert, his only son, at the age of twenty-one became sole proprietor and editor of the *Gloucester Journal*. From the beginning of his editorship, Raikes used his newspaper as a means for helping those he found naked, starving, and rotting in jails. He begged for them, he followed them when they were deported, and he sought to impress upon the minds of his readers concern for unfortunate people whom society by neglect turned into criminals, later relieving itself, in many cases, of responsibility for them by hanging them.

Year after year, Raikes exerted himself in behalf of these unfortunate people, yet found it difficult to accomplish much for them. Over and over, he failed in his attempts to help adult criminals.

His failures set him thinking, and he reached the conclusion that the thing to do was to prevent the making of criminals. Accordingly, at the age of forty-five, after having worked for nearly a quarter of a century to eliminate vice by dealing with adults, he began what he called "a new experiment" of "botanizing in human nature."

In the streets of Gloucester were neglected and ragged children, playing, quarreling, cursing, and fighting on Sundays. During the week these children worked in factories, for there were no child labor laws. On Sundays they were free on the streets in a "slum of moral filth." Raikes knew these children, their homes, and the habits of their parents. Realizing that it was useless to appeal to the parents, he conceived the idea of applying his maxim, "vice is preventable," to work on behalf of the children. Convinced that vice was caused by idleness, which in turn was caused by ignorance, he concluded that vice could be prevented by instructing the children.

Accordingly, in 1780, he started his first Sunday school in Mrs. Meredith's kitchen in Sooty Alley, so named because chimney sweeps lived there. His pupils were from the lowest levels of society and from places of the worst reputation. Some were so unwilling to attend his school that he marched them there with logs of wood tied to their feet so that they could not get away. He paid Mrs. Meredith to instruct these wretched children. The boys were bad and the girls were worse, so she gave up the work after several months. Raikes then transferred the children to the kitchen of Mrs. King with Mrs. Mary Critchley as teacher. She seemed to be better able to handle them and for more than two years carried on the work before Raikes made public what he was doing.

The children, who ranged in age from six to fourteen, were required to come with clean hands and faces, hair combed, and with such clothing as they had, though Raikes sometimes provided better clothing and shoes. Order was maintained; Raikes himself "strapped or caned" the boys for misbehavior; the girls were disciplined in other ways. The children were kept in school from ten to twelve in the morning, then went home, returned at one o'clock, and, after a lesson, were taken to church. Following the church service, they were taught the catechism, then sent home about five o'clock, being charged to go quietly without playing in the streets. Well-behaved pupils were given rewards of Bibles, Testaments, books, games, combs, and clothing.

In time Raikes started a number of Sunday schools in the different slum areas of Gloucester. At first he used women for teachers, paying each a shilling a day. They did not do all the teaching; the more advanced pupils acted as "monitors" or teachers of the younger ones. For some time the church in general took no interest in the schools; Raikes said it was six years before the clergymen gave him any assistance. An exception seems to have been the Rev. Thomas Stock, a rector in Gloucester and a relative of Raikes by marriage. Of him Raikes says, "He went around to the schools Sunday afternoon to examine the progress made, and to enforce order and decorum among such a set of little heathen."[6]

The design of Raikes's schools was not to teach the Bible but to teach reading, writing, and religion to poor children for the purpose of bettering their lot and bringing about reform in society. From the beginning, however, the Bible was used as a text in his schools, as it was at that time in secular schools. The ultimate objective of the schools was to form character, and the Bible was considered the essential means of doing this. Raikes's movement aimed at popular religious education for the poor whom the church was neglecting, and the Bible was the main textbook. The efficacy of religious education in cleaning up the slum life of a wicked city was demonstrated by his experiment. Out of it grew also a plan for national popular education.

For three years Raikes regarded his work as an experiment. Only after he was satisfied that it had passed the experimental stage did he make it public. Prior to doing this he sought and received advice from many men. John and Charles Wesley and George Whitefield were his personal friends and counselors. When William Fox, William Wilberforce, and James Hamway visited him, he explained his plan, took them to the schools to see and hear what was being done, and sought counsel of them as he did of all whom he deemed capable of assisting him. Once he was convinced of the practicality of his attempt to bring about reform among children, he published in his newspaper on November 3, 1783, a brief notice of the success

[6]J. Henry Harris, *Robert Raikes, the Man and His Work* (Bristol: J. W. Arrowsmith, n.d.), p. 165.

achieved in improving the behavior of children who had previously been allowed to run wild on Sundays.

This account was copied by London newspapers. The *Gentleman's Magazine* also published a letter of Raikes of November 25, 1783, and a little later another report was given in a magazine edited by John Wesley. These notices brought to Raikes a number of inquiries, leading to the publication of his plans in various newspapers and in more London magazines. From many pulpits the story of his work was told and his schools praised. By these means knowledge concerning the character of his work was rapidly spread. His plan was widely adopted, because it commended itself to thoughtful and philanthropic minds in a day of mounting evangelical missionary spirit. Also the principle of voluntary instruction and management, which soon became ascendant in Raikes's own schools, adapted the Sunday school to the needs of poor communities while offering to lay individuals opportunity to serve in a manner unknown to them up to this time.

However, there was opposition to the Sunday school movement, especially on the part of churchmen. Some questioned the usefulness of Sunday schools; others condemned them as dangerous and demoralizing institutions and agents of the devil. The Archbishop of Canterbury called together the bishops to consider what should be done to stop the movement. William Pitt thought seriously of introducing into Parliament a bill for the suppression of Sunday schools. In Scotland, teaching on the Sabbath by laymen was pronounced a violation of the Fourth Commandment. Those who fostered schools among the poor were condemned and their teachers were persecuted by the church. Churchmen believed the Sunday school would make for disunity in the church. Some of the English nobility opposed the educating of people of the lower class on the grounds that they would become dissatisfied servants and demand better pay. Worldly-minded people took a stand against the Sunday school because they thought it would end their amusement.

But opposition only served to make friends for the Sunday school. It brought the new movement to the notice of people, calling attention to the need for it and the good work it was doing. Though some opposed, the new institution had the support of many influential people. Among the better classes there were many who gave it their approval. Even the queen placed on it the stamp of royal favor by sending for Robert Raikes and learning from him firsthand the story of his work and its progress.

It was given to Raikes to live to see the success of his "ragged school"; by the time of his death in 1811 Sunday schools were widely established in England, where their total attendance amounted to 400,000 pupils. Thus this man of benevolent disposition and strong purpose who had worked hard in behalf of poor and needy children developed a movement destined to become a tremendous agency for God and the cause of Christian education throughout the world.

One element contributing to the early success of this movement was the position Raikes had as the editor of a newspaper, with the opportunity this gave him to make widely known the good outcomes of his undertaking. Another element that contributed markedly to the rapid development of the movement was the active support given it by John Wesley. From the beginning of Raikes's work, Wesley was in close contact with it. While most clergymen were either openly hostile or apathetically indifferent to Sunday schools, Wesley was actively interested in them and very friendly to them. Following Zinzendorf, Wesley stressed work among children. He recognized the Sunday school as "one of the noblest instruments which has been seen in Europe for some centuries, and will increase more and more."[7] In this confidence, the founder of Methodism made the Sunday school an integral part of his great undertaking. Thus to the philanthropic aims which motivated Raikes were added those of evangelical fervor. The latter were of consequence not only in determining the nature of the Sunday school but also in helping mightily in starting it on its worldwide ministry.

A third important factor in the early success of the Sunday school movement was the work of the Sunday School Society which William Fox founded. Fox was a prosperous London merchant who believed that every person in the world should be able to read the Bible. As he journeyed about England, he found many poor people who had no Bible. When he presented them with a copy, he often discovered that they could not read it, so he proposed to friends the founding of a society to teach all children of the poor to read the Bible. The magnitude of the undertaking, at a time when only one in twenty persons could read, seemed so great that

[7]Trumbull, *op. cit.,* p. 118.

those with whom he consulted gave him little encouragement.

At this juncture Fox heard of the success of Raikes's Sunday schools. After corresponding with Raikes, he decided that the plan of using Sundays for instruction could best accomplish his own purpose. Accordingly, in 1785, he and a few influential friends founded in London the Sunday School Society for organizing, encouraging, and supporting Sunday schools throughout England. Later the society extended its work to Wales, Ireland, and the British colonies. Its method of operating was to rent rooms or buildings in communities where the poor needed instruction, to employ teachers, and to maintain schools. The society provided free Bibles, Testaments, and other books needed by pupils and had each school inspected by competent visitors.

During its life of twenty-seven years, the Sunday School Society formed or aided hundreds of Sunday schools in which thousands of pupils were taught, and gave away multiplied thousands of Bibles, Testaments, spelling books, and reading books. Its refusal to use voluntary teachers and to sell instead of give its literature to schools led to exhausted funds, long struggles, and final dissolution.

Other Sunday school societies were founded after 1785. The practice of using voluntary teachers became general, and instruction of the poorer classes continued to be the special purpose of the movement. Its introduction into the churches was slow, coming only after years of waiting. However, improvement in educational method and procedure began to be made. William Brodie Gurney, an earnest young worker, wondered why Sunday school teachers should not be gotten together to "improve the method of instruction, and stimulate others to open new schools in London."[8] Gurney and two of his friends called a meeting on July 13, 1803, and formed the London Sunday School Union. Its chief objects were "to stimulate and encourage the education and religious instruction of the young"; "to improve the methods of instruction"; "to promote the opening of new schools"; and "to furnish literature suited for Sunday schools at a cheap rate."[9]

The growth of this organization was slow but it faithfully kept in

[8]Edwin Wilbur Rice, *The Sunday-School Movement, 1780-1917, and the American Sunday-School Union, 1817-1917* (Philadelphia: The American Sunday-School Union, 1917), p. 22.

[9]*Ibid.*, p. 23.

view its chief objects. About 1805 it had four publications—a *Plan for Forming Sunday Schools,* a *Guide to Teachers,* a *Catechism in Verse,* and a *Reading Primer.* Later it issued a periodical, *The Repository* or *Teachers' Magazine,* which was of good educational quality. Through the years, in harmony with its union or interdenominational character, it issued publications for use in its affiliated schools. In London and throughout England local unions were formed as auxiliaries. Each of these was represented by a secretary and three members who, with twenty other members chosen at an annual meeting, directed the work of the Union. The formation of new schools was promoted and aid was given schools in housing and equipment. The Union also rendered service by way of developing plans for better Sunday school buildings and in loaning money or granting aid to schools for making improvements. Supplies were furnished members at special prices, and grants of publications were made when funds were available.

The London Union promoted teacher training by circulating works on principles of education, by conducting training classes, by operating a Sunday School Union College for Teachers, by issuing normal handbooks, and by carrying on correspondence classes. The Union was active in publishing lesson materials for use in Sunday schools, in promoting Bible reading, and in producing periodicals for Sunday school pupils. In 1921 the name was changed to National Sunday School Union, to accord with the enlarged ideals and purpose of the organization. Its new aim was to center upon "everything bearing upon the welfare of the young." Great Britain was divided into ten districts, each with a local council. The National Council had about sixty members, consisting of the officers, ten members from local councils, twenty chosen at the annual meeting, and twenty from the denominational bodies. Financial, publishing, and publicity departments were enlarged.

The Sunday School Movement in America

America was settled by those who believed firmly in the necessity of religion and education for welfare and happiness. And many of the early Americans were committed wholeheartedly to the principle of the freedom of the individual to worship God according to the dictates of his own conscience. In such a climate the idea of the modern Sunday school found favor. In fact, before 1780 schools were held on Sunday which were like the Sunday school. As is the case with all great spiritual movements, the idea of this one was more or less clearly existent in many minds and became concrete in a number of instances. Schools in which the chief instruction was from the Bible were conducted in widely separated places. In their essential features these schools, though they existed before Robert Raikes's day, were like those founded by him. The movement started by him served to make the form popular and led in time to its general adoption.

Though claims have been made for the earlier existence of many Sunday schools, only an occasional local church tolerated any such school for children in the church. Ministers regarded themselves as the leaders in spiritual instruction and were loath to have inexpert laymen take part in it. Only gradually did laymen come to be used as aids in imparting Bible knowledge; the practice spread slowly even after familiarity was gained with Raikes's movement. The churches were suspicious of it, partly because it had originated in England, and because Americans were on their guard against any invasion of their religious liberty. Accordingly, the new movement was at first opposed by the churches. However, individuals accepted it as a means for the moral and religious education of children of all classes. Thus it became largely a movement sponsored by laymen upon a union basis, conducted not as a part of the organized work of the local church, yet not wholly in opposition to it.

Eighteenth-century conditions in America were similar to those in England. Though checked in part by the revivals of colonial days, religion and morals had generally declined. Skepticism, infidelity, and atheism thrived, bringing disorder and wickedness of many kinds. Education, which had begun so auspiciously in the colonial period, had declined until popular education and the educator were not held in high esteem. At the close of the Revolutionary War, education was at a low ebb. Naturally, the period of war did not advance the cause of religious education, and the strong influence of atheistic or deistic France was definitely against religion. There was scarcely anything to offer the young and the unlearned except the catechism. So, despite the fact that ministers were few in number, the catechetical method prevailed. Actually, the clergy had no other means of religious education except the sermon, so, in the very nature of things, children were much neglected.

However, many thoughtful people in America realized that the best way to eliminate ignorance, to train citizens in virtue and morality, and to combat social evils was to teach the Bible. Firmly convinced of the importance of knowledge of Bible truth as a basis of sound national life, these people were fearful lest ignorance and its baleful effects, manifest in the cities of Europe, would come to prevail in the cities of America. The time for Sunday schools was ripe. It was realized that the Sunday school could do what cathechetical instruction had not done and could not do. Ignorance and evil could be removed and the life of the people improved by reaching the masses of children through Bible study.

When the Sunday school movement first took hold in England, America was wrought up over problems connected with the founding of the nation. Once the Constitution was adopted in 1787, order took the place of disorder. But there were great problems in the educational field. Even before the end of colonial days the religious control of education had begun to weaken. Forces became operative which were to result during the first half-century of national life in the passing of education more and more out of the hands of the church into the control of the state. The Sunday school offered an educational opportunity the church was losing through its weakening hold on the schools. Since the churches were not yet ready to grasp this opportunity, it was practically necessary to establish the movement on a voluntary basis. Christian philanthropists, eager to do all they could to remove ignorance and vice and to better the lot of the common people through Biblical instruction, did what the church would not do.

From 1785 to 1815 a fair number of Sunday schools based on the English model were started. The fact that the first of these was founded in Virginia is perhaps accounted for by the absence of educational opportunity for the common people in the South. In 1785, William Elliot set aside each Sunday evening as a time for instructing his own children and the servants and slaves working on his plantation. Neighbors' children were invited to attend his school also. It had for its object the preparation of pupils to read the Bible. This was read and explained, and much of it was memorized by teacher and pupils. In 1786 the second Sunday school was established in Virginia by Francis Asbury, who was much under the influence of John Wesley. The teaching of slaves was the main purpose of this school. In 1790 the Methodist Conference in Charleston, South Carolina, urged the establishment of Sunday schools for all children that could be reached, with teachers appointed by church officials. Poor attendance, however, soon led the conference to return the work to voluntary lay leadership.

While this was happening in the South, interest was spreading in the North without church sponsorship. By 1791, the Sunday instruction of needy children had begun in Philadelphia, New York, and Boston, and occasional Sunday schools were developing in the East and as far west as Pittsburgh. Persons interested in the movement soon recognized the futility of trying to advance it through a series of uncoordinated local efforts. Because there were no free public schools, children everywhere were growing up in ignorance, which led to depravity and vice. Sunday was employed for the worst of purposes: the depravation of morals and manners. Those concerned about these conditions saw the necessity for united effort in seeking to bring about the betterment of social conditions.

Accordingly, in 1790, a group of Philadelphia citizens of various faiths united in forming the "First Day or Sabbath School Society" for the purpose of instructing the young by teaching them "from the Bible" and "from such other moral and religious books as the society might, from time to time, direct."[10] Rooms were rented in different parts of the city and teachers secured to conduct schools on the plan followed in England. The real purpose of these schools was to improve the morals and the religious character of the pupils, not merely to teach reading and writing. All reading lessons were from the Bible, and primers and spelling books approved by the Society had only content from the Scriptures. This society did a great work among underprivileged children and had strong influence not only in connection with the Sunday school movement but also in promoting the idea of free public schools for the state.

For around forty years the modern Sunday school movement was promoted independently of the church as an organization. The church regarded the Sunday school as a philanthropic effort concerned with the work of improving the moral condition of ignorant and neglected classes outside the church. Many church leaders

[10]*Ibid.*, p. 45.

maintained that it was a desecration of the Lord's Day to hold a school on Sunday. And it was honestly thought by some that the Sunday school would hurt the influence of the church. A pastor in Connecticut said of a class held in his church on Sunday, "You imps of Satan, doing the devil's work, I'll have you set in the street." Many churches throughout the land would not allow a Sunday school to be conducted in their buildings. In the more enlightened communities, church officials rented church buildings to Sunday schools until it came to be realized that the movement was of value to the cause of Christ.

But more and more the laity were feeling the need for applying the Gospel the church proclaimed. The achievements of the First Day or Sabbath School Society led to the organizing of other non-denominational or union societies. In 1804, a number of women of different denominations formed a "Union Society" for the purpose of giving religious training and instruction to poor female children in Philadelphia. In 1808, persons belonging to different congregations in Philadelphia organized the Evangelical Society to promote "the knowledge of and submission to the Gospel of Jesus Christ among the poor in this city and vicinity."[11] What was done in Philadelphia, then the largest city in America, was being duplicated in other cities.

Before long the beneficial effects of the Sunday school movement became so evident that the attitude of the church grew more favorable to it. After 1810, churches began to allow Sunday schools to be held in their buildings without requiring them to pay rent. However, to avoid giving the school a sectarian basis and thereby limiting its usefulness, interdenominational or union organizations did not always accept the offer of use of church buildings. As soon as churches lent their favor to the movement, schools began to be formed under denominational supervision. There was, however, no widespread acceptance of the Sunday school on the part of the church until after the War of 1812. Then schools spread rapidly not only in the cities and the large towns but also in the small villages of nearly all the states. Over the entire nation organizations were formed outside the great centers. Sunday schools continued to be independent of the church or an appendage to it rather than a recognized part of its local work, for many in the church still

[11]*Ibid.*, p. 51. Quotation from Constitution of the Evangelical Society.

questioned the wisdom of making them an integral part of the work of the church. Hence, Sunday schools, though often held in churches, were of necessity conducted in partial or total independence of church control.

In 1816 laymen in New York, stimulated by the results of experiments in Philadelphia, formed union societies for promoting Sunday schools on the voluntary basis. Similar unions were soon formed in Boston, Hartford, New Haven, Albany, Utica, Princeton, Charleston, Columbia, and Pittsburgh. The rapid increase in the number of Sunday schools and of local unions for promoting them led to a feeling of need for closer association of workers. The desire for some central source of information about progress, methods of operation, and improvement of Sunday schools developed in various parts of the country. The idea of combining schools for common improvement and progress, which was spreading everywhere, became concrete in 1817 with the organization of the Philadelphia Sunday and Adult School Union, an association of workers from at least ten local societies.

Though founded locally, the scope of the activities of this Union was national. This fact and the recognition of the worth of the contributions made by national unions in England, Scotland, and Ireland served to make definite the idea of a union in America national in name as well as in reality. So, after seven years of formative work, at the annual meeting of the Sunday and Adult Union held on May 25, 1824, the name and the constitution of the American Sunday-School Union were unanimously approved by clerical and lay delegates from fifteen or more of the twenty-four states then existing. From the day it was thus named until and including the present this Union has been and is a most effective agency in Sunday school promotion.

The constitution of the American Sunday-School Union gave these as the purposes of the organization: "to concentrate the efforts of Sabbath-School Societies in the different sections of our country; to strengthen the hands of the friends of religious instruction on the Lord's Day; to disseminate useful information, circulate moral and religious publications in every part of the land, and to endeavor to plant a Sunday-school wherever there is a population."[12]

[12]*Ibid.*, p. 79. Quotation from Constitution of the American Sunday-School Union.

In the charter obtained in 1845 the object of the corporation was stated thus: "to establish and maintain Sunday schools, and to publish and circulate moral and religious publications."[13]

The Union has always been careful not to stress the doctrines and tenets of any particular sect or to take part in theological controversies. Its constitution provided that only laymen could be elected as members of its Board of Managers. From the beginning until the present its program has emphasized the basic doctrines held in common by evangelical Christians. It was asserted that affiliation in union required "no sacrifice of principle; no compromise of duty; no interference with the internal management of smaller associations" but did require that "all discordant elements must be banished" and that "union with Christ and union with each other form the basis of the American Sunday School Union."[14]

As Christian laymen, it was—and yet is—the belief of members of the Union that they could teach "the essential truths of our common faith, without reasonable offense to anyone touching matters of unessential importance."[15] They declared that without being disloyal to the churches to which they belonged they could "unite to teach the truth that Christ taught and as plainly as he taught it. For, be it always remembered, that if we differ respecting the true construction of some of the gracious words that proceeded out of his mouth, we say only just what he said, leaving those who read or hear to judge of his meaning. . . . In the doctrines of the supremacy of the inspired Scriptures, as the rule of faith and duty—the lost state of man by nature, and his exposure to endless punishment in a future world—his recovery only by the free, sovereign and sustaining grace of God, through the atonement and merits of a divine Redeemer, and by the influence of the Holy Spirit—the necessity of faith, repentance, and holy living, with an open confession of the Saviour before men, and the duty of complying with his ordinances of Baptism and the Lord's Supper—in these doctrines we find the essential and leading truths of the Christian system; in the reception of these doctrines we agree, and with God's help, we endeavor to teach and inculcate them on all whom we can properly reach."[16]

[13]*Ibid.*, p. 80. Quotation from Act of Incorporation, Section 2.

[14]*Ibid.*, p. 80.

[15]*Ibid.*, p. 80.

[16]*Ibid.*, p. 80.

Thus the American Sunday-School Union originated as a voluntary uniting of consecrated Christians of different religious views and creeds, cooperating for the purpose of teaching the truths of the Bible to those otherwise unreached by the Gospel. One of its general objectives has been to start Sunday schools in needy areas, in destitute sections, especially in pioneer settlements. The Union never has aimed to overlap in any way the work of the organized church. It has always taken as its primary task the teaching of the Bible, not the preaching of the Gospel. It has always sought to bring to the attention of the local church any communities not receiving a preaching ministry and to aid the church in reaching those communities. Another of its general objectives has been to promote Sunday school work in villages and in rural areas where people are so divided in religious prejudices or so irreligious that successful Bible study is possible only on the basis of the presentation of common elements of Christianity. The Union has always assumed that cities and the larger towns with their many churches should take care of their own local needs.

The Union has sought to gather and disseminate information concerning the best methods of Christian education and systematic courses of Bible lessons. It has used all possible means for instituting popular, united, and intelligent Bible study; it has published and widely circulated the Bible and wholesome Christian literature, especially in needy and neglected communities, at or below cost of production. An objective of the Union has been to render helpful and Christlike service in connection with family groups belonging to its Sunday schools. It has always held that, far from lessening the responsibility of parents for the spiritual instruction of their children, the Sunday school greatly increases their Christian responsibility. Always the Union has observed the plain rules of Christian courtesy, endeavoring to keep its promotional activity nonsectarian and interdenominational. In furtherance of this aim, it has sought to place each Sunday school it starts under the denomination best able to conduct it effectively, or under whatever denomination a majority of its pupils decide it should be placed.

For more than forty years the Union was the central agency of progress in Sunday school work in America. The devoted laymen who formed its Board of Managers, with its officers, carried to success a series of enterprises that made the Sunday school a respected institution accepted by the churches of the nation and acknowledged as a major interest by every denomination. It is beyond the power of any historian to set forth adequately the part the Union has played in promoting and maintaining the work of God through the Sunday schools of the United States.

Readings

BENSON, CLARENCE H. *A Popular History of Christian Education.* Chicago: Moody Press, 1943.

BREWER, CLIFTON HARTWELL. *A History of Religious Education in the Episcopal Church to 1835.* New Haven: Yale University Press, 1924.

BROWN, ARLO A. *A History of Religious Education in Recent Times.* New York: Abingdon Press, 1923.

BROWN, MARIANNA C. *Sunday School Movements in America.* New York: Fleming H. Revell Company, 1901.

COPE, HENRY F. *The Evolution of the Sunday School.* Boston: Pilgrim Press, 1911.

DEBLOIS, AUSTIN KENNEDY and GORHAM, DONALD R. *Christian Religious Education: Principles and Practice.* New York: Fleming H. Revell Company, 1939.

The Encyclopedia of Sunday Schools and Religious Education (JOHN T. MCFARLAND and BENJAMIN S. WINCHESTER, Editors-in-chief). New York: Thomas Nelson and Sons, 1915.

Articles on:

"Protestant Episcopal Church Sunday School Work," C. S. Lewis, pp. 828-833.

"Middle Period of Sunday School History," H. F. Cope, pp. 1025-1033.

"London Sunday School Union," W. H. Groser, pp. 1045-1048.

FERGUSSON, EDMUND M. *Historic Chapters in Christian Education in America.* New York: Fleming H. Revell Company, 1935.

HARRIS, J. HENRY. *Robert Raikes, the Man and His Work.* Bristol: J. W. Arrowsmith, n.d.

HASTINGS, JAMES (ed.). *Encyclopaedia of Religion and Ethics.* New York: Charles Scribner's Sons, 1955-1958.

Article on: "Sunday Schools," Theodore Gerald Soares, XII, 111-114.

MURCH, JAMES DEFOREST. *Christian Education and the Local Church.* Cincinnati: Standard Publishing Company, 1943.

———. *Cooperation without Compromise.* Grand Rapids: Wm. B. Eerdmans Publishing Company, 1956.

The New Schaff-Herzog Encyclopedia of Religious Knowledge. New York and London: Funk and Wagnalls Company, 1908-1914.

Article on "Sunday Schools," Edwin Wilbur Rice, XI, 151-164.

Person, Peter P. *An Introduction to Christian Education.* Grand Rapids: Baker Book House, 1958.

Price, J. M., Chapman, J. H., Carpenter, L. L., and Yarborough, W. Forbes. *A Survey of Religious Education.* New York: The Ronald Press, 1959.

Rian, Edwin H. *Christianity and American Education.* San Antonio, Texas: The Naylor Company, 1949.

Rice, Edwin W. *The Sunday-School Movement 1780-1917, and the American Sunday-School Union, 1817-1917.* Philadelphia: The American Sunday-School Union, 1917.

Trumbull, H .C. *Yale Lectures on the Sunday School.* Philadelphia: John D. Wattles, 1888.

B. F. Jacobs was one of the initiators and outstanding leaders of the international Sunday school movement during the last quarter of the nineteenth century.

(Courtesy of the National Sunday School Association)

9

The Sunday School—Its Development, Expansion, and Decline

WITH THE FOUNDING of the American Sunday-School Union, the Sunday school entered upon a new era of development and expansion. The principle of separation of church and state resulted in increasing elimination from state schools of religious teaching. Christian people were faced, therefore, with the problem of how to provide religious instruction for their children. The Sunday school was one solution. At first, the church did not want the Sunday school, particularly because of its lay leadership. However, the church was in dire need of some means for accomplishing the task the public school was relinquishing. Moreover, it was evident that the Sunday school would succeed even if opposed. Consequently, the church had every reason to adopt and use it.

Sunday schools multiplied fast from 1814 to 1824. However, these were years of experimentation when unsystematized modes of procedure were being used to some extent and when individuals to a greater extent were trying to find some sort of wholesome training for children. Trial and error experiments resulted in crude schools quite unrelated to one another, with no ordered curriculum. There was little attempt at classification of pupils, and the teaching was done by lay persons who, though pious and properly motivated, were usually untrained and inexperienced. In spite of its weaknesses, the Sunday school was making an impact on the thinking of church people.

Soon after the organization of the American Sunday-School Union, almost all the denominations took steps to extend Sunday school work within their churches. In 1825 the Baptists started an organization which developed into the American Baptist Publication Society, the name by which it has been known since 1840. The Congregationalists also formed in 1825 an organization which became in 1868 the Congregational Sabbath School and Publishing Society. In 1827 the Sunday School Union of the Methodist Episcopal Church was organized. The Lutherans organized in 1830 a society for carrying on Sunday school work. Other denominations formed similar unions and societies later. These were not rivals of the American Sunday-School Union but were formed for the purpose of promoting Sunday schools under denominational control. All of these organizations have, almost without exception, cooperated harmoniously with the American Sunday-School Union.

Their founding marked the beginning of development and progress. The era they ushered in was one of growth, of organized efficiency, and of far-spreading evangelical activity which resulted in the conquest of America for Protestantism. This period of national development, which took place largely through Union activity, was completed by 1872. Following it came a period of expansion of the Sunday school into a worldwide institution; this expansion, which occurred through the work of conventions, associations, institutes, councils, and organized denominational Sunday school activity, extended from 1872 to 1903. Then followed a period during which the modern Sunday school in America became an institution for religious education characterized by inner integration and outer efficiency.

The founding of the Religious Education Association in 1903 and the creating of the International Council of Religious Education in 1922 were events which meant much to the development of the Sunday school as an educational institution. However, the elimination of the evangelical element by these organizations was fatal to the advance of the Sunday school. Under the blight of liberalism the movement, after a century of continual advance, came to a halt about 1916. After this year there was a decline in Sunday school enrollment in American churches until evangelicals assumed responsibility for promoting Christian education centered in God.

Development Through Union Activity

The remarkable development of the Sunday school was due largely to the zeal, insight, courage, and statesmanship of the leaders of the movement. Chief among these were the managers, officers, and missionaries of the American Sunday-School Union, the central agency of Sunday school progress for more than four decades. Though opposed and resisted, these devoted laymen planned and carried out successfully a series of enterprises that made the Sunday school an effective agency of Christian education, accepted by churches of every denomination throughout the nation. In spite of bitter attacks, the Union persistently continued to promote the Sunday school cause, maintaining strongly the principle of united evangelical effort.

The Union spread rapidly through county and state auxiliaries. By the end of 1825, eighteen months after it was founded, it had nearly four hundred branches in twenty-two of the twenty-four states, nine of these being state unions. These tributary unions did much to promote the Sunday school idea, to enlist and train leaders, and to stimulate the churches to activity. All held annual conventions for consideration of Sunday school problems and for discussion of means whereby the work of schools might be improved and extended.

One of the first acts of the managers of the Union was to conduct a thorough and systematic survey of Sunday schools throughout the world. This survey brought reports from schools in every one of the states and territories of the United States, in British America, in South America, in the West Indies, and in most of the countries of Europe. The returns deeply impressed the managers with a feeling of the immensity of the task confronting those who would bring to the young that knowledge of the Bible which would keep "our population" from becoming "a turbulent mass of moral pollution." The survey also brought to attention the need of Sunday schools for the help and the cooperation of churches and their pastors, leading the managers to urge upon pastors and officers of churches the importance of sponsoring Sunday school activity.

As an outcome of this survey, the Union took action to make definite advances along the lines of:

1. Education, by providing a system of lessons, a decidedly ju-

venile literature, a complete equipment for the school, and definite information about principles and methods of teaching.

2. Organization, by promoting teachers' meetings in the local school, by forming county and state unions among schools and teachers for inspiration, counsel, and mutual improvement.
3. Extension of Sunday schools, by employing general agents and missionaries and providing a medium of communication for and between all Sunday school workers.

Previous to the forming of the Union, Sunday school lessons were very unsatisfactory. Most of them were either from the catechism or were verses from the Bible or from hymns chosen and memorized without understanding of meaning on the part of pupils. Individual pupils memorized hundreds of verses. Interest was stimulated by the giving of Scripture text cards as prizes and, when a certain number had been accumulated, a Bible or a New Testament. But in harmony with principles being enunciated by educators, practical experiments began to be made in Sunday schools along lines broader than mere memorization. Prior to 1820 many works were prepared, with questions, covering the most important portions of the Old and the New Testaments. These were different from the ordinary catechism; they were in harmony with the fundamental principle that all lessons ought to be based directly upon the Bible instead of being man-made statements of truth.

From 1820 to 1823 Sunday schools placed less stress on excessive memorizing. To get away from the stultifying procedure of memorizing without understanding, a system providing lessons of ten to twenty Bible verses to be used by all schools was developed and tried out by the New York Sunday-School Union Society. This Limited Lesson System was heartily received by workers in New York and was introduced into most of their schools. In 1825 the American Sunday-School Union issued a list of select lessons of like nature for one year, with a view to giving schools in places other than New York an opportunity to test the new system of study. This system was received with much enthusiasm wherever it was tried.

It involved the use of the same lesson text in the whole school, with the possible exception of the infant class, unable to read, and a few advanced Bible classes. In response to a general call for the "select uniform system" various revisions of the course were made, and each successive revision helped to improve the system. In 1827 a Five Year Cycle of Select Scripture Lessons was issued. This set of lessons included Judson's Questions, a series of questions prepared by Albert Judson to facilitate the study of the uniform system of lessons. The Union issued in 1828 a set of helps entitled *Select Questions,* a work developed by Judson and several other workers, with many improvements added and more attention given to the grading of instruction. Another revision and further improvement in grading followed in *Union Questions,* to aid teachers in adapting instruction to pupils. The cycle of lessons was extended from five to seven years, then to eleven years, with a twelfth year devoted to a general review of the entire Bible. The helps and *Union Questions* on the uniform lessons were repeatedly revised prior to the first National Sunday-School Convention in 1832.

Thus the Union, within a few years after it came into being, developed a system of uniform lessons for Sunday schools which possessed features similar to those of the later International Sunday-School lessons. It was a "uniform series" providing for comprehensive study of the Bible, it was intended for use in all schools everywhere, and it called forth and was accompanied by graded helps. It was much used in Canada, and the same lessons were introduced into the Sunday schools of England through reprints. So this series actually was the first international system of Bible study. The regard in which these lessons and the lesson books based on them were held is shown by the fact that their circulation ran into the millions. These uniform lessons were continued in the *Union Questions,* revised from time to time, and used in schools of different denominations as well as in undenominational, or Union, schools. They were commended as the best then known by the first and the second National Sunday-School Conventions, held in 1832 and 1833. The National Convention of 1859 requested the Union to revise and reissue these questions, considering them still adaptable for use in most Sunday schools.

About 1840 the larger denominations began to publish series of lessons for the purpose of emphasizing doctrines peculiar to each denomination. This broke up the uniformity of lessons throughout the country. There followed what was termed "the Babel Series" of Sunday school lessons. Some schools of America used the lessons prepared for schools in England from 1842 on, by the London Sunday-School Union, and some of the larger schools developed independent lessons based on this London series. The *Sunday-School Teacher* of Chicago, churches, and individuals issued series of lessons which were used simultaneously in different parts of the country. These were the connecting link between the Select Uniform Lessons of the Union and the Uniform Lesson System so generally used after 1872.

In 1800 there was very little juvenile literature. The American Sunday-School Union recognized that religious literature for the Sunday school was a necessity and at once set about the task of creating juvenile literature of a moral and religious nature and of arousing a taste and a demand for it. The managers of the Union adopted high standards with respect to the character of its literature. It was required that every production bearing the imprint of the Union contain "Gospel truth," and be "free from gross errors"; be "thoroughly biblical and evangelical"; "popular in style" while "pure in tone, serious rather than sensational; be filled with the spirit of the Word"; be graded and adapted to the developing mind of the child; and be thoroughly American in content and coloring. The literature they sought to develop was to be comprehensive in its variety, including history, biography, travel, narratives, discourses, poetry, hymns and songs, and conversations. This literature was to be made attractive with engravings. To increase the demand for it, the price at which it was sold was low, even below cost.

By 1830, the Union had published two hundred bound volumes. In 1845, it began to make libraries of one hundred bound volumes available to Sunday schools at the low price of ten dollars. This original hundred-volume library was followed by three others, all of which were used by a large number of schools. Thus the Sunday school library preceded the public library; the former was also widely and gradually established before any states ever began to encourage libraries in public schools.

The Union performed a service of tremendous value to Sunday school progress by securing the writing of many new hymns for youth and by publishing hymn books. Its first hymn book was repeatedly revised and 250,000 copies were sold before 1846. That the young might understand the meaning of hymns, the Union issued manuals of hymns and music. Also, to supply the great lack of hymns the child could understand, successive collections were published, different in type, with adaptation made in terms of the stages or steps in the development of the child's mind. The Union spared neither labor nor expense to bring music to the highest possible standard.

To promote real progress in Sunday school work, it was necessary to combat indifference through dissemination of information concerning the purpose of the school, its methods of functioning, and modes of extending it. Recognizing this need, the managers of the Union established the *American Sunday School Magazine,* a publication designed to cover the whole field of Christian education. It was for all who were interested in the cause, whether from the standpoint of the church, society, or the family. Its aim was to record the work of Sunday schools everywhere, to consider the best methods of conducting them, to discuss questions pertaining to their management, to deal with educational matters, to give suggestions for the spiritual training of children in the home, to encourage parents and Sunday school teachers through giving actual examples of how divine truth works in human lives, and to stimulate all to take part in the Christian education of the young.

Along with the publication of this monthly magazine, the Union sent out at irregular intervals a considerable variety of letters, circulars, and pamphlets to inform people about the design, importance, and activities of the Sunday school. The Union published also a small illustrated periodical for children and a third magazine for beginners. The subject of Christian education came to be of such great interest as to lead the Union to start in 1830 the publishing of a large weekly periodical, *The Sunday-School Journal and Advocate of Christian Education.* It treated every phase of Christian education and contained also explanations upon and applications of the Select Uniform Limited Lessons then in use. This magazine was published until 1859, when it was succeeded by the *Sunday School Times* and later by the *Sunday School World,* a magazine for teachers which continues to the present time as a publication of the Union.

Besides these journals, various illustrated periodicals for youth, the advanced, the intermediate, and the primary lesson papers, and a *Scholar's Companion,* all printed by the Union, were forerunners of the quarterlies which soon became universally popular. The Union also issued a handbook on the lessons for pupils. The Union's aids on Bible study were so highly appreciated that they had an immense circulation. In addition to these ordinary helps for Bible study, the Union added Bible dictionaries, books on Biblical antiquities, Bible geography, Bible and church history, commentaries, and other treatises on Biblical interpretation, written by leading scholars of the day. These publications, besides giving the Sunday school movement marked impetus, were productive of wonderful spiritual results.

While the Union was thus serving the cause of the Sunday school and Christian education so effectively through the printed page, it was also carrying on a campaign of education and organization that meant much to the cause. Union leaders sent out able instructors and lecturers to introduce better principles and methods of instruction and to inspire deeper interest in the work of the Sunday school. Such activity stimulated enthusiasm for Bible study and aroused zealous endeavor in Christian education.

On the organization side, the Union sent out agents to establish Sunday schools in towns and villages where there were no Sunday schools and to organize the Sunday school forces. These agents formed county and state unions among schools and teachers for inspiration, counsel, and mutual improvement; they collected funds for promoting the general cause; they distributed circulars and pamphlets; they gave addresses; they did everything they could to provide information and to stimulate activity in every phase of Sunday school work. Always, they stressed the feasibility and the advantage of cooperation and the grouping together of people of different denominations for the common end of teaching the fundamental truths of Christianity.

From the time it began, the American Sunday-School Union recognized the importance of training teachers. At its very beginning it started *The American Sunday-School Magazine* to acquaint teachers with ways of improving their teaching and to give them information that would make them more efficient. Two years after its beginning, it endorsed the plan of its New York auxiliary to establish a school for Sunday school teachers. When institutes for public school teachers became popular around 1840, leaders in the Union were quick to start Sunday school institutes as a means for improving teachers in its schools. Many such institutes were held. In them special attention was given to consideration of the development of the mind of the child and ways of adapting instruction to the stages of mental growth. The institute plan of training teachers so grew in extent and importance that the Union, in 1871, appointed a Normal Secretary to direct the training of teachers for Sunday schools. Institutes continued for many years to be most useful in promoting knowledge of best methods of reaching child and adult minds with the truths of the Gospel.

One object of the American Sunday-School Union was "to endeavor to plant a Sunday school wherever there is a population." Along with their effort to secure cooperation of all interested in Christian instruction in all parts of the country and their general plan to give information through publication activity, the managers developed and carried out plans for extending the Sunday school. They engaged in an active campaign to enlist and commission Sunday school missionaries for service in every part of the growing nation. This nonsectarian work was continued through the years and is being carried on at the present time. It is impossible to estimate the value and the influence of the contribution made by hundreds of men and women who have served as missionaries of the American Sunday-School Union. Thousands of churches originated from their work and many more were strengthened and enriched by it. High tribute is due to achievements of these humble servants of God who, in decade after decade, have labored to bring the truth of God to the otherwise unreached throughout rural America.

The Sunday and Adult School Union employed the first missionary in 1820. The growing needs of the work led, in 1824, to the commissioning by the American Sunday-School Union of six paid missionaries "to establish new Sunday schools; visit old ones; revive, animate and encourage such as were languishing; organize auxiliary unions; explain the objects of the Society and . . . extend its usefulness."[1] In a short time growth of the work led the managers to form a Committee on Missions to supervise missionary activity. At once, thirty-five missionaries were employed.

On the basis of information gathered through a survey of the western part of the country, the Union at its annual meeting in 1830 launched a most ambitious enterprise to expand its missionary

[1]Edwin Wilbur Rice, *The Sunday-School Movement, 1780-1917, and the American Sunday-School-Union 1817-1917* (Philadelphia: American Sunday-School Union Press, 1917), p. 93.

work. The decision was that the Union would "within two years, establish a Sunday school in every destitute place where it is practical throughout the valley of the Mississippi."[2] This area of about 300,000 square miles is now occupied by twenty states; it had at that time an estimated population of 4,000,000, of which 400,000 were children and youth. The survey had shown that there were in the whole area approximately 1,500 Sunday schools supported by various sectarian agencies.

Union workers divided the area into districts and assigned missionaries to fields within these districts. The outcome of the work done by the Union was the establishment of Sunday schools in nearly five thousand small communities and the conversion to Christ of fifty thousand or more people. A library, costing about ten dollars, was furnished each Sunday school that raised five dollars for this purpose, with the result that many thousands of books were put into circulation. Thus, in addition to the contribution made to the cause of the Sunday school and to spiritual life in the Middle West, there was added a tremendous effect on general education. This vast campaign did much to influence thousands of young people to seek an education, with the result that state and civic leaders were stimulated to provide adequate educational facilities for children and youth in all the states of this wide area.

The success of the Mississippi Valley enterprise led the Union in 1834 to project another in the South on a similar scale. Here in an area of 330,000 square miles was a population of 4,000,000, of which 800,000 were children and youth. Few of these were members of Sunday schools, and most were growing up without benefit of general education. Motivated by the feeling that Sunday schools could help compensate for lack of educational opportunity existing in the South, thousands of people all over the nation contributed to the Union project. Though difficulties not met in the West were experienced in the South, much was accomplished. A large number of Sunday schools were organized, churches were strengthened, Bible study was much increased, and one thousand libraries of 120 books each were especially prepared and placed all over the area. Thus the Union made also to the spiritual and the educational life of the South a contribution of untold value.

During its first twenty years, the American Sunday-School Union

[2]*Ibid.*, p. 196.

laid strong foundations for healthy Sunday school growth, formulating principles and adopting policies best suited to the needs of the movement in the light of developing experience. During the next twenty years, its leadership was challenged. Beginning in 1826, the major denominations started to turn against Union effort by founding societies of their own with a view to making the Sunday school a church auxiliary for stressing particular doctrinal teachings.

Parenthetically, notice should be taken of other developments during the period the churches were turning toward the Sunday school as a way of meeting the need for Christian education. The churches were facing the problem of finding a type of school suited to the purpose, but because there were many misgivings concerning the suitability of the Sunday school, two efforts were made to carry on Christian education in some other way. One of these was that of Horace Bushnell who published in brief form a treatise entitled *Christian Nurture* which he expanded in 1861 into a book with the same title. His plea was for a conception and a practice of Christianity which would center evangelism and Christian education in the family. Though his book aroused great interest, it did not influence the churches to adopt a family-centered type of Christian education.

The second effort was the attempt by the Presbyterian Church to establish a complete system of schools under church control. This involved a venture to promote parochial schools. Other non-Catholic denominations had also tried to establish parochial schools after colonial days, but the Presbyterian effort was the most ambitious one. In 1846, and again in 1847, the General Assembly approved the idea of parochial schools, with the goal of having such a school in every congregation. Over two hundred sixty Presbyterian parochial schools were started as day schools in which secular and religious subjects were taught in combination. However, the system was a failure, and it was abandoned in 1870. The significance for Christian education of these efforts is that the churches were finding impossible or impractical three means of giving religious instruction—the public school, the family, and the parochial school—and were turning to the Sunday school.

By 1859 it had become evident that promotion of the Sunday school movement under Union direction was a thing of the past. The output of literature by the denominations was replacing Union literature; the treasury of the Union was empty; and many of its auxiliaries had been dissolved. In these circumstances, the Union wisely gave way to "National Convention," turning over to the latter supervisory guidance of over 3,000,000 Sunday school pupils.

However, the Union has never ceased its main task of organizing and sustaining Sunday schools and of publishing and distributing Christian literature. The missionaries of the American Sunday-School Union, working in most of the states of the nation, are today starting Sunday schools in many rural communities and unchurched neighborhoods. The Union continues to emphasize personal and general evangelism, with the result that each year thousands of youth and older persons are led to confess Christ as Saviour. Members of the Board of Officers and Managers, as well as every member of its missionary force, avoiding purely controversial questions and those related to sectarian differences, continue to present Christ crucified as the only hope for fallen man and to base everything they do in Christian education upon this central fact. In addition to its Sunday school work, the Union today conducts hundreds of daily vacation Bible schools, has a Home Department which reaches isolated families in remote areas with Christian publications and Bible truth, and holds many Bible conferences for rural young people.

Development Through Convention Activity

The Sunday school movement has never been a narrow sectarian movement. Robert Raikes, who started it in its modern form, was a layman, and laymen were for a long time its chief promoters, especially in America. This is not to say that ministers had no part in promoting it. On the contrary, a number of ministers from Wesley's time on did much to encourage and guide Sunday school development. However, only after many years did the churches officially assume an important role in controlling the Sunday school. The great conventions were primarily for laymen and were planned and conducted by laymen with the aid of a few outstanding ministers who had gotten a vision of the possibilities of Sunday school work. Laymen are not as much inclined toward sectarian matters as are ministers, and laymen controlled Sunday school conventions.

For thirty years after its transplantation to America, the Sunday school was an institution seeking recognition and favor. Sunday schools grew in number through the work of societies formed to establish them, and each school maintained connection with the body by which it had been organized. Many of the local unions, as auxiliaries of the American Sunday-School Union and the societies preceding it, held annual meetings which were like Sunday school conventions. However, most Sunday schools of the early period were small and scattered, with little opportunity for their workers to learn how the cause was operating elsewhere or to obtain inspiration for new effort and greater devotion to that cause. Whatever new ideas and encouragement for service these workers received came to them through their local union and in some cases through visits of a representative of the society of which the local union was a part.

Local conferences and conventions were held prior to 1820. After that year, these became more numerous for the purpose of considering various aspects of Sunday school work. The first convention representing societies from all parts of the country was held in Philadelphia in 1824 to consider forming a national organization; its outcome was the formation of the American Sunday-School Union. Conferences or conventions were held on the anniversaries of the Union in 1826, 1828, and 1830; these were attended by representatives from the auxiliary unions in different states. The one in 1828 was attended by delegates from fourteen states who gave attention to various suggestions for enlarging the scope of Union operations. Representatives at the 1830 convention considered the Mississippi Valley mission; it was followed by conventions or meetings in every important city in America, held for the furtherance of this project.

The Sunday school union of Hartford County, Connecticut, held regular annual meetings after 1823. In 1831, a convention of Sunday school workers in Mexico, New York, organized an association which held conventions under the direction of a committee of their number. A notable county convention was conducted by Stephen Paxson for Scott County, Illinois, in 1846. Paxson later became a missionary of the American Sunday-School Union—a missionary who organized hundreds of Sunday schools and aided other hundreds. He was one of the fruits of the Mississippi Valley enterprise; as an unsaved man he had, at the insistence of his little daughter, attended a Sunday school. As a result, he was converted and became zealous in starting Sunday schools to bring to others the blessing he had received. Out of his zeal for creating an interest in Sunday schools while feeling himself unable to teach people what they needed to know about the operation of Sunday schools, he conceived the idea of gathering together in a convention for the exchange of ideas, people of education and capacity and those who were ignorant and incapable. Denominational prejudices made the calling of an interdenominational gathering hazardous, but Paxson succeeded in holding a good convention.

The results stimulated repetition, and the practice of holding conventions spread from county to county. These conventions were the historical beginnings of the later system of county, state, national, and international conventions and the associations that grew out of them. Massachusetts called its first state Sunday school convention in 1855 and New York its first one in 1857. Connecticut also organized a state convention in 1857. The first Illinois state convention was held in 1859.

While these developments were taking place, a group in Chicago were infusing into the Sunday school movement evangelical fervor. Benjamin Franklin Jacobs, a zealous young Christian, came to Chicago from New Jersey in 1854, and two years later Dwight Lyman Moody, another zealous Christian, came from Boston. Both men threw themselves earnestly into the well-established Sunday school work of the city and ministered to many phases of need. These and other leaders had an important part in the revival movement of 1857 and 1858. William Reynolds, of Peoria, joined their number in 1861. After the Civil War ended, they—Mr. Moody especially—sought to make Sunday school work more and more a power for God and salvation. In advance of the sixth annual session of the Illinois state convention, Moody and Jacobs started a revival which awakened the convention and the state. Hundreds were converted at the convention and soon thereafter and were started in lines of evangelistic effort all over the state. The outcome was the revivification of the Illinois state convention, with greatly increased attendance and greater impetus to Sunday school work throughout the state.

Three national conventions were held prior to the Civil War and the opening in 1869 of the later series of triennial conventions.

The Board of Officers and Managers of the American Sunday-School Union had proposed in 1832 a national convention "for the purpose of considering the principles of the institution; the duties and obligations which attach to the several officers of the Sunday-schools; the best plans of organizing, instructing and managing a Sunday-school in its various departments, and such other topics as may pertain to the general objects of the convention."[3] Because many denominational leaders were opposed to the Union, the managers themselves did not call the convention but arranged for a meeting in Philadelphia of representative Sunday school leaders. These planned thoroughly and issued a call for a national Sunday school convention in the city of New York in October, 1832.

This convention was attended by two hundred twenty delegates from fourteen states and four territories. Nearly all the outstanding Sunday school men of the time participated in the discussions which covered the whole range of current methods and problems. So important and varied were these that many of them were not sufficiently discussed to reach a conclusion, while others were barely mentioned. The delegates, therefore, proposed that another convention be held in Philadelphia in 1833. Following so closely upon the first, this second national convention was not so largely attended. However, various committees appointed at the first convention brought in elaborate reports on topics assigned them, and many important Sunday school problems were discussed.

These two conventions dealt so thoroughly with problems relating to the organization and administration of Sunday schools that desire for another national convention did not find strong expression for nearly three decades. During this interim, however, numerous states and counties held annual or other conventions for inspiration, diffusion of information, and consideration of local interests in Sunday school work. These were fostered largely by the American Sunday-School Union for the purpose of advancing the extension of Sunday schools and for improving them throughout the country.

The nationwide religious revival of 1857 and 1858 aroused the interest of Christian people in various enterprises, including the Sunday school. On the proposal of the New York State Sunday

[3] *Ibid.*, p. 353. Quotation from minutes of a stated meeting of the American Sunday-School Union held April 10, 1832.

School Convention of 1858, a call was issued for a national convention to be held in Philadelphia in 1859. Every evangelical Sunday school in the United States was invited to send at least one delegate. The response was hearty and general, so this third national convention was well-attended, indicating a much higher level of general interest than had been manifest in the first two conventions. Unlike those earlier conventions, this one planned for its succession; a nonpartisan lay committee was appointed to call another national convention in 1861; this one was to make similar provision for calling another, and so was each succeeding one in turn. Thus began a central leadership of the Sunday school movement other than that of the American Sunday-School Union. The Union heartily endorsed this convention idea, printing in its new weekly, *The Sunday School Times,* a complete report of the proceedings.

War conditions made impractical and impossible the holding of a national gathering of Sunday school workers in America in 1861 or in the years immediately following. However, in 1862, a general Sunday school convention held in London, England, was attended by four hundred fifty delegated workers from a number of countries, including the United States. This convention considered the history, objects, and methods of the Sunday school with a view to improving and extending Sunday schools in all lands. After the Civil War ended, the matter of another national convention was frequently discussed at state conventions and elsewhere. At the Illinois annual convention in 1868, B. F. Jacobs, Edward Eggleston, and others agitated for a renewal of the Philadelphia convention. As a result, a conference of Sunday school workers meeting later in Detroit delegated a committee from their number to call "an International Sunday-School Convention." Finding that the committee appointed by the 1859 convention was yet in existence, this Detroit committee worked with it to call a convention for 1869.

This Fourth National Sunday School Convention was held in Newark, New Jersey. Officially, it was not an international convention, but it was such in character, with visitors present from Canada, England, Scotland, Ireland, Egypt, and South Africa. Delegates from twenty-eight states and four territories were in attendance. Four men—B. F. Jacobs, H. Clay Trumbull, John H. Vincent, and Edward Eggleston, who from this time on were nationally prominent in the Sunday school movement—were active in this convention. It was carefully planned, was conducted with marked ability, and aroused great enthusiasm. Field reports were heard from many states, from denominational Sunday school societies, and from the American Sunday-School Union. The chief subject of discussion was the promotion of teacher training through institutes and normal classes. The convention expressed strong disapproval of the conception that the Sunday school was in any sense a substitute for family or pulpit instruction or that it should be considered as independent of the church.

At this convention a plan was set up for dealing with each separate convention as a separate enterprise, to be promoted during the interim between conventions by an executive committee whose life automatically expired at the end of the convention it had called. During the interim between conventions, local and denominational workers were to carry on without interference. This arrangement eliminated the fear, present during Union years of leadership, of some central group becoming so powerful as to be able to dictate policy in spite of minority opposition. It made possible the uniting of most evangelical groups for promotional purposes. Thus began that series of triennial national and international conventions, becoming quadrennial in 1914, which went on for many years.

The Fifth National Convention was held in Indianapolis in 1872. Two important actions, starting the movement for the formation thirty years later of the International Sunday School Association, were: enlargement to include delegates from all the states and provinces of North America, and the election of a statistical secretary, thus providing the first staff officer of a continuing organization. A third noteworthy act—one marking a most significant event in the history of Sunday schools and of Christian education—was the adoption, after much discussion, of uniform Sunday school lessons and the appointment of a lesson committee to make selections for the following seven years.

The First International Convention met in Baltimore in 1875. Delegates from twenty-seven states and Canada attended. The spirit of fellowship between these two countries and between workers from the North and the South was emphasized. The lesson committee reported remarkably rapid acceptance of the uniform lessons. Dr. John H. Vincent stressed the educational factor by a plea for systematic normal teaching. The statistical report showed a Sunday school membership of 6,500,000 in the United States and 300,000 in Canada.

The Second International Convention in Atlanta in 1878 emphasized still more the spirit of fellowship, was told of the continued success of the uniform lessons, chose a new lesson committee of fourteen members, and expressed much enthusiasm for united Sunday school effort. Dr. Vincent advanced the idea of a plan for graded Bible study to supplement the uniformity of the new lessons.

The Third International Convention, meeting in Toronto in 1881, inaugurated, at the suggestion of B. F. Jacobs, interdenominational work which led later to the establishment of the International Sunday School Association. The London Sunday School Union was represented at this convention.

The Fourth International Convention, 1884, met in Louisville. It was a gathering with a large attendance and was of better quality than preceding ones. Reports showed that there was little territory in the United States and Canada unreached by Sunday schools, the total of whose membership was 9,146,028 pupils, of whom 8,712,551 were in the United States. One full session was given over to discussion of primary Sunday school work, and the organization of a national union of primary workers was announced. The third lesson committee of fourteen members, with the addition of five corresponding members from Great Britain and France, was appointed to select lessons for the years 1886-1893.

The Fifth International Convention, 1887, in Chicago, continued the high standard set in the preceding one. Again a session was devoted to discussion of primary work. The Home Department was presented for the first time. Recommendations for general advance were approved, including one calling for a world Sunday school convention—the initial step toward the later organization of the World Sunday School Association. The first World Sunday School Convention met in London in 1889. Thereafter, it met as regularly as conditions of war and peace permitted; altogether there were twelve such meetings, the last one being held in Oslo, Norway, in 1936, with three thousand delegates from sixty nations in attendance.

The Sixth International Convention met in Pittsburgh in 1890. Two sessions were devoted to primary work. At this convention the fourth lesson committee was appointed. After much debate the committee was increased to fifteen, with representation from additional denominations, and it was instructed to furnish temperance lessons for the first two quarters and alternative temperance and missionary lessons for the last two Sundays of the third and fourth quarters.

The Seventh International Convention held in St. Louis, 1893, saw the beginning of a challenge to international convention leadership under the dominance of B. F. Jacobs, who was most ambitious for the expansion of every possible form of international activity. An independent organization, the Field Workers' Association, held an all-day preconvention session, and a second independent organization, the International Primary Union, demanded a special session on the convention program. The success the uniform lessons had been having, now modified by the issuing in 1892 of the rival Blakeslee lessons and by other evidences of revolt against uniformity, aroused earnest debate. However, no action was taken to change instructions to the lesson committee.

The Eighth International Convention, meeting in Boston in 1896, had the largest number of delegates present in the history of international conventions. D. L. Moody conducted an opening devotional period each day, and many inspiring addresses gave numerous indications of continued progress in Sunday school work. At the sessions of the International Primary Union, held simultaneously, marked advances in method were indicated. This Union was reorganized at this time, with a view to affiliation with the convention. The fifth committee was chosen to select lessons for 1900-1905.

The Ninth International Convention, 1899, meeting in Atlanta, was marked by steps to consolidate the international work. The Field Workers' Association became the Field Workers' Department of the International Convention. The International Primary Union became the International Primary Department. There was interest in the establishment of an international teacher-training department, though it was decided not to take this step. Teacher training for its own constituency became the first activity of the new Primary Department. The convention created the office of general secretary and called Marion Lawrance to fill it. This act marked the virtual establishment of an International Sunday School Association, for it provided a continuous organization instead of one that terminated with the adjournment of each convention.

The Tenth International Convention, 1902, was held in Denver. It dealt with two major issues. One was the demand for a two-year beginners' course of lessons and for a course of advanced Bible lessons for college students and others wishing to progress beyond the uniform course. The latter was disapproved, but the former was favorably referred to the sixth lesson committee, appointed at this convention. This favorable referral constituted the first break in the uniformity of the convention lesson system established thirty years before.

The second issue was the choice of a successor to Mr. Jacobs, who had been the international leader for many years. The man chosen was W. N. Hartshorn, whose qualifications, experience, and innumerable friendships well fitted him for leadership of the convention. However, unlike Mr. Jacobs, he was not cautious in respect to consideration of denominational self-assertion. So devoted was he to the cause of the Sunday school, which he considered to be a divine cause, that he deemed there would be no opposition to it from any quarter. Mr. Lawrance stood with him. In their enthusiasm, they conceived that there were no limits to the jurisdiction of the International Convention, that all differences of opinion relating to the progress of the Sunday school would be resolved in frank and brotherly conference, and that the upbuilding of Sunday schools would win from the denominations full approval and support. Accordingly, they proceeded to create a staff for executing the policy of the International Convention.

At the Eleventh International Convention, held in Toronto in 1905, on the recommendation of the Executive Committee the name of the body was changed from "convention" to "association" and decision was made "that proper steps be taken for incorporation." Thus came into being a continuing body, leading the Sunday school forces of the nation, including denominational ones, through an executive committee which was virtually a permanent board. At once this supradenominational leadership proceeded to enlarge the staff, broaden the functions of the body, and carry its educational program into all Sunday schools.

In 1903 the Religious Education Association, which was to exert great influence on religious education for several decades, was formed to promote education in religion and religion in education by gathering together those who were firm believers in religious education. The organization attracted outstanding churchmen and educators from many denominations. These men represented varied points of view in education, but all agreed that the church was not taking seriously enough her task of religious training and was not using in this training the best educational materials and methods. This association created new interest in religious education and developed sentiment in favor of better methods for carrying it on. The Association's annual conventions and its magazine, *Religious Education,* became a powerful factor in molding public opinion. However, the Association's service to the cause of true Christian education was harmful instead of helpful, because its members were for the most part men of extremely liberal tendencies whose contributions were not in accord with the faith of those who accepted the Bible in its entirety as the Word of God.

The Twelfth International Convention, held in Louisville in 1908, was marked by evidence of the growing power of the Executive Committee through the Association's newly established office in Chicago, its salaried official force, its policies of management, and the increasing unwieldiness of the convention as a deliberative body. By resolution this convention commended the uniform lessons and voted to continue them. Another resolution directed the seventh lesson committee, chosen at this convention, to continue to prepare and develop the uniform lessons but also to provide a thoroughly graded series for the whole school.

Shortly before the Louisville convention met, the General Conference of the Methodist Episcopal Church set up its own Board of Sunday Schools to do its own standardizing and promoting of Sunday schools, teacher training, and development of Sunday school specialization. The Methodist action was only part of a general reaction against the International Sunday School Association. There was at this time a general stirring of educational interest within the denominations, due to a feeling that close adherence to the uniform lessons and other products of the nineteenth century precluded proper educational advance. The summer schools and the annual conventions of the Religious Education Association were responsible in large measure for this feeling of dissatisfaction. The outcome was the formation in 1910 of a new society for the promotion of Sunday school work. This was named "Sunday-School Council of Evangelical Denominations." Originally it was composed of the official representatives of nineteen denominational Sunday school boards and agencies of publication. Later it came to include in its membership thirty or more denominations.

Thus for the first time in the history of the Sunday school, the denominations began to act together. The first annual meeting of the organization was held at Nashville in 1911. Besides holding general sessions, the Council worked in four sections—editorial, educational, extension, and publication. In all four of these phases of work, denominational workers found much in common. In educational matters especially, the definite purpose of the new organization was to make its associated denominations all together, and each for its own membership, the real leader of the Sunday school cause.

Actually, the formation of the Council was a protest against the assumption of legislative powers affecting all by a few in a permanently organized body. Control by a legally incorporated board of managers was just as objectionable now as it had been in the days of the American Sunday-School Union, prior to the period of convention ascendancy. This was especially true when new educational movements appealed to denominational workers who were becoming aware of the importance of religious education and seeking to carry it on in the light of current educational practice. A convention was a mass meeting, composed of representatives from individual schools everywhere who could freely express themselves and take united action, with authority ceasing when the convention ended. An association was a permanently organized body, with continuing authority and legislative powers that meant disappearance of representation on the part of individual schools and loss of a free expression of views by rank-and-file workers.

At the Thirteenth International Convention in San Francisco in 1911, the Executive Committee adopted a set of bylaws giving the International Association a written constitution—something it had not yet had. These bylaws set down the historic power of the convention to elect its own officers and executive committee. However, "all questions pertaining to the policy of the Association" were assigned to the executive committee, which was also to elect the Lesson Committee, to consist henceforth of sixteen men. The powers thus assumed had since 1872 been effectively exercised by a large and representative convention; hereafter issues which had previously been freely debated were to be in the hands of an incorporated group composed of a few men. The graded lessons, which had been issued by the lesson committee in obedience to the Louisville resolution, formed the principal subject for discussion at this convention, but those in power in the Association disapproved of the principle of grading, especially if it meant the introduction of material from other than Bible sources.

Between 1911 and 1914 the relations of the Association and the Sunday School Council were largely cooperative. Committees from the two bodies and from the American Sunday-School Union conferred on issues of interest common to the three. Friction was somewhat eased, and points of disagreement were frankly considered. A joint standard for Sunday schools was completed and accepted. Nevertheless, the Council held firmly to its predetermined way, insisting that the making of lesson courses and matters involving general policies, methods, and standards in the organization, administration, and educational supervision of the Sunday school were matters in which Sunday school leaders of the churches as such must have a part.

The Fourteenth International Convention met in Chicago in 1914. It was planned on a vast scale, with many conferences and numerous gatherings in addition to the sixteen main sessions. The evangelical basis of the international fellowship was reaffirmed, and misconceptions as to the effects of incorporation were removed. As the outcome of much prior conferring, the ascendancy of the convention over its executive committee was stated and exemplified in action. Thus the Association and the Sunday-School Council of Evangelical Denominations began to understand each other better and to move toward a common program. The first step in this direction was the reorganization of the International Lesson Committee to provide a larger representation from the denominations. As reconstituted it was to have eight members elected by the International Sunday School Association, eight elected by the Sunday School Council of Evangelical Denominations, and one member for each denomination having a general Sunday school curriculum committee. At this convention the interval between conventions was extended from three to four years.

The Fifteenth International Convention met in Buffalo in 1918. On the whole, the preceding quadrennial had brought notable progress in Sunday school activity, but it also saw in the two rival organizations such advances in leadership power that harmonious activity was made increasingly difficult. The new lesson committee, now representing the denominations and their ideals, completed the graded course of lessons, which some denominational publishing houses accepted and used. However, independent publishers and some of the denominational houses continued to use the uniform lessons. During the quadrennium, Association leadership had been reorganized for greater efficiency. Its educational department presented at this Convention the results of advances in teacher training and in young people's work. The Council likewise had adopted a new standard for training teachers and a program for young people's work. Also, it had made advances in setting age limits for the various departments of the Sunday school and in formulating aims for the different age groups.

A goodly portion of the progress of the two organizations had been secured through friendly conference with each other, yet there were tensions. However, it was realized by many leaders that in a cause so Christian as the Sunday school, there should be unity, that there should be a common seeking for peace rather than power. The Sunday School Council of Evangelical Denominations was even less democratic than the Association, though the former had had its origin to some considerable extent in a reaction against rule by a few in the latter. Before and during the Buffalo convention, conferences were held with a view to reconciling differences. After the convention, Dr. Walter S. Athearn, Chairman of the Association Committee on Education, who, like earlier leaders, envisioned Christians unitedly studying the Bible, published an article, "Organized to Defeat Democracy: Shall the American Sunday School Be Prussianized?" Both organizations saw that radical compromise of some sort was a duty each owed the cause, whatever their individual tendencies were. In 1919, a joint committee of the two organizations agreed on principles for a complete merging under a new charter and with a new name. The Council at its annual meeting in Chicago in 1922 accepted these principles.

At the Sixteenth International Convention, meeting in Kansas City later in 1922, the Association also adopted the recommendations of the joint committee. The name given the merged organization was "The International Sunday School Council of Religious Education." After 1924 the name was "The International Council of Religious Education." To many the word "religious" was objectionable, for it was equally applied to non-Christian as well as Christian groups. However, attempts to substitute "Christian" to make possible distinctively Christian education, proved unsuccessful. Ideal unity was not obtained through the merger; Southern Baptists, the Church of England in Canada, the Lutheran General Synod, and the United Evangelicals refused to enter the organization. The number of denominations concurring at Kansas City was thirty-one, and at least forty-four eventually entered.

The merger agreement provided for a Committee on Education of not more than sixty members and for a series of professional advisory sections covering children's, young people's, adult, field, directors of religious education, denominational editors, denominational publishers, and other forms of specialization. The number of sections became fifteen in 1925. Each group was given representation on the Committee on Education, to which it was to report its findings and recommendations.

In addition to opposing "religious" rather than "Christian" education, evangelicals in the churches also opposed the elimination of Bible content and the introduction of experience-centered lessons. Now that strong emphasis was placed on the annual meeting of denominational specialists who all too frequently were liberal in outlook and enamored with man-originated views on education, enthusiasm for Sunday school work vanished and interest in the old-time convention waned. Instead of the fervid zeal, devoted loyalty, and humble consecrated service which once characterized lay workers, a coldly professional spirit prevailed. To many, the Council was a professional aristocracy with vested rights and privileges. The result was a definite lack of confidence on the part of thousands of people who had been loyal participants in Sunday school work. Though the Council was supported by most of the denominations, many individual churches did not favor it. Workers standing for true Christian education, especially in avowedly evangelical churches, could not condone in an organization things opposed to their faith, much as they desired to work unitedly in the Sunday school movement.

The Decline of the Sunday School

The result was a decline in the growth of the Sunday school. From 1916 to 1940 there was a decrease both in enrollment of pupils and in the number of Sunday schools. Dr. Clarence H. Benson said in 1943, "Government figures indicated that despite the increase in population, Sunday school enrollment has decreased 12.6 per cent between 1926 and 1936."[4] Helen F. Spaulding, Associate Director of Research of the International Council of Religious Education, said in an article in *The International Journal of Religious Education* for November, 1950, "Sunday school enrollment showed a healthy and continuous growth during the first third of the century, then during the thirties something happened; momentum slowed down and some of the religious bodies actually registered a loss. It was not until 1947 that there were definite signs of recovery."

During the earlier years of the present century, the Sunday school had its "Golden Age." The Sunday school was Protestantism's most important single agency for doing the work of God in the world. It is pertinent, therefore, to ask why it underwent decline after 1916. This question has its basic answer in the fact that leadership became liberal in theology. From 1903 onward a group of professionally-minded people constituting the Religious Education Association exerted a strong influence which was very potent in leading to the formation of the Sunday School Council of Evangelical Denominations in 1910. In 1922 these professionalists gained ascendancy in what came to be known as the International Council of Religious Education. As a school, the Sunday school is responsive to educational trends, but it is more than a school; it is an institution with a purpose that is primarily spiritual. Closely related to the church, the Sunday school is much influenced by movements in theology. The outcome of the 1922 merger was the opening of the door to unevangelical theological factors, with resulting tension between the rank and file of the Protestant laity and the professional leadership of the religious education movement which was liberal in outlook.

Liberalism blights. It denies that Jesus is God and deals with Him as a mere human being. It holds that the Bible is a fallible book, subject to inconsistency and error, not worthy of acceptance in its

[4]Clarence H. Benson, *A Popular History of Christian Education* (Chicago: Moody Press, 1943), p. 338.

every part. Liberalism teaches that the natural state of man is good and that conversion is therefore unnecessary—that through education, all the good, the true, the pure, and the noble elements within the pupil can be brought to fullness of development. It believes that righteousness and truth and moral sanctions are not fixed and absolute but that through education changing values can be discovered and thus man will be led ever onward and upward.

Evangelicals hold that man is a lost and sinful being, standing in need of salvation through the grace of God, which alone can fit him to live in harmony with the will of God. They believe that the Sunday school is fundamentally spiritual in purpose and in educational process. They accept the Bible as the infallible revelation of God and base all education upon it. They emphasize spiritual experience involving crisis, conflict, and choice as essential in the forming of Christian character. While willing to accept whatever is good in education, psychology, and pedagogy, they are unalterably opposed to substituting anything developed by the human mind for the growth in grace and the knowledge of the Lord Jesus Christ which is the fruitage of conversion and of obedience to God and the teachings of His revealed Word.

Liberals in the Religious Education Association and the Federal Council of Churches in America were important factors in religious education. They had strong influence in determining the policies of the International Council, which came to be committed more and more to the liberal view. In the organizational structure, which in 1950 became the Commission on General Education of the National Council of Churches, were many evangelicals. However, the evangelical position was definitely not the official view of the organization. Though dissatisfied with the Council, evangelicals did not express themselves unitedly. Some hoped to reform the Council. Some started other organizations. Some gave up their interest in the Sunday school. The outcome was bad in its effect on Christian education.

This effect was manifest not only in a decrease in Sunday school enrollment and interest in general but also in a concomitant spiritual illiteracy which evangelical Sunday schools could have done much to prevent. Never can a leadership which holds rationalistic views of God's revelation to man inculcate in the young the teachings of the Christian faith. Destructive criticism of the Word of

God, be it by modernism, Neoorthodoxy, or whatnot, is bound to deprive multitudes of that knowledge of the truth of God which is the backbone of the faith that once prevailed in this country.

Modernism was deeply entrenched in America and was a strong factor in its bearing on Christian education. Coupled with this basic cause of the decline of the Sunday school was the allied influence of secularism. Modern education was permeated with the Greek spirit of admiration for human achievement. This made for the idea that classical culture must be the foundation of education, especially on the higher levels. Moreover, modern philosophy was rooted in Greek philosophy, to which it constantly turned back for inspiration and guidance. It is little wonder therefore that education has been influenced much by human instead of divine ways of thinking.

All too frequently religious educators have been much enamored with the ideals of Greek culture. The result was that the influences which weakened Christian education in the Middle Ages wrought anew their baleful effects in the minds of many people. A great deal of the philosophy, psychology, and science which have gone into modern public education is anything but evangelical and, in many cases, it is definitely anti-Christian. There have been those in Christian education who, assuming that the public schools use the most effective methods, have turned away from the Christian emphasis to adopt secular methods they think are superior.

Admittedly, Christian educators can learn much from the public schools, but always the need is for careful discrimination on the basis of actual worth to the cause of Christ. Definitely, the public school is a secular institution employing the temporal. In the nature of things, it but reflects the spirit of the age, which has little regard for God, ignores Jesus Christ, neglects the Bible, and centers interest upon merely human values. Where Christian education followed public education blindly, it failed to realize its true objective of preparing pupils for the kingdom of God. Also, there has been overemphasis upon social factors, causing the Christian school to forsake its God-given purpose. Worldly-minded church school leaders have not proved to be a heavenly benefit to the cause of Christ.

In this connection, note must be made of a third factor that helped to bring about the decline of the Sunday school. Some who stood for true Christian education were responsible for conditions contributing to such decline. There have been evangelical leaders who refused to forsake the old ways, to adopt anything new in methods and materials. Unaware that new times make for new conditions and new needs, they clung to the old instead of adapting their ways to current circumstances. The Sunday school cannot ignore true progress in education; in days of streamlined trains and jet planes it cannot follow the methods that were suitable to times of the oxcart. Doctrinally sound Sunday schools have been hampered in their work by inadequately prepared teachers. Pupils going five days a week to well-conducted public schools staffed by thoroughly prepared teachers, using the very best materials, are not much inclined to attend on Sunday ill-equipped schools taught by inefficient teachers who work with inferior materials and follow no method in their teaching.

A fourth hindrance to the advance of the Sunday school has been ecclesiasticism. All through history progress in Christian education has been hindered by ecclesiastically controlled agencies. It was so in the days of Jesus, of Luther, of Raikes, and of Jacobs. Every development met the determined opposition of ecclesiastical power because there were sectarian tenets to be observed and vested interests to be safeguarded. Every movement of advance was judged, not in terms of real merit but by the effect it might have on the organized body. True Christian education must be based upon God's ways of working, not upon human ideas and human organizations. God's method is men, not ecclesiastical machinery.

At any rate, it was an undeniable fact that the Sunday school was on the decline. The emphasis being carried out was liberal in slant. Christian lay leaders, missing the inspiration and the vitalizing spirit furnished by the great conventions, had lost their enthusiasm and zeal. What could be done? One answer to this question was the organizing of the National Sunday School Association, the formation of which is treated in the next chapter.

Readings

BENSON, CLARENCE H. *A Popular History of Christian Education.* Chicago: Moody Press, 1943.

BOWER, WILLIAM CLAYTON. *Christ and Christian Education.* New York: Abingdon-Cokesbury Press, 1943.

BROWN, ARLO A. *A History of Religious Education in Recent Times.* New York: The Abingdon Press, 1923.

DeBlois, Austin Kennedy and Gorham, Donald R. *Christian Religious Education: Principles and Practice.* New York: Fleming H. Revell Company, 1939.

The Encyclopedia of Sunday Schools and Religious Education (John T. McFarland and Benjamin S. Winchester, Editors-in-chief). New York: Thomas Nelson and Sons, 1915.

Article on "Sunday School Conventions," E. M. Fergusson, pp. 296-310.

Fergusson, Edmund M. *Historic Chapters in Christian Education in America.* New York: Fleming H. Revell Company, 1935.

Ferm, Vergilius T. A. (ed.). *An Encyclopedia of Religion.* New York: The Philosophical Library, 1945.

Articles on:

"Sunday School Movement in the United States," pp. 744-749.

"Liberal Theology," pp. 442-443.

"Modernism," 498-499.

Gaebelein, Frank E. *Christian Education in a Democracy.* New York: Oxford University Press, 1951.

Hastings, James, (ed.). *Encyclopaedia of Religion and Ethics.* New York: Charles Scribner's Sons, 1955-1958.

Article on "Western Church," R. Martin Pope. Part 3. Development of theology and religious thought in the Church of the West. XII, 732-736.

Lotz, Philip Henry. *Orientation in Religious Education.* Nashville and New York: Abingdon-Cokesbury Press, 1950.

Murch, James DeForest. *Christian Education and the Local Church.* Cincinnati: Standard Publishing Company, 1943.

The New Schaff-Herzog Encyclopedia of Religious Knowledge. New York: and London: Funk and Wagnalls Company, 1908-1914.

Article on "Modernism," W. L. Bevan, VII, 428-429.

Price, J. M., Chapman, J. H., Carpenter, L. L., and Yarborough, W. Forbes. *A Survey of Religious Education.* New York: The Ronald Press, 1959.

Rian, Edwin H. *Christianity and American Education.* San Antonio, Texas: The Naylor Company, 1949.

Rice, Edwin W. *The Sunday-School Movement 1780-1917, and the American Sunday-School Union, 1817-1917.* Philadelphia: The American Sunday-School Union, 1917.

Warkentin, Elmo Henry. "The History of Revitalizing the Sunday Schools of America through the National Sunday School Association." Unpublished Master's thesis, Wheaton College, 1958.

The Commission on Research in Christian Education, an important arm of the National Sunday School Association, has as its objectives the stimulation of professional growth in the field, the direction of the formulation of a philosophy of true Christian education, assisting in production of suitable textbooks for institutions of higher learning, and giving guidance to the NSSA in its Christian education policies.

(Courtesy of the National Sunday School Association)

10

The Sunday School—Background of Its Decline and Its Reemergence in Christian Education

As was emphasized in the early portion of this book, the history of Christian education has a twofold aspect, the divine and the human. Intermingled with these two is the history of the influence of the enemy of God, of man, and of righteousness. Had man never yielded to Satan, history would undoubtedly be a record of a gradual ascent to ever higher levels of development such as man is prone to think can be achieved through a human program of education. The entrance of sin made redemption a necessity. Because of the corruption due to sin, nothing man can do for himself by way of developing his powers and capacities avails to make him what he himself wants to be or what God would have him be. One thing and only one can effect in a being marred by sin the change which makes upward development possible. That is the creating of a new spirit —a new nature—by God.

"Where sin abounded, grace did much more abound." God in grace made Himself man's Redeemer. Man is not a devil, therefore he is redeemable; he did not originate sin, but became its victim through being deceived by a cunning enemy. Even as a fallen being, man feels sin to be something foreign to him and seeks continually but unavailingly to free himself from it. Blinded by sin, man is unable to perceive his own corruption, so he believes there is good within himself and he exalts his own nature. As long as he feels sufficiency in himself, he will not lay hold upon the sufficiency which a merciful, loving, and gracious God provides for him through redemption in Christ.

As was said earlier, God's program of education is designed to bring man to recognition of his own insufficiency. History shows that God's education of man ever moves upward. It is a truly progressive education, for each fresh beginning is an advance over the old; each new stage following collapse due to the failure of man carries in it the seed of something better for the future. "But this is all of God's work, not human 'progress,' no ascent of the creature out of the depths into the heights, but a condescension of the Creator out of the heights into the depths; no development of human powers until the unfolding of the highest, ideal humanity, but a leading on to divine, eternal goals through mighty acts of Divine intervention in love and power."[1]

It was God's plan that man be dependent on Him, that he have Him as the source and the center of his whole life and of all his activity—in securing knowledge and in everything else. Instead, man made self the center, the source of knowledge, of happiness, and of redemption. He justifies himself, he commends himself, he finds sufficiency in himself, all his thoughts center upon himself, and all his activity is directed toward achieving by self and for self. Consequently, the program of education he carries on of himself—be it called Christian or not—has man, not God, for its center. In making it so, man is aided, encouraged, and abetted by Satan, his own and God's enemy.

Those who follow their own thinking instead of humbly accepting the revealed will of God are proud of their ability to reason and exalt themselves in what they think they understand and know. They forsake the way of simple and complete trust in God's revelation, of wholehearted acceptance of the truth He gives, and of total dependence upon Him as the only source of true knowledge. They follow "the way of Cain"—the way of emphasis upon human development and accomplishment apart from God, the way of man proud that he knows so much and can do so much—instead of "the way of Abel"—the way of absolute dependence upon God, the way of complete reliance upon Him as the only source of knowledge and wisdom and redemption.

[1]Erich Sauer, *The Dawn of World Redemption* (Grand Rapids: Wm. B. Eerdmans Publishing Company, 1953), p. 54.

The Bible in the Sunday School

Anything and everything done in education by those who humbly and faithfully follow "the way of Abel" is in harmony with and advances the program of educating man that God is carrying on through the ages. These adhere to the letter of the Bible, or verbal inspiration of the Scriptures as originally given man by God. They not only believe the Bible as the inspired authentic Word of God, but they believe also that Jesus Christ is the living Word, the Son God sent into the world to be the Saviour of men. In Christian education, these who thus honor God place emphasis upon gaining a personal knowledge of God through Jesus Christ and upon knowledge of His will made known in His revealed Word. This Word is to them the only authoritative rule of faith and practice for man in this world. They teach the Bible with the threefold purpose of bringing those taught to Christ in salvation, building them up in Christ unto sanctification, and sending them out for Christ in service.

This was not the purpose of the Sunday school in the beginning. Its original design was to teach reading, writing, and religion to poor children. Robert Raikes began the Sunday school for the purpose of imparting knowledge to wretched children with a view to improving their moral condition. In his Sunday schools he sought to eliminate ignorance, which he had concluded was the cause of vice and degradation among the children of his native Gloucester. However, from the first the Bible was used as a text in Sunday schools, as it was at that time in secular schools also. The reason for this was the twofold recognition that character is the ultimate objective in education and that the Bible is the essential means for building character.

So, though the purpose for which it was used should have been a higher one, the Bible was the chief textbook of instruction in the Sunday school from its beginning. Parochial schools used catechisms, creeds, and confessions, but Raikes and his followers made these secondary to the Bible, which they recognized as the source of true knowledge. Raikes also made a marked change in methods of instruction. In his day the Christian world had no ideal of religious education other than the memorizing of a catechism. Raikes sought to inculcate understanding of the Bible. He and those associated with him prepared books with illustrations and stories designed to interest children and teach them the meaning of Bible truth.

The chief manual used in Raikes's day, aside from the Bible, was a book he printed, *The Sunday Scholar's Companion.* Its content was Biblical, consisting of simple lessons based upon the Old and the New Testaments and teaching man's duty to God and to his fellows. It contained also some history having to do mainly with the Creation and with man's fall and redemption. The four parts were graded with a view to meeting the needs of pupils as they advanced in knowledge. This simple Scripture reading book was widely used. There were few Bibles at that time on account of their cost.

In spite of the efforts of Raikes and his coworkers to make the Bible meaningful, the question-and-answer method was the method most commonly used during the eighteenth century. It involved the giving of standard answers to theological questions. Just after the beginning of the nineteenth century, there was a period when indiscriminate memorization of Bible verses was the method used by many Sunday school workers. As the number of public schools increased and took on the function of teaching secular subjects, the Sunday school concentrated more on the Bible.

Though new catechisms were published during this period, they were not used by many of the lay leaders in the rapidly increasing number of Sunday schools. Instead, these leaders relied on the Bible. Children were urged to memorize as many verses as possible—verses of their own choosing. Sunday school sessions consisted of little more than the recitation of scores or hundreds of texts memorized without regard to any principle of selection. The practice of giving rewards of tickets, or cards of several colors indicating exchange value, added zest and served to give an appearance of success to the program.

Workers who loved God's Word were seeking means of Bible instruction suitable to the Sunday school and in harmony with sound educational principles. Bible memorizing, catechetical instruction with answers verbally exact, and a mechanical "verse-a-day method," stressed later, all showed the need for something new. The step in advance was taken about 1810 by Dr. James Gall of Edinburgh in a plan he called "Nature's Normal School" where "normal" means "natural," or "according to nature's law." The plan involved presenting a series of lessons, each consisting of ten to twenty verses—a "limited lesson" too long to memorize but too short to read without pausing to think of its meaning and application.

That is, Gall originated the method of selecting as a Sunday school lesson a Bible passage of instructional value suited to general class discussion. With each lesson, he provided explanations, questions, and answers, to direct the attention of the pupil to all phases of each verse's meaning and its application to life. Thus Gall brought into the Sunday school the limited lesson which has been used ever since and is used to this day. Other writers of lessons have greatly improved, but none have attempted to change, the limited-lesson method of Bible teaching.

Gall's system was much used in Great Britain. Introduced into America with high praise, it did not win great favor. In both lands it was criticized. For one thing, the lessons were entirely detached, without connection or continuity. Moreover, the system overemphasized direct catechetical questions and gave so many practical lessons that the attention of the learner was distracted, preventing him from grasping the truth presented. Some of Gall's works were offered to the American Sunday-School Union, which used their features in a revised form to develop the lesson helps on the early uniform limited lessons for Sunday schools.

Commended strongly by the London Union, Gall's method became popular with British Sunday schools, displacing memoriter learning. However, sharp criticism of the deficiencies of Gall's method led to its being partially supplanted by the Training System of David Stow, which won many advocates, especially those interested in infants' and beginners' classes. Stow emphasized the value of combining the interrogative, the illustrative, and the elliptical methods of teaching and applied his principle to Biblical as well as to secular instruction.

Each of these systems had its advocates, but both of them were soon supplanted by other methods. The London Union was seeking in all possible directions for the best ways of imparting Bible knowledge. This was true of other Sunday school societies, too. During these years their lists of lessons changed annually and were largely experimental. Various systems, which overlapped one another, were used more or less simultaneously in different localities. Most of these systems were introduced into America but, after being used by a few Sunday schools, were discarded. None of them was adopted generally.

In this country also, similar overlapping systems were developed and used experimentally. For a time, emphasis was placed upon lecturing and storytelling, though the era of such emphasis was shorter than the era of memorizing had been. Those most concerned that the Bible be taught effectively in the Sunday school saw that something more was needed. On January 1, 1825, the New York Association of Sunday School Teachers began a series of selected lessons for the next four months on the theory that "all lessons in Sabbath schools should be selected."

The American Sunday-School Union issued in the same year a card of lessons for the entire twelve months. In 1826, the Union published the first of its lesson books, the most systematic yet produced. These were used widely for many years. They were the beginning of systems of connected and consecutive Bible study in Sunday schools. They were not based upon Gall's system, though it had some influence in shaping the helps that came about 1830. In time the Union issued a series of thirteen small question books, covering the entire Bible and graded to meet the needs of pupils of various ages.

The method was the same in each—printed questions, with or without answers, and references to bring out Bible meaning. The questions were skillfully developed, and, in the upper grades, the Biblical knowledge called forth was considerable. Educationally, they were much better "helps" than many that were later furnished to classes. The basis of the system was a *Child's Scripture Question Book,* covering all of Biblical history. The twelve books which followed covered the Bible; five were on the Old Testament and six on the New Testament, and the last was a general review. The introductions stressed the value of uniform lessons for the whole Sunday school with graded use in the classes, the advisability of dividing the lessons if they were too long, and suggested monthly reviews and teachers' meetings. In the introduction to most of the volumes appeared this sentence in italics: "The great object of a book of questions is to excite the mind to a careful and thorough examination of the Scriptures." The teacher was encouraged to "ask many questions not in the book" and "to explain the meaning of each verse."

These Union lessons were widely used but never held complete sway. They were followed by lessons which put special emphasis on denominational distinctions in doctrine. Each denomination issued lessons of its own, stressing its creed. Independent publishers planned lessons to suit their particular constituencies. Writers and publishers competed to provide means to help teachers. Quarterlies and Sunday school materials took the place of the use of the Bible. Semi-Biblical commentaries were produced for the use of teachers in the Sunday school. Extra-Biblical materials introduced in the Sunday school began to compete with Biblical materials. The period from 1840 to 1870 was a period of turmoil known as the "Babel era." The lessons were material-centered, neglecting the growth and needs of pupils in relation to Bible truth. From this confusion arose the demand for improvement of Sunday school lessons.

The rise of the Sunday school convention led to revival of the Union's ideal of a standardized system of lessons which had been on the verge of realization when the confusion of the Babel period began. The main factor in this development was the application of the normal school method of training public school teachers to the training of Sunday school teachers. The leader in this movement was Dr. John H. Vincent, who founded in 1865 *The Chicago Sunday-School Teachers' Quarterly*. A second important influence was the teacher institute idea which Sunday school leaders applied to their work. A favorite topic of discussion in Sunday school teachers' institutes was uniform lessons for the same school. The agitation of this idea among teachers laid the basis for the emergence of definite changes.

As teachers became better trained, they demanded better organization of content for teaching; unitedly they began to insist on the elimination of confusion and on more planning in lesson lists and such helps as would enable them to teach Bible truth more effectively. The outcome was the adoption of the Uniform Bible Lesson System. In bringing this to pass, Dr. Vincent had a direct part. In 1866 he began publication in the *Quarterly* of a two-year course of "uniform" lessons on the life of Christ. These lessons were short sections of eight to fifteen verses, with home readings, golden texts, and explanatory notes. Designed to lead pupils back to the Bible, which had been largely supplanted by other content, these lessons were more helpful to teachers than any previously published. In 1867, Dr. Vincent was succeeded as editor by Dr. Edward Eggleston, who promoted the uniform policy on a national scale. Changing the name of the *Quarterly* to *National Sunday School Teacher,* he published therein a National Series of Lessons.

For some years, B. F. Jacobs had been deeply impressed with the advantages of the scheme of lessons started by Dr. Vincent. Becoming enthusiastic over the possibility of having the Sunday school world united in the study of one lesson for the entire school and the same lesson everywhere, he persuaded Dr. Eggleston and Dr. Vincent, who had become editor of a rival series of lessons called the Berean Series, to compromise and to cooperate with him in developing a uniform series of lessons for the year 1872. This series was in use nearly four months prior to the meeting of the National Sunday School Convention of that year.

So general was the movement in favor of uniformity that, when Mr. Jacobs made in this convention the proposal to create one International Lesson Committee, the proposition was supported almost unanimously. The following year the famous International Uniform Bible Lessons made their official appearance. The Committee formed to issue these aimed to provide lessons designed for direct study of the Bible itself. To this end, the Committee published no helps, only a list of Bible lessons, leaving to denominational and independent publishers the supplying of helps. The principles of the system, in reference to the Bible, were these: (1) The selection of short sections, complete in themselves for the Bible lessons; (2) uniform lessons for the whole school; (3) the covering of the entire Bible in a cycle of six or seven years; (4) alternations quarterly or semiquarterly between the Old and New Testaments.

The inauguration of the uniform lesson plan was one of the most significant events in the history of the Sunday school. It marked a great step forward in its day and the new lessons made possible an era of marvelous Sunday school progress. The appearing of lessons without commentary made urgent the producing of lesson helps. Publishers—private and denominational—soon put out a variety of helps, some good and some not so good. In general, they reflected clearly a move away from the older mechanical methods of instilling Bible knowledge in the direction of helping the pupil to grasp meaning through explanation and illustration. For about twenty years, the uniform lessons seem to have been productive of real Bible study.

But in spite of improved teaching helps and in spite of the fact that for more than a generation after 1872 the great majority of Sunday schools used them, there were objections to the Uniform Lessons. Dissatisfaction with them grew as the Sunday school came to be more and more the chief agency for inculcating Bible knowledge. The basic objection was that they resulted in so fragmentary a study of the Bible that knowledge of it was not comprehensive and complete. General grasp of a particular book or of the trend of a historic period was almost entirely lacking in the average Sunday school. Through the enterprise of energetic publishers, lesson helps became so numerous that the purpose of the system was in part frustrated, and the Bible was once more largely supplanted by lesson materials.

The plan of having a common passage of Scripture for all ages did not prove in practice to be a satisfactory arrangement of Biblical material, either for adults or for children. It left the Sunday school program fundamentally unchanged—material-centered instead of pupil-centered. The impartation of a specific body of knowledge continued to be the chief educational objective; adaptation to specific age needs was necessarily limited so long as the practice of using a uniform lesson for all ages was followed. As the scientific method in general education began to impinge upon the Sunday school, Christian educators sought methods of instruction designed to help the pupil understand the relationship of the lesson to his life. During the last fifteen years of the nineteenth century, educational workers promoted more and more the idea of "teaching the pupils" instead of "teaching the lesson."

The graded principle, which adapted lesson content to the needs, interests, and abilities of those taught and which was recognized in secular education as an absolute essential, had long had its sponsors among Sunday school workers and writers. In 1872 when the Uniform System was adopted, a plea had been made in the Convention for graded lessons but, after discussion, the uniform lessons were adopted. As time went on, opposition to the Uniform System grew, finding expression in two directions: one group sought to attain their end by developing courses independently of the Lesson Committee while another group tried to work through this Committee.

In the first group were certain denominational leaders who had for years been developing their own lesson systems. Some denominations had excellent courses of well-graded lessons, but sectarian emphasis precluded their being used generally. To this group belonged also pioneer educators who were courageous enough to produce series of lessons adapted to the needs of pupils. One of these was Dr. William R. Harper, a distinguished Biblical scholar and a pioneer in modern methods of Bible study. Given a free hand to demonstrate the graded principle in the Hyde Park Baptist Church in Chicago, he, with the aid of the faculty of the divinity school of the University of Chicago, of which he was president, prepared for each grade of pupils lessons suited to their needs. His completed work was widely used by schools of many denominations.

Another pioneer who created a series of lessons as a protest against the Uniform System was Rev. Erastus Blakeslee. His six-year course soon won favor and found its way into schools of nearly all denominations, being popular not only in the United States but in foreign countries as well. Later, Mr. Blakeslee prepared a completely graded series of lessons which, upon his death in 1910, was taken over for publication by Charles Scribner's Sons and became known as the Completely Graded Series.

The group that worked with the Lesson Committee in the movement for graded materials had for a leader Mrs. J. Woodbridge Barnes, an outstanding primary worker. In 1884 the National Primary Union had been formed; in 1887 its name was changed to the International Primary Union. An avowed purpose of this group of women was to secure a better selection of material for younger children through working within the organized Sunday school movement. After repeated efforts, they succeeded in obtaining from the Lesson Committee a list of optional primary lessons for 1896.

The New Jersey School of Methods for Sunday School Workers was also an effective agency in securing graded lessons. It was in this school that Mrs. Barnes proposed to students this question: "What do we wish our children to know about the Bible before they are twelve years of age?" Together they worked out an outline which became the basis of the graded lessons of the Elementary Department of the Sunday school. These were approved by the International Sunday School Convention in Denver in 1902. It was also in the New Jersey school that Miss Margaret Cushman developed a system of kindergarten lessons which many teachers began to use in 1899. The success of these had no small part in influencing the convention in 1902.

All along, the International Sunday School Association had been unwilling to allow the term "International Lessons" to be attached to primary materials and would not approve of any plan for advanced lessons. However, friends of the graded materials persisted in their efforts. Mrs. Barnes, in patient, persistent manner, with much tact and foresight, accomplished what many desired but seemed unable to bring about. She was Superintendent of the Elementary Division of the Association. In 1905 she succeeded in getting on the program of the International Convention a series of lectures dealing with childhood and adolescence, thus bringing to the attention of delegates the principles underlying the demand for lessons adapted to graded needs. In 1906 Mrs. Barnes was granted permission by the International Executive Committee to cooperate with the Lesson Committee and those who were planning graded lessons for the primary and junior levels. Immediately she organized a Graded Lessons Conference which was attended by age group workers and others interested in the movement for graded lessons.

At this conference the needs of children of various ages were considered, appropriate subject matter for courses was described, and plans were made for the organization of lessons according to the principle of grading. These plans called for revision of the beginners' course accepted in 1902, to be followed with a three-year primary course and a four-year junior course. The plans covered nine years of graded material, to the completion of the average pupil's twelfth year.

The proceedings of this conference were transmitted to the International Lesson Committee which in turn submitted them to the Executive Committee of the International Sunday School Association. The outcome was the drawing up of resolutions recommending the continuance of the uniform lessons but calling also for "the preparation of a thoroughly graded course covering the entire range of the Sunday school." These resolutions, submitted to the Louisville Convention in 1908, were passed without a dissenting vote. The Lesson Committee, which prior to this time had prepared outlines for only the Uniform Lessons, was now directed to prepare a second system to be called the International Graded Series.

Thus there became available a closely graded system of lessons—one offering a separate unit of study material for each grade or year. Several leading denominational publishing houses organized a syndicate for joint production of these lessons. These were first used in Sunday schools in 1910. Graded lessons rapidly won their way and were extended to include all ages. During the organizational upheaval of the early part of the twentieth century, various denominations and some independent publishers issued series of graded lessons also. With the formation of the International Council of Religious Education in 1922, organizational unity was restored. Such restoration did not, however, result in lesson unity. The Council never tried to stop the trend toward multiplication of lesson materials. Instead, through its Professional Advisory Sections, it sought to make available knowledge of educational principles upon which specific groups could develop lessons in accord with their particular beliefs. The outcome was the situation existing to the present day: most religious groups have their own lessons which, in the case of graded ones, are standardized according to the Council's scheme of departmentalization for the various ages.

Later, a modification of the closely graded plan brought into being a third series of lessons—the departmental or group-graded. Many Sunday schools are small, making it difficult to divide the pupils into separate classes for each of the different grades. Yet small schools can profit from doing graded work. In such schools gradation needs to be on the departmental basis instead of by single ages and grades. The group plan made the department instead of the grade the unit of the Sunday school and provided a uniform lesson for the department. This lesson covered essentially the same subject matter as was included in the span of the closely graded courses for that department. The International Council of Religious Education adopted the group plan and gave it the same standing as the closely graded type of lesson.

A Turning Away from the Bible in the Sunday School

The aim of the Sunday school as expressed by its outstanding leaders during most of the last half of the nineteenth century was twofold: the conversion of the pupil and the imparting of Bible knowledge. The uniform lessons were wholly from the Bible, which was accepted as the revealed Word of God and the source of spiritual life for pupils. Always there were members of the Lesson Committee who accepted the authenticity of the Bible and who sought to follow "the way of Abel" in the preparation of lessons for the Sunday school. In the early years of the present century these were distinctly in the majority.

However, the minority on the Committee were part of a larger group who, in the later years of the preceding century, began to forsake the ideal of imparting Bible knowledge. These became possessed with a desire to get results in actual religious living on the part of pupils, that is, to build religious character. They made religious education and character education synonymous terms. They considered appropriate as lesson material any and all content that had promise of calling forth religious response. Hence they advocated inclusion in Sunday school lessons of much extra-Biblical material, such as inspirational biography, studies of social problems, and other content of current import. Along with this, they placed strong emphasis on pupil activities for molding character through creative experiences.

The Graded Lessons Conference had taken as the general purpose of graded lessons this principle: "to meet the spiritual needs of the pupil in every stage of his development." It was the conception of many age-grade workers that to achieve this end it was advisable to include in the Sunday school lessons extra-Biblical content such as the lives of missionaries and other Christian heroes. When such material was introduced, much opposition arose. The outcome was a compromise authorizing two lesson courses, one to contain only Biblical material and the other to have extra-Biblical content. Some denominations chose the outlines containing non-Biblical material and other denominations chose those with only the Biblical.

The graded lessons made for the entrance of another factor from which the uniform lessons had up to this time been immune. Some of the writers of the syndicate formed to publish the former set forth in the lesson helps liberal views that raised questions as to their acceptance of the Bible as the authentic Word of God. This made these lessons unacceptable to some denominations, so these inaugurated their own series, selecting denominational writers to prepare lesson helps.

By 1910 it was rather generally deemed that lesson writers, though they should not discard the Bible, might well go outside the Bible for teaching materials. The closely graded lessons contained much that was Biblical, but they had also a great deal of content drawn from other sources—Bible-related, history, biography, literature, and nature. And there had been a shift in emphasis; the Bible was to be used, not for its own sake primarily but to meet the needs and the problems of pupils of the age level where it was taught.

In 1915 the International Lesson Committee was reorganized to permit representation from the denominations. The new representatives stood for two types of graded lesson series and would probably have abolished the uniform series. However, the latter still had advocates, and for the sake of harmony a modification of the uniform lessons was agreed upon. To preserve the principle of uniformity, a common golden text, common daily Bible readings and, so far as possible, a common portion of the Scriptures was retained. Separate lesson topics were selected for four age groups—Primary, Junior, Intermediate-Senior, and Young People-Adult. Since 1918 this series has been known as the International Improved Uniform Lessons. The failure of those who developed these lessons to use a larger portion of the Bible or to meet the needs of all departments of the Sunday school has made the lessons the subject of the same criticisms as have been directed against the uniform plan from the beginning.

Dissatisfaction with this series and the general feeling that it was inexpedient to have three lesson systems—a closely graded, a departmentally graded, and a uniform—led to the appointment of a committee to survey the whole field. After a most thorough investigation, this committee made a report in 1920 which was adopted in 1922. The recommendations provided for graded lessons Biblical in content that would give the pupils good, workable knowledge of the Bible and provide a cycle of three years for each group. The groups were to be Primary, Junior, Intermediate, Senior, and Adult, including young people. There were to be two series of lessons in the new system, group graded (called International Group Lessons) and closely graded (called International Graded Lessons). The former were to replace the Improved Uniform Lessons, beginning January 1, 1924.

The last recommendation was amended, for allegiance to the uniform lessons was strong, and vigorous protests were made against abandoning them. Therefore, it was decided to continue them for the time being. So the uniform lessons remained in the field and, before group-graded lessons could fully take their place, a development occurred which caused many Sunday school workers to continue to use them. This new development was the outcome of the impact of contemporary theories of science, education, and liberal theology.

The enlarging of the lesson committee had meant the bringing in of those who strongly favored the graded principle as against the uniform plan. For the most part these were liberal rather than conservative believers. They grew in prestige until their influence dominated the lesson committee and led to marked changes in Sunday school lessons. The factor that bore most definitely upon the thinking of these members of the lesson committee was the popular vogue of the pragmatic philosophy of which John Dewey was the leading exponent. This philosophy, spun out of the thought of man and exalting an unfounded sense of human sufficiency, had tremendous effect on education, including religious education.

The key word in education based upon pragmatic philosophy is experience—the experience of the individual, not the experience of the race. Applied educationally, experience is gained through projects—constructive, problematic, or purposeful in type. Experience-centered lessons are those which carry out the experiences of the individual, with no reference to the experience of the race. Education founded on such a conception is religious, not Christian, for it does away with the Bible.

As the outcome of a well-organized movement to introduce the project method of teaching into religious education, Sunday school lessons came to be made up of social projects. The leading denominations discarded the lesson recommendations of the committee of 1920 and began to construct experience-centered lessons—lessons marked by absence of the Bible. By 1922, the year of the forming of the International Council of Religious Education, thousands of Sunday schools had ceased to give instruction based on the Bible. Methodology and man-made ideas had so fascinated writers of Sunday school lessons that they practically eliminated the Bible in their planning of lessons. The experience-centered lessons turned out to be lessons with much of man's supposed knowledge and little of God's revealed truth in them.

The influence of Dewey and of what came to be known as "progressive education" led to the exaltation of humanism with its social philosophy. In place of the Bible were put projects in which the pupil adventured in the experience of "Christian living." The Christian life, far from being the outcome of the operation of the Spirit of God in the heart, comes, it was said, through the reconstruction of the pupil's experience. Much stress was placed on the "social gospel," remaking the social order, and setting up the kingdom of God here and now. In classes for young people and adults there were substituted for Bible content lessons in sociology, economics, and political science, with projects for building a better world.

Since 1930, Sunday schools throughout the country have been making large use of this type of lesson materials. The substitution of these experience-centered lessons for the International Group and Graded Lessons left the orthodox constituency of the churches without Bible-centered lessons. When this situation was brought to the attention of denominational publishing houses, they suggested that those who did not like what was being published should return to the uniform lessons. To avoid the use of experience-centered lessons with virtually no Bible content, thousands did turn back to the Uniform Lessons in spite of the shortcomings these have.

The International Council of Religious Education, after its formation in 1922, was the most influential agency in the field of religious education—today quite generally called Christian education. Under the leadership of the Council, the most marked feature was the continuing professionalization of religious education, a movement first finding organizational expression in the founding of the Religious Education Association in 1903.

A change in the conception of the educational function of the church has accompanied the emergence of a professional group devoting themselves consciously to working on problems of religious education in a secular state. During the present century it has come to be realized that the Sunday school is only one means by which the church carries on its program of Christian education. There has been an awakening to the fact that the whole church must be a school, because all persons within the fellowship and the reach of the church need to be taught. The church performs its educational function in many ways and at many times. Also, it is being realized more and more that the home is the basic institution for teaching Christian truth. In the recognition that parents must share with their children what they themselves know and believe, publishers are developing Sunday school lessons for the family.

For Protestants in general, there are at the present time two types of Sunday school lessons: uniform and graded. The former, set up in six-year cycles, has two aims: to provide for study of the Bible as a whole and to center upon those portions which afford best teaching and learning values. Each year there are included some aspect of the life or teaching of Jesus and some challenge to Christian living. Actually, only a small portion of the total content of the Bible is given, and certain doctrinal passages are never included. Graded lessons differ according to their source. Some of them center on the Bible, but interpret it from the liberal point of view. Some are excellent educationally, but have no truly Christian content.

In 1950 the National Council of the Churches of Christ in the United States of America was formed by twenty-nine denominations with the merging of the Federal Council of the Churches of Christ in America and seven other religious organizations, including the International Council of Religious Education. The National Council functions through four main divisions: Christian Education, Christian Life and Walk, Home Missions, and Foreign Missions. The Division of Christian Education is comprised of a Commission on General Christian Education, a Commission on Higher Education, and a Joint Commission on Missionary Education. The Commission on General Christian Education directs and controls the production of most lessons now used in American Sunday schools.

The National Council set up committees for uniform lessons and for graded lessons respectively. The former has about seventy members, representing thirty denominations in the United States and Canada. It works under the direction of a chairman elected triennially by the Commission on General Christian Education and an executive secretary who is the director of the Department of Curriculum Development of the Commission. The second committee has approximately one hundred members appointed by the denominations planning to use the outlines produced. The number of denominations participating in the work of the committee varies from time to time, but usually is more than twenty. Its chief officers are a chairman elected triennially by the Commission on General Christian Education and an executive secretary who is the director of the Department of Curriculum Development of the Commission.

The theological emphases and the educational principles of the National Council in the field of Christian education are a matter of serious concern to many people. Among the writers of Sunday school lessons produced by the Council are men and women who deny the infallibility of the Word of God and who question its accuracy and authority. There may be leaders in the Council who are disturbed over this condition. And there are likely writers and others engaged in the production of National Council lessons who desire to stand for the truth as revealed by God. However, it is evident that their influence is not predominant, that the policy of the National Council as a whole is not in the direction of acceptance by simple faith of that knowledge which has its source in God.

Directly and indirectly the National Council exercises control over the production of Sunday school lessons. It wields direct influence through its official organ, *The International Journal of Religious Education,* a magazine that forcefully presents Council thought and policy in Christian education. The Council also influences directly, through the numerous conferences on Christian education it holds, a number of Protestant denominations which do not belong to it. Representatives of such denominations are invited to these conferences and encouraged to participate in them. In the third place, the Council exerts direct influence effectively, though somewhat intangibly, through graduates of institutions of higher learning who, having specialized in religion and Christian education, are recognized by lesser writers as "scholars" and "authorities." Through these means the National Council is gaining more and more control over everything having to do with what is today called Christian education.

Indirectly, the National Council exercises controlling influence over Sunday school lessons by means of the uniform series, the system of lessons most widely used by Protestants. Many denominations make use of them, several commentaries on them are published each year, syndicated treatments of them appear in weekly and daily papers and, through the World Council on Christian Education, outlines on them are made available for Sunday school lessons in more than fifty countries other than the United States.

The outlines of the uniform lessons are copyrighted by the National Council. Through the copyright the Council exerts tremendous influence and control. Member denominations pay nothing for use of the outlines. But all other denominations, having millions of members, all independent publishers, and other groups wishing to use the outlines in any way must obtain permission of the Council and pay a royalty for the privilege of using them. Thus is provided a potent means by which the Council can influence Sunday schools.

Many evangelicals use the outlines. Evangelicals serve on the Uniform Lesson Committee of the National Council, taking for granted that since the basis for the uniform lessons is the Word of God, the Lord will bless its use, whatever interpretation the liberal members place upon the Bible passages selected. However, modernists, neoorthodox adherents, and social gospel advocates are adept in selecting passages of Scripture suitable for their purpose, omitting others, and arranging them so as to set forth the doctrines they wish to teach. As did Eve, so men do today. Instead of accepting as fact and truth what God says, they twist the meaning to fit their own fancy and desire. Rather than receive in simple faith the plain teaching of the Word of God, they so slant His statements and so select them as to make them support their preconceived ideas. The virtual effect has been the elimination of the Bible as God's revelation.

The Bible Brought Back into the Sunday School

The Bible is the center around which evangelical Christians unite in fellowship and cooperative action. The early Christians were "one in Christ"; they had real fellowship together and they worked together harmoniously in the service of their Lord. So long as the Word of God was honored as such, there was spiritual and temporal unity among believers. But with the coming of apostasy, divisions appeared. When church conformity was stressed above adherence to the truths of divine revelation contained in the Scriptures, the church degenerated. But evangelical Christianity did not die, for God never leaves Himself without a witness among men to the truth He has revealed. But insofar as its visible state was concerned, evangelical Christianity went into eclipse. It did not again appear as a bright shining light visible to men in general until the time of the Reformation.

This light shone in many places. While different doctrinal emphases resulted in various church groupings, the Bible was common to all. Believers regarded one another as brethren on the basis of their faith in Christ and obedience to Him in accordance with the Holy Scriptures. Those called Protestants stood steadfastly for the basic teachings of the Word of God. These teachings included the inspiration, authenticity, and sufficiency of the Bible; the universal priesthood of all believers; the right and the duty of private judgment as to the meaning of the Scriptures; the Trinity; the incarnation, the nature and the work of Christ; the fall of man and the necessity for the new birth; justification by faith; the work of the Holy Spirit in conversion and sanctification; the immortality of the soul; and future rewards and punishments.

From the beginnings of Protestantism there was a measure of cooperation among church bodies which accepted these basic teachings. However, dangers and threats from without and intolerance, pride, selfishness, and bigotry from within the denominations were hindrances to the progress of the Gospel of Christ. These conditions caused Christian leaders to realize the need for united effort in carrying on the work of God. The outcome was the founding in 1846 of the World Evangelical Alliance, through which Protestantism accomplished much in behalf of religious liberty, observance of the Lord's Day, evangelism, temperance, human freedom, and the application of Christian principles in government and society. The Alliance established a World Day of Prayer and a Universal Week of Prayer. It united in fellowship those who were one in

Christ and helped to break down denominational intolerance, selfish ambition, and bigotry.

For about fifty years the Alliance presented a united front for the truth revealed by God in the Scriptures. Near the end of the nineteenth century, certain individuals in the Alliance, influenced by German rationalism and enamored with the social gospel, tried to inject into the organization ideas of their own based upon doubts of the authenticity of the Scriptures and the deity of Christ. When the Alliance refused to depart from the evangelical faith, these liberals withdrew and organized, in 1894, the Open Church League. In 1900 this became the National Federation of Churches and Christian Workers.

During the early decades of the present century, German rationalism and ideas of the social gospel much affected religious life. The result was a new interpretation of Christianity known as "liberalism." This grew rapidly and challenged orthodoxy in every area of thought. The outcome was much controversy—in theology, which was practically revolutionized; in philosophy, which became materialistic; in psychology, which turned from purposivism to mechanism; and in education, which, discarding the Bible and Christ, became a man-centered process. Liberalism penetrated all phases of life and all institutions of Christendom, causing a tremendous defection from the revealed truth of God.

The World Evangelical Alliance, due to unwise policies and to overseas domination, had lost the wholehearted allegiance of the churches. Liberals who had organized the National Federation of Churches and Christian Workers conceived the idea of founding a union of Christian churches. So in 1905 they brought forth the Federal Council of Churches of Christ in America. Beginning with thirty-two denominations in its membership, the Federal Council was for some years fairly representative of organized Christianity, and it accomplished much for the Christian cause. From its inception, cleavage between liberals and evangelicals was evident, but both parties sought to keep their differences from hindering attempts at Christian cooperation. Well-intentioned evangelicals worked with the Council in the hope that liberalism would soon run its course and pass away.

The Federal Council came to be recognized generally as the official voice of Protestantism. Though largely under the influence of liberal leadership, it considered itself the spokesman for all of Protestantism. Yet, evangelicals found that its virtual monopoly not only restrained the freedom of noncooperating denominations but often promoted liberalism at the expense of Bible-believing, Christ-honoring Protestants. Of these there were at least twenty million. Since they had in the Council no true representation of their doctrinal position, they had no alternative but to found an organization of their own for cooperation and united action. So in 1942, at a national conference convened in St. Louis which was attended by more than two hundred evangelical leaders representing thirty-four denominational, missionary, and educational organizations, steps were taken to form an evangelical association. Plans were consummated the following year in a meeting in Chicago with the founding of the National Association of Evangelicals, which established as a basis for fellowship and cooperative action the unqualified acceptance of the Bible as the Word of God.

It was from this background of controversy, reaction against liberalism, and renewal of efforts toward united evangelical action that the Bible was brought back into the Sunday school. Within a few years after liberalism started to have effect in the churches, there was evident a decline in attendance and spiritual power. This decline had a definite and deleterious effect on the Sunday school. This institution, which in the last fifty years of the nineteenth century had undergone marvelous growth, began as early as the first decade of the twentieth century to show a decrease in enrollment.

Moreover, the activity in the International Council of leaders with a liberal theological slant caused unrest and dissatisfaction among evangelicals in the churches. Evangelicals were also greatly concerned because the literature produced by religious educators showed a lack of emphasis on the necessity of the new birth. In addition, Christian lay leaders missed the fervor and the inspiration of the great Sunday school conventions. After 1922, conventions had become for the most part conferences of professional leaders instead of meetings for considering the best ways of reaching men with the Gospel and for nurturing the life of God in the soul.

For some years disturbed evangelicals were not united. Though all agreed that something should be done, they did not agree on what ought to be done and how to do it. Some were in favor of trying to reform the International Council. Some started independent smaller agencies. Others felt that a new national Sunday school organization ought to be formed. Not until 1939 was there any united evangelical move of importance. In that year a group of independent publishers held a conference to discuss the uniform lesson situation in relation to the International Council. All of these publishers, as well as many denominational publishers, were becoming increasingly dissatisfied with the Council's lesson outlines.

Among the causes of such dissatisfaction with these outlines were the liberal theological and progressive education approach, undue emphasis on social gospel teachings, the use of topical lessons and the choosing of unrelated Bible passages to set forth ideas not taught in the Bible, failure to provide a comprehensive view of the Bible, lack of emphasis on fundamental Christian doctrine, too little stress on evangelism, adherence to principles basically humanistic in emphasis and naturalistic in application instead of evangelical and scriptural, and the failure of the lesson committee to consult evangelical editors and publishers who produced most of the Sunday school literature based on the uniform lessons.

The meeting of 1939 was a protest meeting of a group that took no action. It served to convince evangelical leaders more fully that they ought to form some kind of organization for united action. The result was the founding of the National Association of Evangelicals, as was told above. Among the men who took a leading part in forming this Association were a number who were much interested in Christian education in general and in the Sunday school in particular. The year it was founded, the Board of Administration of the Association considered the possibility of developing a new evangelical system of uniform Sunday School lessons.

In 1944, at a meeting in Columbus, Ohio, called by the Church School Commission of the National Association of Evangelicals and attended by independent publishers, denominational publishers and editors, and leaders of interdenominational and undenominational organizations, two proposals were made: first, new uniform Sunday school lesson outlines should be produced; second, the task of producing them should be committed to a new national Sunday school association organized on evangelical bases. The adoption of a graded curriculum for weekday schools was also considered, as was the formation of a strong permanent Christian Education Committee.

As an outgrowth of the Columbus meeting, a conference was held in Chicago in 1945. More than a hundred leaders in the field of Christian education attended. At this time a temporary organization of the National Sunday School Association was effected. The resolutions passed called for a national Sunday school convention in Chicago in 1946, cooperation with the National Association of Evangelicals, an invitation to all evangelicals to participate in the Association, adoption of the doctrinal statement of the National Association of Evangelicals as that of the Sunday School Association, and the formation of a committee to draw up a constitution for the new organization.

The board and the committees of the National Association of Evangelicals cooperated fully with the temporary executive committee of the National Sunday School Association in making plans for the preparation of new uniform lesson outlines, for the first convention, and for formulating a constitution. The first convention was attended by Sunday school workers from thirty-five states and two Canadian provinces. Delegates were united concerning the necessity for founding a national organization for reviving the Sunday school. The convention adopted a constitution for the National Sunday School Association, elected officers, approved the new uniform lesson project, and provided for a program of expansion. The Association was made an affiliate of the National Association of Evangelicals, thus settling the future relationship between the two organizations.

The purposes of the National Sunday School Association are set forth thus in its constitution: "To revitalize Sunday schools; to promote and encourage the study of the Bible; to foster Sunday school conventions; actively to encourage progress in all phases of Christian education; to publish, print, distribute, sell, and otherwise deal in books, papers, periodicals, etc. necessary in the furtherance of the purposes of this Association; to establish a central bureau for Sunday schools with which various churches, denominations, conferences and Sunday school associations may be affiliated; and to secure cooperation and unity of action in promoting Sunday school work in general, nationally and internationally."

In carrying out these purposes, the first concern of the Association was its uniform lesson project. To see the weaknesses of the series put out by the International Council was easier than to correct them. Most leaders in the task of developing new lessons did not favor the uniform principle, preferring the graded or departmental principle. However, the practical situation was that most Sunday schools were small, and the majority still used the uniform system; only this fact made these men willing to develop an evangelical uniform series.

So urgent was the felt need for evangelical lessons that when the lesson committee, which had done considerable work on the project, made a report to the first convention in 1946, that body expressed its unanimous and enthusiastic approval of the uniform lessons proposed. Use of these was first made on January 4, 1948 by a million pupils across the United States. Today, over three million pupils are using the lessons provided by twelve or more publishers, and the number is steadily increasing.

The following are the principles guiding the production of these lessons:

1. The name of the lesson series shall be *The Uniform Bible Lesson Outlines,* prepared by the National Sunday School Association.
2. The curriculum shall be Bible-centered in content. The text for study shall be related to, and in harmony with, the context both in letter and spirit.
3. The supreme purpose of the series shall be the winning of every pupil to the Lord Jesus Christ and the submission of his life to the will of God.
4. The lesson shall be directed to the teaching and training of the pupil for Christian character and service.
5. Recognizing the limitations of the theory of gradual development as the solution of problems of character, the curriculum will keep clearly in view the important place of crisis, conflict, and choice in the making of Christian character.
6. Each cycle of lessons will be six years in length.
7. Cycle content will consist of selections of Scripture: approximately 40 percent from the Old Testament, 40 percent from the New Testament, and 20 percent topical lessons. Three quarters in each year will be devoted primarily to instruction in a body of Bible truth, and one quarter will be devoted to further emphasis on application.
8. The selection of lessons shall be determined primarily by

the nature and capacities of childhood, with necessary adjustment to adolescent and adult life.

9. Topical lessons shall be limited in number and always grounded in Scripture.
10. The schedule of lessons shall be geared to the major observances of the church year.

Three committees responsible to the board of the Association are involved in the preparation of the lessons. The Central Committee consists of nine members chosen annually by the Board of Directors. All members are divided into initiators and collaborators. The former, after basic decisions have been made by the whole committee, make initial drafts of assigned sections of the cycle of lessons, four years in advance of use. After the whole committee has approved these drafts, the collaborators assist in completing final drafts. The General Committee consists of the members of the Central Committee and representatives of all publishers who produce lesson materials based on Association outlines. This committee considers the final drafts of the outlines and makes recommendations as to the character of the lessons and the policies under which they are produced.

The Advisory Committee of One Hundred examines critically the work of the Central Committee in final draft and makes further recommendations relative to corrections and changes. This Advisory Committee is chosen with the greatest care by the board of the Association so as to be representative of evangelical Protestantism. Its members represent denominations, publishers, pastors, educators, and Sunday school teachers and leaders. Following a careful review of all comments and recommendations on the final draft, revision is made by the Central Committee. This goes to the Board of Directors of the Association for approval and official permission for release to publishers, editors, and writers.

The third cycle of lessons, covering the years 1959 to 1964, is now in use. It has never been the purpose of the National Sunday School Association to push uniform lessons above graded ones but rather to fill a need. Graded lessons provided by evangelical publishers are promoted with equal zeal by Association leaders; they subscribe to the view that the graded principle is more educationally sound. Recently the board of the Association has been considering the issuance of graded lessons. These are being used more and more by evangelicals, many of whom have turned to graded courses issued by such publishers as Scripture Press and Gospel Light. At any rate, in seeking to meet a need, the Association has produced in its uniform lessons a series which may have caused the International Council emphasis to be much more evangelical.

Though a primary purpose of forming the National Sunday School Association was to produce lessons that give the Bible its rightful place, most of its emphasis is now on leadership services. One of the Association's major projects is sponsoring Sunday school conventions. It is recognized by the Association, as it had been by devoted Sunday school workers of past years, that conventions are a powerful means of putting life in the Sunday school, of promoting and encouraging Bible study, and of developing and maintaining interest in vital Christian education. At conventions, many people get a vision of what the Sunday school can do, are stimulated to activity, and receive instruction for work. Each year, beginning in 1945, at least one national convention has been held. In addition, the Association sponsors state, regional, city, denominational, and local church conventions. These serve in no slight way the great and important purpose of helping to keep burning brightly the light of evangelical Christian education.

The conventions have two types of meetings: the inspirational mass meeting and the instructional sessions. Conventions have been a fertile field of service; through them the Association reaches, inspires, and helps to train a large number of Sunday school workers. Since 1949 the results of the study and experience of national convention speakers and leaders have been made available in the form of mimeographed papers, constituting annually a volume of the *Sunday School Encyclopedia.* This has become a major means in the purpose to provide leadership education for workers in the Sunday school.

Summer conferences are another means of leadership education. The Association not only sponsors these but also sets them up and conducts them. These are a very successful project, for they bring valuable benefits to those attending, lead to the organizing of other conferences, build up interest in conventions already organized, and help to unite Sunday school workers.

The Association serves evangelical Sunday schools by means of a monthly publication, *Link,* which contains stimulating helps for pastors, Sunday school superintendents, and teachers. It also supplies information on coming conventions (national, state, area, city, and denominational), news items, charts and graphs, and information about Sunday school work in general. The Association provides service literature of value to the cause of the evangelical Sunday school. It maintains a free consulting service for Sunday school workers. It encourages, helps, and organizes city and state Sunday school associations whenever and wherever possible, whether or not these affiliate officially with the National Association, as some fifty have done. As part of the many and varied services performed by the Association, three special weeks are sponsored each year—National Family Week in the spring, National Sunday School Week in the fall, and Youth Week in January.

As means for carrying out its purposes, the Association has set up three Commissions—the Commission on Research in Christian Education, the Youth Commission, and the Camping Commission. The objectives of the first named are to stimulate professional growth, to direct in the formulation of a philosophy of true Christian education, to assist in producing suitable textbooks for institutions of higher learning, and to give guidance to the National Sunday School Association in its Christian education policies. The Youth Commission aims to serve the needs of youth through both denominational and interdenominational organizations. The purposes of the Camping Commission are to unite evangelicals engaged in camping, to share knowledge and experience about camps and camping, to provide helpful services, to encourage high standards, and to perpetuate a Christ-centered philosophy of camping.

Other commissions are to be set up as soon as conditions permit. There is scarcely any limitation to the number of areas in which work helpful to the cause of evangelical Christian education could be carried on. Some under contemplation for which commissions might be formed are: music, adult work, children's work, audio-visual education, Christian publications, evangelism, home and family, leadership training, missionary education, vacation Bible school, and weekday Bible instruction.

The National Sunday School Association has given strong impetus to the reemergence of the Sunday school as a factor in true Christian education. Acting in the capacity of coordinator for more than forty denominations with a constituency of over thirty million evangelical Christians, the Association is a force for infusing life and power, directly and indirectly, into Sunday school work, thus benefiting millions of Sunday school pupils. Emphasizing the Bible as the revealed will of God, the Association makes the purpose of the Sunday school to be that of leading pupils to Christ in salvation and teaching and training them to live in submission to the will of God and in harmony with it. The Association regards man as God's creation, marred by sin and therefore in need of regeneration by God. It looks upon pupils as beings capable of recognizing truth and error and of choosing between them, with capacity for knowing God and for developing mentally, morally, and spiritually in relation to Him.

In accord with its evangelical, Biblical stand, the Association holds that the teaching of the Sunday school must acquaint the pupil with God's will. This is contained in only one authentic and infallible book, the Bible, which must be taught as God's inspired and authoritative revelation to man. Content for teaching must be selected to meet the needs and capacities of the pupil. The curriculum must have the Bible as its center, but this may be supplemented by extra-Biblical material suitable for acquainting pupils with life as they must live it. The content taught must allow for crisis, conflict, and choice as essential elements in the forming of Christian character. There must be ample room for suitable expressional activities.

In its emphasis upon training for church and school the Association acknowledges the worth of the contributions of Christian authorities in education, psychology, and methods. However, the fundamental requirement is that the teacher be a Christian in the real sense of the word and that he live what he professes. By all means, he should have special training and be thoroughly familiar with the objectives of Christian education. He should have a good growing knowledge of the Bible and should be able to lead his pupils to a clear understanding of its truths. He should be open-minded, be able to understand pupils, have real love for them, and be concerned about their eternal welfare. Teaching that does not bring the pupil into vital relationship with Christ, build him up in Christ, and send him out to win others for Christ falls far short of fulfilling the purpose and goal which true Christian education has had throughout its history.

Readings

BENSON, CLARENCE H. *A Popular History of Christian Education.* Chicago: Moody Press, 1943.

BROWN, ARLO A. *A History of Religious Education in Recent Times.* New York: The Abingdon Press, 1923.

DEBLOIS, AUSTIN KENNEDY and GORHAM, DONALD R. *Christian Religious Education: Principles and Practice.* New York: Fleming H. Revell Company, 1939.

The Encyclopedia of Sunday Schools and Religious Education. (JOHN T. MCFARLAND and BENJAMIN S. WINCHESTER, Editors-in-chief). New York: Thomas Nelson and Sons, 1915.

Article on "History of the International Graded Lessons," Ira M. Price, pp. 469-477.

FERGUSSON, EDMUND M. *Historic Chapters in Christian Education in America.* New York: Fleming H. Revell Company, 1935.

FERM, VERGILIUS T. A. (ed.). *An Encyclopedia of Religion.* New York: The Philosophical Library, 1945.

Articles on:

"Religious Education," pp. 649-650.

"Pragmatism," pp. 601-602.

GAEBELEIN, FRANK E. *Christian Education in a Democracy.* New York: Oxford University Press, 1951.

HASTINGS, JAMES (ed.). *Encyclopaedia of Religion and Ethics.* New York: Charles Scribner's Sons, 1955-1958.

Article on "Pragmatism," F. C. S. Schiller, X, 147-150.

LOTZ, PHILIP HENRY. *Orientation in Religious Education.* Nashville and New York: Abingdon-Cokesbury Press, 1950.

MURCH, JAMES DEFOREST. *Christian Education and the Local Church.* Cincinnati: Standard Publishing Company, 1943.

———. *Cooperation without Compromise.* Grand Rapids: Wm. B. Eerdmans Publishing Company, 1956.

QUALBEN, LARS P. *A History of the Christian Church.* New York: Thomas Nelson and Sons, 1933.

RICE, E. W. *The Sunday-School Movement, 1780-1917, and the American Sunday-School Union, 1817-1917.* Philadelphia: The American Sunday-School Union, 1917.

WARKENTIN, ELMO HENRY. "The History of Revitalizing the Sunday Schools of America through the National Sunday School Association." Unpublished Master's thesis, Wheaton College, 1958.

WORRELL, EDWARD K. *Restoring God to Education.* Wheaton, Illinois: Van Kampen Press, 1950.

The Administration Building at Concordia Teachers College, River Forest, Illinois. This college is one of two terminal schools owned and maintained by The Lutheran Church—Missouri Synod for the purpose of preparing full-time professional educators for its elementary and secondary schools and colleges, the largest parochial school system in American Protestantism.

(Courtesy of Concordia Teachers College)

11

Organizations for Religious Education

WHETHER right or wrong, it is the considered opinion of the author that it will be helpful at this point in the narrative to view in a general way for purposes of orientation the history of religious education as it has unfolded in America. Such a view necessarily calls for repetition of some of what has gone before and a preview of what is to follow. Having taken this general view, the remainder of the book will be devoted to the history of organizations (other than the Sunday school) for religious education—education too often merely religious but sometimes Christian. A general view makes evident the interest Protestants have had in religious education and shows the various types of organization they have utilized for giving religious instruction.

From the time America was settled until 1787, the year the Constitutional Convention met, life in general and education in particular were prevailingly Christian. God was recognized as Creator; man was seen as the crown of His creative activity, a creature made in His image and likeness, capable of knowing God, of entering into fellowship with Him, and destined to live not just for a little span of time but for all eternity. The Bible was accepted as the Word of God; it was the supreme authority in faith and morals, the foundation for all obligations and relationships of life. Its precepts were taught in the family, sermons brought its teachings to bear on civic and political developments, and the civil law was based upon its moral codes.

Education, whatever its level or form, was essentially religious.

In New England the typical elementary and secondary schools were controlled by the state but the church had a large part in them and their goals were religious rather than civic. In the middle colonies, schools were of the parochial type in which religious and general education were combined. In the southern colonies, the typical school was the private school, largely under parental control but strongly influenced by the church. The colleges founded prior to 1787 had as their basic purpose the training of ministers for the churches; Bible and theology were the chief subjects taught in them. Thus in all schools—elementary, secondary, and higher—the Bible was central in the curriculum. In fostering a program of education that gave God and His Word first place, the schools of early America did what the Christian church had been doing from its beginning.

The early national period, that is, the period from 1787 to about 1850, was characterized by the secularization both of life and of education, with the result that God was left out. A number of factors contributed to the change from placing God at the center of life and education to ignoring Him and His Word. Chief among these were sectarianism, intellectualism, and statism. Divisions in Christianity made impossible a united impact on community and state, led to conflicts between sects as to what religious teachings should have place in public education, and resulted in elimination of the Bible and all religion, as such, from the public schools. The outcome of Horace Mann's controversy with church leaders in Massachusetts was a law excluding sectarianism from the schools of that state. After 1835, most other states enacted laws against sectarianism. It was, of course, no loss to do away with sectarianism but the accompanying exclusion of religion had most deleterious effects.

Following the Revolutionary War there was a time of infidelity and loss of interest in religion. This condition made possible the coming into America of the rationalistic philosophy prevalent in Europe after the French Revolution. This philosophy regarded ignorance as the source of vice, crime, and all social evils; it held that these would disappear with intellectual enlightenment, the outcome of education. In the words of Frederick Eby, "intellectual enlightenment became a fanatical enthusiasm, a new religious faith for the salvation of the masses." Thus many of that day, as has been the case ever since the days of the Garden of Eden, became possessed with a false estimate of man's capacity and resources, which led them to substitute for the pure knowledge of God the results of man's thinking.

The spread of rationalistic philosophy led eventually to other intellectual developments antagonistic to simple faith in God. One of these was the activity of atheists and agnostics. These organized in 1876 the National Liberal League which had for a purpose the severance of all connection between government and Christianity or any other religion. Particularly it advocated "the discontinuance of religious instruction and worship in the public school." Then toward the close of the nineteenth century naturalism began to exert influence in public education. This made schools in various parts of the country an avenue for the propagation of anti-Christian teachings. Within the scope of naturalism experimentalism arose under the leadership of John Dewey to speed the advance away from God toward secularism in education.

A third factor contributing to secularism was the expansion of government control over education. In colonial days the church was in charge of education. When the Constitution was written, it was deemed wise to provide for separation of church and state. As a consequence of such separation, religious instruction was gradually eliminated from the public schools. The state recognized the necessity of education but, being committed to a policy of separation of church from state, it developed a public school system under its control. More and more this system was divorced from religious influence. In the name of freedom from sectarian control, religion was taken out of the public school.

The results of secularism were damaging to spiritual, social, moral, and political life. Children educated under a program that ignored God and religion naturally regarded the spiritual as unimportant. There was loss of a sense of life's meaning and worth, and a vacuum was created in the realm of values. The outcome was disintegration in many areas of life, followed by a multiplicity of evils such as psychological maladjustment, marital difficulties, decline in morality, and a vast amount of criminological disturbance. Without God the schools could produce neither ethical character nor good citizens. The consequence in every phase of life was corruption and looseness in conduct.

Recognition of the dire results of secular or nonreligious education led to efforts to give the Bible a place in the public school. The difficulty in the way was the need of preserving the principle of separation of church and state. However, as the Bible was honored in courts, prisons, inaugurations, and other phases of public service, it seemed only reasonable to give it a place in schools, where the young were trained for life. Accordingly, the majority of the states adopted the practice of at least allowing it to be read in their schools. A report of the Office of Education issued in 1951 showed the legal status of Bible reading in the public schools to be as follows: thirteen states required it; seven specifically permitted it; eighteen tacitly permitted it; three assumedly forbade it; and seven definitely forbade it. Obviously, the mere reading of the Bible, much as it is to be desired, is no adequate means for coping with the effects of secularism in education.

Another plan was to have classes in religion in the public schools —classes in which factual data from the Bible, church history, and comparative religion were presented in an objective manner by regular teachers on the same basis as language, literature, science, and all other subjects. This plan, of course, would not savor at all of true Christian education. Inevitably, the personal convictions of the teacher influences his presentation. An objective presentation of factual data from a merely intellectual point of view will have no effect in the spiritual life and character development of the pupil. The teaching of the Bible merely as literature or history robs it of its true spiritual value and makes it only a secular subject.

Yet a third plan for bringing into the public school the religious influence so needed to combat the effects of secularism was that of dealing with religion objectively wherever it was met in other subjects such as literature, history, and social studies. The conception was that teachers could in this manner find opportunities to stress needed spiritual and moral values. The objections to this plan are essentially and obviously the same as those mentioned in the preceding paragraph.

During the early national period there were other movements designed to bring religious elements into the lives of the young. As was shown in the three preceding chapters, the Sunday school became the religious school of America. Introduced before the nation was founded, it assumed greater and greater importance as secularism mitigated against religion. Particularly under the leadership of the American Sunday-School Union, the Sunday school served a function in Christian education not always fully appreciated. For more than a hundred years the Sunday school was the chief and almost the only agency for the religious education of Protestant children and youth. The churches, seeing that the teaching of religion was increasingly being left to them, turned to the Sunday school, which they had not hitherto warmly favored. Denominations began to establish boards of education for promoting Sunday schools.

However, misgivings concerning the suitability of the Sunday school led to efforts in other directions. One of these was the attempt by Horace Bushnell to make the family the chief agency of religious education. A second effort was the endeavor of some Protestant groups, notably the Presbyterian Church, to establish parochial schools. Though the Presbyterian program failed, other Protestant groups have established, and continue to maintain, day schools in which religious and general subjects are combined in one curriculum.

A third movement, one destined to exert profound influence in later years, had its beginning near the end of the early national period. This was the organizing of Christian youth. Prior to 1800 some few attempts had been made to do this, but the nineteenth century saw the start of a number of organizations for young people. The most direct forerunner of modern youth societies was the Young Men's Christian Association. Organized in London in 1844 and brought to America in 1851, it furnished the pattern for other similar organizations. The Young Women's Christian Association, also started in England, was introduced into America in 1858. Before these became so thoroughly secularized that they could render slight service to the cause of religious education, they were a source of helpfulness to that cause.

From about 1850 to 1900, the chief feature of religious education in America was the growth and the continuing spread of the Sunday school. The churches, faced with the problem of finding a way to impart religious instruction, turned more and more to developing the Sunday school as a means for meeting the need. One aspect of this development was the effort to train lay teachers. As early as 1827 need had been expressed for a school "for the training of

Sabbath school teachers." However, it was not until 1861 that the plan of teacher institutes was adapted by Dr. John H. Vincent to the training of Sunday school teachers, as was noted in a previous chapter. Out of the teacher institute idea grew the Chautauqua Sunday school summer assembly, begun in 1874, in which the element of normal training of Sunday school workers was predominant. The idea spread rapidly throughout the country, becoming a permanent factor in Sunday school work. Teacher training persists today in what is known, particularly in religious education circles, as leadership education.

Other aspects of the development of the Sunday school as a religious education agency were the association and convention and the development in curriculum. The former were largely lay projects, nondenominational in character, representing the organization of Sunday school interests by areas—local, state, national and, ultimately, international. Associations and conventions contributed to religious education numerous elements that were given concrete embodiment by the churches. The development in curriculum led to the adoption of the uniform lesson system which, though opposed at first, has provided the principal basis for Bible study for many people over many years.

Another general feature of the last half of the nineteenth century was group movements among young people in the churches. Commonly known as young people's societies, these were in their earlier history inspirational rather than educational, but leaders soon recognized the need for a constructive educational program and organized courses of study for local societies. The United Society of Christian Endeavor was started in 1881 by Rev. Francis E. Clark, pastor of a Congregational church in Portland, Maine. This nondenominational society was so successful from its very beginning that the large denominations soon developed youth organizations of their own. In the course of time smaller denominations followed suit, though some made the Christian Endeavor their society. For many years now scarcely any church has been without a young people's organization of some kind. The young people's society has made worthwhile contributions to the program of religious education.

Camping as a phase of modern religious education also had its start in the latter part of the nineteenth century. Camping is known to have begun as early as 1880, when a Rhode Island church held a camp for its members. The Chautauqua summer program, the evangelistic camp meeting, the Salvation Army Fresh Air Camps, and camps conducted by the Young Men's Christian Association were all steps on the way toward Christian youth camps sponsored by denominations and other organizations for the past several decades.

An institution which today is wielding constantly increasing influence in Christian education is the Bible institute or Bible college. This originated near the close of the nineteenth century as the outcome of new interest in the Bible, awakened by the preaching of great men of God. The original purpose was to train men who might stand between pastors and people in local churches. Gradually, however, the purpose came to be to train men and women for service as missionaries, as pastors in smaller churches, and as workers in Christian education.

And still another institution originating prior to 1900 was the vacation church school, often referred to as the daily vacation Bible school. As was the case with the Bible institute, this became more prominent during the twentieth century.

With the beginning of the present century, religious education started to develop markedly in many directions. As the nineteenth century drew to a close, there had been increasing dissatisfaction with the character of the Sunday school, almost the only agency of religious education. Most Sunday schools were ungraded and were staffed by teachers who knew nothing about principles of education and who ignored the simplest laws of learning and teaching. But with the turn of the century, there began a development of educational interest which led eventually to the emphases prevalent today, such as the daily vacation church school, the weekday school, the youth fellowship, summer conferences and camps, the denominational boards and publications, various interdenominational publishers with publications that are helping mightily the cause of evangelical education, programs in local churches, and departments of religious education in theological seminaries, many colleges, and Bible institutes.

Liberalism had deeply affected Protestantism, causing many to forsake both rationalism and orthodoxy and to seek a reinterpretation of the Christian faith. In Europe some so desired to arrive at an intellectually satisfying faith that they retained little connection with the Christian Gospel. Others held to a truly evangelical faith but tried honestly to keep their minds open to intellectual problems. In America, Emerson and the New England liberals had potent influence. Belief in the goodness of man and the perfectibility of human nature and the power of education to bring about a good society aroused impatience with a theology that stressed human depravity. Members of the churches became divided into two groups, eventually to be called modernists and fundamentalists. Between the two were many people who neither agreed with the theology of the liberals nor were willing to accept everything the fundamentalists stood for.

The Sunday school with its large interest in conversion and its relatively little concern about education and learning grew to be more and more intolerable to those who saw the value of education. Also, advances in educational method in the public schools served to make people critical of the Sunday school.

An outcome of the working of these forces of protest was the formation in 1903 of the Religious Education Association. The object of this organization as stated in its constitution was: "To inspire the educational forces of our country with the religious ideal, to inspire the religious forces of our country with the educational ideal, and to keep before the public mind the ideal of religious education, and the sense of its need and value." The Association has no organic connection with any church; it admits to membership adherents of any and all faiths, Christian and non-Christian, and leaders of a variety of professions in addition to those of education and religion. Its members have not hesitated to take their stand for religious education and have been energetic in investigation and in making known the results of experiments in the field. The bimonthly journal, *Religious Education,* published by the Association, presents the views of scholars and the findings of research on problems of religious education. The Association has had a large influence on religious education in America, and this influence continues to be vigorous.

But, because it was so unrelated to the church and because it chose in the beginning to ignore theology, the Religious Education Association never contributed much to Christian education directly.

Evangelicals were quick to brand as unchristian both the Association and the movement for which it stood. Anyone who undertook to bring educational principles into the church was likely to be considered an enemy of the Gospel of Christ. Thus the religious education movement became identified with liberal theology, and religious educators, whatever their theological faith, found welcome and support only among the liberals. Evangelicals, insisting upon the central place of the Bible, the converting power of the Gospel, and the necessity of doctrine, resisted the efforts of religious educators. The result was that for about three decades little progress was made in the field of Christian education.

Another significant feature in the history of religious education has been the rise since 1905 of denominational concern for religious nurture. Within the denominations, boards of education established trained, professional staffs for promoting religious education. Because the nature of the International Sunday School Association gave little opportunity for denominational leaders to participate, these formed in 1910 the Sunday School Council of Evangelical Denominations. These two organizations were competitors until 1922 when they merged to form the International Sunday School Council of Religious Education—later shortened to International Council of Religious Education.

The term "Christian education," proposed but rejected at the time the International Council was formed, has supplanted the term "religious education," though much going by the name is religious instead of Christian. The International Council continued in existence, expanding as conditions demanded, until in 1950 it merged with other denominational agencies to form the National Council of the Churches of Christ in the United States of America. The Division of Christian Education of the National Council carries within itself the interests of six former church agencies, of which one is the International Council of Religious Education.

The outgrowth of world conventions, held since 1889, was the World Sunday School Association, formed at Rome in 1907. Due to recognition of the fact that Christian education is concerned with areas other than Sunday school work, the name was changed in 1947 to the World Council of Christian Education; in 1950 the words "and Sunday School Association" were added. This organization holds world conventions, regional conventions, and institutes;

publishes a quarterly magazine, *World Christian Education;* carries on curriculum projects; engages in leadership training of nationals; promotes effective use of audio-visual materials; distributes curriculum materials in needy countries; and promotes Christian education in other ways.

The early part of the present century saw extension of the movement to restore the Bible to education. This took the form of weekday religious instruction given public school pupils on released time. Begun in Gary, Indiana, in 1914, the movement spread rapidly, reaching into many states. The prevalence of the practice caused the International Council of Religious Education to organize the Department of Vacation and Weekday Schools to encourage and promote religious education work done by these two types of church schools.

After a general apostasy in the early part of the century, there has been evident since 1930 a strong concern about Christian doctrine, Biblical content, church relatedness, evangelism, and family life; and new curricula have been developed to further these. There has also been a new emphasis on youth work and on work with adults. Demand for a type of school suited to the job has led to experimentation with schools as well as with curricula. Daily vacation church schools have been conducted in numerous variations as have also weekday schools of religious education. There have been extended sessions of the Sunday school and many denominational and nondenominational variations of the young people's society. There have been church nurseries and church kindergartens, and Christian day schools have grown in number. Sunday evening schools, Saturday schools, the graded church, and the junior church are among the activities the church carries on with the purpose of educating youth.

A marked feature of the present century is the professionalization of religious education. This is reflected both on the academic and on the vocational side. Since the early 1920's, there has been remarkable increase in offerings in religious education by universities, seminaries, colleges, Bible colleges, Bible institutes, and training schools set up to prepare personnel to work in the field.

Religious education today offers to both men and women a variety of vocational opportunities as denominational and nondenominational workers with children, with youth, with adults; as teachers of religious education in training schools and in institutions of higher learning; as writers of curricular materials in publishing houses; and as directors of religious education in local churches and denominations. This last profession is one that has arisen since 1907 to provide trained leadership, especially in the local church. The director of religious education, called quite generally the director of Christian education, has come to be a standard member of the congregation's professional staff, providing efficient administration of the varied phases of the educational program of the church.

In recent years there has been increasing awareness of need for an adequate philosophy of Christian education, a curriculum and a school suited to the work of Christian education, and teachers and other workers qualified to teach effectively the truth of God. That Christian education is necessary is generally recognized, but only an education based squarely on the Word of God is Christian. Those committed to this position must beware lest what is called "Christian education" become an area for the application of theories, ideas, or philosophies not of God but of men.

Among the many issues confronting Christian education today none loom larger than those concerned with the characteristics and the development of human beings and the recruitment of teachers who can teach Christian truth effectively. Organization, administration, materials, and philosophical concepts are necessary and helpful, but the most difficult and complex factors are people. In Christian education, God, not the pupil, is the end; the goal is that the pupil, a sinner in need of redemption, become, as a redeemed sinner, like God. For this to be realized, it is necessary to know the pupil, his age and developmental level, his ways of learning, and his individual characteristics and needs.

The second issue concerns the selection of teachers. The function of the teacher as a Christian is to reveal God. Above all else, he is a witness, showing by life and by lip the likeness of Christ whose he is and whom he serves. As a teacher, the effective Christian teacher functions as one who serves God in accord with recognized principles of education. He loves his pupils and instructs them as carefully and tenderly as if they were his own children. He has insight into educational problems and understanding of learners and their needs.

For Christian education, the means for resolution of issues such as these come from two major sources: (1) basic understanding derived from the Word of God about the nature of human beings and about man's relationship to God and to man; and (2) learnings from educational psychology and philosophy about the growth, development, characteristics, needs, and methods of training persons of various ages.

Increasing awareness of needs in Christian education has led colleges, universities, and seminaries to give work dealing with the philosophy, the theory, and the practice of Christian education. Evangelical colleges began near the end of the second decade of the present century to introduce courses in this field. Typically, their offerings consisted of three courses: one devoted to the consideration of basic principles, a second dealing with organization and administration, or practical aspects, and a third one on missions. The purpose of this last course was to acquaint the student with the progress of the Gospel through the ages, to awaken his interest in the responsibility of the Christian to the lost of earth, and to equip him to discharge his individual responsibility as a Christian in meeting the need of men for salvation.

From these small beginnings the movement to include Christian education in the program of institutions of higher learning grew in momentum and in scope of offerings. Colleges everywhere took up the work, and courses grew in number and in variety. So numerous are the offerings that a college student can major in the field and have conferred upon him a Christian education degree. After a few years various universities also began to include work in Christian education. Today students in considerable number major in Christian education not only for the baccalaureate degree but also for graduate degrees.

More recently departments of Christian education have been established in theological seminaries. Not only are candidates for the ministry being required to take work in Christian education but students who so elect are trained to become directors of Christian education. Many churches now employ directors trained in colleges, universities, and seminaries to promote the teaching of the Bible in the Sunday school and in other church organizations and to direct a program of Christian education not only for children but for adults as well. As was mentioned, these institutions of higher learning are making to Christian education a notable contribution both along academic lines and in connection with vocational preparation.

Protestant Day Schools

From this background of the history of religious education in general, it is now relevant to consider more particularly the history of the chief institutions and organizations by means of which religious education, and more especially Christian education, is being carried on at the present time. The first in historical sequence of these institutions and organizations is the Protestant day school.

The church-related day school existed long before America was settled. In one form or another, it has been a characteristic of Protestant education from the beginning. Wherever the Reformation spread, education was a part of it, and the church exercised strong influence upon all types of schools in all Protestant countries. That is to say, all schools were in a real sense "church-related."

This was very true of the early schools of America. The first settlers came to obtain freedom of religion, so their communities were usually church-centered. Accordingly, the institution in which they trained their children was under the direction of the church, as a matter of course. Until well within the nineteenth century, church schools prevailed. Recognizing the right of the church to carry on education, the state assisted the church in this function. At the time the Constitution was adopted, education was not considered a function of the state. The Constitution was framed with a view to government encouragement, not government control, of education.

During the first quarter of the nineteenth century, some general interest developed for a system of state education. There were those who became convinced that education conducted unsystematically by a number of churches for varied religious ends did not meet state or national needs. The result was a bitter controversy between the religious forces and those who favored state-controlled education. The first leading educator to fight for the latter was Horace Mann, "the father of the present American public school system." Through the work of Mann, influenced by what he had seen in Prussia, there was introduced a system of general education supported and controlled by the state.

Divorced from religion, this program committed America to secularism. Mann possessed great courage, broad vision, practical ability, and high ideals of education, but he was an avowed Unitarian. He denied the supernatural in Christianity and believed in the innate goodness of man, claiming that he is capable of development morally and religiously through education. Accepting the liberal rationalism of Europe, he adhered to a naturalistic philosophy concerning man. Upon this he built educational theories revolutionary in character.

At the time education came under control of the state, few people were aware of the far-reaching implications of the change. These few led in a revival of the Christian school. About the middle of the nineteenth century a number of Christian schools were founded. However, the movement was of short duration, for, though the few were convinced regarding the evil consequences of omitting the religious emphasis, these consequences had not yet come. Moreover, early public schools were for the most part Christian to a considerable extent, and it seemed they would remain so.

By the third quarter of the century, education under state control had become quite general, and most church schools had been displaced. A number of the churches swung over to the support of state schools. Foremost among these were the Methodists and the Presbyterians. Other churches, though agreeing in principle with the theory of the state school in a democratic nation, chose to maintain their own systems. Among these were the Mennonites and the Friends. Later, other Protestant systems came into being, including those of the Lutherans, the Seventh-Day Adventists, and the Christian Reformed. For the most part, however, church-related schools largely disappeared. By 1920 nonpublic-school enrollment in elementary and secondary schools was only 7½ percent of the total enrollment of all schools of these levels.

Today American education is far from the principles of truth and right taught by the Christian church. Though better and more efficient methods are being used and though education has accomplished and is yet accomplishing much, wrong philosophies have ascendancy. Man and the world, not God, are taken to be the fundamental source of truth. To a large extent, American education is man-centered. As Walter Lippman said in 1941, "Day after day young people are subjected to the bombardment of naturalism with all of its animosity to Christianity. In the formative years of their lives, or at least during the period of their education when their ideas are crystallizing, they must listen and absorb these ideas of man, the world and religion. With these facts before them, why do Protestants wonder that Christianity has so little influence over young people?"[1]

Widespread dissatisfaction with state schools is evidenced by the rapid increase of attendance in church-related schools during the past quarter century. The new fact in the situation in the last five or ten years is a marked increase in the number of elementary and secondary schools conducted by churches or by groups of Christians. The cause of this trend is the realization on the part of Christians of the fulfillment in history of prophetic words uttered by Dr. A. A. Hodge, of Princeton Theological Seminary, in the midst of the movement to introduce state education:

> A comprehensive and centralized system of national education, separated from religion, as is now commonly proposed, will prove the most appalling enginery for the propagation of anti-Christian and atheistic unbelief, and of anti-social nihilistic ethics, individual, social, and political, which this sin-rent world has ever seen. . . . It is capable of exact demonstration that if every party in the state has the right of excluding from the public schools whatever he does not believe to be true, then he that believes most must give way to him that believes least, and then he that believes least must give way to him that believes absolutely nothing, no matter in how small a minority the atheists or the agnostics may be. It is self-evident that on this scheme, if it is consistently and persistently carried out in all parts of the country, the United States system of national popular education will be the most efficient and wide instrument for the propagation of atheism which the world has ever seen.[2]

The Christian day school is a reaction against what has happened in consequence of the separation of education from religion. A non-religious state school may not be atheistic in its purpose, but it is so in its effect. The true Christian school instills the Christian faith. It is not just a school with an added class in religion but one in

[1]Walter Lippman, "Education versus Western Civilization," *The American Scholar*, Spring, 1941.

[2]A. A. Hodge, *Popular Lectures on Theological Themes* (Philadelphia: Presbyterian Board of Education, 1887), pp. 283 ff.

which the Bible is the center and core of every subject taught and learned, though the Bible itself may not always be used in class. Protestant parents may send their children to church-related schools because of the relatively low teacher-pupil ratio prevailing in private schools, because private schools do better teaching, or for other reasons, but the dominant reason for the existence of day schools is the religious motive.

Those who advocate Christian day schools are in general not antagonistic to the public school. They recognize the need for it from the purely national point of view, and they stand ready, as citizens of their country, to bear their responsibilities with respect to it. They decry, however, the secularism and the naturalism which have permeated this system of education. They are grieved that the Bible is left out of the education of the child in the public school. They are also conscious of the fact that the ultimate goal of life is citizenship in Heaven and that their greatest responsibility is to prepare their children for this higher citizenship. Since a Christian education cannot and should not be provided in public schools, they see it is their duty to establish schools for giving education needed by man as an eternal being.

As was said at the beginning of this section, those who first came to America were accustomed to church-related schools in the lands from which they came. This was particularly true of the Anabaptists, whose forefathers in Switzerland and Germany saw the need of, and had, their own Christian schools, of those of the Reformed persuasion, who reflected a strong Netherlands background, and of the Lutherans, whose schools have followed Lutheranism the world over. In European countries where the Lutheran Church was the state church, Lutheran doctrines were taught in the public schools; in other countries, schools were maintained independently by Lutheran congregations. The courts of the United States have sanctioned church-related education, upholding the right of Christians to conduct their own schools out of the recognition that the training of the child is first a parental privilege and responsibility.

Mennonites took steps to organize a school as early as 1701. Christopher Dock, who came from Germany to Pennsylvania about 1714, devoted himself unceasingly to the labor of teaching, with little regard for compensation. Mennonites established many Christian day schools during the eighteenth century. They were most careful in selecting teachers of the right faith and in choosing textbooks with suitable content. But, as the state school movement grew, Mennonite schools gradually ceased to exist. For about fifty years few of them were maintained. However, with the growth of secularism and the trend of American education away from God and the Bible, Mennonites have been impressed with the need for Christian schools.

Bishop Swartzentruber of Iowa, with a vision of this need, wrote as follows in 1915: "Our greatest need is well established Church schools, staffed with talented teachers of our own members, who are sound in the faith, and able to teach others also."[3] He pleaded for church schools in every community where there was a church, echoing the conclusion to which other church leaders had also come. The first of the new schools was organized in 1928 in Greenwood, Delaware. The movement for such schools increased in strength, spreading across the nation. In 1959, Mennonites reported 160 Christian day schools with an enrollment of 8,893 pupils.

Mennonite schools are under the direct control of the various congregations and are financed by freewill offerings and tuition—mostly by the former. When Mennonite parents are inclined to question the necessity of the financial burden entailed by Christian schools, they are enjoined to ask themselves if their children are worth more to the state than to the church and to consider them in the light of eternity. Mennonite education is founded upon these convictions: God is the source of all truth, natural and supernatural; the task of the church is to teach that God may be glorified and that every child may be brought to Christ; parents are responsible for the training of their children in the ways of the Lord; children should be taught all things needful, both spiritual and material. To achieve these objectives great care is taken to see that everything in the school, curricular and extracurricular, all interactions, all relationships, and all interpretations, are truly Christian.

The first schools organized within the circle of the Christian Reformed Church were established near the beginning of the nineteenth century. The organizational arrangement of these schools was different from that of the Mennonite schools, for they were founded not by the church but by parents and individuals locally organized

[3]*Christian Day Schools for Mennonite Youth* (Lancaster, Pa.: Lancaster Conference Schools, Inc., 1945), p. 20.

for the purpose. So committed to the principle of the Christian day schools were Christian Reformed people that the number of schools grew through the years until more than half of the children from their homes attended their schools. In 1920 these parent-controlled schools of Reformed or Calvinistic persuasion were brought together in the National Union of Christian Schools. The purposes of the Union as set forth in its constitution are: to establish normal schools and to write textbooks; to maintain a school magazine; to raise the standard of education; to keep salaries of teachers adequate; to maintain a teachers' agency; to seek uniformity in teacher appointments; and to propagate Christian education, especially through conferences and conventions.

The basis of the doctrinal position of the Union is the Reformed or Calvinistic world and life view. These are its principles: all life and all instruction should be God-centered; man, created in God's image, must think God's thoughts after Him; man has dominion over all creation; in Adam all men sinned and so live apart from God; through Christ, man is a new creation, but sinful ways still cling to him; all believers are supplied with an adequate knowledge of God through nature and the Bible; education is redemptive, a bringing into conscious subjection to God what has been redeemed in Christ.

Organizers of the Union enunciated four principles in their insistence upon parent-society control of education: God makes parents responsible for the training of their offspring; this responsibility must be borne personally or in union with other persons having the same responsibility, apart from any intermediary, be it church or state; neither the state nor the church is qualified to give rounded instruction to children—the former, in this country, must not have anything to do with religion, the latter being concerned fundamentally with spiritual work, cannot prepare youth for temporal life; the parent-society-operated school may have the aid and the interest of the church, but the church should not dominate the school, for a school board charged with the task of managing a school is the proper agency. In 1960 the National Union of Christian Schools had 233 member schools with an enrollment of 57,310 pupils.

Of all Protestant denominations, the Lutherans, especially the Missouri Synod and the Joint Synod of Wisconsin, have developed the most elaborate and the most extensive system of education. Other Lutheran bodies, like the Slovak Evangelical Lutheran Church, the Evangelical Lutheran Synod, the American Lutheran Church, the Augustana Synod, the National Evangelical Lutheran Church, and the United Lutheran Church in America, while concentrating more on higher education, do have some elementary and secondary schools. The total number of such Lutheran schools in 1960 was 1627 in which were enrolled 194,605 pupils.

Lutheran schools are parochial, that is, they are operated by parishes—sometimes by a single congregation, sometimes jointly by two or more congregations. Thus each school is under the direction of a local church or churches, and under the specific supervision of a pastor. Lutheranism was early an American form of worship and was strong by the time of the Revolutionary War. Following the example of him from whom their church took its name, Lutherans in America manifested from the first keen interest in education. At the time of the Revolution, Lutheran synods had more schools than congregations. Nearly every pastor was called as pastor and teacher; this meant that he was to teach the parochial school of the parish. Lutherans who came to America during the gradual advent of public schools continued to establish their own schools. In the early period, the same log cabin served as church, school, and parsonage. Not infrequently the Lutheran school was the only school in the community. It then tried to accommodate children of non-Lutherans also.

When the Missouri Synod was organized in 1847, it listed among its chief purposes the promoting of parochial schools and the training of teachers. Prior to this, in 1843, an institution to train teachers and pastors had been opened at Altenberg, Missouri. In 1846 a second pastor and teacher training school was founded at Fort Wayne, Indiana. In these, pastors and teachers at first received the same training, because such common preparation was demanded by conditions of rapid growth. From these beginnings the work of teacher training has moved forward until today it is being carried on chiefly in two outstanding institutions of college rank—Concordia Teachers College, River Forest, Illinois, and Concordia Teachers College, Seward, Nebraska. From 1847, when there were 14 schools with 764 pupils, until the present, growth of Lutheran schools has been rapid. In 1960, the number of Missouri Synod schools was 1322 with 159,566 pupils enrolled.

Along with growth in number of schools and pupils, there has been progressive development of organization for the purpose of improving the system of education. As now set up, the Missouri Synod has a Board for Parish Education charged with the task of directing Christian education, formal and informal, from the cradle to the grave. This Board through its Executive Secretary guides, in a general way, parochial schools as one of several agencies of Christian education within the Church. However, the unit—the local church—that conducts a school has the final word in all matters pertaining to the school. Details of administration are committed to a Board of Education of which the pastor of the church is an advisory member. The pastor is commonly appointed the visitor or supervisor of the school for the Board and congregation. In addition there are synodical districts with a circuit visitor who supervises both the congregations and the schools of his circuit. Within each district is a Board of Parish Education with a superintendent who cooperates with the circuit visitor to keep the schools functioning properly.

Every teacher and every administrator must be a believer who is in accord with the doctrinal statements of the Synod. Every subject in the curriculum is interpreted from the Christian point of view. A stated philosophy of Christian education is supposed to be the foundation for all teaching and the guide to every course. This philosophy lists these truths of divine revelation: there is only one God who exists as a single essence in three persons; man, created in God's image, sinned with the result that every person is born in sin and deserves the wrath of God; through the death of Christ man's sin is forgiven if he repents and believes on the Son of God; thus man is regenerated and lives in fellowship with God through love, coming finally to eternal bliss.

Next to the Lutherans, the Protestant body that has done most in the realm of the Christian day school is the Seventh-Day Adventist Church. This Church reported in 1960 schools to the number of 1346 and an enrollment in them of 60,302 pupils. The Adventist school organization is similar to that of the Missouri Synod. Local churches conduct their schools with the assistance of conference superintendents. Seventh-Day Adventists have as an ideal the education of youth, especially children, in church-related schools while they live in their homes with their parents. They believe, however, that as children grow older, they may advantageously be placed in boarding schools where deans of residence serve as "parents." Accordingly, this church manifests considerable interest in boarding academies.

Seventh-Day Adventists have always placed stress on the harmonious development of the physical, mental, and spiritual powers of the individual. In their boarding schools they combine daily physical work with intellectual study. The aim is to build into character the qualities of industry, integrity, orderliness, and dependability. They maintain that, inasmuch as the ultimate goal is citizenship in Heaven, the real objective of life and education is to bring about in man the restoration of the image of God.

Until recent years the situation in elementary and secondary education among the larger Protestant denominations has not been favorable to the Christian position. These churches did found colleges and seminaries, and they supported some preparatory schools but practically no elementary schools. In 1955 the Presbyterian Church in the U.S.A., which in 1846 and 1847 had devised an elaborate but short-lived plan of education for nurturing children in the Christian faith, took official action in favor of public education, expressing the determination "to work for better schools and to press for better communication between church and school."[4] In connection with this action, the General Assembly enunciated principles which place upon the home the basic task of nurturing children in Christian truth and link the church with the home in educating for Christian living. The Methodist Church has also been a loyal supporter of the public school.

Yet at the present time Presbyterian churches are among those who are showing interest in church schools, especially nursery and kindergarten schools. Other churches manifesting like interest are the Southern Baptist, the United Presbyterian, and the Protestant Episcopal. All of these are now operating a number of schools. The Episcopalians had in 1960 a total of 477 elementary and secondary schools. This denomination and the Southern Baptists are

[4]Official statement, *The Church and the Public Schools,* approved by the 169th General Assembly of the Presbyterian Church in the United States of America (Philadelphia: Board of Christian Education, June, 1957), p. 23.

launching Christian day schools very rapidly, as are also some of the other larger and a number of the smaller denominations.

In addition to what is being done by the churches, many evangelical parents and interested friends are uniting to establish independent Christian day schools. Associations of such schools are being organized to advance the interests of members and to provide a united front. Among these associations are the California Association of Christian Schools, the New England Association of Christian Schools, the Los Angeles Baptist Mission Society, and the National Association of Christian Schools.

This last organization was founded in 1947 by the National Association of Evangelicals to promote the establishment of new elementary and secondary Christian day schools throughout America and to provide a service function to all who unite with it. Any school willing to subscribe to the doctrinal statement expressing basic beliefs held in common by evangelicals may become a member. Each separate school is allowed to determine its own detailed doctrinal position and its own type of organization. Dr. Mark Fakkema, who had given the cause of the Christian day school valiant service through the National Union of Christian Schools, served as Educational Director of the National Association of Christian Schools until 1960. In this capacity he continued to promote energetically the Christian day school movement. Upon his resignation in 1960, he was succeeded by John F. Blanchard, who had for some years been outstanding as a leader in the field.

The appeal of this movement lies in deep and fundamental principles. Of these the basic one is that God has made parents primarily responsible for the child. The Bible teaches that the child belongs first of all to the parents who brought him into the world. The child is not the property of the state, nor are the parents merely servants of the state to nurture the child until the state sees fit to take control of him. This is not to say that neither state nor church has responsibility for the young, but it does say that both have secondary, not primary, obligation. Parental responsibility implies certain rights, one of which is the right of parents to educate their children as they believe God would have them educated. This is a natural right, not one given by the state. No parent who honors God should be obliged to expose the children God gives him to a type of education that dishonors God.

Courts do not confer on parents their rights but they have upheld them as being natural. The dictum of the Supreme Court of the United States handed down in the Oregon case is: "the child is not the mere creature of the state; those who nurture him and direct his destiny have the right, coupled with the high duty, to recognize and prepare him for additional obligations." Furthermore, the court stated that private and church schools were "engaged in a kind of undertaking not inherently harmful, but long regarded as useful and meritorious."[5] It is the obligation and the right of the state to see that every child receives adequate education, but the state ought not dictate as to who shall give it or how it shall be given.

As the number of Christian schools increases, opposition to them is arising. Though there is concern about the effects of schools that ignore God, there are people who seem to be more concerned that the public school thrive without hindrance. Prominent public men are leveling attacks against nonpublic schools, charging that they are founded upon a philosophy opposed to democratic principles. There have been educators who sought to cast upon people who believe in nonpublic schools the suspicion of disloyalty to American ideals.

Educators are not the only persons who speak against private schools. Among such are Protestants who have attacked private education in recent years. The action of the General Assembly of the Presbyterian Church was referred to above. The Methodist and the Congregational churches have, to a lesser extent, voiced opposition to private education. At a meeting of the Christian Education Division of the National Council of Churches in 1958, the Director of the Division, Rolfe L. Hunt, declared that "an increase in the number of parochial schools poses a bigger threat to American unity than racial segregation." Other churchmen have also voiced opposition to schools conducted under church auspices.

Opposition is not always direct; attempt is made by indirect means to thwart the efforts of those who would conduct Christian schools. The National Citizens Commission for the Public Schools promoted extravagantly the rapid construction of new public school buildings that taxes might be so high people could not afford to send their children to private schools. State departments of education seek through legislation to set impossible standards for private

[5]*Pierce* v. *Society of Sisters,* 268 U.S. 510,535 (1925).

schools. Professional educators discredit private schools by citing statistics twisted to show that graduates of public schools do better in college than those from private schools. In California a major attempt was made during 1957 and 1958 to withdraw tax exemption from private elementary and secondary schools.

According to the Wall Street Journal, the next socio-political battle will be one started by public school leaders to abolish private schools. The Journal says, "Private schools have always been an annoyance to public school officials, although so long as these were small and few they could be suffered. But one of the marked trends of recent years has been the growing dissatisfaction of the public with public school education and the growing tendency of middle-income people to seek something better for their children. And what was better were the private schools."

Under the influence of the naturalistic and relativistic philosophy of John Dewey there has grown up a bureaucracy of educators which nurtures socialistic tendencies. This bureaucracy has, by means of professionalism, compulsory attendance, financial legislation, formulation of educational philosophies, development of school practices, designing of curricula, and the writing of textbooks, so come to dominate education that local control is today an illusion. An all-powerful and machine-like bureaucracy of educational leaders, organizations, and associations operates, whether by conscious design or not, to thwart actual local control and to promote indirectly greater and greater centralization of educational power.

American public schools are socialized schools and, being such, they are politically controlled, even apart from legislated federal control. With government monopoly over the educational program, the political group that is in power upholds and promotes the ideology its leaders support. Herein lies the source of the evil that sponsors of Christian schools combat, maintaining that the child belongs, not to the temporal order of Caesar but to the eternal kingdom of God.

Readings

Byrne, H. W. *A Christian Approach to Education.* Grand Rapids: Zondervan Publishing House, 1961.

DeBlois, Austin Kennedy and Gorham, Donald R. *Christian Religious Education: Principles and Practice.* New York: Fleming H. Revell Company, 1939.

Eby, Frederick. *The Development of Modern Education.* New York: Prentice-Hall, Inc., 1952.

Elliott, Harrison Sacket. *Can Religious Education Be Christian?* New York: The Macmillan Company, 1940.

Ferm, Vergilius T. A. (ed.). *An Encyclopedia of Religion.* New York: The Philosophical Library, 1945. Article on "Parochial Schools," pp. 561-562.

Gaebelein, Frank E. *Christian Education in a Democracy.* New York: Oxford University Press, 1951.

Hastings, James (ed.). *Encyclopaedia of Religion and Ethics.* New York: Charles Scribner's Sons, 1955-1958. Article on "Secularism," Eric S. Waterhouse, XI, 347-350.

Hyde, Floy S. *Protestant Leadership Education Schools.* New York: Bureau of Publications, Teachers College, Columbia University Press, 1950.

Lotz, Philip Henry. *Orientation in Religious Education.* Nashville and New York: Abingdon-Cokesbury Press, 1950.

———, and Crawford, L. W. *Studies in Religious Education.* Nashville: Cokesbury Press, 1931.

Lutheran Cyclopedia (Erwin L. Leuker, editor-in-chief). St. Louis: Concordia Publishing House, 1954.

Martin, Renwick Harper. *Our Public Schools, Christian or Secular.* Pittsburgh, Pa.: National Reform Association, 1952.

100 Years of Christian Education. Fourth Yearbook, Lutheran Education Association. River Forest, Illinois: 1947.

Person, Peter P. *An Introduction to Christian Education.* Grand Rapids: Baker Book House, 1958.

Rian, Edwin H. *Christianity and American Education.* San Antonio, Texas: The Naylor Company, 1949.

Smart, James D. *The Teaching Ministry of the Church.* Philadelphia: The Westminster Press, 1954.

Smith, Hilrie Shelton. *Faith and Nurture.* New York: Charles Scribner's Sons, 1941.

Taylor, Marvin J. (ed.). *Religious Education: A Comprehensive Survey.* New York: Abingdon Press, 1960.

Van Dusen, Henry Pitney. *God in Education.* New York: Charles Scribner's Sons, 1951.

Vieth, Paul H. (ed.). *The Church and Christian Education.* St. Louis: The Bethany Press, 1947.

Symbol of the link between past and present in the Bible school movement is Moseley Hall, men's residence in the contemporary style at Nyack Missionary College. The first Bible school in the United States, Nyack is one of three Bible colleges regionally accredited and is the only such school accredited by the National Association of Schools of Music.

(Courtesy of Nyack Missionary College)

12

Bible Institutes, Vacation Bible Schools, and Weekday Schools of Religion

THE NINETEENTH CENTURY was a great century for Christianity from the double standpoint of rapidity and extent of its spread. Latourette, in his treatise, *A History of the Expansion of Christianity,* found it necessary to devote three of seven volumes to telling about expansion from 1800 to 1914. Of this period he says, "In geographic extent, in movements issuing from it, and in its effects upon the race, Christianity had a far larger place in human history than at any previous time."[1]

Bible Institutes

It was in the latter part of this great century that a movement began which has had potent influence in extending Christianity geographically, in serving as a source of other means for advancing the cause of Christ, and in bringing to bear upon the lives of many people the message of the Gospel. This is the Bible institute movement, which has been accorded scant attention despite the fact that Bible institutes exist in considerable number and provide education for thousands of youth and adults, many of whom become Christian workers at home and abroad. Histories of education give Bible institutes scarcely any notice, encyclopedias make no mention of them, libraries have no books on them, and magazines publish few articles on them.

[1]Kenneth Scott Latourette, *A History of the Expansion of Christianity* (New York: Harper & Brothers, 1941), Vol. V, Introduction, p. 1.

One reason for this silence lies perhaps in the difficulty of defining the term "Bible institute." The term is used to cover a great diversity of types, ranging from teacher training classes conducted by a local church in evening sessions to accredited colleges carrying on work through academic years. Some are supported by denominations; others are faith institutions dependent on God and voluntary contributions. Some are housed in poor quarters; others have plants worth millions of dollars. Some have a few inadequately trained teachers; others have faculties with training comparing favorably with that of faculties of fully accredited liberal arts colleges. The curricular offerings of some do not command educational respect while others have courses making possible specialization in different areas, leading to three-year diplomas or to four- and five-year college degrees. This variety in schools called "Bible institutes" makes it difficult to treat the subject.

A second reason for the scant attention given Bible institutes lies in the education they stress. First of all, this is definitely evangelical, and there are writers who do not approve this emphasis. Bible institutes are without exception evangelical. The education they give honors God and deals with the temporal in the light of man's responsibility to God and dependence upon Him. Faith has precedence over intellectualism; revealed truth is all-important; knowledge gained through human reasoning apart from divine revelation is discounted. The English Bible is the principal textbook; this is studied as the infallible Word of God. Thus students are led to build a Biblical philosophy of life instead of one founded on naturalism and materialism. Man is presented as an eternal being living in a moral and spiritual universe and answerable to his Creator, who in grace has redeemed him through Christ, in whom all of life becomes unified through faith.

It has to be admitted that not all teachers have put into effective practice the kind of education the institutes stress. There have been individual emphases upon special points of view and private interpretations without adequate foundation in facts. Such emphases and interpretations have sometimes affected students in ways not in accord with typical Bible institute education. There are students who know little of what they talk about, some who have inordinate zeal but little knowledge, some who become so lifted up in pride over what they think they know as to be unable to support truth without dogmatism, and some whose stand for truth is repulsive and unpleasant.

But Bible institutes, even with their shortcomings, turn out students who believe the Word of God. Only people who are serious Christians, seeking education that will prepare them to serve the Lord effectively, are admitted as students. The environment of a Bible institute, the courses offered, the personal influence of consecrated teachers, the atmosphere of campus and classroom, and the large place given practical training in Christian service by most institutes serve to develop students who are truly evangelical in character, outlook, and conviction. In a world given over to materialism and secularism, these and the institutions whence they come do not attract a great deal of attention.

Though the Bible institute movement has a short history, it has a long past. The course of the history of the Christian church is marked by similar educational movements. Always, teaching has been an essential and vital factor in carrying on the work of the church and in promulgating the Gospel. At intervals, movements arose to do formally the teaching that was necessary and needed at the time. The first of these came during the second, third, and fourth centuries in the form of catechetical schools, which were an advance over catechumenal schools. The latter were designed to instruct believers preparatory to church membership; the former had for a purpose the inculcation of Christian truth to satisfy the thirst for knowledge which members of the church had, so that they would not be obliged to drink from the streams of pagan learning. Though catechetical schools did not give definite training for the ministry, it was but natural that those trained in them should become workers and leaders in the church.

Some of the most brilliant teachers of the time taught in these schools. The church in this period was fighting for its life; its teachings were being subjected to most searching criticism as Roman scholars, men of massive intellect, sought for truth. These brilliant Christian teachers were trained in Greek philosophy, and they expressed the Christian message in terms of that philosophy. The catechetical schools, located in various large cities of the Empire, were filled with students. Christianity thus developed a literature on doctrine and practical living which made it possible for the church to put into the minds of youth that which would enable them to withstand assaults made by men who relied on human reason alone.

This teaching epoch of the second, third, and fourth centuries was of tremendous importance. There was a similar epoch in Ireland from the sixth to the eighth centuries. Patrick went to Ireland from England about the year 432 and evangelized the country. Though a man of limited educational opportunity, he encouraged learning, laying the foundations for an Irish church that was devoted to the Word of God. A man of the Book and not of traditions, one who believed in the teachings of the Bible and not in the doctrines of men, he gave the impetus that kept the lamp of Christianity burning during the centuries when darkness prevailed elsewhere. The chief subject of instruction in the schools of Ireland was the Bible. Missionary emphasis and evangelistic zeal were strong, and students dedicated to the cause of Christ went forth from them into a large part of Europe.

There were a few here and there who, through the following centuries, continued to teach the simple, unadulterated truth of God, but no similar strong emphasis upon teaching occurs again until the intellectual awakening of the Renaissance and Reformation. In the sixteenth century a great Christian educational movement much like the Bible institute movement made its appearance. It was a movement to give instruction in Christian truth to the many instead of the few. Prior to this time, popular universal education was unknown and, to a considerable extent, undesired; people in general depended mainly on knowledge that could be transmitted orally. But when men began to rely on the Bible instead of the church as the seat of authority, the common people were seized with a desire to study the Scriptures for themselves. Reformation leaders saw clearly the necessity of instructing as many Christians as possible.

The invention of printing made universal education possible. The result was the greatest period of advance in Christian education since the second century. Within a short span of time, Christian school systems were founded in Germany, in Switzerland, and in England. The outcome was the transformation of the people of northern Europe into a Bible-reading people dedicated to universal Christian education.

It was these people who came to America, bringing with them the dedication that made American education Christian from the beginning. It was these people who recognized the need of training for doing effective Christian work. Harvard, Yale, and Columbia were founded to train Christian leaders. The influence of people dedicated to Christian education was felt not only in higher education, where the purpose was to train ministers, but also in every other phase of education: instruction in reading and in Christian truth in the home, in the apprentice system, in the town schools, and in the Latin grammar schools which prepared boys for college. The Christian emphasis was unmistakable in the first public schools of America.

For its first two hundred years American higher education gave large place to the Bible and to the preparation of students for Christian work. With the expansion of society, many new subjects were brought into the college curriculum, and the number of college graduates entering the ministry gradually decreased. Since Biblical and theological studies were being displaced, the major denominations began, shortly after 1800, to establish seminaries to train their leaders. It was altogether in order to elevate the level of education required for entering the ministry, but the unfortunate outcome of the total situation was that the great majority of college students, unable to get seminary training, were deprived of opportunity for Bible study.

With the establishment of state universities and land-grant colleges after the Civil War, higher education was further broadened to include preparation for agriculture, the mechanical arts, and various other professions. The application of the principle of separation of church and state often resulted in the exclusion of Bible subjects from these schools. Thus an increased number of people received a college education but the proportion of those getting knowledge of the Bible became smaller and smaller.

Two conditions involved in seminary education intensified need for the practical training Bible institutes give. One of these was the liberalism that soon came to pervade seminaries, causing much dissatisfaction with them. The other was an impatience with the methods characteristic of seminary education; a considerable number of people in the churches charged that the training given by these institutions of learning was not practical, that it failed to fit men for the work they were to do. There was a demand for shorter and more effective training, for an education that would give practical knowledge of the Bible instead of scholarly theories about it and would use the time spent in studying the church in the past for teaching ministers how to preach the Gospel to men in the present.

Three movements causing Christians to feel keenly the need for education such as Bible institutes give were the Sunday school movement, revivalism, and missionary expansion. The Sunday school was a lay organization staffed by lay teachers. The typical lay teacher had no educational training. With the development of normal school training of public school teachers, the inadequacy of the preparation of Sunday school teachers became painfully evident. As early as 1847, a plea was made to train Sunday school teachers in a manner comparable to the training given public school teachers.[2] Not many years thereafter, Dr. John H. Vincent suggested the idea of Sunday school teacher institutes, modeled after those in vogue for the training of public school teachers. And in the years following he proceeded to organize institutes for Sunday school teachers, starting them in different parts of the country.

Revivalism made a strong impact on America during the nineteenth century. Not only were great campaigns conducted by men like Charles G. Finney and Dwight L. Moody but many local evangelists did a work no one else could do. Though these men had little formal training, they accomplished much for God. As a consequence of evangelism, there was a renewal of Bible reading and a felt need for systematic Bible study. T. B. Madsen, in an article entitled "The Origin of the Bible Institute," published in *The Evangelical Beacon,* November 19, 1946, says, "There seem to have been two leading factors that contributed largely to the establishment of the Bible institute idea: the need for sound, Bible-trained evangelists, preachers, and missionaries, and, consequently, and secondly, the need for institutions that could give systematic and well-rounded Bible studies and subjects closely related to the Bible, to evangelism, and to missionary work."

The vitality generated by the revivals of the nineteenth century expressed itself in a period of missionary expansion. Because of the

[2]Edwin Wilbur Rice, *The Sunday-School Movement, 1780-1917, and the American Sunday-School Union, 1817-1917* (Philadelphia: American Sunday-School Union, 1917), p. 371.

increase in means of travel and communication Christians became acquainted with conditions in heathen lands and were impelled to missionary activity. Many missionary societies were founded. Large numbers of young men, influenced by the revivals, offered themselves to the service of Christ in foreign lands. Many of these volunteers were well adapted for missionary work and quite willing to devote their lives to it, but they needed suitable training for mission work and practical experience in it.

Missionary societies were totally unprepared to give this training and experience. Most of these societies were inclined to send to the foreign field only highly educated men. But there were leaders who, while admitting the need for well-educated missionaries, felt that these were not the only men needed on the field. It was their contention that workers of all classes were needed abroad as at home. Two among those who so thought and two who were foremost in agitating for worldwide proclamation of the Gospel were Dr. A. B. Simpson, of New York, and Dr. A. J. Gordon, of Boston. Both published missionary magazines, and both felt impelled to start Bible schools. Quite independently of these two, Dwight L. Moody, of Chicago, had arrived at the opinion they held of the need for practical training to capitalize on the service of those who were burdened with a spirit of evangelism but who lacked educational training.

Seemingly, Bible schools were the link to form a connection between the need for workers not only on foreign mission fields but also in the homeland and an abundant supply of men ready to be utilized. Schools permeated with liberalism were not producing men who could carry on a spiritual ministry. Moreover, most existing schools had such long courses of study that students were too old and without enthusiasm by the time they were graduated. One after another these three men and others were impressed with the thought of what Christian training schools might do in training lay workers. The plan at first did not involve the preparation of professional leaders; there was no thought of entering into competition with the seminaries. The idea was to prepare spiritual lay workers who could fill the gaps at home and abroad.

Schools similar to Bible institutes existed in Europe long before they made an appearance in America. Germany had such schools as early as the first quarter of the nineteenth century. There were some in Sweden before 1870, the year in which the East London Institute for Home and Foreign Missionaries was founded. However, they did not thrive in Europe; today there are few Bible schools of any size in England or on the Continent. It was in modern America that these schools multiplied in number. The movement has been carried from America to various mission fields, on some of which flourishing Bible institutes are now operating.

Dr. A. B. Simpson founded the first Bible school in America. As early as March, 1880, in an editorial, he said there was need "in every great church in this land" for a missionary training college "where young men may prepare at home for foreign work." Then he went on to say, "A good Missionary Training College would prevent many a subsequent mistake; it would save future years of preparation."[3] A couple of months later he expressed the hope that an Inter-Seminary Missionary Convention to be held in the fall would consider "the establishment of a specific Missionary Training College, to prepare persons who may not be able to take a full scholastic course, for Missionary Service." In this editorial he argued that all who can go should be privileged to find service on the mission field even if they are not university trained.

Simpson's missionary zeal and ardor influenced young people of his congregation to offer themselves for missionary service. Most of these lacked a good education; to prepare for college and then to wait seven more years until they had completed seminary was too much. He had studied and had been impressed by the methods of the East London Institute for Home and Foreign Missionaries. Since there was no school like it in America, he decided to start one to give his own young people basic Bible training for Christian service at home and abroad.

He started the first Bible school in America in 1882 on the rear platform of an old theater in New York City. Two teachers taught twelve students, using for equipment rough benches and crude tables. Christians showed marked interest in the school and, money having been contributed, plans were made for formal organization. About one year after the beginning, the Missionary Training College was opened, with forty students enrolled in day classes and a larger number in evening classes. Thirty completed the first year's

[3]*The Gospel in All Lands, March,* 1880, p. 55.

work, and soon five of the graduates were on their way to Africa as missionaries.

The course of study was three years in length, so arranged as to have each year's work a unit in itself. The course included literary, theological, and practical subjects, with principal emphasis upon the study of the Bible. Within a few years a curriculum was carefully planned, and it has remained basically the same until the present.

Because of rapid growth, the school was moved several times to larger and better quarters. Its name underwent change also until in 1897 the name Missionary Training Institute was given it, and it was moved from New York City to Nyack-on-Hudson. Here on a beautiful campus the school, now known as Nyack Missionary College, is training young people for Christian work, and continues to be a leader in the Bible institute movement.

The school's founder, no superficial educator, gave it enduring direction in breadth of curriculum, in caliber of faculty, and in educational standards, for a record of service fully in accord with the purpose he had in mind. It was not his purpose to duplicate anything then being done in education or to compete with any other institution. His sole motivation was to give laymen thorough Bible training and careful preparation through practical work in order that they might serve God effectively.

The second Bible school, Union Missionary Training Institute, was started at Niagara Falls in 1885 by Mrs. Lucy Drake Osborn. A veteran missionary, Mrs. Osborn, at the behest of young people who came begging her to train them for foreign missionary work, opened her home to students. After some years, the school was moved to Brooklyn. Its outstanding characteristic was a good combination of medical and evangelistic preparation developed by Mrs. Osborn. The school was incorporated in 1891 and grew in size through later years, though it never became large. Some of America's leading Bible scholars served on its staff at different times.

The three-year course included Latin, English, Ancient History, Public Speaking, and intensive Bible study. The plan was to give thorough preparation not only in content studied but also in self-denial and practical training for the life a foreign missionary must live. After thirty years of service fruitful in the training of laborers for the mission field, the school was merged in 1916 with the National Bible Institute in New York City.

In 1886, Dwight L. Moody founded in Chicago the most outstanding of all Bible institutes. The circumstances of Moody's conversion at the age of seventeen set him on the road to winning souls by the method of simple direct appeal. Through deep interest in Sunday school work he caught such a vision of the need of soul-winning that he gave up business and devoted himself wholly to Christian work. His soul-winning zeal in Sunday school and Young Men's Christian Association activity produced many Christians who were without any church connection. Feeling obliged to provide them with a church home, he organized a church which after his death was named the Moody Memorial Church.

Six years of evangelistic work in England and America intensified Moody's already-formed conviction of the need for training men and women in Bible knowledge and soul-winning. He founded Northfield Seminary and Mount Hermon School for Boys on the high school level to enable girls and boys to get an education in a Christian atmosphere. Above all else, students in these schools were instructed in knowledge of the English Bible. Along with such instruction, discipline and influence were designed to develop character and a regard for the worth of service.

For ten years Moody had felt that more personal work should be done by men and women trained for it. He also felt there were many Christians ready and willing to do this type of Christian work if only they were given proper training. He had this work and these Christians in mind when he established the schools at Northfield, intending them to be preparatory schools for a Bible institute in a large city. In January, 1886, he delivered a sermon in which he said, "I believe we have got to have 'gap' men—men who are trained to fill the gap between the common people and the ministers."[4] Following this sermon, a formal decision was made in February to organize the Chicago Evangelization Society, which proved to be the forerunner of Moody Bible Institute.

For a few years prior to the opening of the full-time school, the feasibility of the project was tested by training, in a series of short institutes, lay workers in home visitation, Sunday school teaching, and personal evangelism. The experiments proved that many people were eager to prepare themselves for doing Christian work, so the

[4]Richard Ellsworth Day, *Bush Aglow* (Philadelphia: Judson Press, 1936), p. 264.

school was opened in September, 1889, under the name Chicago Bible Institute, which, after Moody's death, was changed to Moody Bible Institute. Eighty students enrolled the first year, and three times as many the second year. The growth of the school has been noteworthy both in number of students and in the contribution made to the Bible institute movement.

The fourth Bible institute, the Boston Missionary Training School, was founded in 1889 by Dr. A. J. Gordon and others in Boston. The school was launched cautiously "in continuous, strenuous, unremitting prayer," which God honored. Dr. Gordon followed in the train of men who had accomplished much in faith-mission work; as prayer was made, money was received for the needs of the school. As soon as it was opened, there broke forth a storm of opposition. Such opposition has been gathering force with the founding of each new Bible institute.

However, attacks but served to bring the school to the notice of people. Students began to come from all parts of the country, and contributions were made by people who had never seen the school. After Dr. Gordon's death in 1895, it was given the name, Gordon Training School. Shortly after 1900, Dr. Nathan E. Wood, President of Newton Theological Institution, reorganized the school in affiliation with the Institution. In 1914 another reorganization took place, with the result that Gordon Bible Institute was incorporated as a separate school. Today the school exists as Gordon College and Divinity School.

Other Bible schools were started by 1900: Friends Bible Institute and Training School, now Malone College, in 1892; Pennsylvania Bible Institute, in 1894; Toronto Bible Training School, now known as Toronto Bible College, in 1894; Free Church Bible Institute in Chicago, now Trinity Evangelical Divinity School and Trinity College, in 1897; God's Bible School in Cincinnati in 1900; and Bethel Bible Institute in Spencer, Massachusetts, which, after undergoing various transformations, now exists under the name of Barrington College, one of the foremost of such institutions, in 1900.

The expansion of Christianity of the "great century" continued into the twentieth century until 1914. The early years of this century were also a period of great expansion in educational interest, including interest in religious education. The year 1903 marked the formation of the Religious Education Association, which grew rapidly. With its emphasis on education in religion, it provided a challenge to evangelical Christians. At the same time, they became much more conscious of the need for Christian education as they saw the contrast between poorly trained Sunday school teachers and the well-trained public school teachers which normal schools and teachers' colleges were producing in increasing number. Provision for teacher training began to be made in Bible institutes as never before, and it was soon evident that the few institutes in existence could by no means meet the need.

The consequence was the starting of many new institutes all over the country. Most were located in large cities which were strategic centers for the development of evening schools and extension classes. Corespondence courses were offered and conferences were held under the auspices of institutes. They also entered the publication field, issuing magazines of their own and printing other literature. Denominations now began to found Bible institutes. For the most part the schools established prior to 1914 continue to the present day.

World War I brought radical changes in many directions. Morality declined; desire for comforts and luxuries became strong; material prosperity and financial success became the outstanding goals of life. Higher education undertook to provide for these. The social situation favored the promotion by liberals of their views. The long existing conflict between conservatives and liberals now caused a clear distinction to appear between evangelicals and modernists. Many of the former withdrew from churches and organizations which were becoming modernistic. Funds were withheld from modernistic causes and directed to evangelical projects, especially faith missions.

Conditions both favored and opposed the Bible institute movement. On one hand, the situation demanded schools not only to train Christian workers and missionaries but to serve as centers for Bible teaching, which many people had no opportunity to receive in their churches. Evening schools and extension classes increased in number as modernists became more worldly and more enamored with success and temporal prosperity. On the other hand, Bible schools had to meet more indifference and opposition than formerly. Even the older, well-established institutes were tested during the postwar period of conflict and confusion. However, they not only held their ground but even made appreciable gains.

These years saw the launching of a considerable number of new institutes, raising the grand total of such schools by 1930 to nearly sixty. Some of the later ones were weak and did not last long; some served only a local need; others have had a wide ministry and are today noteworthy examples of the effectiveness of education that is Christian.

With the coming of the depression, the sense of social and religious confusion became more real than before. Many avenues of escape from reality were sought by men and women, affording evangelical Christianity opportunity for a period of progress. For this, in its bearing on the Bible institute movement, the founding in 1931 of the Evangelical Teacher Training Association was an important event. This Association set up standards for the training of Sunday school teachers with a view to giving them preparation comparable to that of public school teachers. The Association was the first and, at the time, the only agency affording Bible institutes means for obtaining some kind of uniformity among themselves. Its work and objectives met with the approval of most institutes as well as of some colleges and some seminaries. A large proportion of the institutes became members of the Association immediately, and others endeavored to qualify as soon as possible.

The founding and the success of this standardizing agency gave the Bible institute movement new impetus. In the fifteen years after 1931, many more institutes were started than had been founded in the previous half century of the history of the movement. The Association's work led to some new developments. One of these was the beginning of a trend toward Bible institutes as evening schools only. Another development was the utilization of the Bible institute plan by various denominations. Between 1931 and 1940, thirty-five new institutes came into being, and a number of these were started by denominations, including Mennonites, Baptists, Lutherans, Holiness groups, the Church of God, and the Assemblies of God. While nondenominational and interdenominational schools continue to lead, the number of denominational institutes has noticeably increased since 1940.

A third significant development—probably having little or no connection with the activity of the Evangelical Teacher Training Association—occurred soon after 1931. Columbia Bible Institute, Columbia, South Carolina, secured permission from the state to grant a bachelor's degree in Biblical Education. Later the charter of the school was amended to permit the granting of other degrees. The school, its name changed to Columbia Bible College, thus became the leader of a new movement in Bible institute history. Only one institution, Gordon Bible Institute in Boston, had before this made such a change. Other schools were quick to follow the example of Columbia in a trend that continues to gain momentum.

As the Bible institute movement expands, new schools are being founded in all parts of the country. This is in accord with what has occurred in the past. Bible institutes have never been localized; they spring up almost anywhere. Day schools and evening schools, denominational and undenominational schools, general and specialized schools are found in all sections of America.

No one knows exactly how many Bible institutes there are. Dr. Hubert J. Reynhout found that 167 were known to have been started by 1946. Of these some have been discontinued. Some schools close, some merge with others, and some become liberal arts colleges or theological seminaries. Since new schools have been founded since 1946, it seems safe to say that the number of Bible institutes in the United States and Canada must now be over two hundred.

These vary widely in scope of work and in quality of instruction, but they agree in one respect: they are conservative in theology and evangelical in function. Since the great majority of these schools, once they are established, continue to operate, it must be concluded that the Bible institute movement is permanent, not temporary. Not only are institutes increasing in number but student enrollment in individual schools is definitely on the increase also. Obviously, the future of the Bible institute depends upon the existence of evangelicals in sufficient number to provide students. From what statistics show, there seems to be little reason to doubt that there will be enough young people from evangelical groups to keep the Bible institute and the Bible college in operation in time to come.

Though the Bible institute movement has expanded remarkably and exerted no slight influence in education, it has accomplished these results in spite of handicaps. Of these, one of the greatest, if not the greatest, has been the absence of common standards and of professional association among those who carried on the work of institutes. The Evangelical Teacher Training Association, as was mentioned above, introduced the only standards these schools had. This, however, applied to only one area of their work. Moreover, this organization, obviously, did not function as an association of Bible institutes. Few schools were recognized by any accrediting agency, state or private. Meanwhile, because of rising educational standards, schools were obliged to lengthen and enrich their programs of study. Also, as ministerial candidates sought admission to schools whose original aim had been to train lay workers, more and stronger courses were necessary. Whereas a two-year program once sufficed, now scarcely any schools have a program of less than three years, and an increasing number offer four- and five-year programs, leading to degrees.

It became increasingly apparent that an accrediting agency was needed to function in this movement which had an educational force that could no longer be ignored by those concerned with academic affairs. Such an agency would serve several purposes. For one thing, it would lead to improvement in the quality of Bible instruction and Bible college education. Then, through cooperation with other accrediting associations, it would advance the interests of Bible-centered higher education. Also, it would make available to many societies, boards, departments of government, and other organizations, a list of approved schools. Moreover, it would give prospective students, teachers, and other interested persons a sound basis for choosing among schools. Obviously, it would facilitate the transfer of credits between undergraduate schools and also provide a means of evaluating credits for graduate study. Last but not least, an accrediting agency would encourage schools to maintain their evangelical stand while striving for high academic standards.

So, because it was realized that Bible institutes now occupy, and should continue to occupy, a distinct area in the field of Christian education and because it was recognized that they can best serve the cause of Christ by remaining truly Biblical, an accrediting association was formed in 1947. The name adopted was the Accrediting Association of Bible Institutes and Bible Colleges. This was shortened in 1957 to Accrediting Association of Bible Colleges, though the function was not changed; "Bible" denotes the distinctive emphasis and "Colleges" the academic level. Both institutes and colleges are eligible to membership if they meet the criteria of the Association.

The Association has made commendable progress. Most of the larger and older Bible schools are members. Bible institute education has been definitely strengthened as administrators became aware of weaknesses. Stimulating self-study has made for improvement as schools endeavored to meet Association standards. The Association is recognized by the United States Office of Education and other federal agencies concerned with educational matters. It is a constituent member of the American Council on Education and of the Council on Cooperation in Teacher Education. It is recognized by the National Education Association, by various state boards of education, and by other organizations.

The standards set up by the Association are consistent both with the academic strength demanded in higher education and with evangelical Christian faith. They include stress on general education courses derived from areas giving students the breadth of knowledge and culture needed for effective Christian service. A major of at least thirty hours of Bible and theology is required in all programs leading to graduation. Bible subjects are those whose essential content is Bible, not subjects about the Bible. Theological studies are meant to supplement Biblical studies and to give thorough understanding of Christian doctrine and its application to life and needs. Programs leading to a preaching or Bible teaching ministry require an additional minimum of ten hours in Bible and theology.

The criteria of the Association are revised from time to time, a procedure that both stimulates self-evaluation on the part of member schools and tests the validity of criteria. They were carefully drawn up in 1947 with expert assistance and were revised in 1951, 1955, and 1960. They take into consideration both quantitative and qualitative factors but are structured to focus attention on desirable qualities rather than on minimum quantitative requirements. The criteria are founded on the concept that Christian education embraces the whole personality, so they provide for the physical, mental, social, and spiritual development of students.

The Accrediting Association is made up of a group of member schools in two categories, accredited and associate. Evening schools, which are many in number and often use the name "Bible Institute," are not eligible for membership, though some member schools conduct evening schools as extension programs. Length of program does not determine eligibility for membership. Though an undergraduate program leading to a bachelor's degree may not be less than four years, member schools may offer three-year programs provided they are strictly collegiate in quality and no degrees are granted. Also, a school may offer only the final years of an undergraduate program and require completion of junior college for admission.

Neither does the baccalaureate degree conferred by a school determine eligibility for membership. The Association encourages the use of degrees truly descriptive of the courses offered and will not accredit schools granting degrees that might be misleading in relation either to the rank of the school or to the program of study. It advocates, where legally allowable, the Bachelor of Arts degree, with a Bible major, for the principal program and the Bachelor of Christian Education and the Bachelor of Sacred Music degree for specialized programs. The Bachelor of Theology degree may not be granted for a program of less than five years. It implies that three years of specialized study have been correlated with at least two years of general education.

"Once a member always a member" is not a statement applicable to members of the Accrediting Association of Bible Colleges. To continue as a member, a school must maintain the standards. Both accredited and associate member schools are required to submit annual written reports of their condition and progress. A resurvey is made every five years. Resurvey may be required of any member school whenever the Executive Committee of the Association deems this advisable.

The Association has clarified greatly the concept of Bible institute education. It applies the term "Bible college" to schools that offer "education of college level whose distinctive function is to prepare students for Christian ministries or church vocations through a program of Biblical, general, and professional studies," whether these schools are known as Bible colleges, Bible institutes, or Bible schools. The four- or five-year Bible college differs from the three-year institution in its offering of more liberal arts courses. Yet it is not a liberal arts college, for, instead of providing many fields for concentration, it offers only that of Bible and fields related thereto, such as theology, Christian education, pastoral training, missions, music, church history, and the Biblical languages.

The Bible college does not give full liberal arts training. As a school with a specialized program, it exists primarily to meet the need for well-trained workers in all areas of evangelical activity at home and abroad and as well to accord to the Bible the place it should have in education and life. The unifying factor is the Bible, the study of which orients the student theistically in relation to all areas of knowledge. The Bible college maintains that firsthand study of the Bible is the most effective means of teaching knowledge of greatest worth, of bringing to men light to point the way out of darkness. Along with other Christian colleges and schools, Bible institutes and Bible colleges seek to provide a truly Christian education, since education in America has been almost entirely severed from its Christian roots.

Vacation Bible Schools

A second school developing out of the expanding interest in Christianity and in religious education in the twentieth century was the vacation Bible school. Like the Bible institute, this school had its roots in the preceding century, though it is not altogether clear just when and where the present vacation church school did begin. It is recorded that such a school was conducted in Boston in 1866, but little is known of it. More is known about one that was held in Montreal as early as 1877, the first vacation school held under the auspices of a church. Its program consisted of Bible reading and memory work, hymns and songs, stories, military drill, calisthenics, manual work, and patriotic exercises.

In 1894, at Hopedale, Illinois, a Methodist pastor's wife, Mrs. D. G. Miles, recognizing that the Sunday school was not giving children a thorough knowledge of the Bible, decided to use the long summer vacation to compensate for this lack. She organized and directed an interdenominational school which was held in the public school building and an adjoining park. Each pupil paid an enrollment fee of one dollar and each was expected to bring a Bible. If he had none, the school provided one through the American Bible Society. This school had four divisions, with an assistant for each division. Some activities were for the whole school and some for separate divisions. Included were songs, stories, physical exercises, marches, contests, and dramatic exercises.

In 1898, Mrs. Eliza Hawes conducted a vacation church school in the Epiphany Baptist Church, New York City. This school stressed Bible memorization and Bible stories. A similar school was held the next two summers also.

About 1900, Rev. Howard R. Vaughn, a Congregational pastor in Elk Mound, Wisconsin, started a vacation religious day school. This was organized to parallel the grades of the public school, with Bible content worked out for each grade from the first through high school. The content consisted mostly of Bible stories told by the teachers who were public school teachers. Pupils memorized and retold the stories. Place was given also to missionary content and Christian biography, notebook work, and worship.

However, it was schools held in New York City in 1901 that started the organized movement of vacation school religious education. Dr. Robert G. Boville had observed the Montreal school in operation and had been impressed by what he saw. Later, as Executive Secretary of the New York City Baptist Board of City Missions, he saw what was being done by the schools of the Epiphany Baptist Church. At the same time he became acutely aware of three conditions: the closing of public schools for the summer left idle boys and girls to roam the streets, resulting in delinquency and the creation of social problems; many churches were closed for the summer; and, since this was before the time when colleges and universities held summer sessions, students and teachers in these institutions of higher learning were also unoccupied. Bringing these three together seemed to Boville logical, and by virtue of his administrative position he could do this effectively. In 1901 he conducted five schools with a curriculum including manual work, organized play, Bible and missionary stories, and Bible study. The next summer he promoted ten schools, and in 1903, seventeen.

So great was the appeal that the movement was organized in 1905 as a commission of the federation of churches. In 1907 the National Vacation Bible School Committee was formed, and the movement extended to Philadelphia, Boston, Chicago, and other cities. In 1910, the Home Mission Board of the Presbyterian Church, U.S.A., made vacation schools a part of its program. In 1911, the National Committee was incorporated as the Daily Vacation Bible School

Association for national promotion, with Dr. Boville as secretary. The American Baptist Publication Society adopted vacation Bible schools in 1915. Dr. Boville had carried the movement to China and Japan, so the name of the Association was changed in 1917 to "International Association of Daily Vacation Bible Schools."

The vacation church school was started to gather idle children into unused churches where unoccupied teachers might keep them busy in a wholesome way in a wholesome environment. Soon, however, individual churches saw this school as an opportunity for giving more thorough religious education than they could give through the Sunday school. These churches made such demand upon denominational leaders for assistance that it became necessary for the denominations to prepare materials for use in vacation church schools. Thereupon the International Association of Daily Vacation Bible Schools turned wholly to promotional work. In recognition of the fact that this school was a responsibility of the various denominations, denominational representatives were elected to the Board of Directors of the Association, beginning in 1920.

The International Association contributed much to the progress of the vacation Bible school in this country and throughout the world. It made the school popular when it was concerned mostly with reaching neglected children. Then when the educational purpose superseded the missionary and social motive, the Association joined itself to the educational agency of the churches. In 1923, it became an auxiliary of the International Council of Religious Education, and in 1928 it was merged with the International Council. Thereafter, as a Department of the International Council and later of the National Council of Churches, it carried on its work in a broader field. Thus the vacation church school movement became a component part of the general movement of religious education, with provisions for it in the religious education boards of the denominations.

The development of the vacation church school was rapid. By 1951, its golden anniversary, 62,000 churches conducted such schools, with more than five million pupils enrolled in them. Various reasons account for its popularity. For one thing, it adds appreciably to the amount of time for giving religious instruction. Held for a period of four weeks, it doubles the time afforded annually by the Sunday school. Sessions being long and five days a week, greater thoroughness of instruction is possible. Being a vacation time activity, it challenges leaders to develop a program appealing to parents and pupils as being an adequate substitute for other activities, thus requiring educational excellence. The varied program of the school makes possible practical application to the lives of pupils the truths taught. It helps the Sunday school in several ways: it brings to Sunday school teachers new viewpoints, broadening their outlook and stimulating them to do better work; pupils become more interested in Sunday school lessons as a consequence of increased knowledge of the Bible; often children who attend the vacation school are influenced to join the Sunday school also.

The types of daily vacation schools have varied widely and not always has the aim been clear and definite. Some schools have not been "Bible schools" in that they gave little place to the Bible; some have placed major emphasis on a program of handwork of various kinds. Typically, local churches conduct their own schools, though some unite with other churches in a community school. Schools have met during the spring vacation, in the evenings, in the late afternoon instead of the forenoon, for three days a week instead of five, and some churches in crowded places provide a full day's session. A present trend is to include the whole family in the vacation school, holding it in the evening to make this possible. Today the typical vacation church school term is two weeks.

From the standpoint of true Christian education the vacation church school is still a "vacation Bible school" conducted for the purpose of teaching the Bible to bring pupils to salvation through faith in Christ, develop them in holy living, and challenge them to Christian service. It has many advantages that can be capitalized upon for promoting the cause of Christ among men and women, boys and girls, here in the homeland and wherever a church exists.

Various publishers aid in the effectiveness of such a program by producing sound evangelical materials for use in vacation Bible schools. A number of denominations prepare and publish their own materials, making the content theologically neutral so that churches other than their own may use them. Private publishers such as Scripture Press, Gospel Light, and some others prepare attractive courses which are preponderantly Biblical in content but provide for handwork and workbook activity. Most courses are planned for two weeks, five days a week, three hours a day.

Weekday Church Schools

The vacation church school provides for religious teaching during the summer while children are not attending public school. The weekday church school makes possible such teaching during the school year. Since 1900 the term "church school" has come into rather general use. What was once the "Sunday school" now goes by the name "Sunday church school"; the "daily vacation Bible school" is now the "vacation church school"; and the school giving religious instruction on days other than Sunday is called the "weekday church school." The "Sunday evening school" and the "Saturday school" are beginning to appear. Used in a comprehensive sense, the term "church school" includes all of these and other educational activities of the church. "Weekday church school" is the commonly accepted term for the school conducted by churches individually or unitedly in cooperation with the public school, which either releases or dismisses pupils to receive religious instruction.

The giving of religious instruction on weekdays is no new thing. From the first days of Christianity, classes and schools for instruction in its truths have been held on days other than Sunday. Nor is the movement for weekday religious education something recently developed, for in modern times religious instruction has long been given in parochial schools, catechetical classes, YMCA classes, conferences, and in other connections. But the idea that churches should set up a program of religious education as a part of weekday school life is a new idea, being less than fifty years old.

The weekday church school movement, like that of the vacation church school, had its forerunners. One of these was the vacation church school movement itself, for transition from a school held several weeks during the summer to one of thirty or thirty-five weeks during winter months was logical and natural. It was a Lutheran pastor, Rev. George U. Wenner of New York City, who first proposed that public schools release pupils for religious instruction. In 1905 he suggested a plan for New York City whereby children would be allowed to absent themselves from the public schools on Wednesday or some other afternoon for attending classes in religion in their own churches. Rev. Wenner urged churches to grasp the opportunity thus afforded to give instruction in addition to that given on Sunday.

The plan was discussed but was not largely favored. Later, Rev. Wenner wrote a book in which he presented arguments for released time. Furthermore, he presented the idea to the Federal Council meeting in 1908. There it received halfhearted approval, but virtually nothing was done about the matter. Some weekday schools may have been opened as early as 1909, but scarcely anything is known about them.

In 1912, the Latter-Day Saints established in Salt Lake City, Utah, a church high school using its own building located near the public high school. It offered courses in Bible, church history and doctrine fitting into the schedule of the public school, which gave credit for them. In the next ten years, the Latter-Day Saints built twenty-six more schools, and by 1949 they had over a hundred of these "seminaries." Following the success of this project, similar plans for offering church-controlled credit courses in religion at the high school level were developed in other states.

The most notable of these were the North Dakota and the Colorado plans. Vernon P. Squires was instrumental in getting the North Dakota State Board of Education to adopt in 1912 a plan for giving one half unit of credit in Bible toward the fifteen or sixteen units required for graduation from high school. The courses were taught in Sunday school classes and in youth organizations or taken through individual study, and the examination for credit was directed by the State Board of Education. A similar procedure went into effect in Colorado in 1914. It involved four years of elective study to be done in churches during Sunday school hours under a teacher qualified for high school teaching. Though these plans aroused interest in other states, they did not eventuate in what could be called a movement.

It was in Gary, Indiana, that the movement for weekday religious education had its beginning. The Gary superintendent of schools, William Wirt, convinced of the necessity of instruction in religion for normal development, offered to release pupils from the public schools that they might be given instruction in religion. A number of churches accepted this offer and began weekday schools of religion in 1914. At first these schools were conducted by churches separately, but in 1918 five Protestant denominations united to form a Community Board of Education and to develop a community system of weekday church schools. These were successful from the beginning.

For a few years the movement grew slowly. Schools were started in Toledo, Ohio, in 1916; in Van Wert, Ohio, in 1918; and in Batavia, Illinois, in 1919. Seventy-seven schools were established in 1920 and 131 the following year. By 1930 weekday church schools were in operation in 861 cities and towns, and 260,988 pupils were enrolled in them. Though only sixteen years old, the movement had spread to most of the states. By 1942 it seemed that this plan of cooperation between state and church for the religious education of children was definitely established. Promotional effort was no longer needed, for the school was being accorded much favorable publicity by both the religious and the secular press. Schools were varied in pattern but certain basic principles governed the plan: churches provided curriculum and teachers at no expense to the state; the latter through its schools released pupils for religious instruction on the written request of parents.

During 1944 weekday schools were organized in over five hundred additional communities, and a quarter of a million new pupils were enrolled. Early in 1948 these schools were being operated in all but two states, with an enrollment of above two million pupils. Over half of the cities of the country having a population greater than a quarter million were carrying on weekday religious education. A goodly proportion of the pupils enrolled in these schools were receiving no other religious instruction. The weekday church school movement was presenting to the Protestant church a challenging opportunity.

At this point it may be well to interrupt the course of the narrative to consider why weekday schools were started, why they grew as they did, and what their legal status is. A chief cause of the beginning of the weekday movement of religious education was awareness of the effects of the secularizing of public education. Within the decade beginning about 1870, the Bible was taken out of most public schools. When it went out, the religious element in large measure went also. The consequence was lack of teaching which gives boys and girls knowledge of God and which inculcates obligation to obey His moral laws. The effect of such lack became apparent after several decades in a wave of immorality. Lawlessness, crime, juvenile delinquency, and indifference of people, especially youth, to religion and the church so increased as to cause grave concern as to the outcomes of the secularization of education.

Leaders who shared this concern made efforts to correct what had been done. One form these efforts took was the enactment of laws restoring the Bible to the public schools. From 1913 on, state after state passed laws requiring the daily reading of the Bible in schools. Since this proved wholly inadequate, efforts were made in the direction of providing religious instruction on weekdays for public school pupils. This necessitated cooperation between the schools and the churches; the former had to allow time to be given over to Bible instruction conducted in school buildings, in churches, or in other convenient buildings; the latter were obliged to provide the instruction, inasmuch as the state could not teach religion. The movement, in progress for about thirty-five years, was gaining until 1948.

A second cause of the origin and the remarkable growth of the weekday movement was the new conception of the need to improve the quality of religious education. The standards of general education had risen, resulting in increasing demand for a real school for the teaching of religion. It was realized that more time should be devoted to the teaching of religion, it was recognized that religious education should be given under more favorable conditions, and it was felt that religious instruction must be related more intimately to education in general and to life. It was logical, therefore, to teach it on weekdays as well as on Sunday. Leaders were convinced of the need for teaching religious truth as fully and as efficiently as other subjects that boys and girls study. The weekday school is avowedly educational in nature and in method, that is, it is a *school.*

The movement has been successful by way of increasing interest in religion through reaching the unreached. Weekday religious education seems to catch the favor and good will of parents, who often assist and cooperate. It has been found that weekday schools appeal to a large proportion of the public school population in many localities. No one of the organizations of the church, nor all of them together reach as large a proportion of the youth in many communities as does the weekday church school. It has been found that this school reaches one out of every three children of unchurched families.

The question of the legality of the public school's releasing pupils for religious instruction often came to the mind of those who were not disposed to participate in a movement that was unconstitutional. The conclusion reached by questioners was that the decision of the United States Supreme Court in the Oregon case accorded to parents of all faiths the right to educate their children as they deemed best. It was believed that there was nothing unconstitutional about released time, that it was not violating the principle of freedom, civil or religious.

With the growth of the movement, opposition developed. Lawsuits in different parts of the country called into question the constitutionality of church and state cooperation in conducting weekday schools. Because it was appealed to the Supreme Court of the United States, the matter came to a head in what is known as the McCollum case. For a number of years a "released time" program of religious education had been carried on successfully and unopposed in the public schools of Champaign, Illinois. The program was under the direction of a committee representing Protestants, Catholics, and Jews. It offered instruction in Bible one period a week in school buildings on a voluntary basis, that is, only pupils whose parents requested this instruction could enroll. Teachers were chosen by the committee and paid from private funds. The program was approved by the local school board and was under the general supervision of the superintendent of schools.

Mrs. Vashti McCollum brought suit against the school for this on the grounds that the giving of religious instruction in tax-supported schools is contrary to the First and the Fourteenth Amendments to the Constitution of the United States. The case was lost in the local and state courts but was appealed to the Supreme Court of the United States which, on March 8, 1948, by a vote of eight to one, declared the Champaign plan unconstitutional. In its decision the court affirmed that the Constitution "forbids the commingling of secular with religious instruction in the public schools."[5] Four of the eight justices, in separate and limiting opinions, expressed the opinion that weekday religious programs of education held on re-

[5]*McCollum* v. *Board of Education,* 333 U.S. 306 (1948).

leased time do not violate the constitutional principle of separation between state and religion.

This position was fully sustained in the decision the Court rendered in the Zorach case four years later. In that decision the Supreme Court said, "We are a religious people whose institutions presuppose a Supreme Being" and went on to say that it found "no constitutional requirement which makes it necessary for government to be hostile to religion and to throw its weight against efforts to widen the effective scope of religious influence."[6] The use of school buildings and school facilities was the major factor at issue in the McCollum case, not the matter of cooperation between school and church in giving religious instruction; the decision the Court rendered was not at all adverse to the practice of schools dismissing pupils that they might receive such instruction.

Nevertheless, the 1948 decision came as a shock to leaders in the weekday movement. After it was made, about one fifth of the communities which had conducted weekday programs discontinued them, and the number of pupils enrolled in weekday schools decreased sharply. Many communities, however, continued their programs of religious education on weekdays, some on legal advice and some on the assumption that the ruling in the McCollum case did not apply to them. Once they had recovered from what at first seemed to be a blow, leaders came to the conclusion that Protestant churches should seek clarification of the ruling, help weekday schools conform to it, and set themselves to the task of finding other and better ways that are definitely constitutional to teach the Bible. So what seemed to be a blow to the movement may in the end prove to be a help rather than a hindrance.

The Zorach decision in 1952 opened wide the door for extending programs of weekday religious education. Christian churches and Christian individuals can encourage the practice of excusing pupils from the public school in order that they may be given religious instruction, thus allowing exercise of the rights and privileges of Christian citizens. This decision has given rise to a revived and growing interest in weekday classes in religion. Since the McCollum decision was rendered, little has been done in an organized manner by way of promoting the establishment of new schools, yet there

[6]*Zorach and Gluck* v. *Board of Education,* 343 U.S. 306 (1952).

seems to be a moderate but steady growth in the movement across the country. Schools are being organized in local communities by aroused parents and church leaders. The movement is a national one of significant proportions. Conservative estimates made in 1956 indicated that at least three thousand communities in forty-five states had some kind of weekday religious instruction and that the enrollment in classes for this was approximately three million children.

Whatever it does to stress spiritual and moral values, the public school manifestly has limitations in this area. It is clear that the church must provide for thorough Christian instruction, and released time programs enable churches to give needed instruction during the regular school day. Furthermore, there is definite need for more time for Christian education. One hour a week available through the Sunday school—and usually it is less than one hour—is woefully inadequate, even when supplemented by the vacation Bible school. Some kind of weekday program, whether on released time, dismissed time, after school, or on Saturday, is necessary to meet, even in a measure, the tremendous need for Christian education.

Exposing minds five hours a day and five days a week for at least twelve years during the formative period of life to education that ignores God is bound to have deleterious effects on children, on society, on the church, on the nation, and on the world. Education without God is not true education nor is it right from any point of view. The weekday church school, while it may not be the best means for bringing God into education, has accomplished something toward giving Him a place. To the church that would stress true Christian education, the weekday school presents an opportunity and a challenge, whether that church seeks alone or in conjunction with other churches to place God at the center.

Prophecy is history that has not yet run its course, but the history made in the past and the history being made in the present give seemingly safe grounds for predicting that the history to be made in the future will record much activity on the part of the Christian church in the direction of weekday teaching with a view to gaining headway in the conflict in education between God's revelation and man's reason.

Readings

Blair, W. Dyer. *The New Vacation Church School.* New York: Harper & Brothers, 1934.

Boon, Harold W. "The Development of the Bible College or Institute in the United States and Canada since 1880 and its Relationship to the Field of Theological Education in America." Unpublished doctoral dissertation, New York University School of Education, 1950.

Bower, William Clayton and Hayward, Percy Roy. *Protestantism Faces Its Educational Task Together.* New York: National Council of Churches, 1950.

Brown, Arlo A. *A History of Religious Education in Recent Times.* New York: The Abingdon Press, 1923.

Butt, Elsie Miller. *The Vacation Church School in Christian Education.* New York: Abingdon Press, 1957.

Byrne, H. W. *A Christian Approach to Education.* Grand Rapids: Zondervan Publishing House, 1961.

Cope, Henry F. *The Week-Day Church-School.* New York: George H. Doran, 1921.

———, (ed.). *Week-Day Religious Education.* New York: George H. Doran: 1922.

Eby, Frederick. *The Development of Modern Education.* New York: Prentice-Hall, Inc., 1952.

Edman, V. Raymond. *The Light in Dark Ages.* Wheaton, Illinois: Van Kampen Press, 1949.

Getz, Gene A. *The Vacation Bible School in the Local Church.* Chicago: Moody Press, 1962.

Gove, Floyd S. *Religious Education on Public School Time.* Cambridge: Harvard University Press, 1926.

Hoag, Frank Victor. *The Church's Unique Opportunity in Week-day Religious Education.* Milwaukee: Morehouse Publishing Company, 1927.

Latourette, Kenneth S. *A History of the Expansion of Christianity.* Vol. V. New York: Harper & Brothers, 1943.

Lotz, Philip Henry. *Orientation in Religious Education.* Nashville and New York: Abingdon-Cokesbury Press, 1950.

Martin, Renwick Harper. *Our Public Schools, Christian or Secular.* Pittsburgh, Pa.: National Reform Association, 1952.

MONROE, PAUL, (ed.). *A Cyclopedia of Education.* New York: The Macmillan Company, 1911-1913.

Articles on:

"Religious Education," V, 145-150.

"Bible in the Schools," I, 370-376.

MURCH, JAMES DEFOREST. *Cooperation without Compromise.* Grand Rapids: Wm. B. Eerdmans Publishing Company, 1956.

PERSON, PETER P. *An Introduction to Christian Education.* Grand Rapids: Baker Book House, 1958.

PRICE, J. M., CHAPMAN, J. H., CARPENTER, L. L., and YARBOROUGH, W. FORBES. *A Survey of Religious Education.* New York: The Ronald Press, 1959.

REED, LENICE F. "The Bible Institute Movement in America." Unpublished Master's thesis, Wheaton College, 1947.

REYNHOUT, HUBERT J. "A Comparative Study of the Bible Institute Curriculums." Unpublished Master's thesis, University of Michigan, 1947.

SHAVER, ERWIN L. *The Weekday Church School.* Boston: The Pilgrim Press, 1956.

STAFFORD, HAZEL STRAIGHT. *The Vacation Religious Day School.* New York: The Abingdon Press, 1920.

STOKES, ANSON PHELPS. *Church and State in the United States.* Volume II. New York: Harper & Brothers, 1950.

STOUT, JOHN ELBERT, and THOMPSON, JAMES V. *The Daily Vacation Church School.* New York: The Abingdon Press, 1923.

TAYLOR, MARVIN J. (ed.). *Religious Education: A Comprehensive Survey.* New York: Abingdon Press, 1960.

THAYER, V. T. *Religion in Public Education.* New York: The Viking Press, 1947.

VIETH, PAUL H. (ed.). *The Church and Christian Education.* St. Louis: The Bethany Press, 1947.

WHITTEMORE, LEWIS BLISS. *The Church and Secular Education.* Greenwich, Conn.: Seabury Press, 1960.

Sir George Williams led the founding of the Young Men's Christian Association in London, June 6, 1844, "for the purpose of forming a society, the object of which is to influence religious young men to spread the Redeemer's Kingdom amongst those by whom they are surrounded." The first YMCA was established in America in 1851.

(Courtesy of George Williams College)

13

Young People's Societies, Extrachurch Organizations, Camps, and Conferences

THE LAST CENTURY and a half has witnessed the creation of many Christian organizations. While this has been the outcome in part of the human tendency to organize, there have been deeper reasons also for bringing into being new organizations. The period covering the last half of the eighteenth and the first half of the nineteenth century was one of transition. New ideas and new ways of thinking and doing took the place of old habits of thought and action. This was true in the political realm, in the industrial realm, and in moral and religious life.

These three forces were interacting factors basic to the formation of Christian organizations. The industrial revolution, by bringing in the factory system, caused the massing of people together under conditions that made organization necessary. The development of democracy with its emphasis on liberty and equality provided part of the motivation essential to harmonious cooperation of individuals on equal terms. The religious force, expressed especially through great revivals, stressed the infinite worth of the individual and thus strongly encouraged the forming of organizations giving promise of human betterment.

A fourth factor involved in the creation of new Christian organizations was the Church. The Founder of Christianity left only one organization, His Church, and to it He committed the task of bringing to men the Gospel of salvation. Jesus called and trained twelve men as a nucleus. He gave them no form of church organization, but He did give them a life and a message from God. Jesus' ministry on earth was a threefold one of preaching, teaching, and healing. He preached the kingdom of God, urging men to repent and enter it. His main activity was teaching; everywhere and always He taught men the ways of God. He taught the disciples, He taught individuals at any and every opportunity, and He taught the multitudes whenever occasion arose. The third aspect of His ministry was healing. He healed, not for the sake of healing but to symbolize His spiritual and saving work, using healing as a means for bringing souls to God. He instructed the disciples both before and after the cross to do the same three things: preach, teach, and heal.

In short, Christ's purpose was that the church glorify God, educate and train its members, and be a light to the world, restraining sin and bringing men to God in redemption. Though its organization was simple and quite loose, the early church fulfilled the purpose of its Founder. It assumed responsibility for bringing the Gospel to all it could reach; it taught members; educated children in the home; it made God the center and the motivation of all of life. The result was that the church grew naturally from within and not only drew people to itself but was a force in the life of the world. Every member and every congregation represented God and propagated the Gospel by lip and by life.

But the modern church as a whole neglected the Lord's commission to teach. The result was lack of Bible knowledge, growth of secularism, and prevalence of liberalism. Failure to inculcate spiritual truth has led to little teaching in the home and to lack of concern about the eternal welfare of others. The outcome, in the words of one writer, has been "spiritual stagnation, institutional fossilization and general secularization."

Because of the failure of the modern church, organizations have sprung up outside of the church to do the work it should be doing. Especially when the church was not giving heed to the spiritual needs of children and young people, effort was made outside it to meet that situation. Usually the purpose was to bring the Gospel to some one group, such as a particular social group that is either unreached or inadequately reached. Often, efforts are directed toward meeting the needs of youth of a particular age—children, young people, high school pupils, college students. In scope, efforts range from those of one person in a local community to international action by large organizations. Some organizations cooperate with the church as much as they can, some definitely refrain from having anything to do with the church, and others work with the church or not, depending on circumstances.

There are organizations which were started outside of and apart from the church which the church eventually took over in some measure. Of these the most notable is the Sunday school. This was started because of the dire need of underprivileged children—a need the church was doing nothing to meet. At first, most church leaders opposed the Sunday school, but as its value became evident, they began to allow schools to be held in connection with the church. Once merely tolerated, the Sunday school has developed until today the tendency is to integrate the program of the church into one whole in which the Sunday school loses its separate identity. While this is coming to pass in some churches, there are still many instances in which the Sunday school continues to function quite independently of the church.

From the standpoint of church relationship young people's societies have also had somewhat of a checkered history. The first youth organizations were started wholly apart from the church to meet the spiritual and social needs of young people. Later, what might be called "semichurch" organizations came into being. Finally the church itself began to create youth organizations. Today scarcely any denomination or local church is without its young people's society.

In addition, there are the extrachurch organizations alluded to above. Most of these have been started among the evangelical constituency of the Protestant church. Essentially, the aim of these is evangelistic rather than educational; typically, evangelicals put strong emphasis on evangelism—sometimes to the neglect of Christian education. However, no organization carries on its work without rendering educational service. All organizations educate; the leaders, the committees, the various activities all contribute to the learning situation—usually from the standpoint of informal instead of formal Christian education which is no less actual for its being informal rather than formal.

Manifestly, it is not possible to treat in one chapter the history of all organizations included in the classes mentioned above. From the maze selection must be made. Inasmuch as this is a history of Christian education, the aim is to include those organizations that have greatest bearing on Christian education. Groups definitely organized on a nationwide or at least a statewide basis rather than groups sponsored by an individual or by a few persons working in a circumscribed area are given primary consideration. For the most part, only groups working in the United States are considered, though some whose scope of activity reaches throughout the world are included. Slight attention is given groups not definitely evangelical in nature and aim.

Young People's Societies

Most existing youth organizations were formed in the nineteenth century. However, these had antecedents in various earlier endeavors to unite youth for spiritual purposes. The history of such organizations begins in the Netherlands in 1586 with the appearing of meetings of young men for instruction in Bible. In Paris, in 1628, some students met together to study the Bible. There were societies for young men in New England from 1677 on; one founded in 1678 existed for one hundred fifty years. From 1678 to 1738 there were in England societies for young men banded together to fight against laxity in morals, profanity, desecration of the Sabbath, gambling, and all forms of debauchery.

Christian organizations of students first appeared at Harvard in 1706. It was about this time that Count Zinzendorf founded societies for young men at Halle and at Wittenberg, calling them "choirs." In 1729 Charles Wesley started at Oxford the "Holy Club," a society of young men who sought through prayer, religious conversation, and study of the Greek Testament to attain the ideal in Christian experience.

At Basel in the eighteenth century two pastors of the Moravian Church organized groups of young people and adults of both sexes for spiritual purposes. Many such societies appeared during the first fifty years of the nineteenth century, especially in Germany. But in Scotland, in France, in Switzerland, and in America also, these societies existed. Prior to 1800, they were usually linked with churches; after 1850, laymen were leaders in them. In their meetings Bible reading and study and prayer were the chief, if not the only, activities. Later, social work, including visiting of prisoners, the sick, and the poor, was carried on by most of them. A missionary spirit and the desire for Christian unity also characterized them.

Conditions of life and labor produced by the industrial revolution forced workingmen to organize for their own welfare and benefit. From the friendly society formed for this purpose there developed mechanics' institutions and mutual improvement societies to meet the social and educational needs of the young people of the working classes. In time the high educational and social aims of these societies declined. David Naismuth, feeling the need for a more elevated purpose for them, organized in Glasgow in 1824 the first of a series of "Young Men's Societies for Religious Improvement." Coming to America in 1830, he formed a number of these societies and united them under a board.

About this time the Sunday school began to recognize its duty to minister to young people as well as to children. The result was the adult or senior class movement. This grew rapidly, coming in the course of time to constitute in the form of organized classes an important aspect of the modern young people's movement. The teachers' meeting was a second line of development furnished by the Sunday school; it brought together young people of both sexes to engage in a common task, meeting at stated times for prayer and religious activity, and finding social enjoyment also.

Singing schools or classes were numerous in New England in the later eighteenth and the early nineteenth centuries. These were gatherings of young people for religious singing; they afforded young people opportunity to meet one another in a natural way and to unite in a common enterprise. Temperance societies began to spring up shortly after 1800 and increased rapidly in number during the next half century. Young people, especially young men, found in these the satisfaction of expending united effort in a great cause.

Another aspect of the developing young people's movement was missionary societies which began to be formed near the opening of the century. Missionary effort appealed strongly to young people, and many societies were formed among them. Notable ones were the Baptist Youth's Missionary Assistant Society of New York City, formed in 1806, the Young Men's Missionary Society of New York, an interdenominational organization formed in 1816, and the famous Andover Society originated by five young men of Williams College in the shelter of a haystack during a thunderstorm.

During the developmental period numerous devotional societies were formed among young people. Cotton Mather writes of belonging in 1677 to a society which met on Sunday evenings for the purpose of promoting the spiritual welfare of its members. He urged in books written in 1694 and 1710 the forming of such societies. In 1706 a group of Harvard students, concerned about the decay of practical piety, formed a society with a view to being a blessing to one another and to others. Following the Second Great Awakening, especially from about 1800 on, it was quite common for youth to meet by themselves in prayer meetings. Out of these temporary groups grew organizations formed to carry on religious exercises more permanently.

So for many years before modern youth societies came into being, there existed societies created by groups of earnest young people who sought through prayer, Bible study, and devoted service to know God's Word and to do God's work. It was, however, the Young Men's Christian Association, founded in London in 1844, which became the most direct progenitor of the modern youth society. There were many societies of Christian young men in Europe before 1844; some YMCA's of today can trace their origin to these older fellowships. But it was the English organization which not only supplied the name under which the movement spread throughout the world but which also furnished the distinctive character and the spiritual dynamic for its spread.

George Williams was the leading influence in the formation of the London society. On June 6, 1844, twelve young men met in his bedroom to form a "Society for improving the Spiritual Condition of Young Men engaged in the Drapery and other Trades." Various names were proposed, but shortly after the organization was formed, "Young Men's Christian Association" was the name adopted. The spirit of consecration to its work animating Williams is shown in an entry in his diary made in 1847: "I do solemnly declare from this evening to give myself unreservedly to this Association, to live for the prosperity of the Young Men's Christian Association. I do praise God for having called me by His grace and so blessed me temporally. I do desire to be very low at His feet for all His mercies. I thank Him for the determination of so living as to be useful among the young men of the world. And now, O Lord, I pray Thee to give me from this hour a double portion of Thy Spirit that I may labour and work in this Thy cause that very many souls may be converted and saved."[1]

Organized Bible classes became an important feature of the work of the Association in 1847. A World Conference held in Paris in 1855 adopted this simple statement of faith: "The Young Men's Christian Association seeks to unite those young men, who, regarding the Lord Jesus Christ as their God and Saviour according to the Holy Scriptures, desire to be His disciples in their doctrine and in their life, and to associate their efforts for the extension of His kingdom amongst young men."[2] Educational features were adopted in 1864.

Due largely to the enthusiasm and evangelistic zeal of Williams and his friends and to the fact that each new convert sought to win another for Christ, the Association grew rapidly. Brought to America in 1851, it spread under the leadership of Richard C. Morse and, later, John R. Mott, developing specialized work for city young men, students in colleges, for men in railroad and industrial pursuits, in Army and Navy, among colored young men, and in other departments of service. The original purpose, stated in 1855, was soon broadened. In America, the symbol of the triangle was adopted for spirit, mind, and body to signify effort to reach the whole man, then the young men and boys of the whole world for physical, educational, and religious service. The foreign outreach began in 1889, and secretaries have been appointed in most countries of the world. There is now a World Alliance of Young Men's Christian Associations with headquarters in Geneva, Switzerland.

During the Civil War, the YMCA rendered fundamentally spiritual, or religious, service to soldiers. During the Spanish War, the Association received the formal approval of the military establishment of the United States. In 1917, the YMCA was militarized. The general orders stated that it was to provide amusement and recrea-

[1] J. E. Hodder Williams, *The Life of Sir George Williams* (London: Hodder and Stoughton, 1906), p. 146.

[2] *World Conference Report,* Paris, 1855 (English ed.), p. 23. Quoted by Clarence Prouty Shedd, *History of the World's Alliance of Young Men's Christian Associations* (London: Society for the Promotion of Christian Knowledge, 1955), p. 133.

tion for troops through its usual program of activities. In World War II the YMCA was one of six constituent members for which the USO functioned as agency.

Currently, the Young Men's Christian Association is expanding its activities for families, extending its program to include youth of all ages, young adults, and older men. The objectives of YMCA clubs include stimulation of interest in good government, encouragement of physical fitness, growth in character building through the development of leadership, democratic procedure, interracial and intercultural understanding, and the study of social and political problems in the light of Christian faith and principles.

The Young Women's Christian Association developed alongside the Young Men's Christian Association but with no connection. The former was founded in London in 1855 by Christian women to band young women together for prayer and to provide decent housing and proper companionship for those living away from home. In 1858 the first YWCA was started in America as the Ladies Christian Association "to labor for the temporal, moral and religious welfare of young women who are dependent on their own exertions for support."[3] Since 1872, the YWCA has worked with students in colleges and universities. The International Board of Young Women's Christian Associations was formed in 1887 to include the United States and Canada. Growth of associations, especially student associations, was rapid in both countries. In 1906, because of the feeling that United States associations could work better by themselves, the Young Women's Christian Association of the United States of America was formed. The first world gathering took place in London in 1892, with representatives from the United States, Canada, India, and several European countries in attendance. Two years later the World's YWCA was organized.

Today the YWCA of the United States is at work in community associations in upwards of two thousand communities and has student associations in more than five hundred colleges and universities. Through its national board it sends secretaries to many foreign lands where they assist in programs of leadership training. In the United States it has three main groups: Y Teens, aged twelve to eighteen; Young Adults, employed girls, eighteen to thirty; and

[3]Quoted by Anna V. Rice, *A History of the World's Young Women's Christian Association* (New York: The Woman's Press, 1948) , p. 36.

YW Wives, young married women and mothers of preschool-age children. All three groups engage in educational and recreational activities and projects. Any female over twelve years of age who subscribes to the Christian purpose of the Association may become a member.

Both the Young Men's and the Young Women's Christian Associations were lay movements, essentially auxiliary to the church. This does not mean that there were in the churches no societies for young people during the first half of the nineteenth century; on the contrary, records show that many such societies existed. The two associations, especially the first, furnished both encouragement and pattern for like organizations under the auspices of the church. Two of these that are noteworthy from the historical point of view were the Young People's Association and the Lend-a-Hand Clubs.

The first was founded in 1867 by Dr. Theodore Cuyler, pastor of the First Baptist Church, Brooklyn, New York. This society was composed of young people of both sexes, held weekly devotional meetings, and worked through various committees, such as a devotional committee, a visiting committee, a temperance committee, and a social committee. The purpose of the society was the conversion of souls, the development of Christian character, and training for religious work. It was the starting point for many Young People's Associations all over the country. In particular, it led Dr. Francis E. Clark, founder of the Christian Endeavor organization, to the belief that a young people's society could function well in a local church.

Lend-a-Hand Clubs originated in 1871 under the leadership of Miss Ella Russell. A little book, *Ten Times One is Ten,* written by Edward Everett Hale, caused these clubs to multiply. The book stressed four mottoes: Look up and not down; look forward and not back; look out and not in; and lend a hand. The basic principle of the clubs was that members must not live for themselves. The emphasis the clubs made was that the true Christian spirit is love expressing itself in real service to those in need of help.

Between 1860 and 1881 many societies for young people were formed in various parts of the country. One such organization was the Young People's Baptist Union of Brooklyn, formed in 1877 by fifteen leaders from eight Baptist congregations. Many societies were founded in Baptist churches, some in Methodist churches, in

Presbyterian churches, and in churches of other denominations. Characteristics that either arose or were intensified during this period were: general acceptance of recreational activity, clear recognition of the principle of social service, the associating of young men and young women in societies and, most important of all, the appropriation and the utilization by the church of the young people's society.

From contact with Dr. Cuyler's Young People's Association, Dr. Francis E. Clark, pastor of the Williston Congregational Church of Portland, Maine, had become convinced of the value of the young people's society to the ministry of the church. Accordingly, when a number of boys and girls in his congregation were converted and were willing and eager to serve, he invited them to his home on the evening of February 2, 1881, to consider the forming of a society for Christian work. Many of them responded and, after talking the matter over, they formed a society of Christian Endeavor of about sixty members.

The name was chosen because the purpose of the society was to assist young people in *endeavoring* to live the Christian life. A characteristic feature was the pledge, of which the first sentence is: "Trusting in the Lord Jesus Christ for strength, I promise Him that I will strive to do whatever He would like to have me do; that I will pray to Him and read the Bible every day; and just so far as I know how, throughout my whole life, I will endeavor to lead a Christian life." Other features were the monthly consecration meeting, which afforded members opportunity to share spiritual experiences, and the committee work, which provided outlet for activity. The original committees were the Prayer Meeting Committee, to plan prayer meetings adapted to young people; the Lookout Committee, to win and to care for members; and the Social Committee, to have charge of the recreational and the social aspects of society activity.

The growth of the society of Christian Endeavor was marvelous. Eight months after the first society was formed, a second one was organized in Newburyport, Massachusetts. In 1882, the first convention was held, with six societies represented. The second convention, held the next year, was attended by representatives of fifty-six societies having a membership of nearly three thousand. In 1885, incorporation to include the United States and Canada was completed under the name "The United Society of Christian Endeavor." This name was retained until 1927 when the organization took the name "International Society of Christian Endeavor."

Societies were not long confined to America. Before the movement was five years old, it was introduced into India and China. In 1888 the first society was organized in England, and one was formed in Australia about the same time. Since then, tens of thousands of societies have been organized all over the world. The constitution originally adopted is essentially the same one that has been translated into at least one hundred languages and has been subscribed to by millions of people.

Why did Christian Endeavor grow thus? There are two or three basic answers to the question. In the first place, Christian Endeavor, like the Sunday school a century earlier, brought to a focal point what had been going on over several decades; Dr. Clark, as Raikes had done in the case of the Sunday school, crystallized and popularized a movement of the times. In the second place, Dr. Clark—again like Robert Raikes in connection with his Sunday school—made known to the public the work of Christian Endeavor. In August, 1881, he wrote an account of his society that was published in the *Congregationalist* and republished widely in America and England. He also believed in and practiced wide and persistent advertising. Moreover, Dr. Clark—once more like Robert Raikes—possessed a type of personality suitable to the founding of a work which needed to be done for God.

Christian Endeavor was nondenominational; it made its appeal to any and to every evangelical denomination and sought to relate its work to the denomination as it did to the local church. If there ever was a dream that Christian Endeavor would become the inclusive organization for young people of all evangelical churches, that dream was of short duration. It was soon found that no single type of youth organization or form of activity is acceptable to all evangelicals. Simply because Christian Endeavor was nondenominational and because denominations desired to guide their youth in their own way, it was only a short time until the denominations began to originate youth movements of their own.

The first of these was founded by the Episcopal Church in 1883. It was the Brotherhood of St. Andrew, which had for its double purpose the grouping together of Episcopal men and boys to pray daily for the spread of Christ's kingdom among young men and the effort to bring the Gospel to young men. Today this brotherhood has chapters in about two thirds of the states of this land. Two years after it was formed, a kindred organization, Daughters of the King, was founded for Episcopal young women. In 1888 the Brotherhood of Andrew and Philip was founded under Reformed auspices with the purpose to spread Christ's kingdom among men through emphasis on personal work. Today this has nearly a thousand chapters with about 40,000 members in the United States, Canada, Japan, and Australia.

In 1889 Presbyterian and Methodist denominational youth organizations were formed. The United Presbyterian Youth Fellowship was brought into being by the Sabbath School Committee of the Board of Publications. This fellowship merged with the Westminster Fellowship of the Presbyterian Church, U.S.A., in 1958. The Epworth League was organized in 1889 for Northern Methodists, and five years later for Southern Methodists, to enlist youth in fellowship, study, worship, and service. Since 1939 this work has been done under the name, Methodist Youth Fellowship.

In 1890 the Young People's Christian Endeavor Union of the Church of the United Brethren in Christ was founded by a convention of two hundred pastors and young people's society workers of the denomination. In 1891 a conference of Baptist leaders formed the Baptist Young People's Union of America as a fraternal organization of young people's societies in Baptist churches. Its object was to unify Baptist young people for increased spirituality, edification in Bible knowledge, instruction in Baptist doctrine and history, and enlistment in Christian service. It has been replaced by the Baptist Training Union of the Southern Convention and the Baptist Youth Fellowship of the American Baptists.

The Walther League was formed in 1893 as a general alliance of the youth societies of the Lutheran Church, Missouri Synod. Today it has upwards of four thousand societies. The Luther League of America was established in 1895 to encourage the formation of young people's societies in the United Lutheran Church congregations. It seeks to provide inspiration and guidance in Christian living with a view to encouraging the youth of the church to respond to the love of Jesus Christ with a deep faith and consecrated lives. The League exists in branches affiliated with various Lutheran denominations.

The Baptist Young People's Union, auxiliary to the Southern Baptist Convention, was founded in 1895 to foster and to further the enterprises of the convention. It is the chief agency for informing, enlisting, and inspiring young people, with the purpose of training young Baptists for the fullest service in and through their own churches. Since 1934, the Baptist Young People's Union has been a department of the Baptist Training Union. The Church of God Young People's Endeavor was founded in 1929 "to promote the evangelization, spiritual development, and training in church membership of young people." It has something like three thousand local youth groups with an average weekly attendance of about one hundred thousand young people.

The Baptist Training Union was formed in 1934 by the Executive Committee of the Sunday School Board of the Southern Convention. It has set forth the following educational objectives as its motivating force: Christian growth; increase in knowledge of the Bible; instruction in Baptist doctrine, history, polity, and program; development of skills for all phases of church work, including personal witnessing to the lost; promoting missionary interest and activity. The Union is performing a real educational service, reaching into the greater proportion of Southern Baptist congregations through local unions and by means of a number of training union periodicals and helps, bringing the benefits of Christian education to several million children, youth, and adults.

The Baptist Youth Fellowship and Sunday Evening Programs replaced the Baptist Young People's Union in the Northern Convention in 1941. The Fellowship is the inclusive name given to the youth work of the American Baptist Church, of which the Sunday evening meeting is only a part. The plan is to unify all youth-serving aspects of all Baptist agencies, making each aspect a part of one integrated whole. The Sunday Church School of the BYF is for study, the church service is for worship, the weekday projects are for action, and the Sunday evening meeting is for training.

In 1943 the Westminster Fellowship of the Presbyterian Church, U.S.A., was founded with the purpose of reaching youth in the areas of faith, witness, fellowship, citizenship, and outreach. The

Evangelical United Brethren Youth Fellowship was formed in 1946 to lead young people to an understanding, appreciation, and acceptance of Jesus Christ as their personal Saviour and Lord, to relate them to the total program of the church, to train them for leadership, and to provide them with opportunities to give expression to their faith through service, study, fellowship, and worship.

Within the present century a trend has developed for the youth of many denominations to draw together in united effort. In 1930 the first meeting of the Christian Youth Council of North America was held. Four years later the United Christian Youth Movement was established as a cooperative effort of the national denominational and the national and state interdenominational youth agencies. The youth fellowships joined together in this movement generally build their programs on the basis of five themes meant to be comprehensive—Christian faith, Christian witness, Christian outreach, Christian citizenship, and Christian fellowship.

When the National Association of Evangelicals was founded, a Committee on Youth Evangelism was set up with the purpose of uniting existing evangelistic type youth agencies. However, denominational youth leaders, while friendly to undenominational agencies and entirely willing to cooperate in many ways with them, were committed to an educational approach to youth problems through organizations operated under church supervision. Because it was evident that the two types of youth work could not be served by a single organization in an interchurch body composed mostly of denominational representatives, the Commission on Youth of the National Sunday School Association was formed to operate in relation both to this Association and to the National Association of Evangelicals. The Commission serves denominational and interdenominational youth groups and is of increasing value to youth leaders and organizations, functioning as a clearing-house for common problems and the development of effective methods of youth work and interchurch programs.

In the past twenty-five or thirty years many changes have taken place in youth work as denominations have formed organizations for promoting Christian education in their local churches. A basic change has been the lowering of the age of those participating in youth groups. Whereas young people's societies originally included youth between the ages of twelve and twenty-four, there are now societies for children as well as for young people. These societies have made contributions to Christian education, but their efforts have been fragmentary and disjointed instead of parts of a unified whole.

At present much study is being made of Christian education objectives and curriculum. A manifest cause of weaknesses in young people's societies is lack of objective. Obviously, youth leaders cannot achieve any great measure of real success in their groups unless they understand the true purpose of the society and also its place in the total educational program of the church. Doing the same old thing in the same old way just because it has always been done thus does not produce worthwhile results. New times and new conditions bring about changes in needs; to meet these effectively, study and experimentation are required.

Much effort is being directed to recruiting and training adult workers for youth. It is generally recognized that, while youth can—and should—conduct their own society, adult sponsors are required and that youth and their adult leaders must share responsibility.

Virtually all workers attempt to provide an approach that includes balanced experiences of worship, study, and action. Materials for youth work are available in great profusion. Publications for Sunday evening youth meetings designed to meet the needs of youth in an integrated manner are being produced by various denominational and interdenominational publishing houses. An example of the former is Baptist Publications which began in 1955 to publish Training Union materials that "provide opportunity for training for church leadership and service," with a view to developing mature Christians, "Baptists who know what they believe," "church members trained to serve." Baptist Publications serves about a dozen Baptist denominations.

Among the interdenominational publishers is Scripture Press, which seeks to relate the content of its training-hour materials for Sunday evening groups to the lessons taught in Sunday school. A publisher of promise in this field is the Christian Workers' Service Bureau, founded in 1953 by George F. Santa. Its purpose is "to supply attractive, Christ-exalting, Bible-centered program material for church youth groups." Its philosophy is that the program of the young people's society must be a youth-centered one. While it recognizes that adult sponsorship is necessary, it maintains that active leadership should be in the hands of the youth themselves, with the sponsor standing ready to motivate, to suggest, to support, to guide, to counsel, to help plan. The Bureau stresses expression, training, and service as the threefold purpose of the young people's society. It publishes program helps for children and young people of primary, junior, junior high, senior high, and college age, as well as leadership training books and other helps for youth workers. The Bureau is serving a constantly increasing number of groups in many denominations throughout the United States and in foreign countries.

Extrachurch Organizations

Included in the multiplicity of Christian organizations existing at present are many that were started by individuals or groups to meet the needs of particular classes of people for Gospel ministry. As was indicated earlier, while the immediate purpose for the forming of most of these was evangelistic instead of educational, no one of them carries on its work without something of Christian education being involved therein. The order in which these will be discussed is the logical one of age groups, beginning with those for children and proceeding to those for persons of more advanced ages.

The largest and one of the oldest groups working among children is the International Child Evangelism Fellowship. This was started in 1923 by J. Irvin Overholtzer to win to Christ children not attending Sunday school or church. His own ministry among children convinced him of two things: first, children could be brought to make definite decisions for Christ; second, effectiveness in doing so required organization for carrying on the ministry in a much larger way. After organization, the work grew steadily. Since incorporation in 1937, active branches have been established in all fifty of the states in this country, many parts of Canada, and in fifty other countries. Millions of children have been given the Gospel, and thousands of them have become Christians.

Since 1942 the Fellowship has published a magazine, *Child Evangelism,* which has rendered good service to those who labor among children. In 1945 the Fellowship established the International Child Evangelism Institute to train directors. Two sessions of three months are held each year. In this Institute hundreds of students have received specialized training in Bible and in methods of work. Many of these are serving at home and abroad.

The fellowship is composed of Christian men and women who are members of local churches and who are banded together for the purpose of bringing the Gospel to unchurched children where they are. It has no membership among children; it stresses the need for children who are won to associate themselves with evangelical churches and Sunday schools.

It carries on its program by means of volunteer workers who conduct Good News Clubs, the name given by the Fellowship to its home Bible classes. In addition to these, the Fellowship fosters ministries to children in schools, in orphanages, in hospitals, in the open air, by correspondence courses, by radio, in daily vacation Bible schools, in camps, and in other ways. It conducts teacher training classes, short institutes, and conferences for adults with a view to preparing them to work with children. It carries on a world-wide literature program for teachers and for children. It has developed splendid visual aids for effectively teaching the entire Bible to children.

In addition to its direct contribution to the cause of Christian education this Fellowship has brought to church leaders new ideas for use in their programs. Moreover, it has demonstrated that a leadership adequately trained for effective work can be had for a little extra effort.

A number of organizations founded to reach children conduct their work by the method of Bible memorization. An outstanding one among these is Rural Bible Crusade National which seeks to win rural children by working through schools. A worker visits a school, tells the pupils the plan, and gives them opportunity to sign up for memory work. For memorizing an increasing number of verses of the Bible, a pupil receives progressively greater rewards, culminating in the one of a leather-bound Bible and five days at a summer camp, at no expense to himself, for memorizing five hundred verses. Summer Bible schools are conducted to give instruction to those who have not earned a trip to camp. At camp, in classes meeting each day, children are taught how to become a true Christian, how to live the Christian life, and how to win others to Christ.

Memorizing is done at home; parents hear the verses recited and sign a form, indicating correct recitation. Passages selected for memory work are those leading to conviction of sin and salvation. Many thousands report saving faith in Christ as a direct result of memorizing these passages. Crusade leaders estimate that for each child who recites the verses in a home, four other persons hear the Gospel. Hundreds of memorizers have entered full-time Christian service at home and abroad, and thousands of others fill responsible places in local churches. Follow-up is done through home visitation, personal correspondence, Bible correspondence lessons, and youth publications.

Rev. J. Lloyd Hunter, a missionary of the American Sunday-School Union began Bible memory work in Minnesota in 1918. In 1927 he founded the Canadian Sunday School Mission, which emphasized memory work. After serving in Canada for some years, he came to Illinois, where in 1937 he was instrumental in organizing the Rural Bible Crusade. Under competent advisors, solid foundations were laid for future development, and after Mr. Hunter's death the Crusade was carried forward successfully by others. In 1944 branches in several states were united in a national organization. Since then, the work has been extended into a total of thirteen midwestern states, and about one hundred thousand boys and girls are enrolled each year.

An organization doing essentially the same kind of work as Rural Bible Crusade National is the Children's Bible Mission. This was started in 1935 by Mr. and Mrs. Walter Jensen with the advice and help of Rev. J. Lloyd Hunter. Through Bible memory work and chapel programs it reaches three hundred thousand boys and girls each month in the schools of ten southern states. Many more are reached through radio broadcasts and youth conferences.

Various other groups are engaged in Scripture memory work somewhat on the model of Rural Bible Crusade National. Rural Bible Mission, Inc., is a group which makes a statewide endeavor to reach boys and girls of rural schools in Michigan. Bible to Youth Crusade works mostly among children of miners and farmers in Pennsylvania. Scripture Memory Mountain Mission of Kentucky is doing a worthwhile work among underprivileged children of the mountaineers of that state. Bible Memory Association, founded in 1944 by Dr. N. A. Woychuk, a Canadian convert of Mr. Hunter's mission, is engaged in a very systematic program of Bible memorization, carrying on work throughout the United States, in Canada, and in some foreign countries. This organization has plans for such memorization for adults, youth, and children with booklets for each age group. Those completing a course become graduates.

An organization working among children in a different way is the Youth Gospel Crusade. Founded by Rev. Richard W. Neale, it was incorporated in 1943 and has spread throughout the United States and central Canada. It works only in and through churches; its method is to conduct community-wide campaigns of six or eight days' duration, contacting first the schools and the churches to invite children to come to a church for the meetings. In these, through the use of beautiful equipment, pictures, and magic demonstrations, it aims to bring children to decision for Christ and to help them grow in the Christian life.

The Children for Christ Movement was started in 1945. Its aim is the salvation and spiritual nurture of children for the purpose of getting them into the churches. It conducts home classes, released-time classes, open-air work, club work, summer Bible schools, camps, and rallies, seeking to coordinate all to accomplish the intended purpose. Once a child is saved, he is directed to an evangelical local church.

The Challenger Club founded by Elmer Strouss is an international movement which carries on work in the majority of the states of the United States and in Canada, England, Europe, and South Africa. It seeks to encourage Bible reading and prayer, memorization of Scripture, reading of good Christian literature, and the establishment of the family altar. It furnishes helps and gives suggestions for these and conducts summer Bible schools also. It does not limit its efforts to children; its workers are students in schools of all levels from elementary to university who make contacts through correspondence instead of in person.

Three organizations having purposes consistent with religious education objectives and having policies for local church sponsorship are Camp Fire Girls, Inc., Boy Scouts of America, and Girl Scouts of the U. S. A. The first was founded in 1910 with a view to stressing the spiritual development of girls as essential to a healthy wholesome personality. It emphasizes the following as spiritual values: worship of God, seeking of beauty, giving service, pursuing knowledge, being trustworthy, maintaining health, glorifying work, and being happy. Boy Scouts of America was also founded in 1910. It is concerned with the development of clean habits, wholesome associations, and activities that build character and train useful citizens. All major denominations have endorsed scouting and have established means for integrating the Scout program with the total program of the church. Girl Scouts was founded in 1912. Its program is a spiritual one; the position is that the development of good character and sound citizenship is dependent on recognition of God and one's responsibility to Him.

Two organizations similar to the above three but existing to serve youth in truly evangelical churches are Christian Service Brigade and Pioneer Girls. The Young Men's Christian Association was the pioneer in Christian boys' work. Its first boys' department was established in 1866. As a movement within the church, boys' work had its beginning with William Alexander Smith of Glasgow, Scotland, who organized in 1883 the Boys' Brigade which had for its object "the advancement of Christ's Kingdom among Boys, and the promotion of habits of Reverence, Discipline, Self-respect, and all that tends toward a true Christian Manliness." The Boys' Brigade continues to the present; in 1960 it was reaching about two hundred thousand boys, principally in the British Commonwealth.

Encouraged by William Alexander Smith, Robert Baden-Powell wrote in 1906 *Scouting for Boys,* which received such public acclaim as to lead to the founding of Boy Scouts under Baden-Powell's leadership. The two organizations grew independently of each other, with the Boys' Brigade holding to its original object of advancing Christ's kingdom among boys while the Scout movement avoided religious teaching. The latter has had marvelous growth, claiming nine million members in seventy countries by 1960.

Many organizations for reaching and helping boys were founded after Boys' Brigade was organized. Three of these made contributions to Christian Service Brigade difficult to measure. Of these, the most influence was exerted by the Knights of King Arthur, founded by William Byron Forbush and described in his book, *The Boy Problem,* published in 1901. The second influence was the Highlanders, organized in 1916 by George W. Ollinger. The third was work done among boys under the Oak Hills Fellowship, a home mission serving people of rural areas in northern Minnesota, on the staff of which two of the pioneers in Christian Service Brigade served for a short time. Though the founders of Christian Service Brigade were well acquainted with Boy Scouts, they carefully avoided being influenced by scouting lore or literature. While there is striking similarity between the Boys' Brigade of Scotland and the Christian Service Brigade, the founders of the latter knew virtually nothing of the former. The choice of the word "brigade" was purely coincidental.

The original group of Christian Service Brigade was started in 1937 under the leadership of Joseph W. Coughlin. Soon other groups, or "battalions," were formed; by 1940 there were seventeen of these. In that year Christian Service Brigade was incorporated with the stated purpose "to lead all those whom it reaches into a definite acceptance of Jesus Christ as Saviour and as Lord in every phase of their lives." By 1960 it had grown to over fourteen hundred chartered groups.

Christian Service Brigade carries on a Christ-centered weekday activity and achievement program for boys. From the beginning its purpose has been to win boys for Christ and to prepare them for Christian leadership and service. It works with local evangelical churches, reaching boys through dedicated Christian men in these churches. After boys have been won for Christ, Brigade accomplishes its objective of training through personal guidance by Christian laymen, through instruction in its achievement program, and through the use of older boys as junior leaders.

Pioneer Girls carries on a Christ-centered activity and achievement program for girls. After Christian Service Brigade was under way, girls began to want a club also. In response to this demand, an organization called Girls' Guild was formed in 1939. The name was changed to Pioneer Girls in 1941. The stated aim has always been to exalt "Christ in every phase of a girl's life." The work and the objectives of this organization for girls are the same as those of Christian Service Brigade for boys. Pioneer Girls has grown tremendously; in 1961 there were over 2500 clubs in 1445 churches with more than 65,000 members.

Mrs. Richard Cole, impressed with the need existing among children of junior high school age, founded about 1939 the Key to Life Club organization to carry on work among children of that age. Meetings are held in schools or in homes, led by volunteer workers, and conducted for the purpose of strengthening Christian young people, reaching the unsaved, and bringing young people into the church. Study books and other literature are used. Chapters have been formed in many parts of the United States.

A group originated to reach youth of high school age is the Hi-Crusader Club. Started in 1937 under the sponsorship of the Teachers Christian Fellowship, it has operated principally in high schools of the Chicago area, but it has been extended to a couple of other cities also. Its purpose is to introduce Jesus Christ to high school young persons, then to train, challenge, and encourage those who accept Him as Saviour to live a consistent Christian life. Its activities include the forming of Hi-C Clubs on high school campuses, carrying on a regular program of weekend retreats, Crusader evangelism, radio broadcasts, sports tournaments, a Hi-C chorale, and summer camps.

Special meetings for youth, held as early as 1911 in Great Britain, led to the formation of the National Young Life Campaign of London. In 1937 James Rayburn established America's Young Life Movement, with a view to presenting the Gospel attractively to high school students to win them for Christ and to help them grow in Christ. Beginning in 1929, Lloyd Bryant showed across the country the film "Youth Marches On," stressing soul-winning, and organized large youth rallies in forty cities. In 1931, Percy Crawford began radio broadcasting which developed into the *Young People's Church of the Air.* Jack Wyrtzen and Carlton Booth started in 1940 the *Word of Life Hour,* holding regular Saturday night meetings in Times Square, New York City, week-night rallies in outlying districts, and occasional great regional rallies.

Local rallies began to be held in most major cities. Under the leadership of Torrey M. Johnson, a series of rallies was held in Chicago with Billy Graham, then recently out of college, as the chief speaker. In 1944, Johnson, Douglas Fisher, and Beverly Shea launched Chicagoland Youth for Christ. As an outcome of conferences among various city leaders, Youth for Christ International was organized in Detroit in 1945, to encourage and establish local rallies wherever possible. With the growth of the movement, calls came from other lands, necessitating the engaging of more evangelists. Graham, Johnson, and others went to England in 1946 and established Youth for Christ there. Soon, evangelists were visiting other countries. Great rallies were held in Sweden, Holland, and Ireland. During the summer of 1950 about one hundred gospel teams went to Europe and preached to more than a million people. In 1951 organized rallies were held in fifty-one foreign countries.

Through the years Youth for Christ International has chartered more than a quarter of a million rallies for its members and their nonchurch friends. Its evangelists hold several hundred special youth meetings each year, reaching many thousands of teen-agers. Under Youth for Christ direction teens are banded together in several thousand high school and junior high school clubs to witness collectively for Christ. Recognizing the power of the printed page, the organization publishes a monthly magazine, books, tracts, and other materials. It holds an annual convention, Capital Teen conventions, holiday conferences, area and regional camps, weekend retreats and conferences, and carries on a ministry of film evangelism to instruct, inspire, and challenge teen-age young people. It now reaches into forty-five nations, has its own missionaries in more than twenty countries, and holds World Youth Congresses in various great cities throughout the world.

The Inter-Varsity Christian Fellowship works among youth above the high school age level; its aim is to present "Christ according to the Scriptures" to students on college and university campuses. As early as 1690 there was a voluntary student religious society at Harvard, and when the evangelistic revivals of the eighteenth century reached the college campuses, various societies were formed among students. By 1850 these societies tended to center upon missions, pietism, or theological issues. Beginning in 1857 the student YMCA, and later the YWCA, became the channel for voluntary

Christian student activity, uniting in their campus associations all previous types of societies. Student conferences, evangelism, and missionary interests became dominant—the latter resulting in the organization of the Student Volunteer Movement in 1888.

With the growth of the college population, especially in state universities, it became difficult for these Christian associations alone to serve the religious needs of students. Consequently, denominational student programs began to develop. Finally, in 1944, the United Student Christian Council was formed as a federation of various Protestant agencies and denominational student movements and the student YMCA's and YWCA's. The expressed purpose of the Council is "to further and express Christian unity, to meet and share common responsibility, and to bring students and leaders together in fellowship and prayer around their common task."

Inter-Varsity Christian Fellowship came into being because of opposition of church officials to evangelical preaching. It originated in Holy Trinity Church, Cambridge, England, where Cambridge University students flocked to hear Charles Simeon faithfully preach the Gospel despite the protest of church wardens. As an outcome of his ministry to students, the Cambridge Inter-Collegiate Christian Union was formed. Cambridge students carried the Gospel message to Oxford, where it was heartily received. After World War I ended, the movement grew rapidly, spreading first throughout Great Britain, then to Canada, New Zealand, Australia, India, Scandinavia, other countries of Europe, and finally to the United States ten or fifteen years after the close of the war.

In 1930 Carl Anderson, impressed with the need to reach college and university students with the Gospel, began to distribute Scripture portions and testimonial booklets at athletic games and other student gatherings. His work resulted in the formation of the Scripture Distribution Society through which several hundred campuses were reached. When the Inter-Varsity Christian Fellowship began to extend into the geographical area where the Society was working and it was realized that IVCF met the need which the Society had been meeting, SDS was dissolved in 1948, giving way to IVCF.

Inter-Varsity Christian Fellowship has chapters on hundreds of college and university campuses; each chapter operates as an autonomous evangelical union of Christian students. Inter-Varsity staff members go from campus to campus to stimulate, to encourage, and to guide students in Christian living and serving. Students on a campus have weekly meetings for Bible study and prayer; they also study missions, evangelism, and apologetics. They are active in evangelistic meetings, they do personal work, and they distribute Gospel literature.

Inter-Varsity holds summer training camps to give students leadership training in campus witness and service. In addition, it provides a year-round schedule of conferences throughout the country for college and university students to encourage them in spiritual devotion and living. The work of the United States Inter-Varsity Christian Fellowship is under the direction of a general secretary and a body of workers, including several specialized staff members. Its monthly journal, *HIS*, not only makes a worthwhile contribution to the cause of Christ but is also held in high favor by leading educators.

In addition to promoting Christian education in direct ways, Inter-Varsity broadens its scope of influence by sponsoring Christian education activity in special groups. One of its departments is the Student Foreign Missions Fellowship which promotes the cause of missions among students of Christian colleges, seminaries, and Bible schools. This department has established a number of chapters and groups on campuses across the country. It publishes its own monthly magazine, *Mandate,* which reaches many students with its missionary messages.

A second venture of Inter-Varsity was the forming of a department for nurses, called the Nurses Christian Fellowship. This works in hospitals and nurses' training schools to promote the cause of Christ among nurses. It has many organized chapters and a staff of workers to contact and to guide them. It publishes a bimonthly magazine, *The Lamp,* to bring to members of the nursing profession spiritual help and information of professional value.

Still a third group sponsored by Inter-Varsity is the Teachers Christian Fellowship, started in 1943 to meet the need for definite Christian witness among educators. Local groups meet for prayer, Bible study, consideration of matters of professional interest, and fellowship. Conferences aim at bringing others to Christ and provide opportunity for discussion of educational problems.

Campus Crusade for Christ is another organization devoted to work among college and university students. Started in 1951 at the University of California in Los Angeles, it has grown rapidly. It is carrying on an active ministry on scores of campuses in the United States, and it has already expanded to other countries, including Mexico, Japan, Taiwan, Korea, and Pakistan. Immediate plans call for expansion into still other countries.

The founder was William R. Bright. With Mr. Bright as president, the activities of the Crusade are directed by an Advisory Board composed of nearly thirty outstanding Christian leaders. The United States has been divided into twelve areas; over each of these is a director who guides the work of the organization in his particular area. Strategy involves the division of the entire world into six areas for extension of the ministry on a worldwide basis.

Campus Crusade for Christ is an interdenominational student Christian movement designed to carry on educational evangelism among collegians throughout the world. It stresses the role of the church and seeks to work in close cooperation with churches of all denominations. A staff member must be an active member of a local church, and every student reached by the Crusade ministry is encouraged to identify himself with a local church. Its objective is to win men for Christ, build men up in Christ, and send men out for Christ. Many thousands of students have heard the Gospel through its workers, and thousands have been won to Christ. Hundreds of these are preparing for Christian service, and many are now filling pulpits, serving as missionaries, and engaging in other forms of Christian service.

Campus Crusade uses various methods to win men to Christ and develop in Christian life students and professors through trained men. Evangelistic meetings are held by individuals and by staff and student teams. Bible study meetings are held on campuses. Leadership training courses for Christians are conducted. Christian records and gospel films are used extensively. An international radio ministry has been launched with the objective of beaming to collegians from a number of the most powerful stations on earth broadcasts in every major language.

The Crusade, recognizing the tremendous value of literature, has designed and prepared special materials for communicating to collegians the message of the Gospel. It publishes a magazine, *The*

Collegiate Challenge, adapted specifically for non-Christian students and professors. Thousands of copies are distributed on campuses at home and abroad. The Crusade plans to make this type of magazine available in every major language for distribution to the whole academic world. A Bible study series called "Ten Basic Steps Toward Christian Maturity" has been developed as a means of following up those won to Christ. Other literature helpful to training in Christian living is also available.

Out of its experiences the Crusade has had thrust upon it awareness of need for training Christians in witnessing for Christ. Accordingly, it has established at Arrowhead Springs, near San Bernardino, California, an International Training Institute to give students and Christian laymen instruction in educational evangelism.

Besides organizations that limit their program to persons of a particular age, as do most of those already discussed, there are those that include people of all ages within the scope of their activity. One such is the Bible Club Movement, started in America in 1936. Its method of operating is to gather children, young people, and adults into neighborhood clubs and to teach them, using a four-year course of study that stresses Scripture memorization. During the four years summer camps and conferences are conducted to supplement previous instruction. This organization works in nearly all states of the United States and in some foreign countries.

Another organization seeking to reach people of all ages with the Gospel is Christ for America. It works by means of large evangelistic campaigns in big cities, following well-laid preliminary plans. These involve the rallying, through publicity by every available means, of Christians for support and prayer. Such campaigns have been held in many large cities with very good results not only by way of salvation of the lost but also with good effect on the community through the cooperative and prayer effort.

Camps and Conferences

Camps and conferences, retreats and assemblies of many types currently fill a large place in the program of Christian education, and the movement is growing rapidly. It is probable that a chief causal factor of this growth is modern urbanization of life which leads people to seek occasionally a brief period of freedom from the confinement of city life. Another factor may be the smaller part played by the home in the Christian development of the individual. At any rate, whereas forty or fifty years ago the program of the church outside of its building was, at most, a matter of taking the young people to a camp for a couple of weeks in summer, today the church is making use of camps and conferences for people of all ages throughout the summer, including late spring and early autumn and holding retreats even in winter.

The purpose of any Christian camp or conference is definitely a Christian education purpose; namely, to serve the spiritual needs of people, first of all, for salvation, then for development in Christian life, and finally to give them training for Christian service. Though the purpose is the same, the program of camp or conference is supplementary to the total program of Christian education of which it is but a small part. It is carried on for a limited time, and it reaches relatively few people. However, it wields influence out of proportion to time spent and number reached. The concentrated, intensified, and varied program of a camp, a conference, or a retreat so heightens its effectiveness as to make it a potent formative experience.

The speed with which the camp and conference movement has developed in the past three or four decades has made it a strong force for Christian education. Conferences of many different kinds are being held, and retreats of one kind and another are common. The movement has so proved its value that there is increasing realization of the necessity for making available to many more people, younger and older, the benefits of such experiences.

Camps, as distinct from conferences, are coming to be utilized as a new opportunity for providing Christian education. Camp leaders are not agreed on a definition of camping. However, there is agreement to the effect that it is an experience in cooperative group living in the out-of-doors, a creative educational experience under trained leadership utilizing the resources of natural surroundings. Conferences, as opposed to camps, place emphasis on study. The camp is informal; the conference is more formal. The camp involves groups in activities growing out of and dependent upon a natural environment, while a conference centers on classes, study, and training. The objectives of the camp are achieved indirectly and somewhat incidentally; those of the conference are direct and intentionally purposeful.

Camping was given a place in Jewish history by the direct and specific command of God. The annual Feast of Tabernacles covered a period of seven days during which the Hebrew family was to live out of doors in booths constructed from the branches of trees (Lev. 23:37-44). This feast, observed throughout previous Jewish history (II Chron. 5:3; Ezra 3:4), was kept with unusual solemnity when the people returned to Canaan after the captivity (Neh. 8:14-18). It was religiously observed in Jesus' day (John 7:2). The feast, pointing both backward and forward, had twofold educational significance: it was a memorial of the tabernacle state of Israel during their wilderness wanderings and a figure of the tabernacle state of God's people in this world.

The origin of Christian camping is not clear. As one leader says, "Most of the people in Christian camps have been too busy doing the work for the Lord" to take much note of the history of Christian camping. Some trace it to the camp-meeting movement of the early nineteenth century. The first such meeting was held in Kentucky in the winter of 1799-1800. These meetings, held in the open air rather than in buildings, created a spirit of Christian fellowship. While the Methodists generally took the lead in them, Presbyterians, Baptists, and others were also active. They were community events which brought together most people in rural areas irrespective of denominational connections.

One of the first organized camps was established by Frederick William Gunn, founder of the Gunnery School for boys in Washington, Connecticut. Beginning in 1861 and continuing for eighteen years, he and his wife took the entire student body to camp for two weeks, making the practice an integral part of the curriculum of the school. The Chautauqua movement started by Dr. John H. Vincent in 1874, though not basically a project in camping, was an out-of-doors program of Christian education. As such, it helped to give impetus to the camping movement. In 1880 Rev. George W. Hinckley pioneered a religious camp for boys, and in the same year a Rhode Island church held a camp for its members.

Sumner F. Dudley established in 1885 the oldest existing camp in the United States. Upon his death two years later, the camp, then on Lake Champlain, was named Camp Dudley in his honor and has been in continuous operation ever since under the management of the State Executive Committee of the YMCA of New York. In 1888 Dr. and Mrs. Luther H. Gulick opened a camp for their daughters and their friends—the first camp for girls. It was followed by the establishment of other camps for girls.

The organization that contributed most to the earlier development of the camping movement was the Young Men's Christian Association. It operated a number of camps popularly known as "Y" camps. These early camps were Christian, being conducted for spiritual ends. Most camps of the present follow with certain modifications the pattern established in the early days by the YMCA. Boy Scouts also furnished leadership in camping during the pioneering days of the movement. Camp Fire Girls and Girl Scouts each had a share in popularizing camps. The Salvation Army has for many years conducted camps for mothers and children from the slum areas of large cities, with the purpose of rendering both social and spiritual service.

By 1910 camps and camping had become a noteworthy aspect of the American scene. In addition to the ones mentioned above, many other organizations were sponsoring camps. Included were 4-H clubs, settlements, industries, labor unions, municipalities, fraternal societies, service clubs, schools, and churches. Shortly after World War I denominations began to sponsor Christian youth camps. Today almost every denomination conducts camps and conferences during the summer. Both denominations and interchurch groups, recognizing the potentialities of the Christian camp and conference ground, are following the great move to the out-of-doors. Thousands of Christian organizations are establishing camps.

Typically, these camps follow age-group lines. For children under ten, a day-camp program is beginning to emerge as a specific pattern. Boys and girls are taken each day over a period varying from one to five weeks, to a camping place and then taken home at night. Guidance materials for day-camps have been developed within the past ten years. Resident camping for juniors has advanced markedly since 1950. Camps for junior high boys and girls follow much the same pattern as those for juniors, with groups of size suitable for outcomes in terms of needs. For youth of senior high age, the summer program partakes somewhat of the conference pattern, with the total number of campers broken down into small study groups. In recent years experimentation has been carried on with different patterns of the summer conference. Family camping has grown rapidly since 1950, bringing parents and children together to worship, study, work, and fellowship as families.

Various associations are concerned with promoting and encouraging Christian camping. The National Sunday School Association has a Camping Commission, and there are also camp associations and conferences in different parts of the country. One of these that has always emphasized a Christ-centered camping program is the Western Conference and Camp Association which was founded in 1950. Its purpose was to work with various denominations and interchurch camps and conferences, providing such helps as were possible for those engaged in operating different types of Christian camps. It held regional meetings each year in various sections of the United States and Canada and an annual national convention. Six times a year it published a magazine, *Camp Life,* for the mutual benefit of leaders of Christ-centered interchurch and denominational camps, and it issued a *Yearbook of Christian Camping,* as well as other publications.

At its twelfth annual meeting it was decided that the Western Conference and Camp Association should arrange for a founders' convention to be attended by representatives of various camps and groups to consider the forming of a national or international camping association. At this convention there was created on October 17, 1961, the Christian Camp and Conference Association. This association takes the place of the Western Conference and Camp Association and will carry forward more thoroughly than ever the service rendered by the organization of which it is the outgrowth.

Readings

Byrne, H. W. *A Christian Approach to Education.* Grand Rapids: Zondervan Publishing House, 1961.

Chamberlin, John Gordon. *The Church and Its Young Adults.* Nashville and New York: Abingdon-Cokesbury Press, 1943.

CROSSETT, VINCENT L. "Extra-Church Christian Organizations and the Relation of Their Work to the Work of the Church." Unpublished thesis, Wheaton College, Wheaton, Illinois, 1948.

EBY, FREDERICK. *The Development of Modern Education.* New York: Prentice-Hall, Inc., 1952.

ERB, FRANK O. *The Development of the Young People's Movement.* Chicago: University of Chicago Press, 1917.

HASTINGS, JAMES (ed.). *Encyclopaedia of Religion and Ethics.* New York: Charles Scribner's Sons, 1956.

Articles on:

"Christian Endeavour," Francis E. Clark, III, 571-573.

"Young Men's Christian Association," A. K. Yapp, XII, 835-838.

"Young Women's Christian Association," Emily Kinnaird, XII, 838-841.

JOHNSON, TORREY M. and COOK, ROBERT. *Reaching Youth for Christ.* Chicago: Moody Press, 1944.

LARSON, MELVIN. *Youth for Christ.* Grand Rapids: Zondervan Publishing House, 1947.

LOTZ, PHILIP HENRY. *Orientation in Religious Education.* Nashville and New York: Abingdon-Cokesbury Press, 1950.

MATTSON, LLOYD D. *Camping Guideposts.* Chicago: Moody Press, 1962.

MILLER, RANDOLPH C. (ed.). *The Church and Organized Movements.* New York: Harper & Brothers, 1946.

MURCH, JAMES DEFOREST. *Cooperation without Compromise.* Grand Rapids: Wm. B. Eerdmans Publishing House, 1956.

OSBORN, RONALD E. *The Spirit of American Christianity.* New York: Harper & Brothers, 1958.

OVERHOLTZER, J. IRVIN. *The Children's Home Bible Class Movement.* Chicago, Ill.: International Child Evangelism Fellowship, Inc., 1942.

PRICE, J. M., CHAPMAN, J. H., CARPENTER, L. L. and YARBOROUGH, W. FORBES. *A Survey of Religious Education.* New York: The Ronald Press, 1959.

REIMANN, LEWIS C. *The Successful Camp.* Ann Arbor: The University of Michigan Press, 1958.

SHEDD, CLARENCE PROUTY. *History of the World's Alliance of Young Men's Christian Associations.* London: Society for the Promotion of Christian Knowledge, 1955.

———. *Two Centuries of Student Christian Movements: Their Origin and Intercollegiate Life.* New York: Association Press, 1934.

SHERRILL, LEWIS JOSEPH. *The Rise of Christian Education.* New York: The Macmillan Company, 1944.

STOKES, ANSON PHELPS. *Church and State in the United States.* Vol. II. New York: Harper & Brothers, 1950.

Twentieth Century Encyclopedia of Religious Knowledge (LEFFERTS A. LOETSCHER, editor-in-chief). Grand Rapids: Baker Book House, 1955. Articles on:

"Summer Camps," Martin J. Heinecken, p. 201.

"Young People's Societies," Lefferts A. Loetscher, pp. 1196-1198.

VINCENT, GERALDINE EVELYN. "A Study of the International Child Evangelism Fellowship." Unpublished Master's thesis, Wheaton College, Wheaton, Illinois, 1945.

ZUCK, ROY B. "Training Union Research Project." Unpublished manuscript, Scripture Press, Wheaton, Illinois, 1958.

J. M. Price Hall houses the School of Religious Education at Southwestern Baptist Theological Seminary in Fort Worth, Texas. This is the second oldest school of religious education in the United States and the largest in the world. The school annually graduates well over 100 with the M.R.E. and several with the D.R.E. Over 500 students are enrolled. The school, which will celebrate its fiftieth anniversary in 1965, is accredited by the American Association of Schools of Religious Education.

(Courtesy of Southwestern Baptist Theological Seminary)

14

Leadership Training

God by the Holy Spirit carries on the ministry of His church through those who learn of Christ. Since the church was founded, many changes have taken place in its organization, but never has God changed His plan to use human beings. For doing effectively the work of His church God through the Spirit gives to Christians varieties of gifts and then energizes each Christian to use the gifts bestowed for the good of all. To Him each Christian is responsible for the proper and effective use of whatever gift God has given him; as he thus uses it, the ministry of the church is fulfilled.

Every member of the church needs training without which no gift, faculty, or skill can be brought to perfection in its use. Inasmuch as each Christian learns of Christ and, in turn, shares with others what he learns, each is at one and the same time a leader as well as a learner. Training for leadership applies, therefore, to all in the church, not just to members engaged in the program of Christian education. However, the program of leadership education is usually concerned with those who are responsible for Christian education.

True Christian education follows the model of the Founder of Christianity. Jesus took twelve ordinary disciples and so trained them as to make them great leaders. These twelve were not members of the religious class nor were they learned men; they were simple men from the middle to lower classes. At first, they were rude and very carnal, showing little promise of ever being able to comprehend spiritual truth or to bring to others a true image of the character of Christ. But He educated them lovingly and patiently, dealing in kindly manner with their inferior hopes and obtuse misunderstandings. He devoted much time to their training, keeping them more constantly in His company than the general body of disciples. To these He spoke of the characteristics peculiar to kingdom living, but the twelve He taught in as much detail as they were able to grasp that the deepest meaning of the kingdom can be understood only as the individual accepts for himself the supreme, personal rule of God.

He showed them that the kingdom and eternal life are related to Himself; if men would follow Him, they would know. Little by little, through the ever-present influence of His life on theirs, He led them to find their way to the center of what He taught. He was more important than what He said, and what He was wrought in them His likeness. It was this that prepared them to carry on His work for Him. It was this that made them great leaders—leaders of whom others, even while rejecting the message they brought, had taken note that they had been with the Son of God and learned of Him.

Not human effort and aspiration but the living Christ in hearts and lives is what counts in leadership training for true Christian education. Such training involves far more than acquaintance with effective methods and mastery of a body of content material. More than anything human planning can devise, administration of leadership training requires openness to God that His Spirit may permeate all that is undertaken and done. It is lives possessed by Christ and dominated by Christ—not words and plans and procedures—that are essential in education for God.

While the living Christ dwelling within is fundamental, those intelligently alert to the contribution true Christian education can and should make to the cause of God have always recognized that other qualities also are required for efficient leadership. Moreover, realizing how vitally necessary competent leaders are, they have given serious attention to selecting and training the persons on whom the effectiveness of the program of Christian education depends. This was strikingly evident in the Sunday school, which had been in existence only a short time until earnest workers began to seek ways and means for helping teachers improve the quality of instruction.

From various systems and theories of general education, the Sunday school selected good features. Sunday schools have always been, and are today, heavily indebted to the thinking of great educators and to general education for many of their principles and methods of teaching. Incidentally, it may be said also that public education has been aided much by the Sunday school. It was popular sentiment awakened by Sunday schools that led to the forming of the public school system of England as well as that of some of the states of America. Sunday schools have also made public education stronger and more vital.

During the first fifty years of its history particularly, Sunday school leaders gave careful consideration to every system of education then known. They sifted each theory for helpful features and examined it most critically. Such scrutiny of educational thought convinced these leaders that a great weakness in public education was unqualified teachers and the prevalence of ineffective methods of teaching. Consequently, with the rise of a demand for better training for public school teachers, there was a parallel demand for the training of leaders in Christian education. It was seen that the very life of the Sunday school depended on the adequately trained teacher.

Throughout the nineteenth century this was so persistently urged that many and varied ways of training Sunday school teachers were devised. Another outcome of this urging was the presentation in volumes innumerable of a mass of content quite confusing to the ordinary teacher. During the twentieth century numerous attempts have been made to reach some common standard of achievement in the training of teachers for the Sunday school.

The widening of the scope of interest in Christian education characterizing the twentieth century has led to changed concepts of leadership training. Prior to 1900, Christian education was mostly a matter of Sunday school work directed and controlled largely by lay leaders. Since the beginning of the century, however, it has become a movement of many and varied emphases. This expanded program made absolutely necessary more systematic and thorough training for Christian leadership. More and more it has come to be recognized that the cause suffers when there is lack of consecrated, well-trained leaders.

Recognition of need for professional workers grew, though it has never been assumed that the work of Christian education can be done without voluntary leadership of laymen as well. And it came to be realized that the local church, large or small, must put forth conscious effort to recruit and develop leadership both for its own ministry and for the wider field. The concept prevails that each member of the local church, if he is truly a Christian, is in full-time Christian work, for every true believer is a priest unto God. It is seen that each person in the local church should be growing in his Christian life in preparation for leadership. The task of leaders is to encourage persons of every age to accept as much responsibility in learning, worship, fellowship, and service as their stages in development permit. When leaders share with the individual as he grows through youth into adulthood, a good foundation will have been laid for mature leadership. On this foundation as a basis, specific training can then be given in the particular phase of work to be done.

Along with the change in conception that leadership training is a far broader matter than the training of Sunday school teachers, there has been development in means for training leaders. In addition to the preparation professional workers must receive, it has come to be recognized that every local church ought to have a training program for its volunteer workers. Consequently, it is the practice of local churches, either by themselves or in cooperation with other churches, to provide various kinds of training opportunity. These have to do with two kinds of training: pre-service and in-service. Both are essential; a person needs training in content and in methods by which to do his work before he begins to work, then he needs guidance while in service so that he may make the best possible use of the training given and so that he may meet effectively specific problems arising out of his particular situation.

The history of leadership training in Christian education originates, therefore, with the training of teachers in general education, proceeds with the training of Sunday school teachers, and moves on to the broader training of professional and lay leaders.

The Beginnings of Teacher Training

From the days of ancient Greece until recent times two things required of teachers were moral and religious character and mastery of subject matter. Always it was expected of the teacher that he be sound in faith and morals and that he be loyal to church or state. Though professional training was not instituted until modern times, theorists from the days of Socrates stressed the importance of skill and experience in teaching. Ancient writers, including Socrates, Cicero, and Quintilian, expressed many ideas bearing on pedagogy. Upon foundations laid by these, Erasmus, Montaigne, Ascham, Mulcaster, Locke, Comenius, Vives, Elyot, and numerous later educators built.

From the fourteenth century onward much criticism of schools was directed at the teacher. Increasingly in Europe the need for properly qualified teachers was felt. Richard Mulcaster (c.1530-1611) made the earliest suggestion for the professional training of teachers. It was that university education include a department for the training of teachers which, he said, "is comparable to the greatest professions." In 1599 the Jesuits put plans into operation whereby their teachers were given the most perfect training possible for their work. To the Jesuit order belongs the credit for introducing the practice of training teachers.

Probably the first normal school in the world was the one established at Rheims, France, in 1685 by Abbé de la Salle, who had founded the "Institute of the Brothers of the Christian Schools" to do in elementary education what the Jesuits had done in secondary education. To train prospective teachers for teaching in his Institute, La Salle conceived the new idea of creating a special school where they were given a general education, thorough grounding in religion, and trained to teach in practice schools under the supervision of experienced teachers.

Coming next in point of time was August Hermann Francke's Teachers' Seminar, a training class for teachers established at Halle in 1697. Because of his conception that godliness is an attitude of heart and will coming from faith and because of his recognition of the power of good example as one of the most essential means for inculcating godliness, Francke was impressed with the necessity for well qualified teachers. He therefore initiated teacher training in Germany. In 1738 Johann Julius Hecker, carrying forward the movement started by Francke, established the first regular Seminary for Teachers in Prussia. By the end of the eighteenth century about a dozen such seminaries had been founded in German lands, and normal schools had been established in Denmark and France.

In colonial America the chief qualification required of teachers was soundness of faith. Teachers had to have licenses, but little was asked of them beyond ability to read and write and maintain discipline. There was no systematic plan of training teachers except perhaps a little done by the Quakers by way of the apprenticeship method. Benjamin Franklin made the first definite proposal for teacher training; he wanted it instituted in the Philadelphia Academy. While his proposal did not find adoption in this academy, later academies did undertake the training of teachers. Following the Revolution, academies, seminaries, and high schools concentrated on the training of teachers.

In these, however, as in the teacher training institutions of Europe, the training was largely academic in character, consisting mostly of drill on the subjects to be taught. Professional subjects were seldom taught in these institutions simply because the chief emphasis in teaching was hearing pupils recite what they had memorized. So long as this was the case, there was but little occasion for giving any special training to prospective teachers.

But with the contribution of Pestalozzi to education, the training of teachers took on a wholly different aspect. Pestalozzi declared that education is an individual development, a drawing-out instead of a pouring-in, that the basis of all education lies in the nature of man, and that the method of education must be developed. Pestalozzi was one of the first real teachers. His process was entirely new, calling for a real technique of instruction. The teacher must not only know content but also be able to organize it in terms of the nature of the learner and to direct him in mastering it. This meant a great change in teaching procedure and called for consequent change in teacher preparation.

These new ideas of Pestalozzi led to the making over of the elementary school in the nineteenth century. In the present century a science of education developed from beginnings that had been made by Comenius, Basedow, Herbart, and Froebel along with Pestalozzi. The result was that from 1820 the normal school movement spread rapidly both in America and in Europe. In 1823, Samuel R. Hall opened a private normal school in Vermont and, in 1829, he published his *Lectures on Schoolkeeping,* which attracted considerable attention. The first state normal school was opened at Lexington, Massachusetts, in 1839, and fourteen others were established before the Civil War. Teacher training in these had in view only preparation of teachers for elementary schools, and the instruction was not of college level.

In 1831, Washington College, Pennsylvania, originated teacher training on the college level and the following year New York University appointed a temporary professor of pedagogy. In 1852, Horace Mann, president of Antioch College, offered to sophomores an elective course on the theory and art of teaching. The University of Iowa established in 1873 the first permanent chair of "didactics," and other universities soon followed suit. G. Stanley Hall offered graduate instruction in education at Johns Hopkins in 1881; New York University began graduate instruction in 1888; and in 1889 Teachers College, Columbia University, was chartered.

Because the normal school did not meet the rising standards of the teaching profession and because of the growth of public high schools and the need for teachers in them, normal schools began before the turn of the century to become teachers' colleges; by 1915 this movement was well under way. Summer schools originated about 1872 and were soon taken over by the universities, which have made them important agencies of teacher training. Since about 1910, the universities have also offered such training through extension courses. In 1839, Henry Barnard offered in Hartford, Connecticut, a six weeks' course in pedagogy and elementary subjects; this was the beginning of teachers' institutes which have made a large contribution to teacher training. From the days of Pestalozzi, professional books and educational journals have been fruitful sources of educational experience.

Professional studies in teacher training institutions have become numerous since 1890. Tremendous growth has taken place in technical areas such as methods, supervision, administration, and the application of psychology in education. New courses in education have been developed, and old ones have been subdivided until these exist in profusion. Research has come to be stressed in the graduate education of teachers and school officials.

Since 1900 a science of education has developed to displace, in large measure, the historical and philosophical approach. Teachers and others can profit from the results achieved by the science of education in the study of those aspects of education which can be tested by observation and experiment. However, there are educational values which cannot be made a matter of scientific investigation. Education is a science, but it is more than a science; within its field is content too intangible for scientific study—content that forms part of the rich store of educational wisdom to which many profound thinkers have contributed through the ages.

An outcome of the application of the scientific method to education has been to emphasize in the training of teachers the special knowledge and skills needed in numerous particular fields of service. Specialization has been carried to the point where the trainee may be made a very narrowly educated person from the standpoint of professional knowledge. And professional knowledge has so increased that it tends to crowd out knowledge of the subjects to be taught. Criticisms of teacher training have become so numerous as to cause the present period to be one of evaluation of its bases.

The Training School of Sunday School Teachers

It is in the setting of the training of public school teachers that the training of Sunday school teachers has its place; what was done in the first strongly affected the latter. Seemingly, modern training of teachers for religious ends began in England near the start of the nineteenth century. The Society for the Promotion of Christian Knowledge and its companion Society for the Propagation of the Gospel in Foreign Parts, founded by the Anglican Church to provide, among other things, religious instruction for poor children, trained teachers and supervised schools under their control. Both societies adopted the monitorial system of Joseph Lancaster and Andrew Bell, the principle of which was the taking of older pupils, who had learned their lessons from the adult teacher in charge, to hand them on to the younger pupils. To direct these monitors, head teachers had to have skill in organization and management, so training schools were set up to give it. The stated purpose of the two societies was to make the poor faithful and good church members and to fit them for work in that station of life in which God had placed them.

One of the purposes for which the London Sunday-School Union was founded in 1803 was "to improve the methods of instruction" in Sunday schools. Its leaders promoted teacher training by circulating works on the principles of education, by conducting training classes, and by founding a Sunday school college for teachers, which did not last long. Later, the Union issued normal handbooks, encouraged correspondence classes, maintained a reading room for teachers, and developed a reference library and preparation classes for the training of teachers in different centers throughout Great Britain.

In early American Sunday schools, plans of instruction were simple and crude. Theories of education were in a state of evolution. The first schools in America, as in England, were primarily for the ignorant and neglected, and only a small percentage of these could read. From the beginning teachers were enjoined to spend a portion of each class session giving oral instruction in talks, in lectures, and by personal appeals to pupils. This oral, or lecture, system was accompanied by catechetical lessons—teaching by means of questions and answers. To get away from it the practice of memorizing was begun. Pupils were stimulated to memorize verses from the Bible, hymns, and catechisms. This practice ran to such an extreme as to become almost a craze. The work of the teacher was to listen to pupils recite what they had learned without understanding the meaning of much they were repeating.

It was evident to leaders of the Sunday and Adult School Union that this cramming system and parrot-like recitation was not a good means of instruction. They felt there was a better way, and various methods were introduced with a view to finding it. Educators were still feeling their way through theory and practice toward some satisfactory principles. To exclude the unprofitable plan of memorizing without instruction, from which many schools were dissenting around 1820, a system providing lessons of ten to twenty Bible verses to be used by all schools was tried by the New York Sunday-School Union Society. This Uniform Limited Lessons System commended itself at once to leading Sunday school workers, and it was adopted by the newly formed American Sunday-School Union for use in all of its auxiliaries, within which were included most of the Sunday schools in the United States. To facilitate the use of this system of lessons, teachers' helps were issued on the lessons, adapted to the different grades of pupils. Aids for pupils were also issued. Both these and the teachers' helps were based upon the educational theories of that day.

This uniform system quickly made evident the lack of trained teachers. This difficulty the American Sunday-School Union sought in several ways to remove. It proposed a school for Sunday school teachers, to be conducted by experts. It started the *American Sunday-School Magazine* "to place within the reach of every Sunday-school teacher the improvements in the system and information on subjects which may render their labors easy and efficient."[1] It published a book entitled *The Teacher Taught: an Humble Attempt to Make the Path of the Teacher Straight and Plain,* which emphasized education for God and set forth the object of all teaching as being to make the pupil a believer through the transforming power of His Word.

The first National Sunday School Convention in 1832 suggested the establishing of a National Normal College for Sunday School Teachers, but the suggestion did not go into effect. When institutes for public school teachers became common, some of the foremost national Sunday school workers developed a similar plan for Sunday school teachers. Dr. D. P. Kidder, in 1847, advocated voluntary organizations to instruct Sunday school teachers, similar to those then in wide use for public school teachers, though he felt that the time for such institutions was yet far distant. However, the need for training teachers was widely felt, and many suggestions and efforts continued to be made all over the country.

The first teacher training class was organized in 1857 by Rev. John H. Vincent, then a pastor in Joliet, Illinois. The movement for teacher training was making good headway at this time, but progress was arrested by the Civil War. In 1864, Dr. Vincent led in establishing a permanent Sunday School Institute for the northwest, under the auspices of the Cook County Sunday School Association. R. G. Pardee and Ralph Wells were leaders in holding institutes in other sections of the country. With the close of the War, an era of great advance in teacher training began, and it gathered momentum for years.

In 1866, Dr. John S. Hart published a book entitled The Sunday School Teachers' Institute in which he advocated some general movement for teacher training. In this connection, he suggested that

[1]Address to Friends of the Sunday-Schools in the United States, 1824. Quoted by Edwin Wilbur Rice, *The Sunday-School Movement, 1780-1917, and the American Sunday-School Union, 1817-1917* (Philadelphia: American Sunday-School Union, 1917), p. 370.

theological seminaries make provision for giving such training. It was in this same year that Dr. Vincent recommended the following as standards for a course of study in institutes and normal classes:

First, a series of about fifty lessons, to extend over one or two years:

1. Five lectures on the principles and art of teaching, to be given by a professional and experienced teacher.
2. Ten lectures on the Bible, its history, writers, inspiration, style, evidences, etc., with some simple statements concerning Biblical criticism and interpretation.
3. Ten specimen lessons for infant, advanced, and adult classes.
4. Ten exegetical lessons for Old and New Testament history, from the Psalms, the prophecies, and the epistles.
5. Ten catechetical lessons for concert recitation on Bible history, geography, chronology, manners and customs, etc., covering in comprehensive manner the fields of Biblical archaeology.
6. Five lectures on the organization, management, purpose, history, church relations, and development of the Sunday school.

Second, a prescribed course of reading to insure the careful perusal of the best books on teaching.

Dr. Vincent organized a "normal college" in 1867 which offered a course covering the Bible, its interpretation, its contents, and how to teach the Bible.

American Sunday-School Union workers were making extensive use of Sunday school institutes as a means for improving teachers in their schools. The Union plan of preparation of teachers gave special attention to the mental development of the child and offered suggestions for adapting instruction to the stages of mental growth. In 1871, the Union appointed as Normal Secretary, Henry Clay Trumbull, who had been quite successful in carrying on institute work. In making this appointment, the Union announced that it was but keeping step with "the demand on all sides for special laborers to train teachers for and in their work and to exhibit before them approved modes and appliances of Sunday-school instruction."[2]

In 1874, Dr. Vincent, realizing the need of more time for training than was available in teachers' institutes, started the Chautauqua

[2]*Ibid.*, p. 373.

Sunday-School Assembly with a course of normal study agreeing substantially with that adopted by the normal departments of the Baptist, Presbyterian, and American Sunday-School Union Boards. Sessions lasting for two weeks and covering a course of forty lessons were held each summer. Within a few years the idea spread to many local communities. However, the Chautauqua movement failed to solve the training problem of the Sunday school. The vacation feature and other courses of study took the place of Sunday school courses. But good came from the idea through the working out of standard forms of teacher training lessons by leaders such as Dr. Jesse Lyman Hurlbut.

These efforts to train teachers were concerned more with content and its organization than with development of teaching skill. For the most part, they were efforts so to organize and systematize a body of knowledge as to make it manageable and transmissible by persons with little education and slight teaching skill. It is not to be assumed, however, that there was no good teaching in Sunday schools in those days; what leaders were seeking was improvement, not elimination or supplementation. Sunday school teaching was at least as good as most public school teaching was at the time. And there were ways, as was noted earlier, in which the former contributed to the advance of public education. While these early attempts at improvement overemphasized organization and treatment of content, there came a time when the training of Christian teachers was concerned too much with methods of teaching and too little with the Word of God. Early leaders in teacher training did not seek to educate pupils without giving them the Gospel of salvation. And they did not make the mistake of assuming that training is a substitute for the life of Christ in the soul and the lordship of Christ in the life of the teacher.

The period between 1890 and 1910 was one in which many local congregations took active interest in teacher training. The occasion for this was the prevalence of a type of textbook which aroused much argument. These were brief manuals dealing in condensed manner with the Bible, the pupil, the teacher, and the Sunday school. The books most used were those of Hurlbut, Oliver, Hamill, and Moninger. Their brevity made them popular, and in some churches many adults who had no interest in teaching enrolled for study. Much good was accomplished where these books were used as they were intended to be used—merely as outlines to be supplemented by lecturing and research. However, they were inadequate when used, as they often were, to constitute all the material needed in preparing to teach.

The Assembly Normal Union, organized in 1884, undertook standardization of the work of training teachers. Its course, endorsed by the Chautauqua Assembly and issued in two books, provided for four years' study. Diplomas were awarded upon completion and efforts were made to extend the plan throughout the country. The Illinois Sunday School Association established a normal department in 1886, and other state associations soon did likewise. The teacher training movement was formally recognized by the International Association in 1896. The report of the general secretary, Marion Lawrance, to the Denver Convention in 1902 showed that there were then more than 1,300 normal classes with about 14,000 students and that 1,500 had received diplomas during the year.

The Executive Committee of the International Association appointed a Committee on Education in 1903 and a Teacher Training Section was formed in 1904. The first task of the committee was to formulate standards and rules to govern the granting of diplomas. Up to this time, such matters had been handled by the various state associations, twenty-eight of which maintained teacher training departments, with many of these preparing their own courses of study. To cope with the diversity and confusion that had thus developed, the committee called, in 1908, a conference of denominational leaders for the purpose of improving and unifying the standards for teacher training.

The action of the conference, participated in by all the larger denominations, led to the designation in 1910 of a Standard Course and an Advanced Course. The Standard Course was to cover approximately what was being offered in the manuals in common use at the time. It called for fifty lessons, of which at least twenty were to be on the Bible and a minimum of seven each on the pupil, the teacher, and the school. This course was to cover two years, and no diploma was to be given for its completion in less than one year. The Advanced Course was to consist of one hundred lessons divided as follows: Bible, at least forty; pupil, teacher, school, church, missions, at least ten each; and ten more related to any of these required subjects. This course was to cover three years, with no diploma being given for its completion in less than two years.

After the 1908 conference, the International Association began vigorously to promote the organizing of teacher training classes. From this time, too, the work of training teachers developed rapidly within the denominations as well as through the Association. A number of denominations prepared their own textbooks in accord with the specifications of the courses set forth in the action of the conference. More and more it was seen that the outline studies of Hurlbut, Oliver, Hamill, and Moninger were inadequate. The introduction in 1909 of graded lessons with their avowed aim of meeting the varying needs of childhood, laid a new emphasis upon need for specialization in teacher training.

Though the new courses were a great improvement over the outline studies and though thousands took these courses, they still lacked effectiveness. This was realized by the Sunday School Council of Evangelical Denominations, which decided to revise teacher training standards for its constituents; by the Religious Education Association, which made an exhaustive study and published its views in 1912; and by the International Sunday-School Association itself, whose Committee on Education strongly urged, in 1914, revision of standards.

In 1915, by agreement, former standards were abolished and "only one Standard Course of not less than one hundred and twenty units" was adopted. A unit was defined as "a recitation period of not less than forty-five minutes based upon a lesson assignment by an approved teacher, the lesson assignment to require a minimum of one hour for lesson preparation."[3] The new course covered three years' time, forty units per year. Year I had ten units each on The Pupil, The Teacher, Teaching Values of the Life of Christ, and Organization and Administration of the Sunday School. The courses of Year II were Teaching Values of Old Testament, Training of the Devotional Life, Teaching Values of New Testament, and The Program of the Christian Religion. The forty units of Year III were devoted to Specialization in the Methods of a Particular Department.

This new Standard Course was more than twice as long as the

[3]Clarence H. Benson, *A Popular History of Christian Education* (Chicago: Moody Press 1943), p. 243.

First Standard Course. The increased time was, however, less important than was the added efficiency resulting from the adoption of a specified period for preparation and recitation. Bible content was practically eliminated from the course on the assumption that this was being adequately presented in the graded lessons—an assumption not in accord with the facts, because the Bible was not being taught thoroughly and effectively in the Sunday school. The Association provided an Advanced Course of greater length, requiring as a qualification for entrance a high school diploma and some of the units of the Standard Course.

The Advanced Course made little appeal because of the difficulty of conducting it outside of schools. Therefore, in 1926 the International Council of Religious Education, which in 1922 became the successor of the International Sunday-School Association, made another revision. The Council changed the name of the Advanced Course to Standard Leadership Course and offered most of the subjects of the former Advanced Course as electives, without adding to the number of hours. The content of the Standard Leadership Course included ten units each of Child Study, Pedagogy, Old Testament Teaching Values, New Testament Teaching Values, Message and Program, and Teaching Work of the Church, along with thirty units each of Departmental Work, and electives. This course, with some modification, is used today.

It will be noted that this revision emphasized methodology instead of content, giving training to teach but not giving the trainee anything to teach. The assumption that those taking the course possessed adequate knowledge of the Bible was unfounded for two reasons: first, under the influence of liberalism, the Bible had, to a large extent, been displaced in the Sunday school curriculum; second, instruction in the Sunday school was not thorough. Moreover, the course did not include evangelism and missions, knowledge of both of which is needed by the Sunday school teacher. Finally, the textbooks for the course approved by the Council, whose constituency was by this time prevailingly liberal, were unacceptable to orthodox people. The result was a lag in the teacher training movement. This lag was reflected in the decline of the Sunday school.

However, one denomination, the Southern Baptist Convention, did not experience this lag and decline. Before 1900, this denomination had done nothing by way of training Sunday school teachers. In 1900, the denomination adopted the slogan "A certificate for every teacher" and launched with vigor its own plan for teacher training. This plan has been maintained ever since, being enlarged, as time passed, into a broader program of leadership education. The training course of the Convention has developed through much experiment. Training schools have been used; Sunday school specialists serve as fieldmen; textbooks and manuals have been prepared. A Sunday school manual prepared early offered brief survey studies on management, teaching, the pupil, and Bible; and additional books elaborated on these four. A diploma was awarded for the completion of the manual, a red seal for the mastery of three books, and a large blue seal for the study of four remaining books. A postgraduate course covering five advanced books was added.

The Southern Baptist program has been successful. Its courses have not had scholastic standards as high as those of other training agencies, but it has reached hundreds of thousands of workers in the denomination. The marvelous increase in the number of Sunday schools and the many accessions to the church, even while other denominations were experiencing decline in both of these, testify to the success of Southern Baptist leadership training. The secret of this success lies in the simplicity of the requirements and in enthusiastic and vigorous promotion. Degree of motivation is high, for appeal is made to the heart as well as to the head. Strong emphasis on denominational missions and on evangelism is also a factor.

Stimulated by the success of the Southern Baptists and impressed with the need for an organization that would not only serve the orthodox constituency of the denominations but also put teacher training on a higher plane than any existing agency was then putting it, a small group of evangelical leaders organized in 1930 the International Bible Institute Council of Christian Education. During its first year, the organization sought to work actively with a few of the leading Bible institutes. However, Dr. Clarence H. Benson, the secretary, informed all Bible institutes, as well as colleges, seminaries, churches, and individuals of the purposes and the ideals of the undertaking.

Inasmuch as colleges and seminaries requested membership, the name was changed in 1931 to Evangelical Teacher Training Association. The preamble of its Articles of Organization clearly states its purpose: "We, representatives of Bible institutes, colleges and seminaries in the United States and Canada, in order to foster a closer cooperation among evangelical Christian institutions; to certify to the public our deep interest and concern for Christian education; to provide and promote a common course in teacher training which will give adequate attention to instruction in Bible, personal evangelism, and missions; to recognize and encourage the use of textbooks of approved orthodoxy, do hereby associate ourselves under the following articles of organization."

It is evident from this statement that the Association is committed to the evangelical position and purposes to train teachers in harmony with a distinctly orthodox and conservative theology. However, it has never made the evangelical stand a substitute for scholastic excellence. From the beginning, the Association set itself to maintain high standards and, continuing faithful to its original aims and policies, it has moved forward to new and more efficient levels of teacher training.

At first, the Association offered two courses, a Preliminary Training Course and a Standard Training Course. The first was for the benefit of those who attended community or church classes. It consisted of ninety-six hours, or units, a unit being defined as forty-five minutes of recitation based upon one hour of preparation. The subjects included in this course, each one twelve hours in length, were Old Testament Law and History, Old Testament Poetry and Prophecy, New Testament, Child Study, Pedagogy, Sunday School Administration, Sunday School Evangelism, and Missions. To be approved for giving this course, the teacher had to be a graduate of the Standard Training Course or an instructor in an affiliated institution.

The Standard Training Course was for students enrolled in an affiliated institution. It consisted of 432 hours, or units, a unit being defined as a recitation period of fifty-five minutes and a preparation time of an hour and a half. The studies included were Bible, 144 hours; Personal Evangelism, 36 hours; Missions, 36 hours; Department Specialization, 48 hours; Bible Geography, 12 hours; Biblical Introduction, Child Study, Pedagogy, and Sunday School Administration, each 15 hours; and electives, 96 hours. This course was longer than any teacher training course then in existence and provided adequate instruction in Bible, personal evangelism, and missions. It was so arranged that it could be completed in one year in the day school or two years in the evening school of institutions cooperating with the Association.

Through the years the Association has revised its courses with a view to providing a more effective program of teacher training. Instead of two courses, it now offers three—the Preliminary Certificate Course, the Advanced Certificate Course, and the Standard Training Course. The Preliminary Course is intended for local church and community classes. It consists of six twelve-hour units, three of Bible survey—Old Testament Law and History, Old Testament Poetry and Prophecy, and New Testament—and three of Christian education—Child Study, Teaching Technique, and Sunday School Success, to give the student familiarity with the overall purpose, organization, and program of the Sunday School.

The Advanced Course is suitable for churches or groups that have good teacher training programs and for evening classes in affiliated schools. In addition to the six units of the Preliminary Course, it includes twenty-four units of Bible Doctrine and twelve units each of Bible Introduction, Evangelism, Missions, and Vacation Bible School. For each of the twelve units of the Preliminary and Advanced Courses, the Association has developed textbooks to preserve the message of the Bible in terms of the latest and the best in educational methods.

The Standard Training Course, leading to the Teacher's Diploma, is offered only in active-member schools. It covers a minimum of 24 semester hours. Since it is given only in schools, the content is outlined in general terms to permit emphasis by the particular school according to its type. General areas and the minimum requirements are Bible, 10 semester hours, and Christian Education, 14 semester hours. By Bible is meant the direct study of the Bible, with adequate emphasis on Biblical Introduction, Bible History, and Bible Geography. Christian Education is to include 2 semester hours each of Personal Evangelism and Missions, and basic courses in truly Christian education, not other subjects. The aim of the Standard Course is to give broad basic preparation for leadership in Christian education in local churches, mission fields, and elsewhere.

The membership of the Evangelical Teacher Training Association includes two classes of schools, active and affiliate. Active members are schools fitted by way of stability, size of enrollment, and adequacy of library facilities to offer the Standard Course satisfactorily. Affiliate members are schools fitted along lines such as the above for offering the Advanced Certificate Course, perhaps in evening classes or in connection with community extension programs. The Association is nondenominational; any school subscribing to the doctrinal statement and meeting the requirements and standards set forth in its constitution is welcomed into membership. From the time the Association was organized, membership has progressively expanded. Currently, many seminaries, liberal arts colleges, Bible colleges, and Bible institutes are members.

This Association has meant much to Sunday schools and churches. It has raised the level of teaching wherever its courses have been used and has at the same time emphasized the vital importance of having teaching conform to the Bible as the inspired Word of God. It has helped mightily to uplift the standards of evangelical Sunday schools in North America and elsewhere. It has done more than any other agency in the Sunday school movement of the present generation to promote teacher training. To the cause of true Christian education the Association has made a contribution of no insignificant worth.

The Training of Professional Leaders

Modern Christian education originated as a laymen's movement. The Sunday school, out of which it arose, was started by a layman whose venture was opposed by the clergy. Once they recognized its value, ministers did encourage devoted lay leaders who sponsored it. However, the Sunday school was tolerated instead of being accepted wholeheartedly, for its function and method were still considered inferior to the service rendered by the clergy. Through the years, laymen have been the outstanding leaders, though since the later years of the nineteenth century ministers have been more actively interested in Sunday school work than they had been before.

The rapid development of Christian education in this century made for various attitudes on the part of ministers. Some became openly antagonistic, viewing the Christian education program as a dangerous competitor with the regular program of the church. Others assumed a tolerantly indifferent attitude toward the program of Christian education, looking upon its activities as avenues of lay service which were good but not worthy of their own serious attention. Others became well-meaning but unenthusiastic supporters, recognizing the possibilities. Feeling unable, however, to assume leadership, these sought the services of either professional workers or competent lay workers to carry on educational activity which was seen to be an asset to the church and an obligation to children and youth. Finally, there have been ministers who recognized how vital and necessary Christian education is to the life and work of a church; these have sought not only to prepare themselves for a ministry of which Christian education is an integral part but also to lead their members to awareness of its value and to develop the leadership needed to carry it on.

Not only has much of this leadership been lay, or nonprofessional, in the past but it is such in the present and will continue in the future to be the case for several reasons. In the first place, many churches are so small they cannot have a professional leader—sometimes not even a resident pastor, so the work must be done by lay workers. In the second place, larger churches, though having a pastor and a director of Christian education, need, in addition, many other leaders who, of course, have to be laymen. Furthermore, lay leadership has distinct advantages which the Protestant church cannot afford to lose: Christian fellowship implies assuming of responsibility for expression thereof, including its interpretation to others; rendering service is a means of growth in Christian living; and effort expended on a voluntary basis to bring to others the truth one has come to know commends to them the worth of that truth.

While the lay worker came first and has been the recipient of a goodly proportion of the effort expended in leadership training, pioneers in religious education soon were convinced of the need for persons with specialized training. Therefore, the profession of religious education came into being. To train professional and salaried leaders, chairs of religious education were established in seminaries, universities and colleges, and schools of religious education, previously concerned with the training of lay workers. The Hartford School of Religious Pedagogy, organized as such in

1903 and now called the Hartford School of Religious Education, was the first institution formed with the purpose of training professional leaders. The first college department of religious education in America was established at Drake University around 1910. This most significant movement of preparing teachers of religion in colleges and universities developed slowly for about ten years, then became a rapidly expanding, far-reaching development. From about 1930 on, it has extended into Christian colleges until today there are few, if any, such colleges without departments of Christian education.

Beginning in 1908, leading theological seminaries established chairs of religious education with the definite purpose of giving candidates for the ministry the educational outlook and perspective. It has been the conception that the theological student must be oriented in the principles and methods of religious education in order to be equipped for supervising and promoting the educational work of the local church. This equipping is necessary not only when he, as a graduate, may be serving in a small church where he himself will have to direct the program of education but as well if and when he becomes the pastor of a large church which has a director of religious education, for the work of the church is far more likely to prosper if the pastor has understanding of the educational aspects of its program.

Evangelical seminaries have in more recent years been accepting responsibility for giving their students adequate training in Christian education. As a relatively new subject, this did not for a time receive much attention in their curriculums or a great deal of favor on the part of some faculty members and students. Even where it was accorded attention, the tendency was to add a few elective courses in Christian education to the seminary curriculum. More and more it has come to be recognized that these are not sufficient to give the minister necessary training for leadership of the educational program of a local church.

It cannot be denied that the minister is the leader in the local church. He is at present and he will be in the future the one professionally trained leader in a great many churches. And in those churches which have other staff members, the minister must keep in vital touch with the program of education. Christian education is so basic to the whole work of the church that it is coming to be seen as essential for the minister to have such training as will make him able and willing to accept the place of leadership in its program. It is now realized, therefore, that Christian education, instead of being an appendage to the seminary curriculum, must be one of the centers around which this is built.

It is seen that the minister's training must be for leadership in Christian education, not for doing all of the work. A program must be outlined and promoted; an organization must be set up and its various parts so correlated as to function with maximum efficiency and minimum duplication; workers must be found, inspired, and trained; activities must be directed and supervised. Therefore it is being realized more and more that the minister needs training in the underlying principles and practice of the development of lay leadership. No matter how he is related to the educational program, much of what he does will have to be done indirectly through others. In a very real sense, the minister must be a creator of leaders.

With the rise of Christian education in this century, various professional leaders other than ministers have appeared. Chief among these, and one of the first, was the director of Christian education. The exact time and place of the origination of this leader are not known. His coming on the scene was a gradual process which seems to have culminated when some of the larger churches began employing directors about the year 1909. Of many causes giving rise to this profession, the following are a few: conviction that the church ought to be imparting to young people more thorough instruction in Christian truth and better training for Christian service; changes taking place in religious thought affecting methods of imparting religious truth; changes in social life, rural and urban, necessitating adjustment by the church to new conditions in order to become more proficient; the opportunity presented by the presence of young people in Sunday schools and young people's societies and the awareness that this opportunity was not being grasped as fully as it should have been; and the failure of other institutions, particularly the home and the school, to give moral and religious training.

Because the demands upon the church as the one institution for the religious nurture of youth required greater efficiency and much expansion, it became increasingly difficult for one person to provide all the professional leadership. With the emergence of the new profession, many young men and women began to enlist for this type of Christian service, and churches in considerable number took them on as directors. By 1915 more than a hundred were at work, and others rapidly joined their ranks. Because the work was so new and because of the need for establishing standards for it, the Association of Church Directors of Religious Education was formed in 1913.

Great things were expected from the ministry of the director, but for different reasons expectations were not realized. Mistakes were made both by directors and by churches in the early years of experimentation. In some cases too great a separation existed between the work of the director and that of the pastor. Sometimes directors in their enthusiasm for education became too forward. In some cases there was no clear understanding of what directors were to do; sometimes they were expected to serve as secretaries or janitors. In other cases, when the director succeeded in the work of education, jealousies developed which made harmonious work impossible. Many directors were well trained in technical theory but inadequately trained in the content of Christian belief and in the history and polity of the church. Because results of the director's work were usually not apparent statistically, sometimes his effectiveness was questioned.

Into the midst of this situation there came the financial depression about 1930, causing churches with depleted incomes to drop their employed workers in Christian education—something many churches, because of conditions mentioned in the preceding paragraph, were only too glad to do. Thus Christian education came into a measure of disrepute, especially among a number of influential ministers whose attitudes were widely reflected. The outcome was a definite reaction against this new profession and the blasting of the dreams of what might be expected from it.

Once the depression was over—especially after World War II, the leaders of the church came back to the conviction that in every congregation there is work to be done which requires the kind of service a director can render. In the small church the minister must perform this function. In a larger church a second professional leader is needed to work hand in hand with the minister in developing and maintaining an effective church program which is soundly educational in all its parts. Churches in increasing number are realizing this. Schools training directors, as well as most denominations, report that demand for them is greater than the supply.

Though the history of the profession is not long, it records a change in the qualifications required of a director. Early it was considered that anyone who had had fairly good success in Sunday school and youth groups could fill the office. Today high personal and professional qualifications are stipulated. The qualification basic to all others is a personal experience with Christ as Saviour. Furthermore, the director must be a consecrated Christian, fully surrendered to the Lord and convinced of a call to the work. Directors now in service believe that humility, love, self-control, maturity, cooperativeness, good health, and willingness to learn are other personal qualifications a director should possess.

From the standpoint of professional training, today it is considered ideal for the director to have three years of graduate training —training equivalent to that of the pastor. However, the director should have been specializing in Christian education while the pastor was concentrating on homiletics, worship, and the care of a parish. Though a person may do good work as a director with somewhat less training, especially if he works in a church where the pastor is qualified and willing to guide and help him, the time has passed when a few courses in Christian education suffice to prepare any person to be a professional leader in the field.

With the passage of time, the duties of the director of Christian education have also grown. These vary widely from church to church, but there are certain general duties which are common. While a director works with a board of Christian education, the chief and the central responsibility of the educational task rests upon him. His first function is to make a survey of the congregation, then to formulate plans in the light of results from the survey. He is to promote the educational program of the church and to organize the total educational program, coordinating its parts and setting up a curriculum for the whole. The director enlists and trains leaders, finding, inspiring, and guiding lay workers and preparing them to take their places in the program of activities. He supervises the educational program, seeking to stimulate growth in workers as they work that they may become more proficient in the performance of their duties.

The National Association of Directors of Christian Education was formed in 1961 as an affiliate of the National Sunday School Association. Among the stated purposes of the organization are the following: to encourage personal efficiency and growth in spiritual life, academic improvement, and performance of duties; to provide a national fellowship for directors which will lead to interchange of information and resource materials; to develop professional relationships with teachers of Christian education in institutions of higher learning with a view to contributing to the training of prospective directors; and to foster understanding of the true nature and function of the director's ministry and status in the local church. Membership is open to all professionally employed persons serving in the ministry of education in the local church, even though they have titles other than that of Director of Christian Education.

The wide development of Christian education has made necessary the preparing of a variety of specialized workers. Included among these are a large number of highly trained professional workers to serve denominational boards of Christian education and councils of Christian education, trained staff members and writers for Christian publishing houses, teachers or supervisors of weekday and vacation Bible schools, trained adult leaders and counselors for youth groups, teachers of leadership training classes, professors of Christian education, educational missionaries, directors of city, county, or state Christian education associations, and specialists trained in given fields to give expert guidance to ministers and other local workers.

Humanly speaking, the greatest need of the kingdom of God on earth through all history has been and is today the need for trained leadership. The task of providing such leadership for Christian education—by no means the only but yet an exceedingly important activity of that kingdom—is a gigantic one. It is also a tremendously difficult task. Christian education, far from being an easy discipline, is complex and exacting. It is difficult to give adequate training to an inexperienced worker in his spare time. Jesus chose twelve to be with Him all the time that He might train them. It is difficult to interest people in taking training. Jesus found it so in the case of the apostles. All too few persons ever complete a single course in leadership training; of the great majority who do not, very few ever attend a conference or a convention where they might be given even a little guidance.

There are no shortcuts to truly Christian leadership. The faith upon which true Christian education is founded is demanding, rigorous, and costly. Christians should be faced with this fact, for never will leaders be produced by lowering standards. Real leadership will come only as Christians follow completely the teachings of God's Word. Nothing will be accomplished through mere dreaming or wishful thinking; what is necessary is entire consecration of Christians to God and such devotion to the task He has given that nothing will be left undone which will contribute to truly effective Christian education.

Never in all history has Christian education had such opportunity as it faces today. This opportunity offers a real challenge to an effective ministry for God. "Go ye therefore, and make disciples of all the nations, baptizing them in the name of the Father and of the Son and of the Holy Spirit: teaching them to observe all things whatsoever I have commanded you; and lo, I am with you always, to the close of the age."

Readings

Benson, Clarence H. *A Popular History of Christian Education.* Chicago: Moody Press, 1943.

Brown, Arlo A. *A History of Religious Education in Recent Times.* New York: The Abingdon Press, 1923.

Cubberley, Ellwood P. *A Brief History of Education.* New York: Houghton Mifflin Company, 1922.

Eby, Frederick. *The Development of Modern Education.* New York: Prentice-Hall, Inc., 1952.

The Encyclopedia of Sunday Schools and Religious Education (John T. McFarland and Benjamin S. Winchester, Editors-in-chief). New York: Thomas Nelson and Sons, 1915.

Articles on:

"Religious Pedagogy in Colleges and Theological Seminaries," N. E. Richardson, pp. 908-913.

"Religious Training Schools," Lucy Rider Meyer, pp. 913-917.

"Teacher Training in America," B. S. Winchester, pp. 1079-1084.

Gable, Lee J. *Christian Nurture Through the Church.* New York: National Council of Churches of Christ in the U.S.A., 1955.

GWYNN, PRICE H. *Leadership Education in the Local Church.* Philadelphia: Westminster Press, 1952.

HASTINGS, JAMES (ed.). *Encyclopaedia of Religion and Ethics.* New York: Charles Scribner's Sons, 1955-1958. Article on "Training (religious)," William James Mutch, XII, 415-418.

KRAFT, VERNON R. *The Director of Christian Education in the Local Church.* Chicago: Moody Press, 1957.

LOTZ, PHILIP HENRY. *Orientation in Religious Education.* Nashville and New York: Abingdon-Cokesbury Press, 1950.

———, and CRAWFORD, L. W. *Studies in Religious Education.* Nashville: Cokesbury Press, 1931.

MILLER, RANDOLPH C. *Education for Christian Living.* Englewood Cliffs, N. J.: Prentice-Hall, Inc., 1956.

MULHERN, JAMES. *A History of Education.* New York: The Ronald Press, 1959.

MUNRO, HARRY C. *The Director of Religious Education.* Philadelphia: Westminster Press, 1930.

MURCH, JAMES DEFOREST. *Cooperation without Compromise.* Grand Rapids: Wm. B. Eerdmans Publishing House, 1956.

PERSON, PETER P. *An Introduction to Christian Education.* Grand Rapids: The Baker Book House, 1958.

PRICE, J. M., CHAPMAN, J. H., CARPENTER, L. L. and YARBOROUGH, W. FORBES. *A Survey of Religious Education.* New York: The Ronald Press, 1959.

RICE, EDWIN W. *The Sunday School Movement, 1780-1917, and the American Sunday-School Union, 1817-1917.* Philadelphia: The American Sunday-School Union, 1917.

TAYLOR, MARVIN J. (ed.). *Religious Education: A Comprehensive Survey.* New York: Abingdon Press, 1960.

VIETH, PAUL H. (ed.). *The Church and Christian Education.* St. Louis: The Bethany Press, 1947.

———. *The Church School.* Philadelphia: Christian Education Press, 1957.

Index

D

E

L

M

N

O

P

Y

Z